STUDIES IN
TUDOR AND STUART POLITICS
AND GOVERNMENT

VOLUME ONE

PREVIOUS WORKS BY THE SAME AUTHOR

The Tudor Revolution in Government (C.U.P. 1953)

England under the Tudors, History of England, vol. 4 (Methuen 1955)

(ed.) *The Reformation*, New Cambridge Modern History, vol. 2 (C.U.P. 1958)

Star Chamber Stories (Methuen 1958)

The Tudor Constitution (C.U.P. 1960)

(ed.) *Renaissance and Reformation, 1300–1648*, Ideas and Institutions in Western Civilization (Macmillan, N.Y. 1963)

Reformation Europe, 1517–59 (Collins 1963)

The Practice of History (Sydney U.P. 1967)

England, 1200–1640, The Sources of History (Hodder & Stoughton 1969)

The Future of the Past, Inaugural Lecture (C.U.P. 1968)

Modern Historians on British History, 1485–1945 (Methuen 1970)

Political History: Principles and Practice (Basic Books 1970)

Policy and Police: Enforcement of the Reformation in the Age of Thomas Cromwell (C.U.P. 1972)

Reform and Renewal: Thomas Cromwell and the Common Weal (C.U.P. 1973)

STUDIES IN TUDOR AND STUART POLITICS AND GOVERNMENT

PAPERS AND REVIEWS 1946-1972

G. R. ELTON

VOLUME ONE

TUDOR POLITICS/TUDOR GOVERNMENT

CAMBRIDGE UNIVERSITY PRESS

Published by the Syndics of the Cambridge University Press
Bentley House, 200 Euston Road, London NW1 2DB
American Branch: 32 East 57th Street, New York, N.Y.10022

© Cambridge University Press 1974

Library of Congress Catalogue Card Number: 73-79305

ISBNS:
0 521 20282 5 vol. I
0 521 20288 4 vol. II
0 521 20388 0 set of two volumes
First published 1974

Printed in Great Britain
at the University Printing House, Cambridge
(Brooke Crutchley, University Printer)

CONTENTS

VOLUME ONE

v

Contents

Contents

VOLUME TWO

PREFACE

The papers here collected form a reasonable whole: with the exception of the first (included for reasons of familial piety and because it was the first thing I ever got into print), they revolve around the problems of English society between about 1450 and 1650. This coherence now and again produces repetition, but I may hope that there is not very much of that. I have left out some parts of a quarter century's production: an essay on Henry VIII available as a pamphlet published by the Historical Association, my share in the controversy over the Tudor revolution in *Past and Present* (1963–4) which would look silly without the articles to which I was responding, the greater bulk of even my longer reviews, contributions to encyclopaedias and to the *New Cambridge Modern History*, and several pieces concerned with the study and teaching of history which do not belong here.

In reprinting these papers, I have left the texts untouched, except that I have corrected printing errors, have standardized spelling and capitalization, and in what originally were introductions to reprints of books have omitted a few words appropriate only to that setting. When I first published these articles I sometimes adhered to the original spelling of citations and sometimes modernized; these differences are preserved, without special notice. The footnotes are in substance identical with their original form, but I have recast their presentation which varied so much from journal to journal that standardization appeared desirable in the interests of seemliness. I have also added some new notes, in square brackets, to correct error or draw attention to later developments.

I owe two burdens of gratitude. The first is to those friends whose complaints about the inaccessibility of so many pieces persuaded me to break a long-standing resolution not to produce any such volumes as these; the other is to the Cambridge University Press who bravely and generously decided to publish. I can only hope that my earlier resolve will not after all turn out to have been the right one, and that the Press's decision will not come to be thought of as quixotic.

Clare College, Cambridge G.R.E.
March 1973

ACKNOWLEDGMENTS

The author and publisher are grateful to the following for permission to reproduce material first published by them:

The Journal of Roman Studies (for No. 1)
The English Historical Review, and Longman Ltd. (for Nos. 2, 16 and 19)
The Historical Journal (for Nos. 3, 4, 5, 10, 11 and 17)
The Bulletin of the Institute of Historical Research (for No. 8)
History (for No. 9)
The Economic History Review (for No. 15)
Annali della Fondazione italiana per la storia amministrativa (for No. 18)
The Conference on British Studies, and *The Journal of British Studies* (for No. 13)
Collins (Publishers) (for No. 6)
Yale University Press (for No. 7)
Thomas Y. Crowell Company (for No. 12)
The Louisiana State University Press (for No. 14)
The Athlone Press (for No. 20)

ABBREVIATIONS

Allen	*Opus Epistolarum Desiderii Erasmi Roterodami*, ed. P. S. Allen et al. 12 vols. (Oxford, 1906–58)
APC	*Acts of the Privy Council of England*, ed. J. R. Dasent
BIHR	*Bulletin of the Institute of Historical Research*
BM	British Museum
CHJ	*Cambridge Historical Journal*
CPR	*Calendar of Patent Rolls*
DNB	*Dictionary of National Biography*
EHR	*English Historical Review*
HJ	*The Historical Journal*
LJ	*Journal of the House of Lords*
LP	*Letters and Papers, Foreign and Domestic, of the Reign of Henry VIII*, ed. J. S. Brewer, J. Gairdner, R. H. Brodie, 21 vols. (1862–1932)
Merriman	R. B. Merriman, *The Life and Letters of Thomas Cromwell*, 2 vols. (Oxford, 1902)
Policy and Police	G. R. Elton, *Policy and Police: the enforcement of the Reformation in the age of Thomas Cromwell* (Cambridge, 1972)
PRO	Public Record Office, London
Reform and Renewal	G. R. Elton, *Reform and Renewal: Thomas Cromwell and the Commonweal* (Cambridge, 1973)
Rogers	*The Correspondence of Sir Thomas More*, ed. E. F. Rogers (Princeton, 1947)
Roper	W. Roper, *The Life of Sir Thomas More, Knight*, in *Two Early Tudor Lives*, ed. R. S. Sylvester and D. P. Harding (New Haven, 1962)
StP	*State Papers of Henry VIII*, 11 vols. (1830–52)

TRHS   *Transactions of the Royal Historical Society*

Tudor Constitution   *The Tudor Constitution: Documents and Comment-ary*, ed. G. R. Elton (Cambridge, 1960)

Tudor Revolution   G. R. Elton, *The Tudor Revolution: administrative changes in the reign of Henry VIII* (Cambridge, 1953)

References to *LP* are to numbers of documents, elsewhere to pages. Books for which no place of publication is noted were published in London.

THE TERMINAL DATE OF CAESAR'S GALLIC PROCONSULATE*

The question of the date on which Caesar's command in Gaul expired has recently been reopened by Mr Stevens (below, p. 2, n. 6). His bold and original theories more than justify yet another contribution to the interminable controversy, but they also excuse this attempt at refuting them. This paper is concerned with re-establishing the view, which seemed so obvious to Mommsen and Hardy, that Caesar's governorship was to end on 28th February, 49 B.C. Since the last defence of this theory appeared (p. 2, n. 2), scholars have more and more inclined to the view that the terminal date was in 50, and it will therefore be my task first to discuss in turn their refutations of the 'traditional' view. I propose to deal last with Mr Stevens's theories, and then to suggest a new explanation of the important words of Caelius in *Fam.* 8, 8, 9, since I find it hard to accept either Mommsen's *sanctio* or Stevens's 'appointment-period'. It is hoped that some light may be thrown on the events of 55–50 B.C., and on the motives and actions of the principal actors. I do not, of course, pretend to have found the final answer to the puzzle, but perhaps some useful points may be established.[1]

I 'LEGIS DIES' (*Att.* 7, 7, 6)

First for an attempt to prove that the Lex Pompeia Licinia of 55 B.C. extended Caesar's command in the two Gauls till *pridie Kal. Mart.* 49. This was Mommsen's conclusion,[2] and Hirschfeld[3] and Judeich,[4] who

---

* [*Journal of Roman Studies*, 36 (1946), 18–42.] I owe sincere thanks to Professor M. Cary, the Rev. M. P. Charlesworth, Professor H. Last, and my father, Dr V. Ehrenberg, who all most kindly read this paper in MS and contributed many most valuable corrections and suggestions.

[1] I have to apologize for the arrangement of this paper. The subject is so intricate that it is often necessary to discuss in one place passages and views also relevant in another.

[2] Th. Mommsen, *Gesammelte Schriften* iv, 92–145 (cited here as *Rechtsfrage*). In this he followed F. Hofmann (*De origine belli civilis Caesariani*, Berlin, 1857) whom otherwise he tried to refute.

[3] O. Hirschfeld, 'Der Endtermin der gallischen Statthalterschaft Caesars,' *Klio* iv (1904), 76–87 (*Kleine Schriften* 310–29).

[4] W. Judeich, 'Das Ende von Caesars gallischer Statthalterschaft und der Ausbruch des Bürgerkrieges,' *Rhein. Mus.* 68 (1913), 1–10.

attacked it, were driven from the field by Holmes[1] and Hardy.[2] But in more recent years new attacks have been made on the 'traditional' view: Professor Marsh[3] postulated a date early in 50 as 'legis dies' and was followed, with elaborations, by Mr Stone.[4] Professor Adcock[5] tentatively put forward the claims of 13th November, 50, and Mr Stevens[6] pointed to some date between July and October 50.

(1) *Was there a fixed date?*

Before discussing the actual 'legis dies' one must answer the objections of Mr Balsdon[7] that there was no such date, and that the only way in which the extraordinary commands of the late Republic terminated was by a clause in the laws conferring them that they should not be discussed before a certain date[8] unless the task for which the command was given had been carried out. Mr Balsdon's paper deals with a much larger field than does the present discussion, and a good many of his points are most convincingly stated. But one may doubt whether he has proved that there was no definite *terminus a quo*, and therefore no *terminus in quem*.[9] To his objection that the Romans were a 'practical' people and unlikely to stand upon legal exactitude, it may be answered that they were also eminent legalists, and that both expediency and legal punctilio were satisfied by the arrangement, before 52 B.C., by which legally exact commands were automatically extended by the absence of supersession. The phrase 'exercitum tu habeas diutius quam populus iussit' (*Att.* 7, 9, 4) suggests that there was a definite end set to Caesar's command by the People's orders. More importance must also be

---

[1] T. Rice Holmes, 'Hirschfeld and Judeich on the Lex Pompeia Licinia,' *C[lassical] Q[uarterly]* x (1916), 49–56.

[2] E. G. Hardy, 'The Evidence as to Caesar's Legal Position in Gaul,' *Jour. Phil.* xxxiv (1918), 161–221.

[3] F. B. Marsh, *The Founding of the Roman Empire*[2] (Oxford, 1927), 275–88.

[4] C. G. Stone, '1 March 50, B.C.,' *CQ* xxii (1928), 193–201.

[5] F. E. Adcock, 'The Legal Term of Caesar's Governorship in Gaul,' *CQ* xxvi (1932), 14–26.

[6] C. E. Stevens, 'The Terminal Date of Caesar's Command in Gaul,' *Am. Jour. Phil.* 59 (1938), 169–208.

[7] J. P. V. D. Balsdon, 'Consular Provinces under the Late Republic,' *JRS* 29 (1939), 57 ff., 167 ff. (These articles are cited by authors' names only.)

[8] A somewhat similar conclusion was reached by M. Gelzer (*Hermes* 63 (1928), 113 ff.), who also forgot that supposedly premature discussion was common and passed without remark.

[9] Cf. Mommsen, *Staatsrecht* i[3], 594 ff., for proof that definite termination (*Amtsfrist*) was the usual thing. Balsdon's attack on Mommsen's basic theories seems to me to be only partially successful.

ascribed to Hirtius' testimony about the one summer,[1] and to Cicero's mention of 'legis dies' and 'decem anni'.[2] If we take it, with Balsdon, that the Lex Pompeia Licinia simply deferred the date of discussion by five years (i.e., in his opinion, until 1st March, 50), and that from that moment supersession was constitutionally possible,[3] then the phrase 'annorum enim decem imperium et ita latum' becomes incomprehensible. If anything had been carried, on Mr Balsdon's showing, it was a nine years' command – from 1st March, 59, to 28th February, 50.

The most serious objection still remains, and it is the one on which Mommsen's whole theory of the *sanctio*[4] (which Balsdon takes over in a new form) was wrecked. If no discussion was allowed before a certain date, why did it continually take place? Why did L. Domitius in 58 and 56 (Suet. *Div. Iul.* 23, 1; 24, 1) and M. Marcellus in 51 (ibid. 28, 2) try to start discussions four years, or two years, or one year before the appointed time?

Mr Balsdon tries to save his theory by the supposition that the law contained a double termination clause: no discussion before a certain date unless the task for which the command had been given was finished. Such 'alternative clauses' in laws always raise a doubt. There is no evidence whatever that Caesar in 59 and 55, and Pompey and Crassus in the latter year, received their provinces for the fulfilment of a special task. They were appointed governors to provinces, with special length of command and extraordinary powers, but not 'to wage war against the Helvetii and Ariovistus',[5] or the Parthians, or for any other specific undertaking. Our authorities[6] do not in the least suggest such a possibility in Caesar's case, and we are expressly assured that the Lex Trebonia contained no mention of the Parthian war (Plut. *Crassus* 16, 2). The only bit of evidence which hints that such a clause may have existed[7] is no

---

[1] *BG* 8, 39, 3. Hardy (p. 175) shows that the passage argues a definite end, not a permissive one.

[2] *Att.* 7, 7, 6; 7, 9, 4.

[3] Though Balsdon's attack on Mommsen's interpretation of the Sullan system is serious, it is by no means final. Mommsen does admit the difficulties, but cites as exceptions what to Balsdon become the rule (*Rechtsfrage* 119 ff.).

[4] Mommsen deduced the existence of a clause (*sanctio*) in the Lex Pompeia Licinia forbidding discussion of Caesar's provinces before 1st March, 50, thus enabling Caesar to stay till the end of 49, from *Fam.* 8, 8, 9, and Hirtius, *BG* 8, 53 (*Rechtsfrage* 139).

[5] Are we to believe that the Lex Vatinia would have allowed Caesar's recall in 57 because these enemies had been defeated? L. Domitius – in 58 – could on no account have claimed that the war was over.

[6] Suet., *Div. Iul.* 22, 1; App., *BC* 2, 13, 49; Dio 38, 8, 5.

[7] Suet., *Div. Iul.* 28, 2: 'Marcellus . . . rettulit ad senatum ut ei succederetur ante tempus, quoniam bello confecto pax esset ac dimitti deberet victor exercitus' (for a discussion of

proof: Marcellus, obviously looking for some plausible excuse for recalling Caesar prematurely, found it in the fact that the establishment of peace seemed to make the general's further presence unnecessary. His surprising consideration for the soldiers awaiting their demobilization shows that he was not quoting a clause of the law but merely putting a superficially reasonable case. One may agree that the law made some mention of the task to be performed, that the Lex Pompeia Licinia, e.g., contained a few words about Caesar's difficulties in Gaul and the necessity of continuing him in office there.[1] But one must disagree when this possibility is turned into a legally binding clause and made to explain difficulties which only arise in connection with the theory. If, however, no such alternative clause can reasonably be postulated, the *sanctio*, in whatever form, falls down. One must therefore conclude that Mr Balsdon has failed to discredit the 'legis dies'.

(2) General argument

Before dealing in detail with the objections to the 'traditional' view and the alternative solutions put forward, it may be permissible to review once again the basic reasons for assuming a date which Mommsen considered as 'proven beyond refutation',[2] especially as one or two new points may emerge.

That the Lex Pompeia Licinia renewed Caesar's provincial appointment for five years was conclusively proved by Hardy,[3] who in the process had to throw over Dio's unsupported testimony which speaks of three years (Dio 39, 33, 3; 44, 43, 2). While the three years are demonstrably based on false reasoning,[4] Dio's apparent conviction that Caesar's command ended in 50 deserves some attention, especially as his words suggest that he is contradicting a prevailing opinion. Yet if we here ignore Hardy's insistence on Hirtius 8, 53, and admit that M. Marcellus was trying to recall Caesar before the 'legis dies',[5] the rest of his argument (loc. cit.) supplies the answer. Dio thought that the motion 'ut Caesari succedatur' meant immediate supersession, not – as it did

---

this passage, cf. Stevens, p. 176). Domitius, in 56, may have suggested no more than a recall on the legal day (Suet., *Div. Iul.* 24, 1).

[1] Such words, e.g. as Cicero used in the speech (*de prov. cons.* 35) of which the law was the practical outcome. If Balsdon were right Cicero would have been ill-advised to mention the successes already obtained (ibid. 34).

[2] *Rechtsfrage* 127: 'unwiderleglich erwiesen'.

[3] Pp. 163 ff. His argument is final in many respects.

[4] Cf. Marsh p. 280.   [5] Cf. p. 25.

(cf. p. 8, n. 2) – the appointment of a successor for a future date. He therefore confused Marcellus' proposed date of premature recall – probably 1st March, 50 (*Att.* 8, 3, 3) – with the 'legis dies', and thought that what was proposed was an immediate, and even more premature, recall in 51.

It is not so clear, however, on what date Caesar's second quinquennium started. Mommsen assumed the most straightforward explanation: it was added to the first, which expired on 28th February, 54 (*de prov. cons.* 37), and reached thus to 28th February, 49. This interpretation is the one most easily reconciled with the words of our authorities when they speak of the Lex Pompeia Licinia. The Latin writers[1] use 'prorogare imperium (in quinquennium)' – to vote another (five years') command. Appian (*BC* 2, 17, 63)[2] translates this correctly as ἐπιψηφίζειν ἄλλην πενταετίαν, while Dio (39, 33, 3) employs μηκύνειν, 'to prolong'. Plutarch's testimony,[3] though he cannot be pressed for legal exactitude in his wording, also suggests the vital fact of addition. Thus we may assume that the operative clause of the Lex Pompeia Licinia ran something like this: 'ut Caesari imperium in quinquennium prorogetur'. 'Prorogari' means normally prolongation from the date of expiry,[4] and the word must be twisted at least a little to represent a new grant of office antedating the end of the old. The natural interpretation of our sources is, therefore, that the second quinquennium ran from where the first left off, so that what little we know about the provisions of the law entitles us to claim that Mommsen's date offers the most obvious solution.

There would be no problem at all if our information were no more than these comparatively straightforward statements. But there are a number of other passages which seem difficult to reconcile with the 'traditional' view. Some such passages, i.e. those advanced by Hirschfeld and Judeich, have already been fitted into Mommsen's theory by Holmes and Hardy, and no repetition of their arguments is necessary except where they have been attacked by later scholars.

(3) *Professor Marsh's theory*

Marsh decides that the 'legis dies' was early in 50. He declares that the language of Dio (39, 33) is explicit for 50, and that Appian (*BC* 2, 26 f.,

---

[1] Cic., *Att.* 7, 6, 2; *Phil.* 2, 10, 24; Suet., *Div. Iul.* 24, 1.
[2] Cf. also 2, 18, 65.   [3] *Pomp.* 51, 5; 52, 4; *Caes.* 21, 6; *Crass.* 15, 7.
[4] Mommsen, *Staatsrecht* i3, 636 ff.; iii, 331, 1089 ff., and the examples given in Lewis and Short.

98 ff.) supports him. We have already disposed of Dio and have sought to explain how his error arose. Undoubtedly he believed the end to have been in 50, but it can be shown why he thought so, and why he thought wrongly, and such circumstantial evidence as he produces (it amounts to almost nothing) is obviously shaped to support a view already held. Appian is not much of an aid to Marsh's theory. He does not mention any specific date, and his vague and confused account fits any 'legis dies' that has yet been suggested.

Marsh next takes Caelius' report to Cicero of the compromise proposal of November, 13 (*Fam.* 8, 11, 3), but the detailed discussion of this passage must be reserved for later,[1] when it may be hoped that it may be satisfactorily explained on the assumption that the November talked about was in 49 and the 'legis dies' 28th February, 49. He further repeats Hirschfeld's argument about Cicero's words in December, 50. In two letters (*Att.* 7, 7 and 9) Cicero uses words which at first sight might be taken to show that the 'legis dies' was then already past. Yet Hardy's explanation (pp. 168 ff.) that Cicero was talking about the future is perfectly tenable.[2]

The first passage (*Att.* 7, 7, 5–6) runs as follows:

> Senatum bonum putas per quem sine imperio provinciae sunt? Numquam enim Curio sustinuisset si cum eo agi coeptum esset; quam sententiam senatus sequi noluit' [cf. *Fam.* 8, 13, 2]; 'ex quo factum est ut Caesari non succederetur.... Quid ergo? exercitum retinentis cum legis dies transierit rationem haberi placet?

There seems no doubt that Cicero here meant to express his annoyance at the Senate's failure to supersede Caesar in time, and that the normal date on which a commander would be superseded was undoubtedly the day to which his command ran, his 'legis dies', or later if his successor was late in arriving. If that day had already passed, if Cicero's argument had been that the Senate had failed to appoint a successor on Caesar's (past) 'legis dies', he would surely have said 'ut Caesari non successum esset'. Thus the words 'ut Caesari non succederetur' point to a 'legis dies' yet to come. If it be contended that Cicero was speaking about the Senate's failure, not in the past on the 'legis dies', but in the present, as it were in the thirteenth hour, the reply is that the words do not

---

[1] Below, pp. 19 ff.

[2] His argument loses none of its force when it is admitted that Cicero's ten years did not necessarily mean 120 months, even though he may have been speaking with legal exactitude (Mommsen, *Rechtsfrage* 105 ff.).

say this. The plain statement that no successor is appointed is best taken to refer to the normal date of taking over, not to a belated succession. At their most sober interpretation, the words discussed cannot be dangerous, are indeed helpful, to our view.

The case appears to be strengthened by the words 'cum legis dies transierit'. Mr Stevens has pointed out[1] that the word 'transierit' can be either future perfect (*cum temporale*) or perfect subjunctive (*cum concessivum*). Even if this is admitted, the phrase still appears to refer to the future. Grammatically, it can depend on 'retinentis' or 'haberi', or on 'placet'. The argument that Cicero is talking about a past 'legis dies' can only base itself on the assumption that it depends on 'placet', the meaning then being 'Do I approve, although the day has passed, that. . . .' This does violence to the Latin and makes very little sense; for the point of the sentence was obviously not Cicero's disapproval at this time but the fact of a tenure of power prolonged beyond the 'legis dies' until the elections. The only election which Cicero can have had in mind on 27th December, 50, lay in the future, in the summer of 49. Whether therefore one translates 'Do I approve that he shall have his candidature while still retaining his army, when the day appointed by the law will have passed', or substitutes for the last clause 'although the day has passed', makes little odds. When the elections of 49 came round, Caesar's 'legis dies' would certainly have passed, whenever it may have been. So one may conclude that, though finality is out of the question, this letter points much more strongly to a future 'legis dies' than a past one.[2]

This impression is corroborated by a close study of the other letter (*Att.* 7, 9). Mr Stevens supposes that in speaking as though in a senatorial debate (ibid. 4) Cicero perhaps had in mind the motion of early December, in which case we may assume that even then a speaker might have spoken of a past 'legis dies'. But the whole letter deals with Cicero's plans for the future: he is considering what he is to do, not – rhetorically – the chance that has been missed. The four possibilities (ibid. 2–3) are all in the future (and, by the way, there is no indication

---

[1] P. 196, n. 118.

[2] True, if *transierit* is future perfect Cicero would be saying that in December, 50, the 'legis dies' was yet to come. There are few parallels for a concessive *cum* with the perfect subjunctive. Lewis and Short are silent (p. 496; 2. IV). I can find two examples: Caesar, *BG* I, 26, 2 (cf. ed. Rice-Holmes, p. 30 n.) where the verb in the main clause is in the perfect tense, and Nepos 9, 3, 4, where a concessive meaning is possible but not certain. Quotations for a temporal *cum* with the future perfect and a future in the main clause are numerous: e.g. Lewis and Short p. 491 (2.I.A.3.d.α]), and Cicero, *Att.* 7, 9, 1; *de fin.* 1, 63; *Brut.* 96; *de re pub.* 2, 48. But tempting though it is to claim this passage fully for our view one must admit the existence of some ambiguity.

here that Caesar is already overstaying his allotted time). Clearly and naturally, Cicero is thinking of the approaching, not the past, crisis. As he told Atticus (7, 1, 4), Caesar's enemies concentrated their efforts on preventing the 'absentis ratio', and in the circumstances that could only be done by recalling him before he could use his privilege. Hence the plea ascribed to Caesar – 'habe meam rationem'.[1] As he has the 'ratio absentis' for 49 he considers it unfair to recall him before he has used it (cf. *BC* 1, 9. 32). All the motions concerned with this question, those of 1st March, 50, early December, 50, and 1st January, 49, were attempts to do this. All of them pointed to the future,[2] and it is only reasonable to suppose that all three contemplated the same thing – Caesar's supersession on the 'legis dies'. Cicero was envisaging such a motion with a debate to follow, a motion 'ut Caesari succedatur' which had to be passed – and the veto avoided – by the time his term expired. Finally it may be said that the question 'exercitum tu habeas diutius quam populus iussit, invito senatu?' (ibid. 4) becomes nonsensical if the 'legis dies' is assumed to have passed by December, 50. How could Cicero make the point 'Are you to have your army beyond the date fixed by the people's orders?' if that date lay in the past – if, that is, Caesar was already holding his army longer 'quam populus iussit'? These last words seem to make certain that Cicero was thinking of circumstances in which a future 'legis dies' was an essential condition.

Marsh next cites a passage which seems more dangerous to the 'traditional' view than any yet propounded. On 19th January, 49, Cicero wrote to Atticus (*Att.* 7, 11, 1) 'atque haec ait (sc. Caesar) omnia facere se dignitatis causa. Vbi est autem dignitas nisi ubi honestas? Honestum igitur habere exercitum nullo publico consilio?' As they stand, these words seem to declare that in January, 49, Caesar no longer held his army by the People's 'decision'. But, says Marsh, if the Lex Pompeia Licinia was still in force, then he did hold his army 'publico consilio'. Therefore, the term granted by the Lex Pompeia Licinia had already expired.

The answer is partly to be found in the general tone of the letter. Cicero compares Caesar to Hannibal, he accuses him – in Greek, for greater dramatic effect – of *tyrannis*, of horrors, of 'six hundred other crimes'. It is difficult not to feel that the letter was written under the

---

[1] Probably no more than 'consider my interests'. Or is it an allusion to the 'ratio absentis', and the 'habe tu nostram' which follows a Ciceronian pun?

[2] That 'ut Caesari succedatur' could only mean 'that a successor is to take over at some (future) date' is clearly brought out by Hardy (pp. 176 and 182).

highest emotional stress, with its mass of Greek quotations, classical allusions, and despairing outcries. There is here no sober statement of legal fact. Would the lawyer Cicero normally have used so vague an expression as 'publico consilio' if he meant to say that a law had expired? 'Nulla lege populi Romani' is what we should have expected from him. The vagueness of the statement, together with the expressions of horror at the man who had turned against his country, give us the clue to Cicero's meaning: a monster like Caesar could no longer lead a Roman army with the People's consent. When we then remember that on 7th January the Senate passed the 'consultum ultimum', i.e. virtually outlawed Caesar (*BC* 1, 5, 3 f.), we can see that Cicero was actually basing his opinion on a legal step. The last decision taken at Rome had to all intents deprived Caesar of his army and made him a rebel if he continued to hold it.

But it did not mean that Caesar was no longer proconsul under the terms of the Lex Pompeia Licinia, nor does Cicero say so. Caesar tells us (*BC* 1, 10 f.) that the Senate were prepared to negotiate with him even when he had reached Ariminum, provided he returned to Gaul and dismissed his army. Why should they wish him to go to Gaul unless he was still recognized as proconsul? In other words, the Senate were trying, by a legal quibble, (*a*) not to break the Lex Pompeia Licinia, and (*b*) to fulfil the decision 'ut exercitum dimittat' which had been followed by the *consultum ultimum* (*BC* 1, 2, 6 f.). Cicero's wild words may be a reflection of the official policy or they may be simply a product of rage and fear, but in no case do they prove that the Lex Pompeia Licinia had expired.

Apart from putting forward these passages, Marsh argues that 1st March, 49, cannot have been the 'legis dies' as the two months from January, 49, would, on Mommsen's showing, already have given Caesar his command till the end of 49, and would thus have rendered superfluous the *sanctio* (in which Marsh believes implicitly). For some it is impossible to accept the theory of the *sanctio* (below, p. 23); and a case has been made out[1] that Cicero's argument about the two months (*de prov. cons.* 36 f.) was not quite so convincing as the orator would have us think. At any rate we may well believe that Caesar would make doubly sure. Marsh also shows surprise that the controversy should be thought to have started about two years before time, with the discussions of April, 51. It is quite natural that the question of Caesar's supersession, the problem of how to prevent him from stepping straight

[1] Cf. p. 27, n. 1.

from proconsulship into consulship, should have engaged attention so early, if only because of its importance to his enemies.[1] And in July, 51, Caelius foresaw a two years' wrangle about Caesar's succession (*Fam.* 8, 5, 2). He could only do so at that time if there was reason to believe that Caesar wanted and could stay another two years in Gaul.

It remains to consider Professor Marsh's own suggestion. He puts the 'legis dies' 'early in 50'. He argues that the Lex Pompeia Licinia and the Lex Trebonia were passed at about the same time, and that both laws assigned the respective provinces for five years from the day of their passage. The former point is hardly in doubt, but the latter is much less certain. The two laws did two quite different things: the Lex Trebonia assigned provinces to the consuls of the year (55), the Lex Pompeia Licinia extended the command of an existing proconsul. It has been suggested above (p. 5) that the latter law declared 'ut Caesari imperium prorogetur', but a corresponding phrase could most certainly not have stood in the Lex Trebonia. The one law authorized a fresh *imperium*, the other – by a recognized constitutional custom[2] – prolonged an existing one. The idea that the two laws were in any way similar in content or effect lacks therefore the first basis – a similar purpose. There can be no doubt that the Lex Trebonia, following the precedent of the Lex Vatinia, conferred the *imperium* on the consuls before the expiration of their consulship,[3] though whether from the date of passing cannot be known and is also immaterial. But it does not follow that the Lex Pompeia Licinia became operative on the same date.

Marsh further claims that the 'legis dies' of the two laws must have been roughly the same, considering that equal powers were to be conferred on the three partners by the legislation of 55. But it seems certain that Caesar firmly intended to become consul for a second time after he had finished with Gaul, and that he wished to avoid an interval as *privatus*. It is generally agreed that some steps towards this end, such as the promise of the 'absentis ratio', were taken already at Luca. Pompey would have been extremely undiscerning if he had failed to see that such preparations destroyed any idea of equality which might have been

---

[1] I agree with Stevens that Hardy's suggestion that M. Marcellus was trying to avail himself of a possible doubt as to the continued force of the Lex Sempronia in the hope of avoiding the veto is untenable. The appointments of Cicero and Bibulus in 51 prove that the Lex Sempronia was no longer considered relevant. For a reason for Marcellus' early action, cf. p. 32.

[2] Cf. p. 5, n. 4.

[3] This is conclusively proved by Crassus' departure – *paludatus* – on (probably) 14th November, 55 (*Att.* 4, 13, 2).

contained in the agreement about the provinces.[1] Moreover, the argument[2] that Caesar was the dominant partner before and at Luca is so strong that there is no need to suppose him compelled to allow full equality to his partners. Nor did Pompey have to worry about this point. He knew that in case of need he could secure from the Senate an extension of his command or some other sphere of power which would enable him to stand up to Caesar, a step he took with the prolongation of the Spanish proconsulship in 52. It is very unlikely that the question of equality arose at Luca, and the assumption that the Lex Pompeia Licinia prolonged Caesar's command from 1st March, 54, onwards cannot therefore be attacked through it.

With Professor Marsh goes Mr Stone, whose suggestion for a 'legis dies' – 1st March, 50 – is based on very insecure grounds. Believing in the *sanctio*, he is forced to juggle with it and with M. Marcellus' motion[3] (p. 196). He thinks that Marcellus was not proposing to curtail Caesar's legal term of office but merely to ensure that Caesar would be forced to leave Gaul on or soon after the 'legis dies', which he therefore puts at 1st March, 50. We, on the other hand, disbelieving the *sanctio*, shall be compelled to assume that Dio (40, 59, 1), Appian (*BC* 2, 26, 99), and Suetonius (*Div. Iul.* 28, 2) were right, and that Marcellus was trying to recall Caesar before his appointed time (below, p. 25). In that case, the date proposed by Marcellus (1st March, 50) must have been earlier than the 'legis dies'. Stone does not even succeed in reconciling Marcellus with the *sanctio*. There seems little point in his suggestion that Marcellus was not trying to appoint a successor for 1st March, 50, but merely to reaffirm that date as the legal end of Caesar's command, hoping to have the discussion begin on that date ('finienti' does not mean that). Such a motion would not have been opposed by Pompey, who himself wished the discussion delayed in this manner (*Fam.* 8, 8, 9). Besides, the *sanctio* would still have been broken as it must have been illegal under it to bring up the question in any form before 1st March, 50 (*Rechtsfrage* 139). Nor is it clear why the Senate should be asked to confirm a point known to all, or why opposition to such a step should be so strong. If Stone's argument were correct, M. Marcellus' motion would appear super-

---

[1] Cf. Mommsen, *Rechtsfrage* 127.

[2] Hardy 193 ff., *q.v.* for the authorities. Such, too, is the opinion of Holmes (*RR* ii, p. 74), Ferrero (*Greatn. and Decl.* 2, 59 f.), and, of course, Mommsen (*Hist. of Rome* v, 125: 'in every respect the decisive voice lay with Caesar'). Ed. Meyer (*Caesars Monarchie²* 141 f.), though he makes Caesar largely dependent on Pompey, admits the former's essential superiority: 'so lag die Entscheidung in den Händen Caesars'.

[3] *Att.* 8, 3, 3: 'Marcoque Marcello consuli finienti provincias Gallias Kalendarum Martiarum die restitit (*sc.* Pompeius).'

fluous, its importance inexplicable, and its legality doubtful. Thus he gives no satisfactory explanation for his suggested 'legis dies'.[1]

(4) *Professor Adcock's theory*

Professor Adcock was the first scholar dealing with this problem to abandon the *sanctio*, and his arguments have convinced all later scholars with the exception of Mr Balsdon (above, p. 3). This part of his account will here be accepted, though comment on it must be postponed.[2] But his revival of A. W. Zumpt's suggestion[3] that the 'legis dies' was 13th November, 50, is less convincing. He himself warns us that 'dogmatism is out of place', and is reluctant to make a serious point of the actual date; but what is important is that he considers the end to have been in 50.

His first and main argument is that the events of December, 50, to January, 49, are inexplicable unless the 'legis dies' had already passed. Thus when C. Marcellus proposed[4] that (*a*) successors be sent to Caesar, and (*b*) Pompey be deprived of the Spanish command, the difference in the phrasing and the fact that Pompey's term of office had yet a good time to run suggest to Adcock that Caesar's was already ended. It may be admitted that Marcellus was taking advantage of the rivals' different positions to put his motion in two parts. But since 'ut Caesari succedatur', rendered by Appian as Καίσαρι πέμπειν διαδόχους, meant supersession at some date yet to be fixed,[5] the most satisfactory explanation of this passage is not that Caesar's term had already expired but that the 'legis dies' lay still in the future. Marcellus, one may think, was trying to do the strictly legal thing: Caesar was to leave his province when his tenure was over. It was this legal aspect of his motion which rendered decisive the difference between the two parts into which he divided it: in Caesar's case, a governor would be superseded at the end of his term, in Pompey's some way through it. Marcellus was thus on very strong ground, and the Senate could claim to have acted justly in accepting (*a*) and rejecting (*b*). Professor Adcock's whole interpretation assumes that Caesar's enemies spent all their strength on trying to recall

---

[1] As has frequently been pointed out, a date early in 50 is also excluded by the testimony of Hirtius (8, 39, 3), whose 'unam aestatem' must refer to the summer of 50 (Holmes 52 f.). Stone's argument for 51 (p. 199) does not convince.

[2] For the *sanctio* and discussion of it, cf. p. 26.

[3] *Studia Romana* (Berlin, 1859), 84.

[4] App., *BC* 2, 30, 118. The date cannot be fixed definitely, but it must have been late in November or, more probably, early in December, 50 (cf. Holmes, *RR* ii, 324 f.).

[5] Cf. above p. 8, n. 2.

a man who was already overstaying his time.[1] Surely it would be more reasonable to suppose that they strained every nerve to secure his retirement on the legal day. We are, therefore, justified in taking Appian's account of this motion as actually supporting the view which Professor Adcock thought it discredited.

Then Professor Adcock's second point. He claims that Scipio's motion of 1st January, 49, 'uti ante certam diem Caesar exercitum dimittat; si non faciat eum adversus rem publicam facturum videri' (*BC* I, 2, 6), and the whole turmoil which followed – *consultum ultimum*, appointment of successors to Caesar, the departure of Domitius, etc. – could not have left the Senate with the slightest show of legality if Caesar was still the legal governor of Gaul, and he therefore holds that Caesar's term of office had expired.

It has been argued that the 'certa dies' of this motion must have been 1st March, 49.[2] There was nothing illegal in asking Caesar to dismiss his army by that date if his proconsulship ran to 28th February, 49.[3] Furthermore, an attempt has been made above to show (p. 9) that at this point the Senate, in their demands on Caesar, apparently made a definite distinction between the surrender of his proconsulship and the surrender of his army. Thus even if Scipio's 'certa dies' was earlier than our 'legis dies', the Senate could still claim to have acted legally in that they left the proconsul in his province and merely recalled an army 'no longer necessary'. As for the Senate's precipitate action in not waiting till Caesar showed his mind on the 'certa dies', the second part of Scipio's motion provides the clue. If Caesar resisted he was to be declared a traitor, after which, of course, any action was justifiable against him. It will be objected that he could not start resisting before the date fixed. But it had long been clear to his enemies that there was more than one way for him to disobey orders. As long ago as September, 51, Pompey

---

[1] Cf. also his statement in *CAH* ix, 636: 'Until the command conferred on Caesar ... was at an end it was idle to raise as a vital issue whether Caesar would lay down his command.' The same goes for his 'subjective feeling' (*CQ* 1932, 26) that the situation reached a critical stage towards the end of 50. The situation became critical not because the 'legis dies' had passed but because it was coming near and Caesar's enemies felt their time getting short.

[2] Merrill's explanation of the whole passage (*Class. Phil.* 1912, 248 ff.) sounds reasonable. It seems quite legitimate to assume that a supplementary motion would have mentioned this date.

[3] In effect, though not in law, this motion amounted to a recall. It was probably this proposal that Caesar had in mind (*BC* I, 9, 2) when he spoke of the Senate's attempt to deprive him of 'semestre imperium'. I agree with Hardy (p. 190) that he meant the first half of 49, whether six or four months. Part of a six months' period was officially counted as a whole (Mommsen, *Rechtsfrage* 106 f.).

had declared (*Fam.* 8, 8, 9) that by suborning tribunes to prevent discussion, Caesar was in effect disobeying the Senate. Such must all along
have been the view of the extreme party, and now at last they prevailed.
By their intercession on 1st January, Antonius and Cassius provided
the opportunity. Their veto was regarded as equivalent to disobedience,
and the second part of Scipio's motion now assumed importance.
Caesar could be accused, perhaps two months before the time, of
having refused to comply – 'non fecit', and he could be declared a
hostis. The *senatus consultum ultimum* was the consequence. The occasion
was critical enough to make the Senate do some pretty unconstitutional
things (Caes. *BC* 1, 5–7, 9). Drastic and immediate action was more
important than strictest legality. But it will be clear from all that has
been said that nothing done after 1st January, 49, proves an earlier
expiration for the Lex Pompeia Licinia.

Professor Adcock next points out that Caesar uses every scrap of
illegal action on the Senate's part in his apologia (esp. *BC* 1, 7) but does
not once make use of the fact that he is still proconsul under the Lex
Pompeia Licinia. In all his armoury of propaganda he neglects the most
telling weapon. Adcock therefore concludes that this weapon did not
exist, and that the Lex Pompeia Licinia had already expired.

The answer to this argument has already been given. It has been
argued above that all the Senate proposed doing (by Scipio's motion)
was to withdraw Caesar's army[1] while leaving him in Gaul until his
'legis dies'. Then, when Antonius and Cassius entered their veto, it had
claimed that he had finally put himself beyond the pale, had outlawed
him, and had taken all the obvious steps against him. Caesar might well
attack the legality of this outlawry and its consequences,[2] but he could
not blame the Senate for disregarding the Lex Pompeia Licinia – because
the Senate had not disregarded it. Since the law had not been violated
it was irrelevant to Caesar's argument: what he had to face was the
coup d'état of the Last Decree. The Senate had out-manoeuvred him by
holding to the view that his term of office ran out on 28th February, 49,
when he would be superseded, and that all things done so far were only
the result of his own actual and constructive disobedience.

Professor Adcock's own suggestion for the 'legis dies' (by himself
admitted as no more than probable) is 13th November, 50. To this
Tenney Frank seems to have provided a very strong and almost conclu-

---

[1] Which they had a quasi-legal right to do: Caesar needed no great army in Gaul in 49.
But he does complain about it (cf. previous note).

[2] *BC* 1, 5, 7.

sive answer.[1] It may be added that Adcock's chief reason for that particular date is the supposed equality of the three partners at Luca, and it is hoped that this point has been sufficiently dealt with already (above p. 11). But even if such equality be admitted, it proves nothing for the date of 13th November. The fact that Crassus left Rome on 14th November, 55 (*Att.* 4, 13, 2), does not prove that the date on which the Lex Trebonia conferred the *imperium* on Pompey and Crassus was in November at all. Everything points to a date earlier in the year for the passage of the law,[2] and we should thus have to assume that it contained a later and quite arbitrary date for the beginning of the *imperium*. Moreover, by the Sullan constitution the consuls had probably lost the military *imperium*,[3] i.e. could not levy troops, and Crassus must therefore be supposed to have received the *imperium* at some earlier date, as he would hardly have left Rome until his preparations had at least been properly begun. All this makes 13th November, 50, very doubtful as the 'legis dies'. Professor Adcock's objections to the 'traditional' view have, it is submitted, beeen refuted, and the course of events which to him seemed conclusive for a date in 50 has, it may be hoped, been explained more satisfactorily on the assumption that the end was in 49.

(5) Mr Stevens's theory

Mr Stevens has formed a number of theories to account for the events of 52–49 B.C. among which his view of the 'legis dies' is but a minor point, except that he too declares for a date in 50. He bases it on his other theories, which will be discussed later. He is himself not very insistent on the actual date, 'somewhere between 31st July and 1st October'. If we grant his premise – a 'legis dies' in 50 – his argument sounds ingenious enough. His case rests on the assumption that the attempt was made to have only Caesar's provinces available for allotment when his 'legis dies' came round. This, he tells us, was the reason for the inclusion of Cilicia in the praetorian allotment for 50,[4] and for Bibulus' desire to

---

[1] *JRS* xxiii (1933), 74 f.; cf. *Class. Rev.* xxxiii (1919), 68, and Rice-Holmes, *RR* ii, 248, n. 3.

[2] Dio (39, 33–5) and Plutarch (*Crass.* 15, 7; *Pomp.* 52, 4; *Cato Min.* 43, 1–6) suggest an earlier passage. Cf. also Livy, *Epit.* 105.

[3] Mommsen, *Staatsrecht* ii³, 94. Cf. also Caes., *BC* 1, 85, 8, and Pompey's case in 52 when it was thought better to restore the *imperium* by renewing the grant of Spain.

[4] *Fam.* 8, 8, 8. Stevens (p. 190) challenges us to produce a reason why Syria was left out of the allotment. I suggest that the Parthian danger was considered too great for a praetor to govern this province, which both before and after was one of the most important consular provinces.

leave Syria as late as possible in that year.[1] Thus, he suggests, only Caesar's provinces would have been free for consular appointment between 31st July and 1st October, and somewhere between these two dates we must look for the 'legis dies', on which Caesar was to have been superseded by proconsuls appointed for that date. Whatever may be thought of this explanation of what can after all have been due to other causes – e.g. the lack of ex-consuls necessitating the appointment of a ninth praetor, Bibulus' desire to miss the winter weather at both ends of his command, or his hope that the Parthian danger might be over if he delayed – one must reject a date in 50 in view of everything that has been said and of what still remains to be said.

After this review of such objections as have been put forward against Mommsen's view of the date on which Caesar's Gallic command expired, it is time to turn to Stevens's theory of an 'appointment-period' and to the problem of reconstructing the course of events, especially after 52. There are two remarks made by Caelius which need to be reconciled with the view here put forward.

II 'POMPEIO CVM CAESARE ESSE NEGOTIVM' (*Fam.* 8, 8, 9)

(1) *The 'appointment-period'*

Mr Stevens has formulated a theory which is to explain the significance of the dates of 13th November and 1st March (*Fam.* 8, 11, 3, and 8, 8, 9). He assumes that the Lex Pompeia de provinciis of 52[2] enacted an 'appointment-period' extending between these two dates. Only during that time, he suggests, could the actual appointment of a proconsul or a propraetor take place, while the Senate was free to take the preliminary step of making a province consular or praetorian at any time. Thus a governor could be superseded on any 'legis dies', provided his successor had been appointed and had got his Lex Curiata (made vital by the loss of *imperium* consequent upon the five years' interval) during the previous 'appointment-period'.

The theory is bold. Its most serious shortcoming is, of course, that the fact of its existence is nowhere even clearly hinted at. We know little about the Lex Pompeia de provinciis, mainly because it became obsolete so quickly. But we do know three of its provisions, all affecting Caesar's position: we know that it enacted a five years' interval between

---

[1] *Att.* 5, 16, 4. This point seems also to have occurred to Stone (p. 195, n. 4).
[2] Or the law *de iure magistratuum* (Stevens, p. 180).

magistracy and pro-magistracy (Dio 40, 56, 1), that appointments under it were for one year (*Fam.* 15, 14, 5; cf. 2, 7, 4. *Att.* 5, 14, 1; 15, 1), and that, by making the Lex Sempronia irrelevant, it made possible the tribunician veto in matters of consular provinces. One may therefore pardonably be surprised that so vital a provision of the law as the 'appointment-period', so clear a deviation from traditional constitutional practice, should find no mention anywhere, the more so as it was a provision which, coming into immediate effect, would concern Caesar very closely. It would have been on a par with the provisions that we do know, and the silence of our sources makes us doubt.

(2) Kalendae Martiae

This *argumentum ex silentio* is not, of course, conclusive. We turn to the actual evidence which Stevens adduces to support his theory. He points to the frequent significance of the date of 1st March.[1] In the question of Caesar's provinces this date had been significant since 59 when it became the beginning of his governorship under the Lex Vatinia. The obvious, and the 'traditional', explanation of its importance for the present problem is that, in 49, it was the 'legis dies' of the Lex Pompeia Licinia. Nor do the examples which Stevens quotes prove his case. Cicero's letter of March, 51 (*Fam.* 3, 2, 1), does not prove by any means (as Stevens seems to think) that Cicero already held the *imperium* when he wrote it. It merely shows that he had been informed that he would have to go to Cilicia as governor. He left Rome at the end of April, 51 (*Att.* 5, 1, 1). We do not know at what date between these two letters his appointment took effect by the passage of his Lex Curiata. The case of Minucius Thermus, who was corresponding with Cicero about the appointment of his deputy at the beginning of May, 50 (*Fam.* 2, 18, 2), is even less conclusive. By May, 50, it must have been clear to all provincial governors that they were not likely to be superseded that year, and discussion of a deputy-successor proves nothing for the date of normal succession, the date of taking over, or the date of departure from Rome.

There are indications, however, that after 52 governors may as a rule have got their Lex Curiata about March and left as soon as the spring weather allowed. This would be only sensible, and is suggestively like

---

[1] A possible explanation of both this date and 13th November as of general significance for the provincial allotment is given by Balsdon (pp. 65 ff.).

the practice of the Principate.[1] It is possible that the Lex Pompeia de provinciis may have fixed a date for the usual beginning of the governorship,[2] and may have made it normal for the allotment of provinces to take place at the beginning of the year, followed by a Lex Curiata in March, i.e. perhaps at the beginning of the military year[3] and certainly at the beginning of the open season. But even this little is conjecture. Nothing, however, that we know or may safely surmise about the Lex Pompeia de provinciis shows that no appointment could be made after 1st March. Quite apart from the evidence, it is obvious that such a rigid system would have caused many difficulties: how, e.g., was a *subrogatio* to be effected if a governor died at an inconvenient time?

Though apologizing for his digression, Mr Stevens makes much of Cicero's case; and we must follow him. It is true that from February, 50, onwards Cicero does not seem to regard supersession as likely, but he does so because he fears Curio's blocking of all business in the Senate. It is true also that *Att.* 6, 1, 24[4] shows Cicero aware by 20th February that the provinces would not be dealt with before March, but Stevens reads into the passage the opinion that therefore no allotment was to be expected that year. Such an opinion is not really to be found in the letter. Cicero was mainly concerned about a praetorian province, and praetorian provinces were put into cold storage in September, 51 (*Fam.* 8, 8, 8),[5] and kept there, early in 50, by Curio while he was agitating for his intercalary month and *leges viaria* and *alimentaria* (*Fam.* 8, 6, 5). Cicero's apparent conviction that no successor would be sent only shows that he correctly appreciated the effect of Curio's veto. As for the consular provinces, Cicero had long before been told both that Caesar's provinces were off the agenda till March, 50 (*Fam.* 8, 8, 5), and that Caesar's followers were opposed to discussing Gaul separately from the rest (*Fam.* 8, 9, 5). Throughout the supposed 'appointment-period' Cicero knew that no consular provinces were likely to be discussed. In

---

[1] Cf. Mommsen, *Staatsrecht* ii³, 255, esp.: 'Was den Anfangstermin anbelangt, so fand die Sortition jetzt wahrscheinlich gleich zu Anfang des Kalenderjahres statt, in dem die Provinz zu übernehmen war.' Sortition in January, Lex Curiata and departure in March. Cicero, who did not leave until midsummer, was no doubt delayed by the incorrectness of the calendar: in 51 the seas will not have been open until about May.

[2] Perhaps the end of June, since Tiberius ordered his governors to leave Rome by the beginning of that month (Dio 57, 14, 5).

[3] If Mommsen is to be believed (*Rechtsfrage* 101 ff.).

[4] '...iam enim sciemus de rebus urbanis, de provinciis, quae omnia in mensem Martium sunt collata. ...'

[5] The vetoing of this motion would not have changed the Senate's desire to make Cilicia a praetorian province.

other words, his remark to Atticus did not mean 'the appointment-period is nearly over, and there will be no more appointments', but more simply 'Curio's activities and last September's decisions make it certain that we shall have no provincial business transacted before March.'

Stevens suggests an 'appointment-period' even for prorogation (p. 201 and n. 131). But quite apart from the fact that the passage he quotes (*Att.* 5, 15, 3) does not in the least support his argument, we are given in *Fam.* 8, 5, 2, and 8, 9, 2, the reason for Cicero's beginning to 'canvass actively for support against prorogation . . . in September, 51' – Caelius' warnings that prorogation was a real danger. It should be noted that these warnings came before the whole question of the provinces had been postponed until March, 50 (*Fam.* 8, 8, 5–9). All through the summer of 51 it had to be taken into account that all provincial business could be stopped by Caesar's tribunes, and that this obstruction would continue (*Fam.* 8, 5, 2). Again, things are explained more readily by the known activities of Caesar's tribunes than by the effects of an unknown provision of the Lex Pompeia.

(3) Idus Novembres

Next, the much discussed date of 13th November. Stevens admits (p. 201) that his identification of this date with the beginning of the 'appointment-period' is 'pure imagination', but claims that 'it throws a flood of light on later events'. Other explanations have been offered for this date,[1] none of them final, but Stevens does not supply the answer either, as he bases his on a theory so lacking in proof.

It must be noted first that the date is mentioned only once in the long controversy (*Fam.* 8, 11, 3). In April, 50, Caelius told Cicero:

> In unam causam omnis contentio coniecta est, de provinciis: in quam adhuc incubuisse cum senatu Pompeius videtur ut Caesar Id. Nov. decedat. Curio omnia potius subire constituit quam id pati. . . . Nostri porro, quos tu nosti, ad extremum certamen rem deducere non audent. Scena rei totius haec: Pompeius, tamquam Caesarem non impugnet sed quod illi aequum putet constituat, ait Curionem quaerere discordias. Valde autem non vult et plane timet Caesarem consulem designari prius quam exercitum et provinciam tradiderit.

---

[1] For Adcock's attempt to make it the 'legis dies' cf. above p. 15. Balsdon (p. 67) has given an explanation of the significance of the date which would fit both 50 and 49, but is by no means certain.

The compromise here mentioned never reappears. One will not go far wrong in concluding that it was a tentative proposal (to which Pompey 'inclined'),[1] put forward by that majority in the Senate who, as Caelius says, did not dare let matters get to a crisis. Curio's furious opposition showed them the futility of any compromise which Caesar considered dangerous to himself.

The passage raises three questions: why 13th November, which November was Caelius talking about – 49 or 50, and how can Pompey's attitude be explained. To the first, Tenney Frank would appear to provide an answer (cf. p. 15, n. 1). As to the second, the obvious answer would be: the November of the same year, of 50. But Hardy (p. 210), following Mommsen (*Rechtsfrage*, p. 140, n. 138), made out a case, which Marsh admits 'sounds reasonable in itself' (p. 281), for supposing that Caelius and Cicero knew so well which year was meant (namely 49, the critical year) that exact definition was unnecessary. It is obvious, whatever else may be argued, that the 'legis dies' must have preceded this 13th November, as Pompey could not call it fair ('aequum') to deprive Caesar of however short a period of his legal tenure. Therefore, on our assumption that the 'legis dies' was 28th February, 49, this November must also have been 49. But, it is asked, what in that case about Pompey's fears of a Caesar who was elected consul while yet holding his province? By November, 49, Caesar could expect to have been elected in his absence. Pompey cannot have agreed to a proposal which would have done this very thing he feared.

Yet a study of the passage would seem to show Pompey doing just this, in spite of the commentators who would fathom his mind.[2] Whether 'valde autem' was meant to contrast with the earlier or the later part of the passage makes no difference.[3] The decisive point is the contrast between the proposal and Pompey's attitude, a contrast expressed in 'autem'. If his real desires were being quoted to explain his acceptance of the suggestion we should expect 'enim'. The last part of the passage expresses only Caelius' opinion of what Pompey wanted, not what Pompey himself declared. The meaning is this: Pompey agrees to the proposal that Caesar should be recalled on 13th November (49). He calls this fair because it gives Caesar all he can reasonably ask

---

[1] Stevens (p. 200) makes him joint proposer. But Caelius' language makes it plain that the idea did not come from Pompey.

[2] Cf. Caelius' opinion of Pompey (*Fam.* 8, 1, 3): 'solet enim aliud sentire et loqui neque tantum valere ingenio ut non appareat quid cupiat.' Here, too, Pompey thought and said two different things, and let his true wishes appear to the shrewd observer.

[3] Thus Marsh's objection (p. 281) to Hardy's explanation falls down.

for – an extension of his command and the candidature in absence.[1] He puts a brave face on the situation (which he dislikes) because he knows that 'nostri porro . . . ad extremum certamen rem deducere non audent'. But in reality he is against any proposal which allows Caesar's candidature while he is still in command of his army, and shows plainly that he fears this possibility. Pompey was acting against and despite his fears because some compromise was necessary in view of the Senate's timid mood.

It may be said that the proposal should have satisfied Caesar, and that Curio's furious opposition is therefore inexplicable if this explanation is right. But it is doubtful whether Caesar could accept. If we translate, with Marsh (p. 280), 'Pompey, professing not to be attacking Caesar, but to be making an arrangement which he considers fair to him . . .' we should indeed imply that Pompey could in this case profess himself innocent of hostile intentions towards Caesar. That argues a state of affairs which is neither credible nor fits the situation of April, 50. Thus it is preferable to translate,[2] 'Pompey, as though he were not attacking Caesar but agreeing to a proposal which he thinks fair to him . . .', i.e. that in Caelius' opinion, and in reality, Pompey was attacking Caesar. This becomes obvious when we remember that Caesar feared any period, even six weeks (13th November – 29th December) without armed protection.[3] Six weeks were long enough to re-enact Milo's trial with Caesar in the dock, and once Caesar was without an army his fate depended on his enemies' actual power, not on the technicality whether he still held the *imperium* or not. Curio was bound to resist, even as his master was bound to object.

Thus it is suggested that Hardy's elaboration of Mommsen's theory (that Caelius knew Cicero would understand him to refer to November, 49) will satisfactorily explain this date, the more so as the whole compromise proposal seems to have been dropped almost at once, which would be surprising if 13th November was the beginning of the 'appointment-period' or the 'legis dies'.[4] It can also be shown that

---

[1] Tenney Frank's explanation of Pompey's 'fairness' (i.e. that he proposed to bring the calendar up to date in 49 so that 365 (*sic* – really 355) days would have passed by 13th November), a convincing bit of reasoning (*Class. Rev.* xxxiii, 1919, 68 f.), strengthens the case for a date in 49.

[2] Cf. also Turrell and Purser iii², p. 243 n.

[3] *Fam.* 8, 14, 2; Dio 40, 60, 1.

[4] No explanation has yet been found to suggest that this compromise could have been agreeable to the senatorial extremists, with whom Pompey was already pretty closely connected. They were mainly concerned with preventing the 'ratio absentis'. Was that the reason why the proposal was dropped?

Stevens's explanation makes unintelligible his own conjecture of an agreement ('negotium') between Caesar and Pompey. He supposes that in August, 51, Pompey agreed to hold over the discussion of Caesar's provinces until the end of the 'appointment-period' of 51–50, so that Caesar would be safe until the beginning of the next (see below p. 23). Are we to believe that Caesar would agree to an arrangement which would leave Pompey every show of fairness if he proposed his rival's recall six weeks before he could be consul (if, indeed, Caesar intended to be elected in 50)?[1] Or that Pompey agreed to an arrangement which would leave Caesar some show of justice if, already elected, he prolonged his stay until 29th December, 50? Such an agreement, which could only be made by men of vague minds and a generally trusting disposition, does not fit the situation. There is thus no justification for the theory of the 'appointment-period': it is unnecessary and unconvincing as an explanation of the March and November dates, and unsatisfactory as an explanation for the actions of the chief protagonists.

(4) Fam. 8, 8, 9

There remain the essential passages in *Fam.* 8, 8. Caelius informed Cicero in October, 51:

> ... plane perspecta Cn. Pompeii voluntate in eam partem ut eum decedere post Kal. Mart. placeret, senatus consultum ... factum est ... (§ 4). Illa praeterea Cn. Pompei sunt animadversa, quae maxime confidentiam attulerunt hominibus, ut diceret se ante Kal. Mart. non posse sine iniuria de provinciis Caesaris statuere, post Kal. Mart. se non dubitaturum (§ 9).

It seems probable that the *Kalendae Martiae*, mentioned twice in this letter, are the same, that both refer to 50 B.C., and that in both cases only the *senatus consultum*, not the *successio*, was in Pompey's mind. In § 4 Caelius reports Pompey's inclination to be that after 1st March the Senate should pass a resolution about the end of Caesar's tenure of power.[2] He then transcribes the official resolution which put into operation this 'Pompei voluntas', and follows it with an explanation of

---

[1] Stevens's theory does not exclude the possibility of a proconsul taking out his Lex Curiata at any time during the 'appointment-period', while all preliminary steps could be taken beforehand.

[2] Like Holmes (p. 51, n. 1) and Balsdon (p. 176, n. 44), though independently from them, I take 'post Kal. Mart.' to refer to 'placeret' and not to 'eum decedere'. This despite Hardy's objections (p. 205, n. 1). Pompey was just then only concerned with postponing the discussion. The decree (§ 8) which was the result of his wishes refers only to a debate on 1st March, not to a date of recall.

Pompey's conduct.[1] This 'explanation' is, indeed, highly intriguing. Pompey declared that he could not allow Caesar's provinces to be debated before 1st March (50) without injury to Caesar, but would have no scruples after that date. He then answered to questions about the future that for Caesar to suborn a tribune to block the business of the Senate would be the same as open disobedience to the Senate's demands, and compared any possibility of Caesar's wishing to be both consul-elect and commander to a son raising his stick against his father. 'His vocibus,' continues Caelius, 'ut existimarent homines Pompeio cum Caesare esse negotium effecit.'

Two explanations have been offered for this passage. Mommsen (*Rechtsfrage* 139) postulated a clause (*sanctio*) in the Lex Pompeia Licinia forbidding the discussion of Caesar's provinces before 1st March, 50. Taken in conjunction with the provisions of the Lex Sempronia, this would have assured Caesar of his command till the end of 49, which Mommsen took to be his purpose. Stevens (pp. 178 f.) ascribes Pompey's reluctance to a 'deal' (Caelius' 'negotium') between him and Caesar to the effect that the question was not to be brought up before the end of the 'appointment-period' 51–50.[2] Neither explanation is fully satisfactory. Against Mommsen it has been pointed out[3] that such supposedly forbidden discussions were taking place or being proposed all through 51. This fact, together with the absence of any comment on such blatantly illegal action with the exception of one passing remark in Hirtius,[4] seems to prove Adcock's case: there was no *sanctio*. It should further be noted that, according to Caelius, Pompey's reluctance came as a surprise and as a relief[5] to people: they obviously knew nothing about any legal obstacle forbidding the discussion of Caesar's provinces and thus postponing the outbreak of civil war.[6]

Stevens makes out a more complete case for his view. He translates 'negotium' as 'deal' (Mommsen makes it 'quarrel'), and there is much to be said for this. It is most important to notice, with Stevens, that

[1] Surely a verbatim report of what is briefly stated in *Fam.* 8, 8, 4. Dio (40, 59, 3) must have been thinking of these words when he wrote that Pompey wished Caesar to return 'next year' (50) on the expiration of his command, as he thought that 'ut Caesari succedatur' meant immediate supersession (Hardy p. 173).

[2] Cf. p. 22.   [3] Adcock pp. 20 f.

[4] *BG* 8, 53, 1. This passage is discussed below.

[5] This I take to be the meaning of 'confidentia' (*Fam.* 8, 8, 9). People, disturbed by the evident disagreement between Pompey and Caesar, felt that Pompey's decision had postponed the crisis. (Cf. also Tyrrell and Purser, ad loc., iii², p. 116.)

[6] The same argument applies to Balsdon's explanation of the passage (pp. 175 ff.) which is really only an extension of the *sanctio*.

between 22nd July[1] and the beginning of September, 51,[2] Pompey underwent a complete change of mind. In July he agreed to discuss Caesar's provinces, in September he refused to do so, and his father-in-law, Scipio, mentioned our mysterious date of 1st March.[3] In between Pompey had been to Ariminum (*Fam.* 8, 4, 4). It seems very likely that he met Caesar or an emissary of his there, and that some sort of discussion did take place.[4] But what went on at this discussion?

This is where Stevens's theory becomes less unimpeachable. I can see no justification in *Fam.* 8, 8, 9, for assuming a full deal, an agreement arrived at at this time. People could certainly not deduce any such thing from Pompey's remark about Caesar's possible disobedience to the Senate's orders. And unlike Stevens we cannot see in the father–son simile proof that Pompey thought himself so closely allied to Caesar. No explanation which assumes Pompey to have had himself in mind when he spoke of 'father' is quite satisfactory. Of course, he spoke of 'filius meus', but the whole remark was metaphorical. Who, after all, were the 'Fathers'? A few moments earlier Pompey had spoken about Caesar's relations with the Senate, and it may be suggested that he was still thinking of the Senate. In demanding the 'ratio absentis' while still in command of his army (this was the point raised) Caesar would be disobeying not Pompey, who had no official position with regard to him, but the Senate who could decree his recall before the 'absentis ratio' was used.[5] The significance of the remark would then be that Pompey hardly expected such unfilial conduct from Caesar, but if matters should come to such a pass – well, the father would, of course, prove the stronger. No listener could deduce the existence of a real 'deal' between Pompey and Caesar from these remarks. Hence one may be justified in taking the passage in its most general sense, 'these remarks have led people to believe that there is something going on between Pompey and Caesar'. Pompey's sudden reluctance to discuss Caesar's provinces,

---

[1] *Fam.* 8, 4, 4: 'interrogatus de successione C. Caesaris, de qua, hoc est de provinciis, placitum est ut quam primum ad urbem reverteretur Cn. Pompeius, ut coram eo de provinciarum successione ageretur'. Pompey was present at this debate.

[2] *Fam.* 8, 9, 5: 'Ipse (Pompeius) tamen hanc sententiam dixit nullum hoc tempore senatus consultum faciendum.'

[3] *Fam.* 8, 9, 5: 'Scipio hanc ut Kal. Mart. de provinciis neu quid coniunctim referretur.'

[4] This is Stevens's theory (pp. 178 ff.). His collateral supports, Balbus' visit to Rome and Plancus' presence at Ravenna, have no intrinsic significance and become important only in connection with the theory.

[5] The Senate had also fathered Caesar's greatness by giving him Transalpine Gaul in 59, though Cicero (*Att.* 8, 3, 3) and Plutarch (*Pomp.* 46, 4) ascribe a good deal of fatherhood of this kind to Pompey. But whatever the general implications of the paternity problem, in this passage it is clearly the Senate that is viewed as wielding a father's authority.

and to a smaller degree his references to disobedience and unfilial conduct, would infallibly create the impression that 'something was up'
between these two men which people in general did not know about.
That is all that can legitimately be deduced from Caelius' words.

The only passage which suggests that there was something in the Lex
Pompeia Licinia forbidding discussion before a certain date is Hirtius
8, 53, 1 – 'M. Marcellus proximo anno . . . contra legem Pompei et
Crassi rettulerat ante tempus ad senatum de Caesaris provinciis.' This
has generally been interpreted as proving that Marcellus was offending
against some provision of the law.[1] But one may translate: 'Marcellus
had put the motion, in contravention of the Lex Pompeia Licinia, that
Caesar's provinces be disposed of, before the expiration of his command'
(free, but possible), taking 'ante tempus' to go in general sense with 'de
provinciis' and understanding Marcellus' action to have been premature
because the law gave Caesar a longer command. In other words, the
contents of his *relatio* and not the fact that he 'rettulerat' were premature,
and Hirtius, in his passing remark, expressed himself too concisely. This
is corroborated by other authorities who make Marcellus propose the
premature recall of Caesar (Suet. *Div. Iul.* 28, 2; App. *BC* 2, 26; Dio 40,
59, 1). Hardy (for his discussion of the passage cf. p. 176) throws over the
secondary authorities and prefers Hirtius. But however unfortunate it
may be that a contemporary authority should be made to yield to the
later, Hirtius is easily the least explicit of them all and can most readily
be interpreted so as not to contradict the other sources.[2]

(5) *The possibility of a 'gentlemen's agreement'*

This brings us to the question what it was that went on between
Pompey and Caesar, and here there is frankly nothing for it but conjecture. It is generally agreed that when Caesar and Pompey renewed
the triumvirate at Luca the latter promised to secure for his partner a
privilegium exempting him from the duty to attend his election to the
consulship in person. This promise Pompey redeemed in 52 by the
passage of the Lex Decem Tribunorum, which granted Caesar his
'ratio absentis', and by the codicil of doubtful legality which he added
to his own Lex de iure magistratuum.[3] It was also decided at Luca that

---

[1] E.g. Rice-Holmes in his edition of *BG* (8, 53, 1 – p. 399 n.) and *RR* ii, 299 ff.
[2] For a similar opinion of this passage, cf. Adcock, pp. 20 f.
[3] Cicero (*Att.* 7, 6, 2; 8, 3, 3) seems to have regarded the belated addition to the *lex quaedam*
as effective.

Caesar's tenure of power in Gaul should be prolonged by five years. Surprise has been shown[1] that in 55 Caesar should have expected or wanted another five years of war in Gaul. It is not suggested that he did; but what we know of Caesar entitles us to assume that he would prepare for all the eventualities he could foresee.

At Luca Caesar's position was as follows. If he got another five years from 54 (or on some views from 55) he would have ample time to finish the conquest and settlement of Gaul. Pompey's promise of the 'absentis ratio' could be redeemed at any convenient moment. The question for Caesar was whether he should be elected before or after the date on which his provincial command expired. If before he could make sure of avoiding the dreaded interval as *privatus*,[2] but he would need an exemption from the Lex annalis. If after, i.e. in 49, some means had to be found to enable him to stay in Gaul till the end of 49. It may well have been that Caesar contemplated both possibilities, leaving his choice to depend on developments in Gaul. In such circumstances one may suggest that he exacted another promise from Pompey, namely that, if necessary, the discussion of his successor should be held over until 1st March, 50. As Mommsen has worked out, this would have prolonged Caesar's stay till the end of 49, by which time he could be legally elected consul if Pompey kept his other promise, of the 'absentis ratio'. As against Mommsen, this view then postulates not a *sanctio* contained in the Lex Pompeia Licinia but a private agreement between Pompey and Caesar, concluded at the same time as the agreement which resulted in the Lex Pompeia Licinia, which if redeemed would have had the same effect. This view would seem to resolve several difficulties:

(*a*) That M. Marcellus continually did in 51 what by the *sanctio* he would not have been allowed to do.

(*b*) That Caesar should have expected from 55 onwards to stay in Gaul till January, 48, when the obvious thing for him to do was to leave the province as soon as his task was finished.

(*c*) That a 'negotium' between Pompey and Caesar came as a surprise in September, 51 (which it would not have done if it had been contained in the Lex Pompeia Licinia), and that no one before suggested or seems to have considered any postponement of discussion.

(*d*) That no one ever showed any surprise or indignation at an

---

[1] Adcock, p. 22.

[2] It is assumed here as certain that Caesar was convinced of the danger of even a few weeks not so much without *imperium* as without an army before his entry on the consulship (*Fam* 8, 14, 2; Dio 40, 60, 1).

arrangement which gave Caesar at least ten additional months in Gaul. No one knew about it.

(*e*) It does account for the fact that according to his own testimony Caesar intended to become consul after the legal interval (*BC* 1, 32, 2; 3, 1, 1), and for Caelius' report that he 'feared to leave his army' (*Fam.* 8, 14, 2). If Pompey honoured his promise, the Lex Sempronia assured Caesar of an extension of his command till the end of 49.[1]

Nor need it be surprising that Caesar relied on Pompey's word only.[2] For one thing, the alternative for which this promise was needed, i.e. that he would stay till the end of 49 and have himself elected for 48, must have seemed the less likely of the two in 56, and even the other possibility – election in 50 – needed Pompey's help in getting round the Lex annalis. (Perhaps one may suspect here a third promise, again conditional on what Caesar proposed to do.) Then it must be remembered that the two partners had just concluded a family alliance through Pompey's marriage with Julia, and that the ancients had reason to think her death the beginning of the rupture (cf. e.g. Florus 4, 2, 13). Lastly, Pompey's character, discussed below,[3] suggests that he would stick to his word even when its fulfilment had become quite useless. He did keep his promise about the 'absentis ratio' at a time (in 52) when things were no longer going well between him and Caesar.[4] Moreover, there can be no doubt that civil war became a possibility from 52 onwards and practical certainty in 50,[5] and that if Caesar foresaw such a contingency in 56 he knew from the first that armed power and not verbal agreements would be decisive. He can never have thought that any calculations made in 56 would outlast a serious breach with Pompey. Yet that will not have prevented him from making Pompey promise to take certain legal steps.

---

[1] Stevens (p. 171) and Balsdon (pp. 58 ff.) have tried to tear to shreds Mommsen's other 'guarantee', namely the fact that supersession in March would have been a constitutional anomaly (*de prov. cons.* 36–8). I am not fully convinced of the futility of Cicero's argument and can believe that Caesar may have considered this an additional safeguard.

[2] For what sounds like a correct appreciation of the good relations between Caesar and Pompey immediately after Luca, cf. Plut., *Cato Minor* 43, 10.

[3] Cf. p. 33.

[4] I cannot agree with the novel theory (Stevens, pp. 174, 180 f.; Balsdon, pp. 173 f.; *CAH* ix, 627 f.) that Pompey's legislation of 52 did not work against Caesar. For the re-enactment of the duty of personal attendance at elections was highly inconvenient for Caesar, and Pompey's codicil could be attacked as invalid. The Lex Pompeia de provinciis did put the provinces at the Senate's disposal at the critical time and it was perhaps realized too late that it made the veto possible. At any rate, persistent vetoing could be (and was) dubbed resistance to the State, and force could be used against it.

[5] Cf. e.g. *Fam.* 8, 14, 2.

To sum up, then, it may be contended that Caesar's position after Luca was that he had another five years in which to complete the conquest of Gaul, after which time Pompey's promise to hold over the discussion until March, 50, and to secure the 'absentis ratio' would ensure his safe entry on the consulship of 48. But if the conquest of Gaul should be finished before that time, a senatorial dispensation from the ten years' interval might be secured, the 'absentis ratio' might be ante-dated, and he might become consul while yet holding his provincial command.

(6) Ratio absentis

If, for the moment, we may accept this position as proven, we may ask how its implications would work out in the next five years. Till the end of 53 Caesar was busy in Gaul. Pompey became consul in 52, and Suetonius tells us (*Div. Iul.* 26, 1) that Caesar was suggested as his colleague. Caesar, however, preferred to be given the privilege 'ut absenti sibi quandoque imperii tempus expleri coepisset petitio secundi consulatus daretur'. Mr Stevens is, of course, fully justified in taking this to prove that Caesar intended to be elected before his command expired, a view of Caesar's intentions which is in itself probable enough. He finds confirmation for this in the much discussed passage (*Fam.* 8, 8, 9) in which Caelius tells Cicero that Caesar might, as one of two alternatives, stand 'hoc anno' (i.e. 50, on any literal interpretation). The trouble is that Caesar tells us that he was given the *privilegium* for 49 (*BC* 1, 9, 2). Stevens neglects this important passage.

It is perhaps possible to reconstruct the relevant facts of the first months of 52. At the beginning of the year Caesar considered Gaul 'at peace'[1] and he may well have hoped to stand for the consulship in 50 if a dispens-ation could be secured.[2] Thus he may have answered the tribunes who wished to make him joint consul with Pompey that Gaul was not yet fully settled but that he would like to be consul before his command ended. But early in 52 Vercingetorix's revolt broke out. Clodius was murdered on 18th January (Ascon. *in Milon.* 27). The Gauls heard about it 'quickly' (*BG* 7, 1, 2), i.e. perhaps during the first week of February.

---

[1] *BG* 7, 1, 1. Although Caesar probably only meant that the previous year's rebellion had been quelled, he had every reason to suppose three further years (January, 52, to January, 49) sufficient for final pacification.

[2] Pompey had not yet fully joined his enemies, and the dispensation should not have been difficult to get from one who had himself just received one, even if it had not formed part of the compact at Luca.

The revolt may have been in full swing within five or six weeks after that, say, by the second week of the intercalary month or a little later. Pompey was commissioned to restore order early in the intercalary month (Ascon. 29), elected sole consul on the 24th (Ascon. 31), and moved his two laws *de vi* and *de ambitu* on the 27th (Ascon. 31). Caesar's request, as related by Suetonius, must have come before Pompey's election, or at the latest very soon after. He did not leave for Gaul until after some order had been restored at Rome by Pompey (*BG* 7, 6, 1). This must refer to the events of the intercalary month and points to a departure early in March, which is likely anyhow as he must have got the news from Gaul at the end of the intercalary month. The Lex Decem Tribunorum came at least a little later.[1] Thus Caesar would have had time to rescind his original instructions (if Suetonius is right about them).[2] Such a step, taken with a view to the news from Gaul, would allow us to credit both Caesar's and Suetonius' testimony. As early as August, 51, Caelius prophesied that the circle of intercession and counter-intercession would drag on for 'more than two years' (*Fam.* 8, 5, 2), i.e. he assumed already that Caesar would wish to stay till the end of 49. In fact, there is nothing to show after September, 51, when Caelius indicated something of the sort by his 'hoc anno', that Caesar intended to be elected in 50.

This passage (*Fam.* 8, 8, 9), however, needs some discussion. Caelius' words are – 'itaque iam, ut video, alteram utram ad condicionem descendere vult Caesar, ut aut maneat neque hoc anno sua ratio habeatur aut, si designari poterit, decedat'. Caelius gives it as his own view ('ut video') that Caesar will either 'stay on' ('maneat' must mean – stay on beyond the date on which he could legally be superseded) and give up any idea of being elected this year (50), or, if he should, after all, manage to be elected, leave his province (i.e. before the 'legis dies'). It is significant that the views hitherto given make Caelius misinterpret Caesar. If Mommsen and Hardy were right and 'hoc anno' meant 49 ('the year we are all thinking about'),[3] then Caelius made the mistake of supposing

---

[1] 'Probably in March, 52', according to Tyrrell and Purser (iii, p. lxv). Plutarch (*Pomp.* 56, 1) alludes to it after the co-optation of Scipio in August, 52 (*Pomp.* 55, 11). Dio (40, 51, 2), who puts both at the beginning of Pompey's sole consulship, before the laws *de vi* and *de ambitu*, is in conflict with Livy, *Epit.* 107, Asconius *in Milon.* 31, and Appian, *BC* 2, 25, 96, who all indicate its passage after Milo's trial.

[2] That in the end Caesar did not intend to stand in 50 is further indicated by the facts that at the elections of 50 he had his own candidate in the person of Ser. Sulpicius Galba, and that he visited Cisalpine Gaul early in the year for the sake of the canvass of M. Antonius, not his own (Hirtius, *BG* 8, 50, 1–2 and 4). These points are made by Tenney Frank (*JRS* xxiii, 1933, 74).   [3] Cf. Hardy p. 189.

that Caesar would give way to his enemies' desires not to allow him 'et consul esse et exercitum habere' (*Fam.* 8, 8, 9): he would either stay beyond the 'legis dies', and yet not be elected that year (49) – this, however, does not make sense; or he would secure his election after departing on the 'legis dies' (for 'decedat' suggests that Caelius was thinking of a departure earlier than or on, but not after, the 'legis dies'), but this makes even less sense. In either case, we should have to conclude that Caelius believed that Caesar would give up the 'absentis ratio'. If, on the other hand, we agree with the advocates of a date in 50 for the 'legis dies' and the 'absentis ratio', we again accuse Caelius of making a mistake in supposing that Caesar would leave Gaul before the end of 50, the earliest date on which it is agreed he could enter on his consulship. In either case Caelius would have overlooked what he himself later tells us (*Fam.* 8, 14, 2) was Caesar's view, namely that he thought it too dangerous to leave his army (before, that is, he was consul).[1] On our interpretation, however, we find that Caelius is actually discussing the alternatives which we conjectured Caesar may have been considering as early as 56 (above p. 27): he could either be elected in 50 and stay till January, 49 (he would then 'decedere' two months before the 'legis dies'), or he could wait for his election till 49 and 'manere' until the end of that year. In 51, Caesar was believed to be contemplating possibilities which to a man of his sagacity must have been plain since 56. Our theories are assuming some body and reality.

However, it has been suggested (above p. 28) that, if there was a choice at all, Caesar made it early in 52. How then could Caelius suppose in September, 51, that Caesar was at liberty to avail himself of the 'absentis ratio', either in 50 or in 49? This might be taken to indicate that the Lex Decem Tribunorum mentioned no date at all. That is intrinsically unlikely, and is disproved by Caesar's explicit statement (*BC* 1, 9, 2) that he had been given the privilege for 49 – 'cuius absentis rationem haberi proximis comitiis populus iussisset'. These words are strongly corroborated by Dio,[2] and Cicero's language in *Att.* 7, 7, 6 suggests the same thing. The whole question was really settled by Mommsen,[3] whose argument shows that the Lex Decem Tribunorum must have

---

[1] Cf. here Caesar's offers in 50–49: he always wished to retain at least one legion and one province, or when he did offer to surrender the 'absentis ratio' and to return (*Fam.* 16, 12, 3) he demanded that Pompey should go to Spain. Pompey's absence would free Caesar from the threat of Milo's fate.

[2] 40, 51, 2. The νόμοι here mentioned must be the Leges annales; for the Lex Vatinia or Pompeia Licinia had nothing to do with any lawful time for consular election.

[3] *Rechtsfrage* 125 ff.

given Caesar the right to stand in his absence in 49, though it does not prove that he never intended to stand in 50. It must be shown, then, how Caelius came to think of the earlier date at all. He obviously believed that Caesar would choose the first alternative; for that must be why he put the event later in time first in his letter. Moreover, his words – 'si designari poterit' – clearly suggest that it was not open to Caesar simply to choose election in 50, but that some new measures were needed for this, such as a senatorial dispensation from the Lex annalis and an ante-dating of the 'absentis ratio' by a new tribunician law.[1] The situation may have been as follows. When the Gallic revolt broke out Caesar's first idea, to stand in 50, the idea which Suetonius preserved,[2] was replaced by the decision to stand in 49. But, as is shown by the motion of M. Marcellus, which like all moves against Caesar was an attempt to recall him before the 'absentis ratio' could be used, observers at Rome considered it possible in 51 that Caesar might yet try to revert to the previous position by means of new legislation.[3] When the whole question had been shelved for the time being by Pompey's desire to postpone discussion, Caelius – his use of the word 'itaque' shows that he based his forecast on the events related in the earlier part of the letter (*Fam.* 8, 8, 5 and 9) – decided that Caesar's candidature in 50 was now unlikely. He mentioned it at all only because Caesar might possibly do something during the winter, despite the postponement.[4]

[1] As a rule the tribunes were Caesar's adherents. In 51 surprise was shown at the election of one who professed senatorial leanings (Curio, *Fam.* 8, 4, 2). A new tribunician law would also obviate the now doubtful legality of the old.

[2] If we are right Caesar wrote first a letter to his tribunes, who then started their preparations for a bill with 50 in their view. The whole matter may have been well under way before Caesar asked for 49. It does not seem incredible to me that from an account of these negotiations, preserved in a lost historian (Asinius Pollio?), Suetonius should have quoted the initial letter only.

[3] Having written this I find that Mr Stone, whose purpose was quite different, came to a similar conclusion about this passage (p. 198): 'Caelius is referring to some talk about having a law passed to enable Caesar to stand in 50 for the consulship of 49.'

[4] I admit, of course, that my theory of Caesar's 'alternatives' and 'choice' must be considered tentative and based on conjecture. It does, however, consider all three important passages (*BC* 1, 9, 2; *Fam.* 8, 8, 9; Suet., *Div. Iul.* 26, 1), and seems to offer the only solution of their contradictions. I think that Caesar's own testimony as to the date mentioned in the Lex Decem Tribunorum must stand, and that, at any rate after March, 52, he had no intention of being elected in 50. In that case Suetonius and Caelius were either talking nonsense or allowing for some other possibility, and I feel that the theory offered in this paper does something to combine all these statements into a reasonable whole.

(7) 'Negotium' *between Caesar and Pompey*

The revolt of 52 and the consequent prolongation of his stay in Gaul through the summer of 50,[1] forced Caesar to fall back on 48 for his consulship. This gave him the chance of posing as the upholder of the law (*BC* 1, 32, 2; 3, 1, 1). On the other hand, Pompey's second promise now became important for extending his command till the end of 49. But just when Caesar was ready to demand its fulfilment, the ground was cut from under him by Pompey's legislation of 52, which in effect scrapped the Lex Sempronia and much of the traditional system of allotting provinces. Caesar's only chance now of prolonging his proconsulship was to prevent his supersession by the tribunician veto, made possible by the fact that the Lex Sempronia did not apply.

Probably in April, 51, M. Marcellus began his attack on Caesar's position, i.e. on the 'absentis ratio' and apparently also on the 'legis dies'.[2] Later, Caelius informs us (*Fam.* 8, 1, 2; 8, 2, 2), this motion was put off, the probable cause being Pompey's vacillation and his reluctance to admit the open breach with Caesar. Counsels of moderation did not prevail for long, and on 22nd July the Senate decided that the question of the provinces (which would include that of Caesar's successor)[3] should be brought up for discussion. Nothing happened on the appointed day (13th August) because of the trial of the consul-elect, C. Marcellus (*Fam.* 8, 9, 2). When the matter came up again in September, Pompey twice refused to have it discussed, and first Scipio and then he himself referred everything to 1st March, 50 (*Fam.* 8, 9, 5; 8, 8, 9). We are back at Pompey's change of mind and his probable meeting with Caesar.

It may be suggested that when Pompey met his old partner, or his partner's envoy, he may well have remembered his now useless promise of five years before to hold over any discussion of Caesar's provinces till 1st March, 50, and that he now satisfied his conscience by declaring he would stick to his old bargain. Caesar, he may have told him, could not expect more: every part of the pact at Luca had been fulfilled (and Pompey had incidentally freed himself from all obligations to Caesar). The 'absentis ratio' had been granted – even though in circumstances which made it possible to attack its legal validity, and the discussion

---

[1] In 56 Cicero (*de prov. cons.* 34) suggested the need for two more years to round off the conquest after the real fighting was over.

[2] Dio 40, 59, 1; App., *BC* 2, 26, 99; Suet., *Div. Iul.* 28, 2-3.

[3] *Fam.* 8, 4, 4. 'De successione Caesaris, hoc est de provinciis' proves that the Senate preferred to discuss the general problem rather than the particular.

would be postponed till the agreed date – even though that was now a worthless concession. Such action would have been in character. Pompey was a stickler for minor points of honour and used to set his soul at rest by fulfilling the letter when he ignored the spirit of an agreement. He did so in the matter of the 'absentis ratio' and the codicil he added to his own Lex de iure magistratuum.[1] Similarly, when Clodius began his attack on Cicero, Pompey tried to deceive himself and Cicero by easy promises which he may have considered fulfilled by his apparent innocence in the matter (*Att.* 2, 20, 2; 22, 2: Plut. *Pomp.* 46, 9). Pompey's almost proverbial duplicity[2] suggests a similar attitude of mind: his conscience was untroubled if only he had not himself expressly avowed what was being proposed for him.[3] We also learn that in difficult circumstances he was fond of verbal quibbles (*Att.* 2, 16, 2; Plut. *Pomp.* 51, 7 f.).

Thus, while Stevens postulates a real 'deal' in 51, one may rather suggest that there was no negotiation in the true sense of the word at that time. An old agreement – Pompey's promise of 56 to hold over the discussion of Caesar's provinces if a prolonged stay should become necessary – was resurrected in order that Pompey might placate his conscience and set himself fully aright for the approaching conflict. The 'negotium' of 51, no more than a postponement of the clash which both sides must have seen approaching, gave Caesar nothing of substance; but then he could not expect anything substantial from Pompey at this stage. At least there was no reason why he should not accept this arrangement, which absolved him for six months from the necessity of having all provincial business blocked.

This theory helps us over a hurdle which Stevens fails to take. Everything that happened from 52 onwards (Pompey's legislation, the relations between the Catonian party and Pompey, the senatorial discussions of 51) points to an ever-growing estrangement between the ex-partners. Such is the impression given by Cicero's correspondence (*Att.* 5, 12, 2; *Fam.* 8, 4, 4; 9, 5; 10, 4), by the narratives of Dio (40, 50, 5; 51, 1; 56, 2), Appian (*BC* 2, 23, 84 ff.; 25, 95 ff.), and Suetonius (*Div. Iul.* 27, 1; 28, 3), and by Caesar's brief reference to his relations with Pompey (*BC* 1, 4) which seems to indicate that their friendship began to break down after the death of Julia in 54 (*sim.* Florus 4, 2, 13). That Caesar tried to maintain good relations with his partner and rival as long

---

[1] Cf. Plutarch (*Pomp.* 56, 2–3), who also suggests this acquiescence in a broken promise with a conscience satisfied by its apparent fulfilment.

[2] 'Simulator' (Q.F. 1, 3, 9); 'solet enim aliud sentire et loqui' (*Fam.* 8, 1, 3).

[3] Cf. the cases of the *cura annonae* (57 B.C.), Ptolemy Auletes (56 B.C.), and Pompey's dictatorship (54 B.C.).

as possible (Caes. *BC* 1, 7; App. *BC* 2, 25, 96) is surely no argument against the general worsening of the situation. But Stevens would have us believe that all at once they reforged their alliance. The supposition becomes the more incredible when it is remembered that the next few months showed no relaxation of their hostility. Stevens points out that Pompey returned from Ariminum without the legion which he had lent to Caesar. But Pompey had himself declared that he could not withdraw the legion at once, before he went to Ariminum (*Fam.* 8, 4, 4). If August, 51, saw a true 'deal' between the two men, then why did Caesar labour all through the winter to secure Paulus and Curio? Why and how did the 'deal' break down so completely in a few months, by spring 50? The sequence of events becomes illogical and incomprehensible if we assume a real agreement between the protagonists as late as this. It becomes comprehensible if the meeting in August, 51, resulted in no more than the fulfilment of an old promise which, though it had had a purpose behind it in 56, had now become completely futile.[1]

One last point remains, Balbus' 'sorrow' at Scipio's *sententia* of 1st September, 51, that the Gallic provinces should be brought up by themselves on 1st March, 50 (*Fam.* 8, 9, 5). Stevens (pp. 188 f.) takes this as additional evidence for the 'appointment-period'. But there was probably behind it no more than Caesar's obvious reluctance to have his provinces discussed by themselves. To single them out from the general allotment would be to attack him directly.[2] Moreover, if he could block all provincial business in one go, the Senate would be more likely to give way.[3] Balbus may also have remonstrated with Scipio because the postponement, now after all an illusory concession, was being represented as the fair fulfilment of an old promise. The decree of 29th September (*Fam.* 8, 8, 5), which implemented Scipio's motion, was not opposed by the Caesarian tribunes, because they, too, preferred the small concession of six months' peace to nothing. They, and their master, could at least attend to their preparations for the critical year of 50 B.C. without being distracted by the activities of the Marcelli.

---

[1] The same goes for Balsdon's explanation of the 'negotium' (pp. 176 f.). He, too, would have us believe in friendly relations between Pompey and Caesar in 51. About 50 he says (p. 177): 'The "negotium" had broken down,' but does not explain how or why. I agree with his idea of a 'gentlemen's agreement' (of which I read after I had formulated my own theory), but put it into 56 when we know that Caesar and Pompey were partners rather than in 51 when their relations were strained.

[2] Cf. also Hardy (p. 180): 'It was still possible that in a general debate on the provinces one or both of his provinces might be left out of the settlement, and consular or praetorian be selected from the rest.'

[3] Cf. *Fam.* 8, 9, 2: 'Galliae in eandem condicionem quam ceterae provinciae vocantur,' as an explanation for the general stoppage of provincial appointments which Caelius foresaw.

III CONCLUSION

It may now be asked what has been gained from this long discussion. To begin with, it may be claimed that a more satisfactory explanation has been offered of several passages which have been held to conflict with the 'traditional' view,[1] and this without neglecting the clear evidence for the year for which the 'absentis ratio' was given. It seems also as though the question why no 'legis dies' is mentioned in our sources can best be answered on the assumption that it lay yet in the future when the civil war broke out. All through the negotiations the critical date was too well known to need special mention, and when at last it did arrive, war was already raging and legal questions had lost all significance. If, on the other hand, the 'legis dies' was in 50, the question how it could possibly pass without any attention being paid to it must remain unanswered.[2]

Even more important than these points is the possibility provided by this theory of rationally explaining the activities of Caesar and his enemies. On this showing, Caesar was capable of looking ahead and of laying his plans for future eventualities. Mommsen makes him act rigidly, tying himself down to a definite course without suggestion of modification. Adcock and Stevens virtually assume that he had no plan at all at Luca and simply lived from hand to mouth. The view, on the other hand, here put forward, fits the man much better. And it may be hoped that an answer has been given to the reasonable objection that Caesar, on this theory, is made to rely only on Pompey's word and 'gentlemen's agreements'.

It has also been possible to avoid what may perhaps be called the catastrophic view of Pompey's and Caesar's relationship, i.e. that everything went fairly well until the winter of 51–50, when all at once hostilities flared up. That the protagonists were veiled enemies some time before Pompey finally joined the senatorial extremists during 50 seems certain, and the explanation of the *negotium*, offered above, takes account of this.

Lastly, one may hope to have given a better interpretation of the events of December, 50, and January, 49, than is possible on the assumption of a 'legis dies' in 50. The advocates of the 50 date ask us to suppose that Caesar's enemies reserved the full weight of their attack until the 'legis dies' was past, until, that is, their best chance of achieving their

---

[1] Particularly *Fam.* 8, 8, 9 and *Fam.* 8, 11, 3.
[2] Mr Stevens's answer (p. 208) stands and falls with the 'appointment-period'.

end with a show of legality had gone. Against this, it has been suggested above that by concentrating on the Lex Pompeia Licinia and pressing for Caesar's recall on the 'legis dies' they tried to prevent the 'ratio absentis'. All the motions concerning Caesar's recall become more reasonable if this view is right.[1]

But all Caesar's planning was overthrown by the legislation of 52. Hence the circle of proposal and veto, counter-proposal and counter-veto, which filled the years 51 and 50. With the approach of the 'legis dies', not after it had passed, the Catonian party gathered up its reserves and brought matters to a crisis. Once Pompey's active help had finally been secured (December, 50), they could afford to press their motion for Caesar's recall, to override the veto, and to seek to achieve by war what the veto had prevented them from achieving by the ordinary operation of the Lex Pompeia Licinia. As a result of Pompey's legislation of 52, it was they who could rely on the law in December, 50, though Caesar had the stronger army and the veto. Thus it was not until the actual outbreak of war that the legal question, the question of the 'legis dies', ceased to be of importance.

[1] M. Marcellus, in 51, admittedly tried to recall Caesar prematurely, but he, too, wished to prevent the 'absentis ratio' and made his attempt before, not after, the end of Caesar's command. For the probable reason for his early action cf. p. 32.

I

TUDOR POLITICS

2

RENAISSANCE MONARCHY?*

Not so long ago the sixteenth century could be considered as nearly worked out: perhaps there might be details to fill in, but the outlines stood firm and clear. However, of late, as we have learned more about the middle ages, our confident generalizations about the Tudor period have grown less and less convincing. Was it the beginning of fresh things or the end of old, the first modern or the last medieval century? Or have these terms perhaps no meaning at all? What is the truth about Tudor monarchy? What place does the period occupy in the development of Parliament? Was its preoccupation with religion real or a screen for – at a guess – economic forces? The questions accumulate. The old answers too often fail to accord with new views of the centuries surrounding the sixteenth, and the old methods lead nowhere. There are marked weaknesses in the old approach, with its undue reliance on printed material and its eyes fixed on later political developments, weaknesses which the spread of the techniques of medieval scholarship is constantly revealing. What has to be grasped about the changed thinking in these matters is that there is no question of just correcting points of detail or of discovering a few new facts. A whole complex of underlying ideas, a whole frame of reference, is being discarded. It is this that makes synthesis so difficult. The problem cannot be solved by incorporating some new discoveries into an established and acceptable account, for while there is no quarrel with the old facts there is much disquiet about the interpretations commonly put upon them.

Professor Mackie has therefore had a specially trying task in attempting to fill this gap in the Oxford History of England. He had a choice to make, and he decided, on the whole, to take his stand with the old approach. In this he was very probably wise, for the old view has at least the merit of being complete within its own limits. Preoccupations with foreign policy and general constitutional issues – rather than with the details of economic, social, and institutional development – therefore take up most of the book. There are advantages in this: Professor Mackie

* [Review of J. D. Mackie, *The Earlier Tudors, 1485–1558* (Oxford, 1952), in *EHR* 68 (1953), 276–80.]

39

could concentrate upon telling the story of seventy years of history without having to interrupt the flow with those knotty and difficult chapters which analytical problems demand. What is more, the story has never been better told. Professor Mackie's treatment of foreign affairs makes for uncommon clarity in a field which is often incomprehensible enough, even though one may feel that outlines of European events occupy a disproportionate amount of space. The author succeeds wonderfully in bringing people to life: we know that these men and women once were alive and are not abstractions of paper and ink. In fact, the book will be read with enjoyment for its own sake, which is a fate that befalls few historical publications these days. What makes it specially attractive is its independence of judgment, its understanding of men and their ways. Professor Mackie sees the virtues of a man like Henry VIII without having to gloss over his horrible side; he can be scathing on Henry VII or Cromwell or Northumberland without turning them into monsters that never were. He has no patience with religious persecution one way or the other, though perhaps he handles More and Mary Tudor rather less gently than the makers of the Dissolution. Altogether this is a balanced, sensible, and enjoyable book.

It is when one turns to those aspects of the period which have been much rewritten in recent years that doubts begin to arise. The fundamental difficulty lies in the outmoded conception of a New Monarchy and the notion of a ' Renaissance' in political affairs. We have come to realize that Yorkist or Tudor monarchy was nothing fresh either in aims or methods or doctrine, though perhaps we are in danger of forgetting the changes which the Reformation made in all these. Furthermore, few today would really argue that Tudor rule was despotic, however energetic and arbitrary it may at times have been; it rested on the law. The whole idea of a specifically ' Renaissance' kingship looks odd in the light of the practice of every strong medieval king. It is a hangover from the days when the middle ages were thought of as a closed period – probably deplorable – which gave way round about 1500 to something quite new. As for the humanists like Erasmus, Colet, and More – did their ideas really influence any politicians? And was not Machiavelli the recorder of ancient practices rather than the inventor of new theory? And if so, why continue to discuss these men as though the politics of the times centred upon their writings? All these reflections are caused by Professor Mackie's somewhat uneasy stand between the untenable old view and the as yet only half-formulated new view on these matters. He retains the term 'new monarchy', but attempts to show that the new monarchy only handled old institutions in a new way; even this is doubtful, for often it was a question of handling old institutions in the old way. In either case, the term only confuses and ought to be abandoned. 'The "new monarchy" was the political expression of the Renaissance, and the Renaissance represented the triumph of the facts' (p. 23). But, except perhaps in the arts, the Renaissance represents only an abstraction of the historians which they are now labouring to destroy. 'In the new monarchy the prince was the mainspring of the state' (p. 478). Who, remembering medieval kingship, cannot but feel that this is the essence also of pre-sixteenth century government? Professor Mackie frequently uses the Renaissance to explain things: its individualism is reflected in diplomacy (p. 82), the Renaissance prince had few confidants (p. 202), though Colet's learning was clogged by some errors of medievalism he was a true son of the Renaissance in other ways (p. 246), Wolsey is the type of the Renaissance prince (p. 286), it was a prince's duty in a Renaissance state to make his country self-sufficient (p. 468). The term really has no meaning at all and therefore interprets nothing, unless one believes in that sudden outburst of novelty about 1500 – and that one can no longer do. All these 'Renaissance' characteristics are found in as plain form in other periods, both earlier and later. It is a pity that Professor Mackie could not free himself from an outdated framework. There were new things in the period he discusses – the sovereignty created by the break with Rome, for one – but it does not help to define things as 'Renaissance' because that word begs a question long since denied. In any case, novelty can be an overrated quality.

On points of detail it must be said that Professor Mackie is not very happy when he turns to economic, constitutional, and administrative matters. The chapter on economic affairs is handicapped by excessive reliance on superseded views: the picture here given of the medieval manor and medieval agrarian conditions has much of that fixity and universality which more modern research can no longer accept. It is unfortunate that London's Guildhall is used to prove the identity of gild merchant and town – London had no gild merchant (p. 458). Many would query the notion of a protectionist policy in the later middle ages, and there are moments when the trade in wool seems to be confused with that in cloth. Much of the uncertainty of this chapter may indeed be due to the fact that research in this field is constantly proceeding, but Professor Mackie's endeavour to discount the evidence for limited enclosing once again reflects a reluctance to abandon an old notion.

In constitutional matters the book suffers from the advantages of its arrangement: these things cannot well be dealt with piecemeal, in the course of a connected narrative. The account of the Council, for instance, is spread over three or four places, and there are errors. There was no distinction in Henry VII's time between the Council attendant and the Council at Westminster, but only between councillors happening to be at either place; the Eltham Ordinance did not, as is suggested, exclude from attendance the councillors it permitted to be absent (p. 435); the 'inner ring' was never the following of a great minister but the group of leading men chosen by the king (ibid.); to see in the conciliar committees of Edward VI's reign any link with the later cabinet is to misunderstand both (pp. 497, 532). Professor Mackie says many good and true things on the common law and its rivals, yet he suggests that the conciliar courts administered a 'prerogative law' of their own; they enforced the common and statute law, with a few proclamations thrown in, though they used a different procedure. On the whole, the account of Tudor methods of influence in Parliament is fair and accurate (p. 437), but we still hear far too much of packing. Henry VII's chamber system of finance deserves fuller treatment, as do other administrative changes. An account of the office of secretary which virtually leaves out Thomas Cromwell must be considered inadequate; too much is made of the signet (which played little part in the Tudor secretary's greatness) and the division of the office in 1540. To speak of Henry VIII keeping under his hand 'all the apparatus of an administrative despotism' (p. 434) seems to beg several questions: that king did not administer in person at all, and the institutions of government cannot properly be described in such terms.

There may never be two people with identical views on the Henrician Reformation, but here Professor Mackie displays his knowledge and judgment to the best advantage. If a criticism may be offered it must apply to the wider constitutional interpretation. The Henrician supremacy was personal – the Statute of Appeals made that quite plain; thus, it is wrong to say that Henry asserted the supremacy in ecclesiastical affairs of the king in Parliament (p. 359). The change to a parliamentary supremacy begins under Edward VI. Failure to realize these points has dogged writing on this period, so that it is generally asserted that Elizabeth's Supremacy did not differ essentially from that of her father; Professor Mackie seems to enthrone this error. Nor was Tudor monarchy absolute, except in the Church; in the state it did not 'presage', it embodied, 'the rule of the king in parliament' (p. 363). Otherwise, the story of the Reformation is told with such clarity and fairness that the more ardent partisans of either side will probably think none too well of it. There could be no higher praise.

A book of such length and on so crowded a period will always offer opportunity for carping criticism; it is hoped that this review will not be suspected of a failing which is far from its intentions. Professor Mackie's book will become a stand-by to students of this period and will surely run into many editions; may one plead these facts in justification for listing a number of points – minor but still important – which perhaps ought to be emended in another impression?

The fifth 'duke' of Northumberland on page 16 should read 'earl'; he was born in 1478, not 1487. Henry VII's title was registered and not established by Parliament; there was thus neither *petitio principii* nor illogicality involved in the step (p. 61). The system of covering Household expenses by Exchequer allocations goes back to Edward IV (p. 64); it was not invented by Henry VII, and it never worked. It was Lord Stanley, as correctly stated on page 54, not Sir William Stanley, who put the crown on Henry's head at Bosworth (p. 122). Sir Thomas Lovell was treasurer of the Household, not of the Chamber, early in the reign of Henry VIII (p. 233). The story that Wolsey drove Pace into insanity is discredited (p. 301). The Commons are not likely to have 'chosen' More as Speaker in 1523, any more than they exercised free choice in any other election of a Speaker in this period; this therefore proves nothing as to their disposition (p. 303). The story of Cromwell's entry into the Parliament of 1529 (p. 349), based on Merriman, is inaccurate in several details: it was Orford he tried, not Oxford, and Taunton (for which he sat) *was* a Winchester borough. The instructions which Cromwell received in 1531 were in part for the drafting of bills with the *legal* council; Professor Mackie's conclusions here are invalid (p. 351). The footnote on p. 354 should be to 'The Commons' Supplication of 1532'. Cromwell's titles of vicar-general and vicegerent in spirituals should be kept apart (p. 382); it was as vicar-general that he visited the monasteries, but as vicegerent that he presided in Convocation. There were nineteen, not twenty, privy councillors in 1540 (p. 435). Starkey's first name was Thomas, not Robert (p. 457). St John's office as 'great master of our house' was that of lord steward, not lord chamberlain (p. 494). It is misleading to say that the absolution of the realm under Mary was given parliamentary authority (p. 549); it was recorded in a statement from Parliament, but that is a very different thing. The assertion that the clerk of the Privy Council appointed in 1540 was also to be the king's secretary (p. 626) is a mistake arising out of the appointment of Paget, late the queen's secretary.

Professor Mackie has added Miss Anne Robertson's very useful appendix on the coinage which makes real the common statements on debasement, and an exhaustive bibliography whose only fault is the too frequent description of books as 'standard'. The admirable tables of royal officials will be blessed by all students of the period, and the few errors they contain can be remedied in the next edition. Thus the title of chief or principal secretary was certainly current well before 1540, and Cromwell was appointed in April 1534, not in 1533 (p. 648). The title of lord great master (for lord steward), on the other hand, seems to have become official only in 1539 (p. 649). Thomas Moyle was never chancellor of Augmentations, but one of the general surveyors in the court of Augmentations; and Sir John Baker succeeded Cromwell as chancellor of the Exchequer in 1540, not 1545 (p. 654).

It is a relief to turn back from these corrections in detail to a last general survey of a book which gives much pleasure as well as instruction. For one lasting impression is of great breadth and animation in the telling. Ultimately, one hopes that the fresh labours already referred to will produce a clearer and truer picture of a society and a century which have always held the interest, both professional and lay. In the meantime, Professor Mackie's book takes its place at the end of the older tradition which it concludes in a worthy manner. The new history may well be more professional and more severe, but it will be lucky if it can emulate the skill in presentation and the wide sympathy of this book.

3

HENRY VII: RAPACITY
AND REMORSE*

In my *England under the Tudors* I took the liberty of advancing the view that Henry VII's reputation for rapacity and extortion is probably not borne out by the facts and that his policy did not turn from just to unjust exactions.[1] Though I knew, of course, that this opinion contradicted one held by many since Henry VII's own time I did not imagine it to be provocative; I thought that the work of such scholars as Professors Thorne and Richardson, Miss Brodie and Mr Somerville, had shown the old notions to be quite as mistaken as I maintained. However, I have since discovered that I was too simple in that assumption; in particular, I have been challenged to say how I would dispose of the well-attested facts that Henry VII deteriorated in the second half of his reign into a grasping miser and that he showed deep remorse in his last weeks. The short answer is that I do not regard the first fact as attested at all and cannot believe that remorse in the face of death should be interpreted so trustingly. But, since the issue still appears to be in doubt, I should like to rehearse it here rather more thoroughly. I believe that this historical revision results from an important change in historical method which involves both a more critical attitude to the sources and a better understanding of that age in its own terms.

The consensus of opinion on the earlier view is impressive enough. Bacon, echoing the contemptuous sixteenth-century view of parsimony, accused Henry VII of 'being a little poor in admiring riches' and perpetuated the chronicle tradition that some two-thirds through his reign he began to 'crush treasure out of his subjects' purses, by forfeiture upon penal laws'.[2] Mrs Temperley, using the fuller language of the modern historian, remarked that 'the sensational faults of the later have obscured the patient, meritorious work of the earlier years' and that 'after the critical period of the reign was over, the financial methods

---

* Paper read to the sixth Anglo-American Conference of Historians at London in July 1957 [and published in *HJ* I (1958), 21–39. A reply by Mr J. P. Cooper, ibid. 2 (1959), 103–29, drew the further paper published below as no. 4.]

[1] *England under the Tudors* (1955), 52 and n.

[2] F. Bacon, [*History of the Reign of King*] *Henry VII* (ed. J. R. Lumby, Cambridge, 1885), 213 f., 128.

gradually deteriorated'.[1] Occasionally this view received embroidery, as when H. A. L. Fisher linked the deterioration of Henry's character to the death of his queen and the removal of her influence upon him[2] – that queen of whom Bacon could only say that she 'could do nothing with him'.[3] When Mrs Temperley and Fisher wrote, very little was known of Henry VII's financial and administrative policy and methods; a great deal has been discovered since. Signs of a different interpretation began to appear in Professor C. H. Williams's brief sketch, published in 1936:[4] though he admitted to finding the technicalities of financial administration difficult he was prepared to follow 'the experts'. Even so, the experts had not got very far at that date. Inevitably, I must rest my case in great part on what they have told us since.

Before going on to see how the traditional view arose and to deal with the problem of the king's remorse, it will be best first to attempt to establish the truth about Henry VII's fiscal exactions. The traditional view held that these exactions began by being reasonable and later turned oppressive; while I wish to maintain that from first to last Henry VII pursued a policy of getting every legitimate penny out of his fiscal rights, as re-defined by himself. He did not wait long before he asserted them. Mr Wolffe (who has recently shown that – as has long been suspected[5] – the administrative methods of Henry VII, his 'chamber system', continued and improved Yorkist organization)[6] has made too much of the two years' delay after Henry's accession – two years in which the Exchequer regained some temporary ascendancy at the expense of the Chamber.[7] Household government always retreated at the death of a king, and Henry VII took two years to establish his throne firmly enough to be able to spare time for administrative reforms; yet from the first he continued the essential organization of auditors and receivers for the royal lands,[8] and nearly from the first he instituted his great series of investigating commissions designed to discover his rights in the lands of tenants-in-chief.[9] In 1492 these commissions became more

---

[1] Gladys Temperley, *Henry VII* (1917), 269, 275.
[2] H. A. L. Fisher, *Political History of England*, v (1913), 95.
[3] Bacon, *Henry VII*, 215.
[4] C. H. Williams, 'Henry VII,' in *The Great Tudors*, ed. K. Garvin (1935), 3 ff.
[5] *Tudor Revolution*, 19.
[6] B. P. Wolffe, 'The Management of the Royal Estates under the Yorkist Kings,' *EHR* 71 (1956), 1 ff.　　　　　　　[7] Ibid. 25.
[8] E.g. *CPR Henry VII*, i. 15, 45, 48, 54, 62 etc. (Sept. 1485 to March 1486).
[9] The first recorded commission issued on 15 Jan. 1486 (ibid. 71). The whole subject is discussed in W. C. Richardson, 'The Surveyor of the King's Prerogative,' *EHR* 56 (1941), 52 ff.

comprehensive, and in 1495–6 the whole inquisitorial system was greatly developed.[1] Another wave of commissions covering individual counties or groups of them started in July 1503 and had not spent itself by February 1506.[2] Though it may thus be true that the notorious 'second phase' associated with the arrival in power of Empson and Dudley produced a large-scale resumption of this activity, it is equally clear that by that time there was nothing new about such methods. The king did his best throughout his reign to uncover concealed royal rights and extract the utmost financial advantage from them.

The significance of these investigations can only be understood if one looks at the meaning which Henry VII attached to his prerogative rights. Here we must turn to the lawyers. In 1495 Robert Constable gave a reading on the so-called statute *Prerogativa Regis*, and (thanks to his editor) we now know what Henry did with and to the feudal dues.[3] Professor Thorne has shown that the attention given to this document in this reign was altogether novel. No readings on it before Henry VII; two early in the reign; two, vastly expanding its scope, in 1495.[4] The reason is plain: the first ten years of the reign had witnessed an enormous enlargement of the enforcement of prerogative rights. Professor Thorne holds that this enlargement had involved no abuses of the law, however burdensome the process may have been; the king proceeded by a 'rigorous use of law and logic, rather than by their neglect'.[5] The basic principle was simple. The king's rights fell upon those who held from him in chief in knight's service, and it was therefore desirable on the one hand to discover those who belonged to that class and on the other to add to their number. The commissions of inquiry already mentioned, as well as close attention to regular inquisitions *post mortem*, dealt with the first problem. The second resulted in an exercise of royal power which, though legal, was so extreme that one may question its legitimacy. Every device for turning a mesne tenant into a tenant-in-chief was vigorously exploited. The king's claims were extended from lands to offices, rents, annuities and any other profits held of the Crown, and any grant which did not specify the kind of service upon which it rested was construed to imply military tenure. By permitting men to alienate nearly all, but never altogether all, the lands they held in knight's service, additional tenants-in-chief were easily created. Co-heirs were forced so to divide their lands at the suing out of livery that each

---

[1] Ibid. 56–7.   [2] *CPR Henry VII*, i. 323, 420–2, 437–8, 457, 459.
[3] Robert Constable, *Praerogativa Regis*, ed. S. E. Thorne, New Haven, 1949.
[4] Ibid. p. vii.   [5] Ibid. pp. vii–xi.

retained some land *in capite*. It only remained to enforce the claims of prerogative wardship and primer seisin – by which a small parcel held of the Crown brought all into the king's hands – to extract the utmost benefit from the system.[1] The law could yield the king all sorts of profits. By making *Quia Emptores* applicable to socage lands the Crown lawyers opened a large field of revenue from fines for unlicensed alienation. Alienation itself was given a wide meaning, including, for instance, a lease for years followed by a release, or a disseisin with release to the disseisor; it is worth pointing out that these were devices for escaping the king's control over alienation proper. In all this the king was fighting for recognized rights, even if interpreting them largely; Professor Thorne has even argued that such vigorous application was designed to prevent concealment rather than exact money.[2]

Be that as it may, the very fact that the simple and brief terms of *Prerogativa Regis* could be pushed to such extremes suggests that Henry was not only calling for his due but pressing hard upon all landowners. That he did so by perfectly legal methods is neither here nor there; no one has supposed that he ever resorted to strictly illegal methods. But the accusation traditionally levelled against his later methods – that the law was being exploited by chicanery – surely also applies to a policy which threatened everyone who held land with a visit from the king's tax-gatherers. Nor did these activities pass without protests, though the chronicles do not record them and they are not, therefore, part of the traditional view. Even before 1495 men tried to defeat the king: traverses were occasionally upheld, lands improperly seized into the king's hands were successfully sued out even *cum exitibus*, and decisions were sometimes reversed upon petitions of right in Chancery.[3] Surely it would be simple to suppose that the king always lost in such cases; many more unsuccessful attempts to extricate lands from his grasp must have occurred. Protests also appeared during the time of reaction immediately after Henry VII's death. One act of 1509 complained of the trouble caused 'lately' over inquests *post mortem* held either by escheators or commissions when sometimes false offices had been found and sometimes true ones had been privily changed afterwards.[4] Another act, which specifically ascribed the abuses to Empson and Dudley, accused officers taking inquisitions of falsifying returns so as to find all or part of

---

[1] For all this cf. ibid. pp. xiii–xxi.
[2] Ibid. pp. xliii ff.   [3] Ibid. p. xi.
[4] 1 Henry VIII, c. 8. All references to statutes are to *Statues of the Realm* (1810–28), vols. ii and iii.

the lands to be held *in capite*.[1] It was alleged that parties could not have traverse in law but were forced to sue their livery and thereby admit to a tenancy-in-chief which did not exist. The act provided that traverse was to be accepted and – a devastating attack – that liveries granted under Henry VII were not to be taken as proof of tenancy-in-chief. Of course, these acts spoke of recent troubles and accused the two scapegoats of 1509; but in view of the fact that Robert Constable's *Reading* shows similar and still more extreme practices to be common even before 1495 it is impossible to ascribe any value to that dating. The plain fact is that from the first Henry VII used the law and the machinery of inquisitions *post mortem* and investigating commissions to extract the maximum rights (and revenue) from lands, much to the unquestionable annoyance of the people affected.

Unaware of what the exploitation of feudal rights really meant, the holders of the traditional view believed that after a period of proper if strict exactions (under the guidance of Morton and Bray) the king turned round about 1503-4 to an improper and avaricious use of his power through Empson and Dudley. According to Edward Hall, the chronicler, he did so because he wished to be rid of 'the scrupulous strynges of domesticall sedicion and civile commocion' by depriving his restless subjects of their wealth. But, not wishing to appear oppressive, 'he deuysed wyth hym selfe by what honest meane he might perform it'; and 'it came into hys hed that the Englishmen dyd litle passe vpon the obseruacion and kepynge of penall lawes and pecuniall statutes'.[2] It is surely superfluous once more to prove that the legendary reputation of Empson and Dudley is not founded on fact. Thirty-five years ago Professor Dietz called them 'the king's long arms with which ... he took what was his';[3] Miss Brodie has shown that Dudley was simply an efficient agent of a legal, if oppressive, policy;[4] and Mr Somerville has rightly said of Empson that 'the ignominy with which he is remembered is surely only a measure of his success' in carrying out the king's policy.[5] But that still leaves Henry VII: was he guilty of improper extortion in the last years of his reign? The memory of the skill with which both his son and his granddaughter devolved the odium of unpopular actions

---

[1] 1 Henry VIII, c. 12.

[2] Edward Hall, *The Vnion of the two noble and illustre Famelies of Lancastre & Yorke* (ed. 1809) [hereafter referred to as *Chronicle*], 499.

[3] F. C. Dietz, *English Government Finance 1485–1558* (University of Illinois Studies in the Social Sciences IX, 1920), 44.

[4] D. M. Brodie, 'Edmund Dudley, Minister of Henry VII,' *TRHS* (1933), 133 ff.

[5] R. Somerville, *History of the Duchy of Lancaster* (1953), i. 264.

upon others must make the rehabilitation of Empson and Dudley appear as an indictment of the king. Did he in fact adopt a new and vicious policy round about 1504?

There is, to begin with, good reason to question the dating in the chronicles. We now know that from at least 1500 onwards a committee of the Council, known as the King's Council Learned in the Law, sat regularly as a tribunal under the presidency of the chancellor of the duchy of Lancaster, at first Sir Reginald Bray and later Sir Richard Empson.[1] Since this body was in great part engaged in the enforcement of penal statutes, it is important to note that as early as 1489, long before the first extant signs of its work, the king had prepared the ground with a statute which attempted to put a stop to collusive and feigned actions popular (that is, on statutes penal) designed to bar honest actions against transgressors.[2] Though it may well be that Henry did not succeed in establishing effective machinery until about 1500, it is not true that he only bethought himself of these matters after three-quarters of the reign had passed. Empson became chancellor of the duchy in 1504, and it is possible that the chronicle tradition reflects a tightening-up of policy in that year; but this does not dispose of the evidence for an earlier concern, or of the activities of Reginald Bray himself which were entirely on the same lines as those pursued later.

More important than the question of the date is the meaning of the charge. Taken by itself, Hall's comment is naïve in that it suggests a certain demerit in the king for holding that laws ought to be obeyed and offences against them punished. Statutes penal were statutes which prohibited a stated offence on pain of a forfeiture or a fixed fine. Because the problem of enforcement largely resolved itself into the discovery of the offence, these acts generally offered half the profits to 'him who will sue for it', that is to the informer who denounced the offender.[3] The acts covered mainly economic matters such as the import and export of goods or the regulations governing manufacture. They thus tended to deal with the private concerns of many profit-making individuals; they represented an attempt at control in the interests of a national policy at the expense of men peculiarly hostile to such interference. This naturally made their enforcement very difficult, and it was no blame to the king that he should turn his attention to the fact. Informations on

---

[1] R. Somerville, 'Henry VII's "Council learned in the law",' *EHR* 54 (1939), 427 ff.

[2] 4 Henry VII, c. 20.

[3] For a discussion of the problems posed by these statutes cf. T. F. T. Plucknett, 'Some proposed legislation of Henry VIII,' *TRHS* (1936), 125 ff., and my 'Informing for Profit,' *Star Chamber Stories* (1958), 78–113.

penal statutes were normally heard in the Exchequer which, however, in common with other late-fifteenth century courts, was in no position to make the king's policy effective. As usual, Henry therefore turned to his Council for a new weapon. The establishment of the Council Learned as a regular tribunal is of a piece with the policy which used Council committees to hear the plaints of 'poor men', or, as in the so-called Star Chamber act, to cope with the riotous transgressions of the powerful – the policy which used the royal Council in its protean forms to supplement the insufficiencies of the existing system of law-enforcement.

Its surviving records show that the Council Learned was largely concerned with hearing cases brought by the Crown, and a majority of these cases were on penal statutes. No Tudor tribunal ever had an absolutely delimited jurisdiction, and cases of riot, retaining and even (in one instance) treasonable words came before this body. Its very many prosecutions for failure to take up knighthood may be considered as rather like actions on statutes penal. The tribunal also acted as a debt-collecting agency for the treasurer of the Chamber who summoned defaulting collectors of revenue and others of the king's debtors through privy seals authorized by the Council Learned. Offences committed in office, especially by sheriffs, and the fining of both sheriffs and bishops for letting prisoners escape – the weakness of episcopal prisons was one of the graver and less known obstacles to the restoration of order in early Tudor England – added a good body of business. There were also a few private suits, mostly concerned with lands.[1] The Council Learned was therefore a typical enough court of the early Tudor type: a royal tribunal rather than a regular court of the realm, a weapon of the king's policy rather than a means for settling the subject's disputes. Its main concern was with the enforcement of penal legislation of all kinds; it is here that one must look for a record of those activities which tradition has ascribed to the 'ravening wolves', Empson and Dudley. So far from being the haphazard and wilful doings of a pair of extortioners, they represent the operation of a proper if novel royal commission. Whatever one's view of penal statutes, it cannot be maintained that the enforcement of existing legislation was an improper task for his majesty's councillors.

Contemporaries recognized this, and their complaints were a little more subtle. In the first place it was alleged that the Council deliberately revived ancient laws long since disused. This argument appeared not

[1] PRO, DL 5, vols. 2 and 4. The subject is also summarized in Mr Somerville's article, referred to above, p. 50, n. 1.

only in the chronicles but also in the statutes of the reaction early in Henry VIII's reign which spoke of 'the greate nombre of whiche Statutes penalle have nott ben putt in execucion tyll nowe of late';[1] even Henry VIII's general pardon mentioned 'statutes or ordenaunces made of long tyme past and never put in vre vse or execucion till now of late tyme'.[2] It is no wonder that this sort of vague statement should have bred vaguer generalizations still, such as Mrs Temperley's 'old statutes that mouldered forgotten'.[3] The only remotely precise statement of this grievance does not encourage much credence. It occurs in the *Great Chronicle of London* which, after an extravagant flourish about 'many unlefull & forgottyn statutis & actis made hunderyth of yeris passid', goes on to list 'statutis for huntyng, ffor syllyng and byyng of wollys, for trystyng to Strangers ovyr syxe monythis, ffor payyng of Gold to strangers, for byyng or syllyng of sylkis Rawe, or other marchaundises contrary to ordynauncis of long tyme & owth of myend made'.[4] The statutes are not so clearly described as to make an absolute identification possible, but it would appear that acts of 1485 and 1495 dealt with hunting offences,[5] acts of 1487 and 1489 with wool,[6] an act of 1495 with usury and lending money,[7] one of 1489 (admittedly reviving one of 1478) prohibited the export of coin,[8] and two acts of 1485 and 1504 (both popular with informers) legislated about silk.[9] The enforcement of such acts from about 1500 onwards can hardly be said to have revived forgotten statutes. Even if it be argued that prosecutions no doubt often took place under earlier acts, the list just given shows that every one of the issues mentioned in the chronicle was still very much alive in the reign of Henry VII.

Greater certainty in the matter might be obtained from the entry books of the Council Learned, but these unfortunately rarely specify the offence for which a man was summoned. Now and again one reads of a man charged with exporting uncustomed wool or a customer who had concealed breaches of the customs regulations;[10] much more commonly it is recorded that defendants were called 'to answere to such thinges as shalbe declarid ayenst them'.[11] This was the customary, if ominous, phrase of the privy seal subpoena, not invented then or

---

[1] 1 Henry VIII, c. 4. [2] P RO, C 82/335. [3] Temperley, op. cit. 278.
[4] [*The*] *Great Chronicle* [*of London*], ed. A. H. Thomas and I. D. Thornley (1938), 334.
[5] 1 Henry VII, c. 7; 11 Henry VII, c. 17.
[6] 3 Henry VII, c. 12; 4 Henry VII, c. 11. [7] 11 Henry VII, c. 8.
[8] 4 Henry VII, c. 23; 17 Edward IV, c. 1.
[9] 1 Henry VII, c. 9; 19 Henry VII, c. 21. There is no law in the statute book dealing with raw silk. [10] P RO, DL 5/2, fo. 30. [11] Ibid. fo. 101.

discarded for a long time after. Yet if one cannot show that the cases brought in the Council Learned were certainly on recent statutes, there is no difficulty in demonstrating that such recent statutes existed in plenty. Here is a list, by no means necessarily complete, of acts passed in Henry VII's reign which imposed forfeitures or fines to be shared between king and informer: for tanning of leather, concerning Gascon wines, against the import of silk goods, against exchange of lands without licence, against coastal trade without customers' certificates, against the export of woollens until partially finished, concerning the mint, against butchering within London walls, fixing prices for cloths, hats and bonnets, for the maintenance of drapery, against depopulation, against excessive fishing at Oxford, against the export of coin and bullion, for weights and measures, for the removal of obstructions in Southampton harbour, against usury, against unapprenticed shearers of cloth, against the export of horses, against the malpractices of sheriffs in their courts, against unlawful hawking and hunting, against the unlawful making of fustian, for the reform of the coinage, regulating the work of pewterers, against negligent keeping of prisoners, for the free navigation of the Severn, against cordwainers being tanners, against the import of wrought silk.[1] Add to this list the legislation of Edward IV (occasionally confirmed by Henry VII) and such old but respectably alive practices as distraint of knighthood, and it becomes obvious that to speak of mouldering and forgotten statutes is a grave mistake. The truth appears in the act of 1510 which limits actions on statutes penal commenced by the king to within three years of the alleged offence and by private persons to within one year.[2] What was resented seems to have been not so much the revival of old statutes as the discovery of old offences. The fact is that, earlier steps notwithstanding, only Henry VII systematically developed a policy of control and regulation based on statutes penal; both these and the informations in which they resulted were to have a long history after his day. The various complaints on this score should really be read as expressing on the one hand the self-justification of transgressors who wished it thought that all those laws were in any case long dead, and on the other the perfectly accurate

[1] 1 Henry VII, cc. 5, 8, 9; 2 Henry VII, cc. 7, 8, 12; 4 Henry VII, cc. 2, 3, 8, 9, 11, 19, 21, 23; 7 Henry VII, c. 3; 11 Henry VII, cc. 5, 8, 11, 13, 15, 17, 27; 19 Henry VII, cc. 5, 6, 10, 18, 19, 21.

[2] 1 Henry VIII, c. 4. Six years later another act (7 Henry VIII, c. 3) tried to be easier on the Crown. Under it, where the king alone had power to act, he was to have four years; where both the king and a private person could act the former had two years and the latter one.

feeling that proper enforcement was of fairly recent date. But for this surely Henry VII and his agents deserve credit rather than obloquy.

A more important body of objections concerned the methods employed in enforcing the acts. Bacon's contemptuous description is only the reaction of a common lawyer, and a seventeenth-century lawyer at that, to the irregularities of conciliar procedure:[1] 'Neither did they . . . observe so much as the half-face of justice, in proceeding by indictment; but sent forth their precepts to attach men and convent them before themselves, and some others, at their private houses, in a court of commission: and there used to shuffle up a summary proceeding by examination, without trial by jury; assuming to themselves there, to deal both in pleas of the crown, and controversies civil.' Remove the prejudice, and the passage, read aright, becomes a reasonably accurate description of the king's Council Learned, thus losing its air of generalized illegality. Both Henry VII and Henry VIII proceeded by methods not known to the common law – though it would be hard to prove that they enforced a law not known to the common-law courts – because the regular methods had proved ineffective against the strong and cunning. These proceedings will not have endeared the tribunal to its victims, but that does not prove the victims guiltless. It merely puts the Council Learned once again in the same category as such courts as the early Star Chamber whose unorthodox procedure was retrospectively legalized by an act of 1504.[2]

More serious are the charges that Empson and Dudley packed juries, got up false accusations to extract money by compositions, mixed charges under dead statutes with more proper proceedings, and even attacked the dead through their executors.[3] These charges can be neither denied nor substantiated. It must be remembered that it was easy to fall foul of the penal laws. 'Learned men in the lawe,' says Hall, 'when they were requyred of their aduise, would saye to agree is the best counsayll that I can geue you.' Very likely, and no doubt very shocking to a generation used to the evasive tricks of trials at common law: but was it because the accused was patently guilty or because nothing was to be gained by facing a notoriously rigged trial? The specific cases harped on by the chroniclers are few and seem certainly to deal with people harassed but guilty: such as Sir William Capell and Thomas Kneysworth

---

[1] Bacon, *Henry VII*, 191.   [2] 19 Henry VII, c. 14.

[3] Polydore Vergil has the most rhetorical and least particular version of these charges ([*Anglica*] *Historia*, ed. D. Hay, 1950, 126–30); Hall (*Chronicle*, 502) is rather more specific in his description of 'this pluckyng bancket'.

who (the latter with his two sheriffs) were heavily fined for misdemeanours committed in the office of lord mayor of London. We know that the earl of Northumberland was fined £10,000 (most of it remitted) for abducting a royal ward.[1] Doubtless there were others – even many others. But it is quite impossible to be sure of their innocence. On the contrary, the outraged protests read much more like those of men who know that they are guilty of practices in which 'everybody' indulges and who do not see why the law should pick on them. The enforcement of neglected legislation is likely to produce plenty of squeals.

Empson and Dudley further caused much resentment because they allegedly filled their own pockets and because they relied on informers. It is easy to believe that the two ministers did not go without profit in their proceedings; they would have been somewhat unusual in their day if they had. But it is patently untrue that 'all was doone in the kinges name and yet the most profit came to other mens coffers'.[2] Dudley's well-known account book is proof enough of that.[3] If Dudley made more out of those whom he prosecuted than he handed over to the king, he would indeed have ruined even the wealthy beyond the bounds of possibility. He collected £65,361 for the king in 1506–7; are we to believe that he kept an equal or much larger sum for himself?[4] The point is absurd. Not so absurd is the point about informers. Their employment was necessary but none the less unpleasant; it opened the door to private rancour, secret bribery, false prosecutions and corruption of every sort. Professional informers, or promoters as they were called, took advantage of the government's new stringent policy, and it appears probable that the ministers virtually employed a detective staff of such men. Hall, who lists a number of them, says the worst of the lot was one John Baptist Brimaldi,[5] surely that Brymeley whom Dudley in his will accused of knowing everything – 'all thinges consideryd, [he] mought have delt with me better than he dyde'.[6] No doubt a determined policy of law-enforcement which willy-nilly had to rely on informers and did not attempt to check informations too carefully could be vicious as well as oppressive; but one must always remember that the story as it stands was virtually told by the victims. Later evidence shows how hard the lot of an informer could be and how difficult it was to bring transgressors to heel, especially those who broke penal statutes;[7]

---

[1] *LP* i. 414 (58).
[2] John Stowe, *Annales of England* (1592), 810. He borrowed this from the *Great Chronicle of London*, 335.   [3] BM, Lansdowne MS 127.
[4] Cf. Dietz, op. cit. 39.   [5] Hall, *Chronicle*, 506.
[6] Brodie, art. cit. 152.   [7] Cf. my *Star Chamber Stories*, 78 ff.

it may well be that the stories of horror only describe the efficiency of the Council Learned compared with the Exchequer. Where the tale is so one-sided, and where other equally extreme statements can be shown to be untrue, I would prefer to incline in favour of the Council; I do not believe that many suffered who were genuinely innocent. But those who cannot stomach the promoters may take solace from Lord Herbert of Cherbury's improbable statement that within a few days after the fall of Dudley they all died of shame and the pillory – all, that is, except one Grimaldi, indubitably the redoubtable John Baptist, who in any case sounds as though he were a foreigner.[1]

If it is not true that the proceedings were mainly on out-of-date statutes, and if the stories of improper methods are at least wildly exaggerated, what shall we make of the third charge – that the king enforced the law not because he cared for the law but because he was avaricious and also wanted to lower the mighty? Two very different motives are here ascribed to Henry's campaign. Perhaps I need not spend much time on the second. Among modern historians, at least, Henry VII has generally had much praise for his attack on 'overmighty subjects' of all kinds, and especially for hitting them in the purse rather than the neck. We find it hard to recapture the mixture of horror and awe with which Polydore Vergil regarded the fact that it was the wealthy and powerful who suffered and not the poor.[2] We think it right as well as politic that it should have been so. But this motive, while it is not necessarily in conflict with straight avarice, is also not essentially linked with it. The traditional story, on the other hand, depends on the belief that Henry grew excessively greedy for money as he grew older. In this connection I should like to borrow an argument suggested by Professor Williams who saw a fundamental difference between fines collected in cash and those collected in bonds.[3] These last, he argued, represented not extortion but 'symbols of Henry's devices for good government'. One may perhaps suggest that in the first place they represented a defendant's inability to pay all his fine in cash; but there is nevertheless cogent value in the argument. Dudley, who collected something between £40,000 and £60,000 a year from the activities of the Council Learned, took only about £7,500 to £10,000 in cash: over

---

[1] Lord Herbert of Cherbury, *Life and Reign of King Henry the Eighth* (1672), 7. 'B' and 'G' are very alike in early Tudor handwriting.

[2] Polydore Vergil, *Historia*, 128.

[3] *The Great Tudors*, 18. For an excellent discussion of obligations and recognizances cf. W. C. Richardson, *Tudor Chamber Administration* (Baton Rouge, La., 1952), 141 ff.

three-quarters of his income was in bonds. And it is incidentally worth remark that only a portion of this was derived from the much-resented enforcement of the law: of the £44,882 collected in 1504–5 only perhaps £8,335 can be identified as coming from this source, and even if we add the £11,315 'for causes not stated' we are still left with a large balance from less disputed sources.[1] We are reminded of the words of Sir Brian Tuke, treasurer of the Chamber, who in 1539 pointed out that in the past 'the grete dettes arose vpon lones of money and licences'.[2] Even a purist would be hard put to it to complain of the king's habit of taking security for his loans and promissory notes for the payment involved in obtaining royal licences for various purposes. Bonds – obligations and recognizances – were not money but the promise of money, and in many cases payment depended on future contingencies which might never arise; they must also have resulted in a large number of bad debts. The fate of Henry VII's recognizances cannot be worked out in detail, but we know that bad debts beset the royal finances for many years. All this, however, does suggest that the fiscal motives need not have been uppermost. Of course, the king must have been delighted with any addition to his resources: no one wants to deny his careful husbandry and his determined search after solvency. But the yields were not nearly as large as tradition supposes, and it looks as though Henry faced the unpopularity involved in these measures because he wished to attack all forms of lawlessness and suppress those who thought themselves above the law, rather than because he wanted more money.

Perhaps we are now in a position to pronounce with some confidence on the nature of Henry VII's fiscal policy. Down to about 1495 the king and his ministers were mainly engaged in extending the operation of the royal prerogative and erecting a system which would bring in the maximum return from landed revenues and feudal rights. The system received further elaboration later when the death of its chief agent, Bray, made it advisable to settle specific tasks on selected councillors: in 1503 Sir John Husee was appointed master of wards, and in 1508 Sir Edward Belknap became surveyor of the prerogative.[3] But the main work consisted in the extension of the king's legal claims, and this was quite complete by 1495. In the years that followed it appears that Henry turned to the problem of penal statutes, and from 1500 we know that

---

[1] Dietz, op. cit. 39 f. I have taken the money for pardons (compositions?), fines for escapes, forfeited goods, customs on wine, and fines for hunting and riots, to fall within this category.

[2] PRO, SP 1/133, fo. 245.   [3] Richardson, *Tudor Chamber Admin.*, 169, 198.

an organization for their enforcement existed. These two activities – which in any case overlapped – do not represent a contrast between justifiable right and unjustifiable extortion. Though two different targets were involved, it is clear that both were targets properly constructed for the king's arrows. The most that one can say is that very possibly some of the exactions which resulted from this consistent and determined policy were oppressive and some unjust. A policy designed to restore half-vanished rights and enforce neglected laws cannot escape being harsh at times. But nothing in the discoverable facts hints at excessive injustice, at a change of attitude, or at some deterioration in the king's character after nearly twenty years of rule.

Yet, since this is what the chronicle tradition alleges, it is now necessary to see how that arose. There are in fact quite a few accounts of the reign which contain accusations of the kind here rebutted, but – with the exception of the short notes provided by the *Grey Friars' Chronicle* which says nothing of Henry VII's evil practices[1] – they all stem from two sources.[2] One of these, the London source, consists of C. L. Kingsford's lost 'Main City Chronicle' whose putative existence the editors of the Guildhall *Great Chronicle* have accepted.[3] From this descended not only the *Great Chronicle* itself but also the *Continuation of Fabyan* and other lesser London chronicles.[4] The other strand goes back to Polydore Vergil. Hall's very influential chronicle is almost unadulterated Vergil, but he adds a point or two from the London tradition; Grafton is pure Hall with the addition of Empson's speech in his own defence, the source of which I do not know.[5] Holinshed and Stowe, operative in establishing the story, simply derive from all these.

It is true that both the London strand and Vergil accuse Empson and Dudley of malpractices. But there are differences between them. Only Vergil speaks of the king's sad deterioration after about 1504: the

---

[1] *Chronicle of the Grey Friars of London*, ed. J. G. Nicholls (1852), 29; the same is true of 'A London Chronicle in the Times of King Henry VII and King Henry VIII,' ed. C. Hopper (*Camden Miscellany*, iv), 6.

[2] The chronicles of the reign have been analysed by W. Busch, *England under the Tudors* (1893), i. 391 ff. and by A. H. Thomas and I. D. Thornley in their introduction to the *Great Chronicle of London*. Dietz, *Gov. Finance*, 35 ff., traces the growth of Empson's and Dudley's legend through the accounts, but his investigation is neither precise nor complete.

[3] C. L. Kingsford, *English Historical Literature in the Fifteenth Century* (1913), 99 ff.; *Great Chronicle*, p. lxxvi.

[4] Robert Fabyan, *Chronicle*, ed. H. Ellis (1811), 689; *Chronicles of London*, ed. C. L. Kingsford (1905), 261.

[5] Vergil, *Historia*, 127 ff.; Hall, *Chronicle*, 477, 492 ff., 502 f., 504; Richard Grafton, *Chronicle*, ed. H. Ellis (1809), 236.

allegation of Henry's tortuous motives rests entirely on his authority. The London writers differ considerably. Fabyan and the lesser chronicles confine themselves to relating without comment the troubles of various London worthies and speak with adulation of Henry VII himself: 'euery naturall Englysshman now lyuyng hath cause & ought deuoutly to pray' for his soul.[1] The *Great Chronicle*, on the other hand, remarks on the fault of avarice which alone marred the king's record and gives a detailed denunciation of Empson and Dudley, large parts of which reappear in Hall.[2] It also provides a generous picture of Bray and Morton – rather like Vergil's but different in detail[3] – while there is nothing on this in the other supposed derivations from the lost 'Main City Chronicle'. One difficulty arises from the fact that all these accounts were written after the event; in the strict sense, no surviving chronicle is contemporary.[4] There may thus have been more cross-borrowing than we know of, and the independent value of the two strands may be less than it appears. But leaving this possibility aside, it still seems plain that we have two traditions, one of which (Vergil's) has the full story centring on a change of character in the king, while the other (London) is mainly concerned with the ills that arose from the ministers' activities. And even this is to suppose that the full *Great Chronicle* represents the lost 'Main Chronicle' better than do the shorter surviving extracts – a supposition which, likely or not (I think it is), gives to the traditional view the greatest weight it can possibly muster.

Let us now take the two sources in turn. The London chronicles complain of the ill-treatment of those likely to suffer from an enforcement of economic regulations. The list of statutes given in the *Great Chronicle* significantly includes nothing that concerns landowners.[5] In particular it fails to mention one of the greatest sources of profit for informers, the act against depopulation and enclosure.[6] One would never suppose from it that tenants-in-chief had their grievances too, or that the king's officers had long been extracting money from many to whom statutes penal can have been of little consequence. When the *Great Chronicle* says that 'noon that owgth hadd was wythowth trowble' it meant the wealthy citizens of London. This is not surprising; it is what one would expect of a city chronicle. But since Henry VII's financial policy happened to begin with an attack on landowners and

---

[1] Fabyan, *Chronicle*, 690.
[2] *Great Chronicle*, 334 f.; Hall, *Chronicle*, 502 f.   [3] *Great Chronicle*, 294 f., 325 f.
[4] The fact, well known with regard to Vergil and Hall, is also true of the London chronicles (ibid. p. lxviii).
[5] Above, p. 52.   [6] 4 Henry VII, c. 19.

then went on to attack also those who evaded penal statutes, it naturally appeared to the London interest to have taken a turn for the worse. Thus hatred concentrated on the new agents, even to the extent of exculpating their predecessors, Morton and Bray. Of Bray the *Great Chronicle* says that he had 'much haterede and many an unkeynd & untrewe Report of many of the kynges subgectys, But afftyr his deth they apparceyvid well It was not he that made the Smoke. Ffor he was playn & Rowth In spech & dyd bettyr than he wold make countenaunce ffor'.[1] It was held to his credit that he refused gifts of value and that 'where he took, the gyver was suyr of a ffreend'; his successors took all they could get and belied their friendly words in their deeds. This is judicious praise without enthusiasm; it certainly suggests – what one need not doubt – that Bray was a greater man and better statesman than Dudley, but also that complaints were plentiful even in his time. It does not interfere with the general tenor of the London chronicles which is to ignore the things that did not concern London and harp on those that did.

For the full traditional story Polydore Vergil is much more important. Not that he can be kept entirely distinct from the London strand: he must himself have heard many of the complaints which got into the city chronicle. The first point to note about him is that he did not arrive in England until 1502;[2] that is to say, he witnessed the period of the king's alleged misdoings but knew the first seventeen years of the reign only by report. Even if the report was that of eyewitnesses, the impact on the historian must have been very different. In any case, what were Vergil's sources? As Professor Hay has pointed out, Morton and Bray were clearly among his best informants.[3] Bray is the man whom Vergil described as 'uere pater patriae, homo seuerus, ac ita recti amator, ut si quid interdum peccatum esset, illud acriter in Henrico reprehenderet'. But, popularly, he and Morton had been reckoned corrupters of the king: 'suche is euer', to quote Hall's translation, 'the errour of the common people'.[4] Unquestionably Vergil held Bray in high esteem, and we need not accuse him of deliberately perverting the truth. But it is quite another matter whether his estimate ought to be believed. He may not have thought much of the common people, but the complaints to whose loudness during Morton's and Bray's ascendancy he himself testifies look suspiciously like those later raised against Empson and Dudley. It is hard to escape the obvious conclusion that Henry VII's

[1] *Great Chronicle*, 325.   [2] D. Hay, *Polydore Vergil* (Oxford, 1952), 4.   [3] Ibid. 93.
[4] Vergil, *Historia*, 128 f. (in the collation). Hall, *Chronicle*, 497, is practically a straight translation.

exactions always caused a good deal of resentment, but that his first ministers were diligently whitewashed while his last, sacrificed after his death, were carefully blackened. Even if the different judgments represent genuine differences between the men concerned, it must not be forgotten that Vergil's view of Bray – so much more favourable than that of the *Great Chronicle* and so essential to the notion of a sudden change of policy in 1504 – rested on bias. If he largely relied for his opinion of Bray's ministry on Bray himself – and it does look very much as though he did – then his *History* embodies Bray's apologia, and the king's alleged deterioration is Vergil's deduction from the difference between what Bray told him and what he saw around him. If the dark view of the last years comes from the disgruntled memories of the articulate victims of the king's policy, while the brighter view of the earlier years represents at least in great part the opinion of Henry's chief agent – an opinion which Vergil and others had to set against a contrary popular view – then surely the whole story of deterioration and what follows ceases altogether to be credible.

Yet one last point remains. It has been suggested that Henry VII himself recognized the evil of his ways when in the last weeks of his life he determined to turn over a new leaf and, as an earnest of his intentions, issued a general pardon.[1] That he felt some remorse seems certain, but what it amounted to and what it proves are other matters. The *locus classicus* of this problem occurs in Fisher's sermon at the king's funeral. On the authority of the king's confessor, Fisher told how at the beginning of Lent Henry had made his confession and then promised three things: 'a true reformacyon of al them that were offycers & mynysters of his lawes to the entent that Iustyce from hens forwarde truly and indyfferently myght be executed'; 'that the promocyons of the chyrche that were of his dysposycyon sholde from hens forth be dysposed to able men suche as were vertuous & well lerned'; and that he would grant a pardon 'touchynge the daungers and Ieopardyes of his lawes for thynges done in tymes passed'. He talked often of these intentions and told his 'secret seruauntes' many times that 'yf it pleased god to sende hym lyfe they sholde se hym a newe chaunged man'.[2] Lent in 1509 began on 21 February; the only positive result of these resolves was a pardon issued on 16 April; on 21 April he was dead.

---

[1] In Mr J. P. Cooper's review of my *England under the Tudors* in *Oxford Magazine*, lxxiv (1955–6), 324, the review which first suggested to me that it would be as well to elaborate the reasons for my interpretation of Henry VII's policy.

[2] John Fisher, 'Funeral Sermon for Henry VII,' *English Works*, ed. J. E. B. Mayor (1876), 271 f.

Henry's remorse does not, of course, prove that he thought he had left the path of righteousness for that of extortion some five or seven years earlier: Fisher's words rather suggest that the king had come to regret many of his proceedings throughout his reign. This was not the first time that Henry had felt a twinge of conscience – or worried about his health. In 1506 he had cancelled all debts of 40s. or under and released all those imprisoned for such debts.[1] As long ago as 19 August 1504, just at the time when by the traditional story he should have begun to show his cloven hoof, he had issued a proclamation calling all who had claims against the Crown in respect of any loans, debts, or injury done to them to deliver their complaints within two years to a committee presided over by Richard Foxe, bishop of Winchester, and Sir John Fineux, chief justice of the King's Bench.[2] There is no sign that the proclamation either evoked much response or resulted in any remedy to petitioners, but it proves that Henry showed some awareness of the unpopularity of his policy long before 1509. Nor is it the case that general pardons were unobtainable before the proclamation of 16 April 1509. To cite an example: in Henry VII's last year, only two pardons were enrolled after 16 April,[3] while no fewer than twenty-three appear before that date.[4] These figures do not prove much – many pardons, especially of those obtained under a general proclamation, would not be enrolled – but they do show that it required no proclamation for Henry to grant general pardons. Most of those ordinary pardons were issued for releases to office-holders or for specific crimes; that is, they represented the common insurance policy of the day against later investigation. Some, however, touched precisely those issues for pursuing which Empson and Dudley got their bad names: a citizen and draper of London, pardoned for all offences before a certain day, avoided the prosecutions which the 'promoters' were instigating; the abbey of Lewes obtained a pardon which included the offence of unlicensed alienation; that of Gloucester even got one for offences against the statutes of livery and the forests.[5]

However, if pardoning was not rare, it is still possible that the measure of 1509 embodied a special sort of pardoning and with it a significant remorse. In one respect it may well have been different: pardons under the proclamation were presumably free. One has to say 'presumably'

[1] *Chronicles of London*, ed. Kingsford, 261.
[2] *Letters and Papers of Richard III and Henry VII*, ed. J. Gairdner (1863), ii. 379.
[3] *CPR Henry VII*, ii. 600. The special patent roll of pardons (C 67/53) includes nothing after 1505–6.   [4] *CPR Henry VII*, ii. 594–600, 609–11, 625.
[5] Ibid. 600, 609.

because – in spite of the entry in Steele's *Tudor and Stuart Proclamations* – the proclamation of 16 April does not survive.[1] Its tenor has to be reconstructed from the renewal issued by Henry VIII soon after his accession, on 25 April.[2] From this it appears that Henry VII's pardon covered misprisions, felonies, trespasses, forfeitures, outlawries, certain recognizances and 'diuerse and many other offences doon and committed before the tenth day of April last past'. Henry VIII claimed that his pardon (which specifically excepted debts and accounts) was 'moche more ample gracious and beneficiall' than his father's. It is true that a pardon under the second proclamation was more than half as long again as one under the first,[3] but since the earlier pardon covered a vast variety of things (for instance, felonies, burglaries, rapes, abductions of women, insurrections, rebellions, conspiracies, trespasses of all kinds, forfeitures and concealments, forgeries, etc.) to which virtually nothing seems to have been added in the second, the mere technical elaboration of offences would not account for the claim. It may be that the willingness of Henry VIII to give his pardon free, specifically mentioned in his proclamation,[4] was not anticipated by his father; Fisher, too, does not say that the pardon was to be free, and it would have been well within the compass of Henry VII's sardonic humour to temper his remorse with a little revenue from pardons sold.

However, if this inference be thought unjustified, there are other points in which Henry VIII's enlargement of his father's generosity may lie. The second proclamation contains a specific order that the king's officers were to do justice without fear of the king's wrath 'ner for his lettres if it shal fortune eny suche to be writen to theim in tyme to come to the contrary', or for fear of contrary orders from the Council. These are rather extraordinary admissions of impotence in the face of the existing machinery which one could easily suppose absent from Henry VII's proclamation. His successor also proclaimed his readiness to protect all merchants and craftsmen in the exercise of their trades against wrong-

[1] R. R. Steele, *Tudor and Stuart Proclamations* (Oxford, 1910), no. 51b. The document there suggested as extant cannot be found at the P RO: I am happy to have confirmation of my own disappointment in the search from Mr H. C. Johnson. All that survives is a draft specimen of the pardon as issued (C 82/326), and at present it is not known what Steele had in mind in his entry.

[2] C 82/335 (slightly mutilated but completed from paper copies in SP 1/1, fos. 2–3). This is Steele, op. cit. no. 53; his date (30 April) appears to be conjectural and arrived at on grounds no longer apparent. It is wrong: *Great Chronicle*, 337.

[3] The two specimens are in C 82/326 and 335.

[4] But not entirely free. An act of 1514 (5 Henry VIII, c. 8) ordered that the general pardon should be obtainable on payment of certain small fees only, as ordered by king and Council.

ful prosecutions under ancient laws by officers of the Crown or 'eny persones calling theimself promoters'. The king would see to a 'refor-macion of the great extremyte and Rygour wherwith his said subgiettes haue been greuously vexed and trobled in tyme past'. If, as seems not unreasonable, these points are the improvements on Henry VII's offer, then it becomes impossible to see in this last any remorse or admission that wrongful deeds had been done. Since the proclamation is not extant one can only produce a guess, but the guess receives some confirmation from another document in which Henry VII had a chance of expressing his repentance. This is his will, drawn up on 31 March 1509.[1] Among other things this set up a committee to investigate complaints 'if any persone of what degree so evir he bee, shewe by any complainte to our Executours any wrong to have been done to hym, by us, by our commaundement, occasion or meane, or that we held any goodes or lands which of right ought to apperteigne unto hym'. The complaints were to be effective if grounded in conscience 'other than mater doon by the course and ordre of our lawes', or if it be thought that the king's soul 'aught to stand charged withe the said matier and complaint'. These fair words, already a little doubtful because lawful impositions were exempt – and, after all, the alleged exactions were all legal in form – suffer further from two facts: the king showed himself mainly exercised over any debts remaining payable by him at his death, and the committee included among others both Empson and Dudley.

Whatever Henry VII may have thought due to his soul and his conscience, there is no sign here that he either repented of his doings as very bad or associated the worst of them with a period of deterioration in his last years. His remorse was surely real enough, but it was the remorse induced by fear of death in a conventionally and deeply religious man come to the end of a life necessarily filled with the actions of the statesman and the politician. How many such would have faced death differently if, like Henry VII, they believed in all the teachings of the fifteenth-century Church? Fisher thought it most praiseworthy in the king that he should have shown himself so penitent, sometimes weeping for nearly an hour at a time, displaying an ostentatious reverence for the sacrament of the altar, and so forth.[2] One may or may not agree with his approval, but in any case a dispassionate reading of both Henry's will and Fisher's funeral sermon makes plain that we have here a man's fear of purgatory and hell on account of the things which

[1] *The Will of Henry VII*, ed. T. Astle (1775), 11 f.
[2] John Fisher, *English Works*, 273 f.

both as a ruler and a human being he had had to do, rather than his considered reflections on particular aspects of his policy.

The reaction after Henry VII's death – which expressed itself in the terms of Henry VIII's pardon, in the attack on Empson and Dudley, and in certain statutes already referred to – does not prove anything either. It had clearly at first been intended to go even further: thus Sir John Husee, another of Henry VII's fiscal agents, was originally excepted from the pardon.[1] How very much of a gesture the whole distasteful business was appears well in the outcome. Not only did Wolsey soon revive the administrative machinery of Henry VII, including the court of Star Chamber;[2] but a few years later even commissions to inquire into concealed lands, wardships and the rest issued again,[3] informers continued to ply their trade (as a glance at any of the memoranda rolls will show), fines were collected from penal statutes, and even the Council Learned, though much reduced in weight and vigour, was far from dead.[4] These were the methods which Tudor governments had to adopt if they were to be effective. Henry VII's government was much more effective than that of Henry VIII before 1530 simply because he employed such 'conciliar' methods more consistently, more energetically, and perhaps more ruthlessly. But if they are to be judged they must not be measured against a false standard of morality or constitutionalism. For they were neither immoral nor unconstitutional, resting as they did on the king's just prerogative and the needs of the country. One might condemn them because they caused more unpopularity than they were worth: that seems to have been the opinion of those who advised Henry VIII on his accession. The whole history of Henry VII's reign seems to me to disprove this judgment. Hostile views of these methods have prevailed for so long that Henry VII's reputation looked like being permanently damaged by those very things he thought most conducive to strong and good government in England. Yet by an agreeable stroke of justice he has now recovered a high standing among English sovereigns precisely because he governed well and wisely by methods which those who evaded the law might well resent but which represented no rapacity and required no remorse.

[1] *LP* i. 54(63).
[2] *Tudor Revolution*, 45 ff.
[3] *LP* ii. 1435, 1455, 1595.
[4] *Tudor Revolution*, 143 f., 162, 292 n. 1.

4

HENRY VII: A RESTATEMENT*

In a vigorously argued paper, Mr J. P. Cooper has attacked my interpretation of Henry VII's reign.[1] If the point at issue were only Mr Cooper's view of my methods and scholarship – or, for that matter, my view of his – I should feel neither justified nor inclined to trouble anyone again with these problems. But Mr Cooper is almost as much concerned to prove Henry VII rapacious as he is sure that I am wrong; and the truth about Henry VII's government deserves all the elucidation it may need. If, therefore, I reluctantly recur to an argument in which I have already had an extended say, it is because I believe Mr Cooper to be in error on a matter of first-rate importance; I hope to show that he has arrived at a mistaken view from partial, and partially misinterpreted, evidence. In a field in which things are far from clear or straightforward this is neither surprising nor shocking; it is more disconcerting to find that one who so readily chastises others for their supposed failings should himself be strangely inclined to inaccuracy in discussing other people's views and even in transcribing documents.[2] A self-appointed hound of heaven ought to be more precise in his quest.

I

I must once again state the purpose of my earlier article. I wished to show, in the first place, that modern research had demonstrated how

* [HJ 4 (1961), 1–29.]
[1] Above, no. 3; J. P. Cooper, 'Henry VII's Last Years Reconsidered,' HJ ii. 103 ff. These two articles will be referred to by their authors' names only. All MSS cited here (except original acts of Parliament) are at the PRO.
[2] E.g. the line and a half quoted from Acts . . . of the Mercers in Cooper, n. 36, contains six errors; the last paragraph on p. 121 contains seven and fails to mark an omitted passage; the paragraph from the Great Chronicle on p. 107 omits two words and totals fifteen errors in under eight lines. These inaccuracies do not distort the sense, but Mr Cooper's penchant for cutting his quotations occasionally does even that. Thus when he says (n. 26) that my question with respect to the advice offered by legal counsel – to agree rather than to risk trial – is superfluous, he achieves his effect by reducing my remark by half. I asked whether this advice was due to accused's patent guilt or to the fact that the trial was rigged (the point omitted by Mr Cooper), and the double question retains its point even if counsel were afraid to speak in the cause.

intensive Henry VII's fiscal policy was in the years before 1504, so that it was no longer right to see in that year a serious deterioration from strictness to rapacity, from legality to illegality. Secondly – and secondarily – I suggested that the older view of the king's last years as a period of extortion and greed was greatly exaggerated. As the title of his article indicates, Mr Cooper is almost exclusively concerned with my minor premise: he seeks to re-establish something like the traditional view of the Empson and Dudley era in order to show that a deterioration had set in. For this he claims the support of expert opinion, though he allows me Professor Thorne. But when he quotes Miss Brodie to the effect 'that such a policy must have been oppressive and sometimes unjust is probably true', he does not refer to her careful justification of the king's policy, in a long passage which immediately follows.[1] His citation from Mr Bell seems off the point: no one doubts that the yield of Henry VII's resources increased, a fact which proves nothing as to the justice of his dealings. As for Professor Richardson, the passage chosen by Mr Cooper misrepresents him.[2] It begins with the words 'this[3] new policy was put into operation sometime between 1503 and 1505',[4] and no one reading them in the context of Mr Cooper's article can suppose them to refer to anything but a change in fiscal policy. In fact – as the five lines represented in Mr Cooper's quotation by three dots make plain – the new policy in question was one of administrative rearrangement, a change from casual to more organized methods in government. The reader may determine whether Mr Richardson's views are fairly to be judged from a passage which mentions 'outstanding instances of flagrant miscarriages of justice', or whether attention should not be paid to such wider-ranging verdicts as these:

recognisances and obligations...represent neither a departure from the regular chamber policy nor a change in the developing administrative techniques. An analysis of the records of the chamber...does not show the results to have been either excessive or unduly exploitable.

To brand all these agents as extortioners, as earlier historians have done, is tantamount to a repudiation of the government's entire policy for restoring order and financial stability.

The policy of revival of the feudal prerogative aroused general bitterness, not so much because of particular injustice as from apprehension of its ultimate consequences.

[1] Cooper, 104; D. M. Brodie, 'Edmund Dudley: Minister of Henry VII,' *IRHS* (1932), 155 f.
[2] Cooper, 103.   [3] Mr Cooper has 'a'.
[4] The last five words appear as '1503–5' in Mr Cooper's version.

True, the exactions were sometimes heavy, though not necessarily unjust. Henry VII was a practical sovereign, and his good business sense demanded the full payment of all revenues legitimately due him under his prerogative rights. It was not so much the principle of prerogative power that aroused opposition as the thoroughness with which it was enforced.[1]

It would appear that Mr Richardson takes much the same line as I do, namely that the king throughout laboured to get all his rightful dues, though his policy, in the hands of agents both central and local who were often hard to supervise, could and did lead to isolated examples of injustice. What is in dispute between Mr Cooper and me is the general justice of the policy, not its occasional lapses, and here I would appear to have recent work on my side.[2] It is Mr Cooper, not I, who must defend his interpretation by attacking the expert consensus on this period. Of course, this does not necessarily prove him wrong; though alone, he may be perfectly right. Only the evidence can settle this. I propose first to deal with Mr Cooper's few remarks on my main contention, namely that the earlier years of Henry VII's reign were as exacting as the later, and then to examine his evidence for rapacity in the king's last years.

II

I shall not repeat my analysis of the chronicles, especially as Mr Cooper's only criticism is that I misrepresented the *Great Chronicle* as not contemporary and thereby sought to deprive it of credence.[3] My point, to be tedious, was that since it was not written until after 1512 we cannot be sure that what appears in it is entirely independent of what appears in other chronicles of the same or earlier date. I was not concerned to discredit the London chronicles; I was seeking to understand them. In the process I came to the not surprising conclusion that they concerned themselves very largely with London – even exclusively if one listens to their specific and substantiated grievances. When the *Great Chronicle* talks of others than Londoners it is vague and general in the extreme. I therefore suggested that a deterioration was seen in Henry VII because in fact his policy had turned from a main preoccupation with landed proprietors to an interest in economic offences. The evidence of Robert

---

[1] Richardson, *Tudor Chamber Administration*, 141, 145, 158, 212.

[2] One would not suppose from Mr Cooper's article that I described Henry VII's policy *vis-à-vis* landowners as legal but so extreme 'that one may question its legitimacy' (above, p. 45), or that my remarks on the promoters speak of 'false prosecutions and corruptions of every sort' (above, p. 55).

[3] Cooper, 107.

Constable's *Reading on Prerogativa Regis* shows that from the first the king exploited against the gentry those prerogative and judicial powers which London was to encounter later on, and whether or not there was some increase in activity under Empson and Dudley, there was no change in kind and no deterioration. Prosecutions under obsolete statutes cannot be proved to have taken place by citing, among others, an act of 1473.[1] Reginald Bray, though rescued by Polydore Vergil and the continuation of the reign with its policy, died in much the same odour of villainy as Dudley did later; Morton's Fork does not belong to the 'last years'; the hated informers were active before 1500.[2] The evidence for supposing a severe exploitation of feudal rights before 1504 was recited in my earlier paper.[3] Mr Cooper objects that the expansion of such rights does not prove the existence of malpractices (like the obtaining of false inquests) alleged by the acts of 1 Henry VIII to have been recently committed, and that no evidence of similar things 'has yet been offered' for the earlier period.[4] Ignoring the fact that none has been offered for the later period either, it may be said that Sir Robert Plumpton's well-known troubles with Empson (which turned upon the verdicts of allegedly constrained juries) belong to 1500–2;[5] an inquest of 1493 was traversed successfully after a second inquiry;[6] and one of July 1502 was expressly disallowed because the verdict was feigned.[7]

Then there is Henry's repentance in the last weeks of his life. Mr Cooper reaffirms his view that this demonstrates a recognition of injustices committed towards the end of the reign.[8] He cites in support the king's will and the proclamation of April 1509, claiming that the provisions of the will were unique and that there is no evidence of general pardons being granted without undue charge except under the proclamation. As to this last, on 18 July 1500 one John Corbett obtained a general pardon for all trespasses, offences, contempts and forfeitures incurred by force of any statute for cloth-making, and saving him for the future in all actions, suits, pleas, process and demands to be made

---

[1] Cooper, 108 and n. 29. It is very hard to get facts concerning prosecutions under penal statutes, but the occasional example does not look to be concerned with obsolete legislation. Thus in 1505 a man was pardoned for an outlawry incurred by failing to pay a fine in a qui-tam action arising out of the act of 1 Ric. III, c. 8 (*CPR Henry VII*, ii. 440).

[2] Cf. above, p. 60, and for informing, below, p. 72.

[3] Above, pp. 45 f.   [4] Cooper, 105 f.

[5] *Plumpton Correspondence*, ed. T. Stapleton (Camden Soc. 1839), pp. cvi *seqq.*, 147 ff. Mr Cooper dates the disputed York assizes to January 1505 (p. 106, n. 16). This was the date of the attestation in Plumpton's interest; the assizes were held in September 1502 (*Plumpton Corr.* p. cx).

[6] C 43/1/56.   [7] Ibid. 32.   [8] Cooper, 112 ff.

against him by the king or any other person. He paid no fee.[1] It is quite
true that Henry VII's will took unusual care to secure restitution to those
who had claims against his government, but I repeat that his main
concern was with debts owed at his death, a point made at even greater
length in the will of Henry V.[2] In addition Henry VII certainly ordered
that complaints alleging wrongful detention of lands and other wrongs
be investigated and, if justified, righted.[3] I cannot agree that the will
left much to discretion. The committee appointed to receive complaints
were to act if the matter were 'of grounded cause in conscience other
than mater doon by the course and ordre of our lawes' (that is, constituted a claim in equity not contrary to the Crown's common-law
rights), or if the executors thought 'that in conscience our soule aught to
stande charged with the said matier and complaint' (if, that is, they wished
equity for once to override the law). The stress is clearly on retaining
lawful gains. The investigating committee consisted of nineteen men, six
of whom together with three of the named executors (there was some
overlap between the two bodies) made a quorum. It included four
bishops (among them that great official, Richard Foxe), three office-
holding noblemen, the leading legal counsel, and five leading members
of the Household administration. In effect, the king asked his own
government to investigate complaints against them. The will's intent is
clearly to remedy real grievances, but not to abandon what was just and
necessary; it does not prove Henry a repentant oppressor.

Mr Cooper would have done well to heed a hint in my earlier article
and look at the proclamation of 19 August 1504,[4] issued before the
deterioration of policy is alleged to have occurred. Ordered to be
published in every shire, it declared the king's notable interest in the
administration of justice and his tender zeal for his people: he had

> a speciall regard, mynde and desire in noo maner wyse to doo any wronge or to
> be indebted to any personne . . . ner to haue any mannys londes, goodes ner
> catalles otherwyse than good reason and conscience woll require, or that by the
> due order and cours of his lawes hath be adiuged.

He therefore ordered – 'and for the discharge of his conscience chargith'
– that anyone with a reasonable and true claim on him, either over a

---

[1] C 202/H64/30. General pardons for various offences occur often in the patent rolls;
there are no signs that money was demanded for the majority though payment is recorded
for some. No payment: e.g. *CPR Henry VII*, i. 291, 292, 295, 299, 310, 316; ii. 154, 156,
158, 164, 282–4, 557, 558–9, 570–1 (a list ranging from Oct. 1489 to June 1508). Payment:
e.g. ibid. i. 317, 403.   [2] E 23/2.
[3] E 23/3. This is the original of Astle's not altogether accurate edition.
[4] C 66/594, m. 27d.

debt or over a wrongful invasion of property rights, should present his complaint in writing within two years after the Michaelmas following to one of seven officials named. A fair hearing and speedy remedy were promised. The coincidence in phrasing and sentiment between this document and the later will is very striking: the king's purpose and reservations are the same, and the earlier offer looks quite as good as the later.[1] It may also be remarked that Mr Cooper cannot have it both ways. If he is right in supposing that the king turned significantly remorseful in February 1509, and also in supposing that the levying of fines for outlawry was extortionate, he must explain why Henry is found assessing such fines on at least two occasions in that very month.[2] My argument was never that 'having repented, Henry took care that nothing but verbal gestures should be made'.[3] It was, and is, that Henry's genuine scruples both in 1504 and 1509 reflect a creditable worry about possible injustices, but are careful not to go so far as to surrender any of the Crown's lawful rights. There is nothing in the relevant documents – the will, the 1509 pardon (what little we know of it), or the comments of contemporaries – to contradict this.[4]

There remains the question whether the last years really produced such a crop of serious examples of injustice and ruthless exploitation that rapacity is the correct word to describe the way in which more or less legal rights were then exacted. I shall treat in turn of four particular problems relied upon by Mr Cooper but capable of a more searching analysis: the traversing of offices (inquisitions *post mortem*), the king's bonds and more especially fines for outlawry, Henry VII's relations with London and especially with the Merchant Adventurers, and the meaning of the reaction against his policy after his death. Two preliminary warnings. While the state of the evidence is bad for this reign and much – especially the records of the common-law courts – has hardly been touched, it looks (as one would expect) as though rather more detail had survived from the later years. Thus we can be sure that outlaws were fined in the last years, but can only suspect that similar things may have happened much earlier.[5] Sometimes things work the

---

[1] No case of a complaint received is at present known, though it is possible that some of the traverses of the years 1504–5 (below, p. 98) were connected with the proclamation.

[2] E 101/517/15.   [3] Cooper, 115.

[4] Mr Cooper (ibid.) misapplies the quotation from Coke who was talking about the traversing of inquests, not of outlawries. Fisher's funeral sermon proves that Henry VII had scruples of conscience, not that ills were manifold; and Polydore Vergil explicitly reports only the talk of the time of reaction ('fertur').

[5] Cf. below, p. 78.

other way. Despite all the complaints about promoters under Dudley, the best documented informer is one Henry Toft, described as active in 1496 by the *Great Chronicle*, very busy in the next few years, and called the 'kinges promoter' in 1504.[1] Secondly, it is fatally easy, as Mr Cooper has proved, to ascribe every grievance to the king's policy and to see it invariably involved in the obscure conflicts that lie behind the statements made later. The men whom the Common Council of London excluded for ever from sitting on juries because they had used their office to labour against justice[2] include William Simpson who on 15 May 1501 participated in rendering a false verdict contrary to the king's rights;[3] Dudley himself was in trouble with one of the commissions investigating royal claims in lands because he had failed to sue livery for certain manors;[4] if Stephen Jenyns was Henry VII's nominee as lord mayor of London, he was also a member of the commissions which took Dudley's indictment for treason and conducted his trial;[5] the notorious John Baptist Grimaldi – according to the *Great Chronicle* 'the most crewell & subtyllest wrecch' among all the promoters – obtained as late as October 1507 a pardon for an outlawry which had resulted from his failure to appear at the king's suit to answer to a charge of suspected treason.[6] Sir Robert Plumpton's various encounters with Empson are too complex to be sorted out here; but it may be noted that while he accused Empson of unlawfully maintaining Sir John Rowcliffe at York assizes,[7] he himself was advised to do his best to influence sheriff and jury at Derby, was charged with resisting the king's writ with force of arms, and saved himself by exploiting the king's favour.[8] One can be sure of little except that behind the claims and counter-claims there lay private quarrels and ambitions which took advantage of changing political circumstances; any straightforward acceptance of accusations would seem exceedingly rash.

---

[1] *Great Chronicle of London*, 258; *Select Cases in the Council of Henry VII*, ed. C. G. Bayne and W. H. Dunham (Selden Soc. 1958), pp. lvi–lviii, lx–lxi, 70 ff.
[2] Cooper, 108.
[3] *Cases in the Council of Henry VII*, 75.
[4] Edmund Dudley, *The Tree of Commonwealth*, ed. D. M. Brodie (Cambridge, 1948), 8.
[5] *Deputy Keeper's Third Report*, App. ii. 226 f.
[6] *Great Chronicle*, 337; *CPR Henry VII*, ii. 564. Grimaldi's association with the Crown was not recent: the *Great Chronicle* makes him partly responsible for Capell's troubles in 1495–6 (p. 258).
[7] *Plumpton Corr.* pp. cvi *seqq.*   [8] Ibid. 151; pp. cxi–cxiii.

III

An act of 1510 (1 Henry VIII, c. 12) complained that landowners, attacked in their titles by means of untrue inquisitions, had been prevented from making traverse to the verdict and compelled to sue out livery of lands falsely declared to be held in chief of the Crown. Traverse was in future to be admitted, and liveries in Henry VII's day were not to constitute proof of tenancy-in-chief. The act directed its allegations against Empson and Dudley by name and did not expressly speak of the king's last years, but it may, in fairness to Mr Cooper's case and to the probabilities, be supposed to refer to the years from about 1504 onwards. The point at issue is this. Offices taken either by escheators or special commissions of enquiry established by the verdict of a jury whether the king had any rights in a given property. If the jury found such rights, the lands were at once taken into the king's hands. If the party affected wished to contest the verdict, they could sue in Chancery – by traverse, interpleading, petition of right, or *monstrance le droit*, according to the circumstances of the case – to 'have the king's hands amoved' from the lands, on the grounds that the king's title had been falsely established.[1] The Crown would either, after investigation, concede the claim through the attorney-general, or it would oppose it and the matter would go to the King's Bench for trial by jury.

No doubt Professor Thorne is right in thinking that this procedure favoured the Crown,[2] but before the truth of the charge in the statute is accepted it would surely be as well to investigate the evidence for traverses. This is found in a bundle of Chancery proceedings on the common law side which among other things contains the record of at least forty-eight traverses entered in the course of the reign; two more are preserved by the Chancery of Chester.[3] A total of fifty may not seem vast but is in fact very considerable. The notorious problem of recovering the king's rights concealed during the disturbed times resulted in a good deal of inquiring, much of which must have established incontrovertible claims and would not be traversed.[4] These fifty

---

[1] The law is elaborated in Constable, *Tertia Lectura on Prerogativa Regis*, 70 ff. The simplest method, traverse, was ordinarily available and, to judge from the documents cited below, commonly used; a petition of right was required when the king claimed lands for felony or treason, and *monstrance le droit* (a petition of grace) if the petitioner's title was limited.

[2] Ibid. p. xix.

[3] C 43/1; Chester 7/3, 5. Cf. the table, in chronological order, in the Appendix to this paper.

[4] Cf. Richardson, 'The Surveyor of the Prerogative,' *EHR* 56 (1941), 52 ff., and for a summary above, pp. 46 f.

cases are the absolute minimum; some of the documents in the bundle are too much damaged to have been included in the count, and there is no guarantee at all that this rough collection, which contains almost nothing for the first seventeen years of the reign, was ever complete. However, it proves that the traversing of inquests was entirely possible under Henry VII and happened quite frequently.

The dates of the cases argue further against the statement in the 1510 act. Only twelve concern inquests taken before 1504, but against seven of these offices traverses were not entered until after the alleged change of policy.[1] The majority quite probably arose from the renewed commissions of inquiry which went out in July 1503 and thereafter. No inquest after November 1507 is included. Except for the early ones, there is no sign that procedure by traverse involved any great delays. Though the interval between inquest and traverse varied a good deal it rarely exceeded three years; in eighteen cases it was less than a year, an astonishing record among the leisurely processes of the Tudor common law and no support for the charge that men were prevented from making traverse. There was practically no delay after the first pleading in Chancery. In twenty-one cases the Crown admitted the truth of the traverse, which does not sound like tyranny; of these twenty-one, only two preceded the Empson and Dudley era, and of these one concerned an inquest taken under Edward IV.[2] The reasons given vary; sometimes it is simply said that the facts as stated in the traverse are true or that the king acts 'for certain considerations', but in five cases it is expressly stated that the inquest was feigned, and all these occurred after May 1505.[3] That the procedure by traverse was entirely normal is strikingly illustrated by the fact that the bundle contains one traverse entered by the Crown, incidentally one in which the interval since the office was just over three years.[4]

It therefore appears that the traversing of offices was common and straightforward, and more particularly that it was especially common in Henry VII's last years. This probably reflects the state of the evidence; more is no doubt lost for the 1490s than for the later decade. An additional traverse of 1491 is known only because it involved a wardship bought by Empson: when the grant was traversed by interested parties, it was decided that Empson's bond for the purchase price be held in

---

[1] One of the early inquests (C 43/1/38) may in fact belong to 1507; cf. Appendix.

[2] C 43/1/58. It is, of course, possible that of the twenty-nine contested cases some ended happily for the traverser.

[3] Ibid. 32, 34, 16, 32*, 31.   [4] Ibid. 43.

abeyance until the traverse had been tried.[1] One might suspect more injustice in inquests taken after 1504, but even if this were so the fact remains that many injured parties had their remedy. That the absence of full records does not hide outrageous doings is corroborated by what happened under Henry VIII. The last months of Henry VII had witnessed another outburst of commissions of inquiry,[2] and one would therefore expect some very intensive traversing as soon as the oppressor was dead. Yet the surviving bundle of traverses *temp. Henr. VIII* includes only twelve concerned with inquests of his father's reign, all taken between April 1507 and November 1508.[3] Of these seven were conceded, a larger proportion than appeared in the earlier bundle; but it signifies more that even at the time of reaction five out of twelve could be contested. Moreover, despite the act of 1510 no one apparently attempted to upset older inquests or enter his traverse now that the alleged practice of preventing traverse had been abandoned. If the statute had had the right of it, one would surely expect some traversing of inquests old enough for traverse to have been normally possible in the reign of Henry VII; one would expect people to bring cases in spite of their having sued livery, since that fact was now no longer to be evidence against them. Diligent search in the records may perhaps still turn up something more; the obvious place – traverses in Chancery – yields no support at all for the charges made after Henry VII's death and tends entirely to justify his administration. Dudley comes especially well out of the business. He who was charged with forcing men to forgo their rights is found signing two of the kings' mandates to the attorney-general for surrendering falsely claimed lands and appears on one of the commissions appointed to examine a traverser's claim which was conceded.[4] It is clear that his work as legal adviser to the Crown involved some positive surrender of claims in the interests of justice.

One may ask why the Parliament of 1510 should have accepted a bill with so dubious a preamble; that the bill did not originate in either House appears from the original act in the House of Lords.[5] The answer should probably in part be sought in the general atmosphere of that Parliament, and in part in the fact that Henry VII's inquiries of necessity

[1] *Calendar of Close Rolls 1485–1500*, no. 574.
[2] *CPR Henry VII*, ii. 608, 618, 626, 627 f.
[3] C 43/2/23–32, 35, 37.   [4] C 43/1/10, 30, 32*.
[5] The bill, written by an unofficial scribe, was a petition addressed to 'the Right Honorable and discreet Commons', asking that 'yt may therfore please your discrett wysedomes humbly to be seche the Kynges grace that it may . . .', a phrase corrected after acceptance into 'wherfore be hit enacted' (original act, House of Lords).

turned up a good deal of uncertainty in possession and title which as a rule operated in the king's favour. The history of landed property was never simple, but the fifteenth century naturally complicated it greatly. Before one supposes that a false office always represented malice, one should be aware of the horribly complicated issues before juries at such inquests. A relatively plain case, that of the manor of Stanbridge in Essex, held by one William Benstead, caused trouble enough.[1] In the complicated suits of Sir Maurice Berkeley, the history of some manors back to Edward III had to be proved.[2] Altogether, the terms of these traverses incline one to believe that juries were more commonly bemused by the manner in which the landed classes had played about with their properties than constrained by threats to favour the Crown. The general state of the land law and the evasive ingenuity to which it had given rise, the particular policy of Henry VII to recover the Crown's rights over tenants-in-chief, the insufficiency of inquest juries who, even when they were not got at, could hardly always be aware of the whole jungle of facts – such points readily explain the feelings of men over whom the king had asserted rights they may not have been aware existed when they acquired the lands. We have already seen that Dudley himself fell into this trap. In any case, the available evidence concerning traverses of offices shows that no convincing accusation can be levelled against the king's officers.[3]

[1] C 43/1/32*. On 12 November 1505, a jury found that Benstead had sold the manor to Edward IV for £5, on condition that the vendor died without heirs. Then, however, he enfeoffed four men with it, and on his death some other party still entered upon it. After the inquest, the commissioners naturally seized the manor into the king's hands; but the feoffees traversed the office, and on 8 July 1506 the attorney-general, presenting a royal warrant which stated that the office had been 'but fayned' and that the traverse had been proved 'substancyall & good . . . before our Counsell lernyd', restored the manor to the petitioners.

[2] Ibid. 29.

[3] Contemporary misapprehensions are also strikingly reflected in Lord Chancellor Warham's attitude in 1510, as exemplified in a case cited by Mr Cooper (n. 17) from Keilwey's *Reports*. Long arguments by the judges, turning on the technical question of the form which a petitioner's interpleading should take, ended with a request for a special pardon, but Warham cut the knot by simply quashing the disputed inquest because he believed it to be one which Empson and Dudley had falsely procured. According to the reporter, this was at the time described as unlawful (*contra legem*). In other words, he had used the arbitrary powers of equity because he had a general suspicion that parties had suffered injustice, and his action seems to have been ill considered in this instance. The report as printed speaks of Empson and 'Audley'; no doubt Mr Cooper's tacit emendation to 'Dudley' restores the original meaning.

IV

One of the particular complaints of the *Great Chronicle* touched upon the driving in of debts on bonds, alleged to have gathered momentum in 1506.[1] The *Chronicle* admitted that such things had happened many times since the tenth year of the reign when Sir William Capell's 'trowbyll' occurred,[2] but 'syne Empson & dudley were sett In auctoryte' the summons increased in number. Men were being harried for 'old Reconysauncis & boundis ffor pease or othir suyrtees' in Chancery or Star Chamber or other courts, 'And ovyr all these were lastly sowgth owth alle outelawryes syne the begynnyng of the kyngis Regn' for which grievous fines were imposed. Mr Cooper regards these complaints as justified and grows quite indignant especially over the business of outlawries,[3] but it may be suggested that he ought to have explained what this outlawry was and so have avoided giving a general impression of men victimized contrary to all reason and law.

Outlawry was the last stage in mesne process at common law – the ultimate weapon available to the courts for compelling a defendant to appear and answer the plaintiff's charges so that the case might proceed. If the defendant refused to comply with the first summons, the other party could move through set stages of writs of attachment, writs of exigent, and proclamation of outlawry. This sequence was originally part of the criminal law and continued to be available to the Crown for the securing of a man accused of felony; through the action of trespass it came to be available in civil pleas between party and party and was in particular the normal procedure in an action for debt. An outlaw was therefore, *a priori*, one who kept another (nearly always a subject) from his legal rights. In theory, the consequences of outlawry were very serious: an outlaw forfeited his moveables to the Crown and lost the protection of the law: he could not sue in the king's courts and was liable to arrest as a rebel.[4] But it is hard to bring this vigour into accord with the facts. Outlawry sounded terrible but was regularly ignored without any consequences. In King's Bench, the court, having ordered

---

[1] *Great Chronicle*, 334 f.

[2] This dating of a general grievance by an event in London's history underlines my point that the London chronicles were really concerned with the city's grievances only.

[3] E.g. Cooper, 111 f., 115.

[4] For all this cf. M. Hastings, *The Court of Common Pleas in Fifteenth Century England* (Ithaca, 1947), 169 ff. The old right to kill an outlaw on sight had lapsed. The whole business had lost the terror it had had in King John's time, though that king's doings tend to leap to the minds of historians and others when outlawry is mentioned.

a man's outlawry, would then have to wait until he was caught by the sheriff or surrendered to the Marshalsea, neither (we are told) a frequent occurrence.[1] The historian of the fifteenth-century court of Common Pleas called it a 'long-drawn-out ritual' which took at least eighteen months even if the defendant tried no tricks; it was 'frequently ineffective' and the consequences were nothing so serious as might be supposed.[2] A man could clear himself of it in various ways of which the securing of a pardon was the commonest, and a pardon was automatic if the defendant surrendered himself to the Fleet or the Marshalsea and paid 16s. 4d. in the Hanaper.[3] That in spite of this many men allowed their outlawry to stand rather than face creditors and other complainants indicates how little store they set by this overrated weapon of the common law.

A special grievance was that a man might be proclaimed an outlaw in a shire other than that in which he lived; he might thus not have been aware of the three exigents and have been unable to purge his offence before he was outlawed. This long-standing complaint, convincing on the face of it, was remedied in 1513 by an act of Parliament which ordered that when an exigent issued into such a 'foreign' county the writ of proclamation was to be awarded into the county of residence.[4] The act claimed that by the malice of enemies men had been outlawed in ignorance, but (though this may of course have happened) the real trouble was that the law demanded the issue of process into the county in which the suit had arisen, so that of necessity and without malice a man might easily be proclaimed in a shire in which he owed a debt though he did not reside there. Miss Hastings cites a case of a man outlawed unawares in 1405–6;[5] and in Henry VII's reign, long before Dudley earned his bad name, men were often proclaimed out of their shires.[6]

---

[1] M. Blatcher, 'The Working of the Court of King's Bench in the Fifteenth Century' (unpub. London Ph.D. thesis, 1936), 184.

[2] Hastings, *Common Pleas*, 171 f., 176.

[3] Ibid. 180 f. The traverses of outlawry which the king licensed presumably pleaded one of the other ways of escaping outlawry; suing a writ of error, or challenge on grounds of misnomer. It does not seem unfair that a man who had long avoided his obligations but now under pressure claimed that the process was false should have to pay for his earlier neglect which affected law-enforcement and the rights of others.

[4] 4 Henry VIII, c. 4, in effect made permanent by 6 Henry VIII, c. 4.

[5] *Common Pleas*, 179, n. 43.

[6] E.g. an entry book of outlawries proclaimed in Lincs. (E 36/91) includes a proclamation for felony at the king's suit for men from Lancashire as well as Lincolnshire (p. 31: 1491), one for debt against men from Huntingdonshire (pp. 35 f.: 1491), one for debt against a Northumbrian (p. 57: 1499), and so forth.

The ineffectiveness of outlawry was manifestly a serious obstacle to the proper enforcement of the law and more particularly a problem to creditors, for debt was far and away the commonest cause of these extreme proceedings. If in the last years of Henry VII the king's ministers really instituted a campaign to bring outlaws to heel, they were thus engaged in a very necessary tightening up of procedure, and some exaction of fines was entirely justified: as Miss Hastings says, in the fifteenth century it was still thought right to make 'defendant suffer for his contumacy in not appearing'.[1] Whether special fines were assessed for pardons of outlawry or licences to traverse outlawries only in the last part of the reign, is by no means clear. We happen to have evidence that Sir Edward Belknap, who entered upon office in 1508, collected such fines in 1508–9, to a total of £2910 15s. 5d., much of it in bonds.[2] But we also know that the commissions which investigated the king's rights from early in the reign concerned themselves from at least 1495 with inquiring into outlaws,[3] and we know that the accounts of the treasurer of the chamber from the very first list large sums collected from recognizances, with no details given.[4] It may well be that the explicitness of Belknap's accounts, itself expressive only of a change in administrative technique, distorts the picture.

However, I do not think that this quite answers; it does look as though the last years of Henry VII witnessed a more particular attention to the collection of debts and fines owed to the king. The reason appears readily enough if one looks rather further than the complaints or allows that the king may have had a right to the money owed to him. Henry VII's activities in the 1490s unquestionably resulted in a good many impositions – fines and the like – for which bonds were given while payment was deferred. The *Great Chronicle* itself indicates that its complaint was against the effrontery of those who sought to make a reality out of such commitments; it held it improper that 'old' recognizances for debts to the Crown should be called in. Would the chronicler also have denounced the Merchant Adventurers who in 1501 resolved to get what they could of debts expressly described as 'olde'?[5] The king's recovery of debts is far from well documented, but something may be learned from the records of fifteen extant *scire facias* actions.[6] In these

---

[1] *Common Pleas*, 182.
[2] E 101/517/14, Belknap's account for 1 July 1508 to 10 March 1509.
[3] Richardson, *Tudor Chamber Admin.* 120.   [4] E 101/413/2.
[5] *Acts (of Court) of the Mercers' (Company 1453–1527)*, ed. L. Lyell and F. D. Watney (Cambridge, 1936), 248.
[6] C 43/1: in chronological order 63, 66, 59, 44, 71, 69, 72, 60, 61, 62, 68, 67, 45, 65, 70.

the sheriff was ordered to summon a debtor to show cause why a certain sum, payable at a date in the past and for which the king held a recognizance, should not be recovered. In only one case did the defendant appear and 'nihil dicit in barram siue Retardacionem executionis predicte'; twice debtors denied liability and the case went to a jury; in the remaining twelve instances the Chancery, after repeated failure to secure the debtor's presence, awarded the Crown the right to recover by distress. Three of the cases took place in 1498–1502, for debts of 1496 and 1498; all the remainder were started by writs issued in 1505 and 1506. While this clearly suggests some sort of campaign to secure unpaid debts, it does not prove injustice. The king had waited long enough. Every debt but one had been incurred by 1499 at the latest; one was ten years old when the writ issued. Thus there had been no precipitancy; nor could Henry fairly be charged with asserting claims so ancient that in equity they no longer existed.

Another document amplifies the picture by demonstrating how difficult it was to collect on bonds given in the courts. It is a list of recognizances forfeited in the Exchequer for failure to appear, usually to give security of peaceful behaviour – one of the points in the *Great Chronicle*'s list of grievances.[1] Since the list goes down to the Trinity term of 18 Henry VII, it was probably drawn up in the summer of 1503. The number of entries year by year suggests no particular trend in policy. The busiest years were 4, 6, 10 and 16 Henry VII (1488–9, 1490–1, 1494–5, 1500–1) when thirty-two, forty-three, twenty-three and twenty-six persons gave bonds for totals of £680, £1,873, £1,923, and £680. What really matters, however, is the number of forfeited bonds not yet paid and in many cases not yet put in execution. That nearly all debts incurred to the Crown in the four years preceding the drawing up of the list should remain unsettled is perhaps reasonable; but the Exchequer had also failed with fifty-seven of the 191 who had given bonds in the first ten years of the reign. The figure shows, on the one hand, that collecting these debts was both possible and proper, and on the other that difficulties could be considerable; yet what sort of a complaint is it which maintains that fifty-seven should escape their legal duty when 134 had paid it?

It therefore appears that attempts to step up the collection of debts were made, and legitimately made, after about 1504, though it is clear that many sums remained outstanding to trouble the government of Henry VIII. As late as 1514 a commission was appointed to deal with

[1] E 101/516/17. The bonds were taken of the principal and his sureties.

debts on bonds, many of which must have dated back to Henry VII; though empowered both to enforce payment, to grant respite, and to discharge, it did not end the matter.[1] Henry VII's later policy on bonds cannot, however, be regarded as significantly new: obviously debts cannot be collected until they have been incurred. It still remains possible that in the matter of outlawries the Crown so increased its pressure that the complaints were justified. There is certainly no sign that more pardons for outlawry were issued in the last years than in earlier ones.[2] Indeed, the figures are highest at the beginning of Henry's reign: the sixty-two of 1487–8 were never even approached again, the average thereafter running at round about thirty, with a decline down to twenty-five in 1504–5. Perhaps the thirty-three of 1505–6 represent the results of a new drive, but only twenty-eight issued the year after. The very low figures for 1507–8 and for the seven months of Henry's last year (seventeen and four respectively) no doubt reflect patchy enrolment, for Belknap's accounts provide evidence of fifty-three pardons and licences to traverse between July 1508 and March 1509.[3] It is therefore probable that measures to get outlaws to purge themselves continued unabated to the end of the reign, with possibly a little rise in numbers, and the king's personal activity in assessing fines underlines this.[4] These fines were really in the nature of compositions for the goods of outlaws to which he was entitled; they vary a good deal but do not look outrageous.[5] The accounts also include items paid in by Belknap's deputies in the shires which must represent goods confiscated and sold. Of course, this strict policy was bound to be resented. However, not only was it legal but it was as much an effort to assist the courts as a fiscal

[1] *LP* i. 3226 (8); Richardson, *Tudor Chamber Admin.* 158. As late as the early 1520s a list of unremitted debts to the Crown contained many bonds taken by Henry VII (*LP* iii. 3694).

[2] Pardons for outlawry are nearly all enrolled at the head of each year's patent roll and can be counted easily from *CPR*. A few additional ones are sometimes found later in the roll. A cross-check is possible from such Particulars of the Hanaper Accounts as survive. Though the figures do not tally exactly, they are close enough to show that the patent roll provides reliable evidence. Thus in 7 Henry VII thirty-six pardons paid fees in the Hanaper (E 101/218/4) and thirty-eight appear on the roll; forty-six paid in 1505–6 (Michaelmas to Michaelmas: E 101/219/8), with thirty-three on the roll (August to August).

[3] E 101/517/14.

[4] Belknap's accounts include one for outlawries and other matters 'assessed by his highnesse' (E 101/517/15).

[5] E.g. Richard Marten paid £20 (E 101/517/15, fo. 1) for the pardon of an outlawry for a debt of 40s., all other outlawries in which he stood, and the restoration of his goods and chattels (*CPR Henry VII*, ii. 600).

device; the bulk of the money was received in recognizances for future payment.[1]

Mr Cooper supposes that the charges of deliberately procured outlawries may have been exaggerated but cites a statement from one man that he was compelled to make a fine against conscience.[2] Such cases may have occurred; there is no certainty either way. A man was pardoned in May 1490 for an outlawry procured by malice.[3] What matters is the absence of evidence in Belknap's accounts or elsewhere for many outlawries sued on the king's behalf; nearly all the pardons were for outlawry at the suit of a party; if there was malice, it was private malice.[4] A considered judgment must take account of the fact that outlawry nearly always reflected the difficulty encountered by private persons in obtaining their rights; the outlaw's victim deserves some consideration, too. One must also remember that the collecting of debts and the driving in of outlaws could not happen until the debts existed and the outlaws had shown reluctance to purge themselves. While the policy may have resulted in a few hard cases, it was in general justified and necessary.

V

That Henry VII, and Dudley on his behalf, often found themselves in conflict with the city of London and certain interests in it has never been in doubt.[5] Certain isolated cases in which injustice was committed obviously occurred. That of Thomas Sunnyff,[6] the only one known in which a man seems to have suffered quite innocently, is not likely to have had no companions; Sir William Capell may not have been guilty of the technical offence for which he was imprisoned in 1508.[7] No one maintains that such things were commendable, though to suppose that

---

[1] E.g. fines assessed on 11 Feb. 1509 totalled £193 12s. 3d. of which £73 3s. 5d. was paid in cash (E 101/517/15). Many of the assessments in this paper are crossed out and may have been remitted, but some of those crossed out appear in Belknap's comprehensive account (ibid. 14).

[2] Cooper, 112 and n. 61.   [3] *CPR Henry VII*, i. 309.

[4] E.g. of the ten pardons agreed to on 27 January 1509, one concerned felony and one other may have arisen from a Crown suit; for the last three properly recorded years (1504–7), the patent roll shows three, three, and two outlawries at the king's suit out of twenty-five, thirty-three, and twenty-eight respectively. Henry Wodecock, secondary of the Counter in the Poultry, made a return of all exigents executed there during his term of office, which practically covered the reign; of fifty-three listed only three were at the king's suit, and all these belonged to 1501–2 (E 163/9/9).

[5] Cf. Miss Brodie's remarks in *Tree of Commonwealth*, 5 ff.

[6] Cooper, 120 f.; Brodie, *TRHS* (1932), 153 f.

[7] Ibid.; *Great Chronicle*, 336.

any period of history – and more particularly the later fifteenth century – could be free of persecution by malicious enemies would be naïve indeed. The question of Henry's policy does not turn on Sunnyff's case but on the meaning of his interference with city government and of the grievances felt by the Merchant Adventurers.[1] The conflict between Henry and the city over its charters and liberties, his interference with the election of a sheriff and the influence exerted in favour of Stephen Jenyns, a merchant tailor elected mayor in 1508 against the enmity of those who hated that company[2] – all this cannot be seen in its true light unless one remembers that Henry was trying to trim the powers of franchise holders everywhere and had good cause to do so.[3] The city's privileges were great; its arrogance was greater.

It is scarcely right, for instance, to throw Henry's actions up against him without recalling the sort of attitude exemplified by Sir William Capell who in 1504 high-handedly confiscated the property of a currier who proposed to exercise his trade by royal licence. Whether Capell was within his rights seems more than doubtful; the words with which he was charged (and which were not denied), that the king 'had noon auctoryte to graunte or gyf any suche licence withyn' London, were nothing short of outrageous.[4] It was in this spirit of separatist pretensions that the city wished to revive its liberties after Henry VII's death;[5] more significant than its desire to seek a remedy for infringements is the fact that nothing seems to have resulted from these protests – if indeed they were ever actually made. Henry's support for the Merchant Tailors, much resented as newcomers in city politics, may have been part of a policy to reduce the power of the great companies, or may merely have been due to his desire for the masses they agreed to say in exchange for their charter;[6] at any rate, it lay behind his actions in the shrieval election of 1506 and the mayoral election of 1508 when he favoured one city interest against another. It is possible to regard this involvement in city politics as improper and to side with the powers in possession. Mr

---

[1] Cooper, 109, 110, 126.

[2] For the details cf. Cooper, 110. The act of 1504 transferred control of guild ordinances from mayors and J.P.s to the king's officers. This measure at least said that it was promoted by the Commons and has always been regarded as a sensible attack on the disastrous selfishness of guilds and towns; the use of it in order to burden Henry VII would seem to require some explanation.

[3] For Henry and London cf. also K. Pickthorn, *Early Tudor Government* (Cambridge, 1934), i. 70.

[4] Cf. *Select Cases in the Court of Requests*, ed. I. S. Leadam (Selden Soc. 1898), 7 ff.

[5] Cooper, 110, 117.

[6] C. M. Clode, *The Early History of the Guild of Merchant Tailors* (London, 1888), i. 347 ff., 350.

Cooper does so; but he should concede that he is condemning not a rapacious or vicious development of Henry's later years, but a part of the king's general policy to restore the monarchy and subject privileged persons to the general interest.

The case is clearer still with the Merchant Adventurers. This powerful body gave the king a good deal of trouble and was forced by him (through Parliament) to abandon attempts at creating a monopoly of Londoners; on the other hand, he assisted it by devising a better organization, though one may call this interference.[1] No doubt the Adventurers did not always like the king's policy and contracted some grievances. But the points made by Mr Cooper really will not do. He may be right in supposing that in December 1508 Henry contemplated a new custom on cloth, and he may well say that Dudley's threat of an embargo was high-handed;[2] but in fact the document speaks only of an inquiry 'for the Custume' without any indication that a new levy was intended, and nothing more is heard of it or of the threatened prohibition. Mr Cooper says that the Adventurers resented 'customs and impositions' (by which he means poundage) and were 'anxious to see rates returned to the old values'.[3] But there is no proof at all that the rates of 1507 had led to an increase in the levy; though it is difficult to compare the general statement of rates in the £ given in the tunnage and poundage acts with a book of rates dealing in quantities, the scholars best qualified to judge are clear that the purpose of the new book was not to raise rates (which would have been a breach of statute) but to secure a fair assessment in place of relying, as hitherto, on merchants' sworn declarations of the value of the customed goods.[4]

Not only, therefore, is there no evidence that the Adventurers were justly complaining of new and excessive burdens, but there is evidence that their aims were a good deal less praiseworthy and sensible than Mr Cooper suggests. For the demand of the Merchant Adventurers in the first year of Henry VIII was not simply that 'the subsidy should be reduced to the old rates of the first years of Henry VII'.[5] The Adventurers' first plan was to resist the passage of a tunnage and poundage

---

[1] G. Schanz, *Englische Handelspolitik gegen Ende des Mittelalters* (Leipzig, 1881), i. 340 ff.

[2] Cooper, 109.   [3] Ibid.

[4] N. Gras, 'Tudor Books of Rates,' *Quart. J. Econ.* 26 (1912), 766 ff., holds that the 1507 book did not raise rates. The customs figures of London, where alone the book applied, show no significant increase. Though the yield of the subsidy for 1507–8 is up a bit on the previous year, this is in accord with the national movement of the customs and clearly represents improved trade (Schanz, op. cit. ii. 37, 46; P. Ramsay, 'Overseas Trade in the Reign of Henry VII,' *Econ. Hist. Rev.* 2nd ser. vi (1954), 173 ff.).

[5] Cooper, 126.

bill altogether.[1] When they realized that opinion in Council and Parliament was against them, they contemplated a petition against the granting of a subsidy as heavy as that granted to the late king.[2] The next stage finds them drafting provisos for the subsidy bill of which the first postponed payment till Michaelmas 1510, the second protected the Adventurers against an increase of the rates in the forthcoming statute, and the third limited the penalties for failure to pay the subsidy.[3] None of these appear in the act which passed the Commons on 14 February,[4] and on the 12th the Adventurers began their campaign to secure the one real concession they could now hope for: to have all payments remitted between the death of Henry VII and the day of the new grant, during which time, they argued – and had told the lord treasurer as long ago as August 1509[5] – the king had no right to collect the subsidy.[6]

Though the Council told them at once 'that the Subside shulde be graunted unto the Kyng lyke wise as it was unto his father and in as ample maner, and therfor to labur to the contrary it was but foly',[7] they persisted with petitions and suits and the soliciting of friendly offices till the matter was decided against them on 19 March.[8] The company tried to save something by agreeing that their members should themselves make a return of goods carried in the disputed period, but this naturally proved a dilatory business, and on 17 June the Council ordered the customers to report on those merchants who had not produced a statement.[9] Passive resistance, however, as usually in the Tudor century, earned its reward: on 12 November the Crown agreed to accept by way of settlement two-thirds of the money due. Even so, the Adventurers four days later decided to make another attempt at total evasion, but it would seem that this came to nothing; there is no further reference to the matter.[10]

Thus by far the most serious dispute over the subsidy which is recorded in the Adventurers' books took place in the first year of Henry VIII, during the time of the reaction against Henry VII's policy, and had nothing whatever to do with the late king's exactions. The company had tried the same game at the accession of Edward IV and of Richard

[1] *Acts of the Mercers*, 346 f.
[2] Ibid. 347: they do not want 'to haue the Subside graunted after the extremytie, as it was in the tyme of Kyng Henry the vijth'. The point is clearly not, as Mr Cooper supposes, that they want to return to Henry VII's grant (1485): they want to offer less than that.
[3] Ibid. 348 (8 Feb. 1510).
[4] Ibid. 351; though it did not reach the Lords till the 23rd (*LJ* i. 7a).
[5] *Acts of the Mercers*, 326 f.   [6] Ibid. 348 ff.   [7] Ibid. 350.
[8] Ibid. 358 ff.   [9] Ibid. 372.   [10] Ibid. 380 f.

III;[1] on the former occasion many of them had been 'for their sub-sydie . . . gretely trubled in the Kinges Eschecur',[2] a kind of entry never found under the extortionate Henry VII. Indeed, this king alone had allowed them to get away with it: in 1485 they had paid no poundage between Richard's death and the date of the grant to his successor.[3] It is odd, to say the least, that their struggle with Henry VIII's government should be so presented as to suggest that they had a genuine grievance against Henry VII. The genuine troubles between Henry VII and the city of London were either the consequence of a true political battle over the dangerous independence of the city and its merchants, or (like Sunnyff's case) are found to be isolated excesses with a background of private malice. The tangle of politics also lies, of course, behind the indignation of the city chronicles.

VI

That Henry VII's death was followed by a sizeable reaction against his policies is not disputed; it is also obvious that the mere fact of reaction means little. That grievances existed does not prove their justice, and it is not established that the councillors of Henry VIII, in encouraging these complaints, sought more than popularity for the new reign or a proper treatment for the occasional genuine victim. As we have seen, Henry VII had himself been perfectly willing to offer this last. Henry VIII's pardon was no doubt a little more generous than his father's; on this Mr Cooper and I seem agreed. But the reader may judge whether a charge of making heavy weather applies more suitably to my six lines or to Mr Cooper's half-page discussing the assurance that parties need not fear interference in the future by letters from king or Council.[4] The words may indeed be read as implying that such things had hap-pened in the past, but they must unquestionably also be read as envisaging the possibility of their happening in time to come: through-out the age and beyond it it had to be recognized that thanks to the activities of suitors in high places mandates might go forth which were not properly instructed in the truth of a case. Such interference, for money or favour, happened often enough after 1509; this does not argue, and Henry VIII's proclamation did not say, that Henry VII's government had been guilty of more than inadvertence, while it did say that his own might also conceivably be guilty of that.

---

[1] Ibid. 118 ff., 152 ff.
[3] Ibid. p. xix.
[2] Ibid. 119.
[4] Above, p. 63; Cooper, 116.

Mr Cooper has cited a number of complaints entered after Henry VII's death, but he would surely agree that they must not be taken at their face value without question. Thus Lord Dacre's allegation of wrongful recognizances does not appear to have convinced Henry VIII any more than it convinced Henry VII;[1] there is no record that he received redress. It is true that eleven sets of recognizances are known to have been cancelled by Henry VII's executors,[2] but it is not so likely that many more may have been cancelled without record, for Henry VII's recognizances seem usually to have been registered in Chancery.[3] Perhaps Capell and Kneysworth, released as soon as the old king was dead, were innocent of the offences charged against them, though it seems a good deal more likely that they were let off for popularity's sake.[4] Aylmer's case, however, certainly does not prove what Mr Cooper wants it to prove.[5] Indicted and held in prison during Henry VII's lifetime, Aylmer was acquitted at a trial held shortly afterwards in the new reign. Are we to take it that in Mr Cooper's view (which is that a royal judge regarded the presenting jury's activities as false) an indictment must always be followed by a conviction? That many people felt relief at Henry VII's death is both obvious and comprehensible, and one need not wonder that a general reaction of this sort dredged up some convincing cases of injustice as well as a larger number in which it is far from clear that the alleged victims were not exploiting the turn of events to get at their enemies. What matters is whether it can really be shown that any large-scale rectification was called for, and here Mr Cooper's two major points about the reaction – the general commissions of 1509 and the Parliament of 1510 – deserve rather more critical study.

Mr Cooper is quite right in describing the commissions of oyer and terminer which issued in July 1509 as 'a nation-wide inquiry to redress grievances'.[6] But in this they were not unique. It became something like practice to introduce a new reign with such a survey; at least Edward VI and Mary copied the 1509 example without having any of the special reasons alleged for that year.[7] What is more, it looks as though Henry

[1] Cooper, 114.   [2] Cooper, 113 f.

[3] It is also not true that all the warrants were made 'two years or more after Henry's death'. Only two of them were, and the implied suggestion that this marks a considered rather than a hot-blooded reaction has no support. A good many recognizances were also cancelled because the debts had been paid (e.g. *LP* i. 257 [63, 68, 84]); many of these documents were never called in doubt.

[4] *Great Chronicle*, 336.

[5] Cooper, 109.   [6] Cooper, 117 ff.

[7] *CPR Edward VI*, i. 75 ff.; *Philip and Mary*, i. 27 ff.

VII was the first king to elaborate the occasional general commission of oyer and terminer into a broad inquiry; early in 1495 he issued commissions covering the whole realm except the north, the Welsh border, and the south-east.[1] Earlier still he had set one up to investigate offences in fifteen widely scattered towns.[2] Henry VIII's government, therefore, took over and developed his father's experimental device for increasing the effectiveness of the Crown's criminal jurisdiction. Mr Cooper seeks significance in the 1509 commissions' membership, but this was in no way unusual: such general commissions always included leading nobility and gentry as well as judges and lawyers, with a quorum of these last. Their varying terms of reference are interesting. The towns commission of 1493 included breaches of cloth-making statutes, and one of 1486 offences under retaining acts: the weapon was a most flexible one.[3] However, every such inquiry was in the first place designed to discover and punish crimes. The commissions of 1495 were to try treason, murder, rape, insurrection, rebellion, felony, misprision, negligence, extortion, conspiracy, contempt, concealments, congregations, condonations, riots, routs, illicit conventicles, and other trespasses and offences.[4] To this the 1509 commission added a few more crimes such as champerty, taking of fees from both sides (*ambidextria*), and forgery; it also included maintenance and retaining contrary to the statutes, and regrating and forestalling. In addition it specified trespasses, contempts and offences 'contra formam Statuti de Magna Carta de libertatibus Anglie editi aliorumque Statutorum quorumcunque editorum aut contra legem & consuetudinem regni nostri Anglie quoquo modo factis'.[5] The commission thus covered both a general enforcement of the criminal law and the prosecution of any who had offended against the rights of the subject. This double purpose was quite conscious: when the commissions were revoked it was stated that they had been issued because the king had learned of things done 'to the subuersion of his lawes and the good gouernaunce of his seid Realme' and had wished to invite both Crown and private suits.[6] The Crown purpose looms larger: the first group of offences is detailed and specific,

---

[1] *CPR Henry VII*, ii. 29 ff. Before his day general commissions were seemingly rare, though Henry IV occasionally appointed one for a single county (*CPR Henry IV*, i. 267 f., 313).

[2] *CPR Henry VII*, i. 442.

[3] C 66/574, m. 16d; 563, m. 16d.   [4] C 66/576, m. 20d.

[5] KB 8/4/51, 9/453/69. Mr Cooper's description of the commission's powers is fair enough (pp. 117 f.), though it is not clear why his macaronic rendering of the Latin original should appear as a quotation.

[6] C 82/342/1/576.

the second vague; though breaches of Magna Carta may be reckoned to include oppression by royal officials, this was not mentioned explicitly. Still, it may well be that the commissions were in part designed to give an opportunity for the presenting of just grievances against the king's government.

Whether, however, one can argue from the Council's willingness to hear complaints to the depravity of Henry VII's policy is quite another matter. There is a warning in Polydore Vergil's remark that the proclamation of the commission produced such a flood of doubtful suits that the Council were forced to abandon their intention to redress grievances.[1] What we know of the commissions' work also suggests that there was much more noise than substance in the complaints. Mr Cooper notes that the surviving indictments are those transferred to the King's Bench when the commissions ended, but his apparent opinion that this represents a possibly small part of those found before the commissioners seems improbable. The commissions sat from July to October/November: is it really to be supposed that in that time many men, indicted without being in custody – for that was the general experience of criminal inquiries except after a rebellion or at a gaol delivery – could have been arraigned and tried? Indeed, as late as December 1509 twelve informers imprisoned in London were released on bail: they had been arrested, apparently as notorious offenders, by royal warrant before the issue of the commission, had been variously indicted before the oyer and terminer, and had still come to no sort of trial.[2] Though some cases were no doubt settled in the shires, not far short of 500 indictments survive in King's Bench, a large enough number to confirm that we have pretty full information of the commissioners' discoveries.[3]

Mr Cooper has singled out twenty of these indictments as complaints of abuses in government: not a large number, but even so more than can be accepted. Lord Dacre's (of the South) charge against Chauncy is exceedingly dubious; it so happens that we have the earlier troubles on record and know that Dacre had made a most unconvincing answer to Chauncy's accusation of abuses of power and false imprisonment.[4] Moreover, this was a private quarrel in which the Crown, compelled to take note of complaints even if unfounded, would seem hard to

---

[1] Polydore Vergil, *Anglica Historia*, ed. D. Hay (Camden Soc. 1950), 150: in the concordance.
[2] C 82/343/1/615. Mr Cooper (n. 118) makes nothing of their names, but one of them was the notorious promoter Henry Toft.
[3] KB 9/453.
[4] *Cases in the Council of Henry VII*, pp. xcviii, 123 ff.

blame; it took place in 1500 and proves nothing for the disputed 'last years'. The fact that customs officers sometimes overcharged merchants for their clearance documents does not constitute an indictment of Henry VII's government which could in no circumstances have prevented such lapses. One of the customers' offences and one of three cases of purveyance complained of took place after Henry VII's death.[1] Of the recorded charges against Empson, encroachment on the king's highway is no proof of royal misdoings, while of the other four only one for certain and another possibly concern misdeeds in the last years of the reign.[2] So that the adversary's case may appear as strong as possible, Empson's London indictment may be allowed; however, it remains true that in the end proceedings on it proved inadvisable and were abandoned. Dudley's indictment for Sunnyff's case was just, but that for selling woods and keeping the money again proves nothing about the king's government.[3] That leaves four cases in which one may suspect malicious informing and the empanelling of corrupt juries; whether the law was broken in the private interest or the king's is impossible to say, especially as three concerned the doings of those Hampshire commissioners of whom Dudley also fell foul.[4] The harvest is small. We are left with six relevant complaints (two against purveyors, three against Empson, and Sunnyff's case), with a possible four more referring to malicious prosecutions and inquests. The commissioners' discoveries hardly support a generalized charge of oppressive and rapacious government in the last years of Henry VII.

The termination of the commissions suggests that this came also to be the view of Henry VIII's Council.[5] Mr Cooper thinks they were withdrawn because they encroached on the common-law courts; the argument ignores the fact that commissions of oyer and terminer were a

[1] KB 9/453/277 on 28 April 1509, and no. 24 in June 1509.
[2] Plumpton's case of 1500 (ibid. 142) and the forcible seizure of May 1504 (ibid. 138), even if they show Empson acting in the king's service (which is not certain), cannot be used to substantiate Mr Cooper's case for a worsening of things in the last years; the charge of false imprisonment (ibid. 139) states no year.
[3] Ibid. 461, 140.
[4] Ibid. 154, 157–8, and cf. above, p. 72. This Hampshire commission certainly ran into trouble; of the traverses entered in 1 Henry VIII, four of the seven conceded dealt with its inquests (C 43/2/27–30). But the apparent offender, Sir Amyas Paulet, had caused annoyance as early as 1498 (*Letters and Papers of Richard III and Henry VII*, ii. 76 f.); perhaps it would be wiser to regard these cases, too, as private quarrels taking advantage of the machinery of the king's government.
[5] I possess microfilms of the transcripts of Council records in the Huntington Library which Mr Cooper has used; though his printed version (pp. 121 f.) contains many minor errors and I shall quote from the microfilm, his paper may be referred to for the sake of convenience.

common-law weapon used freely then and later, and it also destroys the logic of his view that the 1509 commissions were part of a reaction against prerogative government. The Council resolved to end the commissions for two main reasons, stated on 11 October in a passage printed by Mr Cooper: one, that the urgent matters were dealt with and nothing more to be expected that could not easily be settled at sessions and assizes, and the other that it appeared from the reports of circuit judges that 'by the demeaner of the people the contynuaunce of the said Oyer Determyne sholde be to them bothe chargeable and painfull'. When the Council reconsidered the matter on 14 November, it did add to its arguments the needs of the central courts, deprived of much business, but also noted that matters brought before the commissions had been petty and not the sort of criminal charges intended. The proclamation of 26 November justified the revoking of the commissions on the ground that their continuance would involve very heavy costs to parties and jury panels; it also claimed that counsel would be more easily available at Westminster.[1] This charmingly ignored the notorious difficulty of deciding cases at the centre which required the verdicts of local juries, but confirms that the chief reason for ending the commissions lay in the annoyance they were causing. It is not clear, therefore, why Mr Cooper should speak so categorically of their 'popularity'.[2]

Altogether, Mr Cooper overdraws the picture of a common-law reaction against either Henry VII's new courts or Henry VIII's commissions, which in any case are alleged to have pursued opposing aims. The decision to abandon Henry VII's 'bye courtes'[3] – presumably the Council Learned and surveyors of Crown lands, and possibly the Star Chamber and statutory tribunals as well – was taken not so much because they were oppressive to the subject but because 'the Kinges Righte and tytell in proces of tyme sholde perishe for lacke of matter of Recordes ... for the kinges highnes cannot be intituled by Recorde but by matter of Recorde in Courte of Authority'. The other reason given – that people could not be lawfully discharged for payments made in those courts – reflects the Exchequer's attitude which led to the series of acts establishing the general surveyors;[4] prerogative courts were not, after all, long in coming back, though the Council Learned seems to have been content with a much less vigorous existence.[5] We can well

---

[1] C 82/342/1/576.
[2] Cooper, 123.
[3] Cited ibid. 121 f.
[4] Cf. *Tudor Revolution*, 46 ff.
[5] Mr Cooper's gibe (n. 121) convicts me of overconciseness. The memorandum of 1531 (*Tudor Revolution*, 162, 438) shows clearly that 'The kinges learned Counsaille' was regarded as potentially in existence, requiring only attention; their activities concerning

believe that much of Henry VII's law-enforcement annoyed those against whom it operated; what cannot be proved is that this resentment embodied just objections to serious or frequent abuses of power by the king or his servants.

Much the same impression of a reaction based on little justified resentment emerges from a study of the first Parliament of Henry VIII whose calling had been delayed until January 1510. The Crown needed money and the king's chief interest should be sought in the tunnage and poundage bill and in the allocation for the Household made in this session. No one can have doubted that the opportunity would be taken to work off complaints, and as Mr Cooper has shown, more was debated than became law. However, his account is not entirely satisfactory in detail. Thus he includes among the bills that failed one concerning perjury; this became 1 Henry VIII, c. 16. Nor has he used the original acts of the House of Lords to assess, as far as may be, the parts played by Lords and Commons in the business. 1 Henry VIII, c. 4 (for limiting the time during which prosecutions for offences under penal statutes were to be admitted) originated in the Commons; the Lords refused to accept the original term set for actions by the king; in the end three years was agreed on.[1] There was then trouble over the duration of the act which the Lords wanted to be till the next Parliament only.[2] In the outcome, there were two bills, identical in terms except that one had the final words 'to the next parlyament' crossed out and replaced (in the hand of the clerk of the Parliament) by 'for euer'; this is marked by the clerk as 'Missa a dominis' and endorsed with the royal veto. In the other, which passed, two words at the end are erased and 'This acte to endure to the next parliament' is written in.[3] Possibly the king, rather than the Lords, overruled the Commons' desire for permanence; the statute lapsed in 1512 until revived by a permanent act in 1515 which gave the king four years.[4] The act for the payment of customs, which permitted denizens to enter wares on behalf of other

---

penal laws and bonds taken 'for any maner offence or forfaicture' show their concerns to be those for which Dudley had employed them. While they were much less organized a body than under Henry VII, they did exist to the extent that they could order appearances by privy seal (ibid. 292, and cf. e.g. *LP, Add.* 932). If the evidence seems thin, it should be remembered that but for the accidental survival of two entry books in the Duchy of Lancaster records we should still be as ignorant of Henry VII's Learned Council, as in fact we were until Mr Somerville's article appeared in the 1939 *EHR*.

[1] *LJ* 5b, 6a, 6b. According to Mr Cooper the Commons' bill granted only one year, but there is no evidence of this. Ibid. 5b only declares the Lords' opinion that the king should have four or three years, 'pars contra partem in unum annum'.

[2] Ibid. 8a.　　　　　[3] House of Lords.　　　　　[4] 7 Henry VIII, c. 3.

denizens,[1] started surprisingly in the Lords and was sent back by the Commons for amendment;[2] since the surviving act started in the Commons, it appears that they drew up a new bill which the Lords then passed after obtaining a further change.[3] The repeal of 11 Henry VII, c. 3, which permitted justices of the peace to hear cases without indictment, started in the Commons but was returned to them before the Lords would pass it.[4] 1 Henry VIII, c. 8 (concerning false inquests rendered by escheators) was a Commons' bill which was passed by the Lords but sent down for amendment; they received it back but another was then substituted for it, which must be the one that passed, though its parliamentary history remains obscure.[5] The limiting proviso, saving certain types of escheators, originated in the Commons.[6] It was the Lords who produced 1 Henry VIII, c. 10, which mainly re-enacted a statute of Henry VI that lands seized into the king's hands must not be let to farm until some time had elapsed, so as to make traverse effective.[7] The act that traverse should in future be admitted reached the Commons as a petition from outside, was passed by them, but received an amendment in the Lords;[8] probably this was the proviso, attached on a separate schedule, which barred victorious traversers from securing the issues of lands during their retention in the king's hands. Thus the actual acts of the reaction could come from either House; there was no sort of plan, three bills dealing variously with inquests and traverses (cc. 8, 10, 12); and while on the whole the Lords look to have been a little more careful of the Crown's rights, the bill against escheators was modified in the Commons.

Some bills in Parliament got nowhere, especially the attainder of Empson and Dudley, left unfinished after some flurried passing to and fro on the last day of the session.[9] The bill against promoters would seem to have begun in the Commons; the Lords desired to record the wretches' names on the parliament roll, but (as Mr Cooper says) this was not done. Still, the bill was read three times; no more is heard of it after 14 February;[10] perhaps we should conjecture an interposition from

---

[1] 1 Henry VIII, c. 5. This is the statute which remedied, in Mr Cooper's opinion (p. 109), a justified grievance in that native merchants had been caught under a law intended to prevent strangers from getting their goods customed at native rates.
[2] *LJ* i. 5b, 6a.   [3] Ibid. 6b.
[4] Original act (House of Lords), and *LJ* i. 7a, 7b, 8a.
[5] Ibid. 4b, 5a, 7b, 8a.   [6] Original act (House of Lords).
[7] Original act (House of Lords). The first and only mention of this act in *LJ* (i. 8a) gives the impression that the bill had started in the Commons.
[8] Above, p. 75.   [9] Cooper, 126 and n. 133.
[10] *LJ* i. 6a, 6b, 7a.

the Council. The Lords disputed a bill for justices of assize, *nisi prius* and gaol delivery,[1] but it looks as though they regarded it as insufficiently wide.[2] Of none of these bills can any trace now be found; on the other hand, the bill for letters of privy seal survives. Received from the Commons and assented to by the Lords after some amplification and a fortnight's delay because they thought it necessary to consider it a while, this bill was firmly vetoed by the king.[3] It was apparently the only one of the 'reaction' bills so treated;[4] its contents explain both the veto and the Lords' long doubts, for (appealing to Magna Carta) it simply proposed to abolish the use of privy seal subpoenas and letters missive, except only for private actions before the Council in the Marches of Wales. In the end the Lords modified it only by limiting its duration to the next Parliament, but the Crown could clearly not accept a statute which would have destroyed all conciliar jurisdiction. Nor, it should be said, would this have been a happy day for the many who sought to gain settlement of their troubles in prerogative courts because the common law could not or would not help.[5]

It is thus obvious that in this Parliament Henry VII's rule received a slap in the face. But not all the resentment concentrated on new or prerogative methods. 1 Henry VIII, c. 10 complained of an abuse already legislated against in 1430; it only held that the month's grace granted by the old statute was insufficient. The bill against justices of assize, whatever its contents, must have attacked an aspect of the common law. Nor is it easy to agree that the statutes themselves prove the justice of their contents. We have already seen that 1 Henry VIII, c. 8 (for traverse) wildly exaggerated the position,[6] a point which should make one chary of accepting the words of preambles as fact. The later act concerning outlawries also laid at Henry VII's door what was in fact a necessary consequence of the common law on the subject.[7] The act against escheators maintained that divers men had 'lately' been dispossessed and troubled by untrue offices found at the instance of escheators and commissioners; yet the evidence of traceable complaints, suits and

---

[1] Cooper, 125.

[2] The matter is very obscure, but it seems that the Lords wished to extend a prohibition to exercise these offices from those who lived in the locality to those who were born there (*LJ* i. 6, 7).

[3] Original act (House of Lords) and *LJ* i. 5b, 6a, 7b (1, 4, 19 Feb.).

[4] One other act was vetoed: it permitted the killing of deer outside proper forest areas (cf. *LJ* i. 5a, 6a, 6b; 29 Jan., 4, 6, 7 Feb.).

[5] The point is familiar: both Star Chamber and Requests really gained their jurisdiction from the demands of suitors, not by royal decree or use.

[6] Above, pp. 74 ff.   [7] Above, p. 78.

traverses does not bear this out. The act repealing 11 Henry VII, c. 3 declares that 'it is manifestely known that many Synestr' and craftely feyned and forged informacions have ben pursued'; yet, however manifest this was, we have found only four charges of false informations entered before the commissions of oyer and terminer.[1] A diligent further search may possibly yet discover more cases, but as things stand it is hard indeed that Henry VII's government should be judged by the unsubstantiated generalizations produced after his death and apparently emanating from interests and individuals who either exaggerated occasional unfairness into systematic oppression or mistook their reaction against law-enforcement for legitimate indignation.

VII

An ill-documented period of history full of energetic action will probably always give rise to disagreement, and Mr Cooper may continue to feel that his interpretation has not been completely disproved. But this much has been shown: there are good grounds for holding that the earlier and later years of the reign did not differ essentially; traverses of inquisitions *post mortem*, despite contemporary and later assertions, were frequent; the policy concerning debts and outlawries, properly understood, was neither extortion nor rapacity; the king's relations with London, which in great part explain his bad reputation, are not to be judged so readily from the city's point of view; and the very real reaction after his death proves only the existence, not the justice, of resentment and did not discover the supposed masses of serious cases. It may be added that the evidence which Mr Cooper collects to create a general impression of corruption – payments for pardons, the possible sale of justice and offices – amounts to saying that Henry VII used the procedures of government to get money, a fact which is not contested; some of it may have been improper, as much of it was no doubt undignified, but none of the examples cited can be shown to mark either oppression or neglect of duty.[2] Dudley's warning against the use of royal letters to interfere in the course of justice, and the supporting evidence of such things happening, is not, says Mr Cooper, to be entirely explained by the proper use of privy seal summons.[3] No

[1] Above, p. 90.
[2] Cooper, 116. Most of this evidence was taken into account by such earlier writers as Miss Brodie or Professor Dietz who arrived at more balanced conclusions.
[3] Cooper, 116.

doubt; but he greatly mistakes the nature of early Tudor society and the problem of securing obedience to the law if he thinks that the king would not have caused at least as much dissatisfaction if he had ignored the petitions of suitors. It must be remembered that what was injustice to the defeated party was commonly justice to the victor.

The charge that I have allowed preconceived notions to defeat the evidence may thus be turned against the accuser. Mr Cooper seems as much concerned to controvert me because he dislikes my attitude to the period as because he distrusts my arguments. If my understanding of the age seems to him 'too narrowly restricted to the interests of the Crown', I cannot help feeling that his is distorted by the false analogy which he draws with the early seventeenth century. Perhaps it is significant that he should be particularly impressed by the appearance among the complaints of Magna Carta and the act of 23 Edward III, c. 3, two mainstays of the Petition of Right. Of course it is important that Tudor monarchs never developed strong kingship into despotism, and it is fair to remember with Mr Cooper that in part this was because their subjects would not let them. However, the signs that their own absence of intent had more to do with it are much stronger. Those who have really studied the reign have, like Professor Richardson, found Chamber finance to be far from essentially unjust, or like the late Mr Bayne have discovered that so far from using novel prerogative means against transgressors the king relied largely on the common-law courts.[1] The events of Henry VII's reign did not take place in a vacuum, or even in the simple context of strict, discovered and defined rights. The king was trying to restore solvency and power to the Crown, but he was also trying to bring peace, justice and order to the realm; rightly he regarded the first as the necessary condition for the second. No more than anyone else would I maintain the position which Mr Cooper ascribes to me – that 'all his actions and policies ... were either just or justifiable'. I have only maintained that his policy was rigorous, thorough and sometimes harsh throughout his reign; that the alleged evidence for a marked deterioration in the last years rests either on the statements of interested

---

[1] *Cases in the Council of Henry VII*, pp. cxiv, cxxvi. In an unsatisfactory summing up of prerogative jurisdiction (Cooper, 120: e.g. the Council tried title to land because it was pressed to do so by suitors, not because it wished to encroach on the common law), Mr Cooper relies largely on Bayne's attack on the Council Learned (*Cases* . . ., pp. xxvii–xxviii). This rests on some serious misunderstandings and such unconvincing arguments as that because Empson and Dudley were charged with oppression, of which there is no sign in the Exchequer records, they used the Council Learned improperly, even though there is no explicit evidence of such doings in its records either.

parties or can be paralleled from the earlier years; and that despite occasional injustice, inseparable from a determined policy in the circumstances of the time, it is a false view which speaks of rapacity and oppression.★

★ [Since this paper was written new evidence has come to light in a list of undue exactions compiled by Edmund Dudley: cf. C. J. Harrison, 'The Petition of Edmund Dudley,' *EHR* 87 (1972), 82–99. This shows that, according to Dudley who had searched his books, Henry VII had imposed excessive burdens on at any rate eighty-four occasions; people had been compelled to enter upon recognizances in quite excessive amounts, their real offences considered. It is now clear that Henry VII had on occasion behaved badly. But not all the cases tell strongly against him, and Dudley's own testimony that the King's 'inward mynde was never to vse them' shows his real purpose. He was anxious to put men under restraints which compelled obedience and discretion; politics, and a growing suspiciousness of reckless behaviour, rather than plain rapacity, would seem to have been the considerations moving him.]

APPENDIX

Traverse of Office, temp. Henr. VII

Ref.: C 43/1	Inquest	Traverse	Conceded	Contested
26	21 March 1486	—	23 May 1505	—
38	24 Oct. 1487[1]	6 Feb. 1508	—	Yes
58	*temp.* Ed. IV	—	24 Nov. 1488	—
29	16 Nov. 1493	17 March 1504	*c.* April 1504	—
56	25 Sept. 1494	10 Oct. 1494	—	Yes
Chester 7/3	11 Dec. 1494	26 Dec. 1494	Yes	—
Chester 7/5	Dec. 1494	'late'	Before 1507	—
12	20 Oct. 1501	11 Dec. 1504	—	Yes
14	2 Dec. 1501	10 May 1508	—	Yes
57	30 May 1502	—	26 Jan. 1504	—
32	18 July 1502	—	25 May 1505	—
53	3 Nov. 1503	1 Dec. 1503	—	Yes
10	8 Feb. 1504	—	16 March 1504	—
35	—	—	17 March 1504	—
37	—	—	17 March 1504	—
46	18 May 1504	12 Feb. 1506	—	Yes
54	13 June 1504	27 July 1504	—	Yes
27	20 Oct. 1504	—	—	Yes
34	20 Jan. 1505	—	4 July 1505	—
19	15 April 1505	10 Feb. 1508	Yes	—
47	15 April 1505	8 May 1507	—	Yes
15	15 April 1505	2 June 1508	—	Yes
43	15 April 1505	5 June 1508	Crown traverse	—
33	18 April 1505	11 Nov. 1506	Yes	—
28	3 June 1505	1 July 1505	—	Yes
21	2 July 1505	—	12 Dec. 1507	—
22	2 July 1505	—	12 Dec. 1507	—
16	23 Sept. 1505	8 June 1508	Yes	—
42	30 Sept. 1505	27 Oct. 1507	—	Yes
17	30 Sept. 1505	12 May 1508	—	Yes
18	30 Sept. 1505	22 Oct. 1507	—	Yes
51	30 Sept. 1505	—	—	Yes
52	30 Sept. 1505	—	—	Yes
39	3 Nov. 1505	12 Dec. 1505	—	Yes
41	4 Nov. 1505	26 March 1506	—	Yes
13	4 Nov. 1505	26 March 1506	—	Yes
50	5 Nov. 1505	28 April 1507	—	Yes
?	—	—	16 June 1506	—
32*	12 Nov. 1505	—	8 July 1506	—
31	20 Nov. 1505	—	4 July 1506	—
40	2 March 1506	July 1508	—	Yes
11	6 March 1506	14 May 1507	—	Yes
48	1 July 1506	1 Aug. 1506	—	Yes
49	1 July 1506	1 Aug. 1506	—	Yes
20	2 July 1506	1 Aug. 1506	—	Yes

APPENDIX

Traverse of Office, temp. Henr. VII (cont.)

Ref.: C 43/1	Inquest	Traverse	Conceded	Contested
30	2 July 1506	1 Dec. 1507	12 Dec. 1507	—
25	12 Oct. 1506	—	6 Feb. 1507	—
23	2 Nov. 1506	8 Nov. 1506	—	Yes
24	Mid-1507	Mich. 1507	Yes	—
37	29 Nov. 1507	28 Nov. 1507[2]	—	Yes

[1] If 3 Henry VII in the record is a mistake for 23 (quite possible), this inquest belongs to 1507.

[2] *Sic.*

5

THE KING OF HEARTS*

No king should be less of an enigma than Henry VIII, bestriding his world, articulate, an author, a man who recorded even his private life in the preambles to acts of Parliament. And yet, just because he so much succeeded in identifying his personality with his age, the problems of that age leave the king himself still the subject of debate. Quite apart from popular mythology, we have had Froude's hero of Protestantism, Pollard's embodiment of statecraft, Catholic historiography's destroyer of all that was valuable in England, and the skilful opportunist devoid of original ideas whom I described on an earlier occasion.[1] Now, in a new biography, worthy of its subject in both size and weight, Dr Scarisbrick parades yet another Henry: great and formidable indeed, a man of plans and purposes, but also frivolous and whimsical, markedly eclectic in both ideas and action, and fundamentally not very competent. It should at once be said that the picture in great part seems true, and it is particularly chastening to have it shown so firmly, and with such a wealth of evidence, that of Henry's famous understanding of his time and his people there is much less evidence than of heedless wilfulness and rash selfishness. This is a badly flawed hero, but a hero none the less. For his vision of the man, Dr Scarisbrick commands the agreement which must follow upon such thoroughly documented learning illumined by subtle insight and genuine historical imagination.

The book undoubtedly supersedes Pollard's 65-year-old book as the best treatment of its subject. If it rather lacks its predecessor's narrative verve, this is mainly because it takes account of so much more and therefore frequently stops to explain. If its general outline is, in some ways, surprisingly like Pollard's, this is because both authors of necessity depended on the same kind of evidence – the evidence calendared in *The Letters and Papers, Foreign and Domestic, of the Reign of Henry VIII* – though Dr Scarisbrick has looked further, added fresh

* [Review of J. J. Scarisbrick, *Henry VIII* (1968), in *HJ* 12 (1969), 158–63.]
[1] J. A. Froude, *History of England*, esp. iv. 238 ff.; A. F. Pollard, *Henry VIII* (1902); (e.g.) R. W. Chambers, *Thomas More* (1935); G. R. Elton, *Henry VIII: an Essay in Revision* (Hist. Ass. Pamphlet, 1962).

material, and done better than Pollard by going behind the calendar to the originals. Political biography is a somewhat limited art form to which nothing significant has been added since the beginning of the century. Pollard was an honest man regardful of his evidence; in his equal but technically superior honesty, Dr Scarisbrick was bound to a large extent to tread the same paths. Benefiting from the massive research of three generations (some of it his own), he has incorporated some new themes and much reassessment, but the framework of the story remains fundamentally unaltered. The young, inexperienced and pleasure-loving king, the dominant cardinal, the assumption of personal rule from about 1528 onwards, the steady progress towards the gradually realized break with Rome, the use in the last years of newly found power and wealth for great schemes of warlike policy – with all this we are generally familiar, nor is the familiar any the worse for being restated so much more intelligently than has been usual.

However, inside this framework there is much change, not only of emphasis but also of fact. Of course, the whole story reads rather differently when the writer holds that Henry was doing unreasonable things without sufficient thought or competence in execution, than when the king's doings are represented (as they were by Pollard) as the achievements of a splendid destiny; but beyond that, Dr Scarisbrick has thoroughly reconsidered some important problems. It is on these that discussion must turn, though even a long review can deal with only some of the fascinating issues. Some of Dr Scarisbrick's analyses command nothing but assent. Thus his chapter on the canon law of the Divorce, the most striking intellectual achievement of the book, shows clearly, and for the first time, what the issues really were and how Henry's failure to grasp a point of law led to the seven years' struggle for success. The discussion of Henry's theology is equally fascinating and convincing; again for the first time, it makes sense of the king's later years by showing that, far from being the pillar of conservative orthodoxy usually described, he was busy composing his own eclectic religion from sources which ranged over a considerable stretch of the spectrum. Dr Scarisbrick demonstrates (for the first time) that Cromwell was destroyed by a lying charge of religious radicalism (sacramentarianism) and comes as close as anyone will to explaining the dark mystery which surrounds the plot against him. The concise account of the Church on the eve of the Reformation skilfully absorbs much recent research and arrives at the most balanced judgment in print. Equally impressive is the very firm demonstration that the establishment of the royal supremacy amounted to a revolution in both theory and practice; the curious notion that it was just a predictable and not very important continuation of existing policy finds no support here. And although the analysis of foreign policy in the 1540s bogs down in that dreary waste of dull negotiations, the assessment of the policy itself as misconceived and ill-executed is beautifully done. To say that this new biography retains much of Pollard's outline is not to say that it is not a more learned, more accurate and better book.

On some other points it is not so easy to agree. The case for seeing in the Pilgrimage of Grace not only a major crisis but a true judgment on the king's doings is overstated (the one lapse into false emphasis), as indeed is the savagery of its suppression.[1] It is pleasant to see Wolsey treated as a great man, but the conclusion that his whole policy was directed towards the maintenance of peace in Europe suggests that for once somewhat rose-coloured spectacles were used by the historian. Nor does Dr Scarisbrick provide evidence for the familiar assertion that Wolsey really created the equity courts and benefited justice: which, since so far there is hardly any, is not surprising. Cromwell's building up of a professional and bureaucratic administration differed from medieval moves in the same direction by his deliberate adoption of the principle that the royal household should be excluded from such work (and the fact that thereafter it was); the attempt to dethrone this 'revolution' has really not been as successful as Dr Scarisbrick thinks (p. 499). Though it is quite true that even in the 1530s the royal supremacy, so personal in the main, partook in measure of a 'parliamentary' foundation,[2] the First Act of Uniformity was nevertheless crucial in that it transferred to the king-in-Parliament the power to make the Church, leaving the supreme head with the more limited power to rule the Church (p. 398).[3] On a point of possibly smaller significance: Dr Scarisbrick adheres to the view that Anne Boleyn's pregnancy preceded the decision to secure parliamentary authority for dissolving the Aragon marriage. But could anyone be certain before late December 1532 that the matter was as urgent as it is here represented, and how does that fact fit with the laborious preparation of the Act of Appeals? Five complete drafting stages (one of them including the king's own

---

[1] More of the Lincolnshire rebels were pardoned than hanged; several men guilty of rebellion were acquitted by juries; the seventy-odd men hanged at Carlisle were summarily executed by the field-commander in accordance with the laws of war, and no one at the time would have acted differently.   [2] Cf. *Tudor Constitution*, 336 n. 3.

[3] 'Modern' sovereignty (legislative authority) now vested in the Parliament; 'medieval' sovereignty (rulership) vested in the Crown.

contributions and their later removal, surely not a matter to be settled very quickly), not to mention two suggested acts of a more specific purpose against Catherine, were all got through before the end of January 1533: at the very least, the order of events is not as unambiguous as this book makes out (p. 313).[1]

All these points deserve to be discussed much more thoroughly than is possible here, but the last leads to the issue which must be considered with care because on it depends one's full acceptance of the Henry VIII delineated in this book. Dr Scarisbrick returns, in effect, to Pollard's view that the king was responsible for the policy which, by stages, separated England from Rome. His was the mind and hand that devised and guided affairs from late in 1529 at least. Certainly, Dr Scarisbrick makes the best case possible for this interpretation; he shows at length how 'imperial' Henry's words were long before the break came, how much the principles apparent later emerge from earlier hints, and how pervasive the notions were which ultimately underlay the drastic action of 1533–4. His assertion that Cromwell 'neither worked alone nor was the true initiator of these royal undertakings' (p. 304) will be widely and eagerly accepted, especially by those who never could stomach the sudden transformation of the evil Machiavellian into a great constructive statesman – though in general Dr Scarisbrick, who calls Cromwell a genius and ascribes to him the energy and vision thanks to which the 1530s 'were a decisive decade in English history', has little comfort for them.

Yet has he proved his important case for Henry's initiative and control? The question is not one very easily resolved by the analysis of evidence, because that evidence must in the last resort remain uncertain. For one thing, nearly all of it – and especially that on which the use of specific words turns – comes from ambassadorial reports behind which there are not only the insufficiencies of the reporter's knowledge but also the problems of translation. For another, so much took place at the time that never got into the record that especially the relations between a king always officially represented as the man from whom everything flowed and the ministers with whom he discussed policy cannot safely be assessed from despatches. Besides, even Dr Scarisbrick, assembling all the evidence there is, cannot and does not claim that no doubt remains.

There are some clues in his own account that all is not well with the interpretation. In the first place, Dr Scarisbrick finds himself forced

[1] [On this point cf. also *Policy and Police*, 179.]

to say of the Henrician Reformation that it was 'a movement of inexplicable halts and starts', that 'at almost every point in the story there are unanswerable questions' (pp. 295–6). Now it would be absurd to deny that some questions cannot be answered, including some of those he lists. But the seeming halts and starts – and despite his assertion that they continue beyond 1532 it is not easy to see in what way this is true – would be less difficult to explain if it were not assumed that the inspiration behind policy was, consistently, one man's. And secondly, there are things about this Henry VIII which do not hold together. Dr Scarisbrick makes very plain how very inept he thinks the king most of the time. Down to 1528, every mad scheme is shown to be Henry's; sane policies come invariably from Wolsey. This lack of foresight and insight becomes strikingly obvious during the earlier stages of the Divorce when Henry, having failed to grasp the one suggestion of Wolsey's which could have ensured immediate success, dreamed up all sorts of schemes without ever achieving anything.[1] If the version of Cromwell's end here given is correct (and it makes very good sense), Henry was completely fooled by his councillors; nor did he allegedly know why Barnes, Jerome and Garret were burned soon after (pp. 380 ff.). That, in Dr Scarisbrick's view, Henry badly mismanaged policy after 1542 has already been noted. Frequently, as one reads, one comes to think of this king as a bit of a booby and a bit of a baby, and I think that in creating this impression Dr Scarisbrick is right. And yet this almost consistently inept man was also the man who, completely in control, succeeded in just about everything he did during the years 1532–40, followed large and largely consistent policies, and thrust his way through every difficulty. Dr Scarisbrick sees the problem and tries to explain it away by making Henry a 'vulnerable and volatile thing', now clever, now obtuse, now certain, now bewildered (p. 383). There is something in this, but it only makes the coherence and determined drive of the Cromwell era even harder to ascribe to the king's initiative. The signs are that Henry really owed far more to others, and especially owed creative ideas to them, than the story suggests as it is here told. It is not going too far to say that, if Dr Scarisbrick is right, just about everybody except Cromwell

[1] E.g. p. 201: 'This magnificent vista [an unworkable plan to use the pope's difficulties in 1528] was, it seems, largely of Henry's creation. It was full of blatant, and probably inept, guile.' P. 206: 'Henry had not the courage to take matters into his own hands and risk a solution which might well have worked.' P. 230: Henry's stupidity alone ruined the efforts of Francis I to help him.

could do with Henry what he would, at least for a time. This does not make much sense.

Yet has not Dr Scarisbrick shown – for this is whence his problem stems – that the king's policy from 1529 was of a piece: that long before Cromwell can be thought to influence affairs Henry was moving on the line which led to the predictable assertion that in the empire of England no foreign authority had any claims at all? Despite the evidence mustered, I remain unconvinced. For one thing, there is a difference between the notion of the territorial empire expressed in the Act of Appeals and the concept of an imperial crown possessed by the king – a small difference, but a real one. The first was novel (so much so that it did not become current), the second ancient. Dr Scarisbrick does not dispose of the view which links the 'imperial' claims of 1530–1 with the king's assertion in 1516 – long before he thought of quarrelling with the papacy – that in his realm he had no superior but God. For once the argument turns uncharacteristically hesitant: 'it surely cannot have been a pre-echo of the Royal Supremacy, a hint of Henricianism which lay dormant for about fifteen years thereafter' (p. 249). Of course not: it pre-echoed the general conviction expressed in 1530 and 1531 that 'somehow' the king ought to be free to do in England as he pleased, a conviction which it required somebody else to turn into a practical policy based on a fundamental philosophy. It is not uninteresting to note, with Dr Scarisbrick, that at this earlier stage the king was talking about possessing specific priestly powers which were not, in the event, to be ascribed to the supreme head. Henry VIII's notion of his imperial crown was a much more mystical, even 'thaumaturgical' idea than Thomas Cromwell's 'Marsiglian' concept of the royal supremacy.

Much turns on the discernible purposes of policy between the fall of Wolsey and the passage of the Acts of Appeals. Despite everything the king was saying, whatever ideas he put forward or picked up, one thing is clear: he throughout endeavoured to get Rome to agree to have the case tried in England. The 'special national privilege' of which he talked so much (p. 265) involved only the right to demand that Rome should dismiss to England all matters touching England; it falls a long way short of the later assertion that God created absolute and self-sufficient authority in the territorial entity subject to a royal and 'imperial' head. All the argument about English immunities and the king's personal dignity, which it was alleged required that the matrimonial issue be settled within the king's dominions, was put forward at Rome and in order to secure a solution by agreement. The argument's unvarying failure led to no new steps at all, only to yet another shot at the same policy. Dr Scarisbrick, as usual, sees the point: as he admits, Henry's claims to autonomy were always accompanied by requests for papal action which implicitly acknowledged his 'complete dependence upon Rome's universal jurisdiction' (p. 289); but this constitutes a dilemma only if one reads these claims to autonomy as embodying already a full understanding of what that autonomy might mean in terms of action by king, Council and Parliament. Yet, when, as early as October 1530 and as late as February 1532, Henry tried to find some way in which Parliament could be employed to solve the problem, the experts denied that there was such a way – until the radical concept of an 'empire' of England legislatively embodied in its Parliament triumphed over the perfectly sound conservative opinions which had set specific limits to the competence of Parliament. And even if Henry (out of his own mind or listening to radical advice?) seemed to grope for some such solution before early 1533, it is still the case that he found himself unable to cut clean through to it until Cromwell was his chief adviser.

If Dr Scarisbrick were right, Henry for at least two years spent much money, labour and ingenuity in trying to arrest the progress of the case at Rome, while all the time he was aware that none of this was necessary because he had autonomy. It is hard to see the point of it all, and Dr Scarisbrick, who unquestionably does as well for his argument as anyone could, does not succeed in explaining his interpretation. Instead he falls back on the supposition that Henry, who already knew the solution to his problem, 'did not yet dare to implement it'. We are to accept that the king 'was running ahead of at least some of his subjects' (pp. 291–2) and therefore, unable to get his revolutionary notions accepted, had to bide his time. No doubt he was ahead of at least some of his subjects, but he was well behind some others, too. What had happened between February 1532, when he met a positive rebuff from the experts, and February 1533, when the Act of Appeals passed a committee of experts, to persuade him that 'the country' was now with him?

The difficulties disappear if one abandons the notion that Henry throughout knew where his 'imperial' claims of privilege and authority could lead him and accepts that what he personally originated was not the royal supremacy properly so called. Nor was he really so firmly or clearly in control during the years 1529–32. I once called that hiatus

'years without a policy', but this, I now think, was wrong. It would
be truer to call them years with too many policies. On one side, there
were men with radical views, highly influential from the first in the
City and the House of Commons;[1] at Court their growing influence
is reflected in the gradual rise of Cromwell and his appointment to
the Council late in 1530. On the other side stood a strong conservative
party who enjoyed the moderately active support of the lord chancellor, Thomas More, had much support among the bishops (whose
resistance to Henry Dr Scarisbrick himself has chronicled), and conducted an active propaganda campaign in and out of Parliament.[2]
But neither of these groups controlled events which were rather in
the hands of the leading councillors, especially Norfolk and Wiltshire,
anxious to secure Henry his Divorce but very reluctant to accept the
radical line in full. It seems likely that in those years the Council
cannot ever have agreed on anything of importance and that Henry
never got straightforward advice; the 'halts and starts' reflect specific
pulls hither and yon applied by conflicting political interests.

That this is not pure conjecture can be shown. The struggle of policies
and parties comes out more clearly for once in the months of February–
May 1532 when Cromwell, by the use of the 'Supplication against
the Ordinaries', succeeded in destroying the conservative party on the
Council, drove out Gardiner and forced More's resignation. This
at least is the most reasonable explanation of the fact (over which there
has been some argument) that, looked at from one end, these manoeuvres seem planned from the start, while from another angle
developments and outcome were unforeseeable and came as a shock,
so that policy can appear to be extraordinarily hand-to-mouth.[3] In
this struggle of parties Henry certainly 'controlled events' in the sense
that what was done resulted from his attempts to balance among the
conflicts of counsel. At the same time his volatile and eclectic mind
(the terms are Dr Scarisbrick's) was seizing on ideas and arguments
which might help achieve the end desired. But to credit him with the
initiative in political planning, or to suppose that, knowing exactly
where he was going, he yet would not go, is to mistake both his mind
and this situation of unresolved conflict right at the heart of the English
government. It was when he came to accept the coherent policy based

[1] Dr Scarisbrick (p. 251) is uncertain whether the anticlerical bills of 1529 were spontaneous
or 'disguised government legislation'. These bills were foreshadowed in city circles
before the Parliament met (cf. below, p. 292).

[2] Cf. below, pp. 165–9.

Below, no. 25; M. J. Kelly, 'The Submission of the Clergy,' *TRHS* (1965), 97 ff.

on a philosophy of the state which Cromwell extracted from the general claims to imperial authority that the conflict ended.

That, at least, is how things look to me, and I agree, of course, that in such hidden matters there will always be more than one possible explanation. Dr Scarisbrick has done great service by reopening the issue, and greater still by his searching analysis of the theological and juridical sources and effects of all that was said and done. Whether or not one can agree with his view of the king as an initiator, his Henry VIII remains a striking and largely convincing portrait. It is good to have so careful a study whose soundness of learning in no way inhibits firm views and brilliance of insight. Pollard has found a worthy successor, and Henry VIII a worthy biographer, however little he may thank Dr Scarisbrick for his skill in seeing beyond the façade which the king presented to the world.

6

CARDINAL WOLSEY*

Few men of eminence and ability can ever have had a worse press than Thomas Wolsey, butcher's son and prince of the Church: Thomas, by the sufferance of God of the title of St Cecily beyond Tiber of the Holy Church of Rome priest-cardinal, legate *a latere*, archbishop of York, primate of England and chancellor of the same. In his own day he was hated for his wealth, ostentation and arrogance. After his fall and death, the dislike of those who regarded him as the embodiment of papal domination was only exceeded by the fury of those who held him responsible for the first steps on the road to the Anglican schism. In the seventeenth century, Lord Herbert of Cherbury condemned him with those measured antitheses, resolving impartiality into hidden bias or lukewarm displeasure, of which he was master;[1] and Laud's opponents, having exhausted more immediate terms of abuse, thought themselves unable to make their point plainer than by comparing Charles I's archbishop to Henry VIII's cardinal.[2] True, some churchmen of the eighteenth century found Wolsey's Laodicean religion and massive pomp most agreeably to their taste;[3] while in the nineteenth a good historian discovered in Wolsey a patriot pursuing the only sound policy for his country, a policy apparently inspired by the principles of Prince Bismarck.[4] But at the present, opinion has relapsed again: a standard textbook qualified its description of his record as 'one of failure' only by supposing that he created a 'tremendous authority', to be used more intelligently by Henry

---

* [Introduction to the reprint of A. F. Pollard's *Wolsey* (Fontana Books, 1965). Copyright © in the Introduction William Collins Sons & Company Limited 1965.]

[1] *Life and Reign of King Henry the Eighth* (1672), 342 f.

[2] H. R. Trevor-Roper, *Archbishop Laud* (2nd ed., 1962), 52.

[3] Richard Fiddes, *Life of Cardinal Wolsey* (1724). That worthy if stuffy author, distrustful of passion and devoutly attached to a settled order in society, even maintained that Wolsey all his life proved zealous in the public and private service of God (p. 529).

[4] Mandell Creighton, *Cardinal Wolsey* (1891), a contribution to the 'Twelve English Statesmen' series. If that number was chosen for specific reasons, rational or mystical, and not because no more contributors could be found, Wolsey was lucky to make the side even as twelfth man.

VIII.[1] For that renewed fall in historians' estimation, this book, now reprinted (one of the major works of Tudor scholarship to appear this century) bears the chief responsibility. Pollard's powerful analysis of the cardinal's life and work left Wolsey with few claims to men's respect or approval, except the doubtful one of having taught Henry VIII how to become the sort of king he turned out to be. To Pollard, Wolsey was a phenomenon rendered significant by what came after, an unwitting harbinger and unconscious pioneer, but also – despite a regrettable private character – a noble patron of justice and administrator of genius. How far can we still agree with him?

In some respects, Albert Frederick Pollard (1869–1948) was perhaps peculiarly ill-qualified to do justice to Wolsey.[2] The product of a long line of Wesleyan ministers, he possessed a sharp and austere mind; somewhat severe and even narrow in his sympathies, he was hard on himself but inclined to be harder on others. Though it is not clear that he adhered to any formal religion, the traditions of nonconformity coloured his thinking more than he knew. In addition he was a liberal, a Gladstonian liberal, in politics who several times tried to enter Parliament (for a University seat) in the interest of what may be called the Asquith–Bonham Carter wing of the declining Liberal party. Belief in Parliament, constitutionalism and the common law – the unquestioned articles of nineteenth-century political faith – determined his attitude to the past; moral tenets of a straightforward kind guided his judgment of the dead as much as of the living. Thus he was little equipped to appreciate the childish flamboyancy, the spirited deviousness of mind, the overpitched ambitions and overcharged emotions which made up so large a part of Wolsey's personality; and he was positively hostile both to the kind of churchman represented by a cardinal of the late-medieval Church and to a statesman who disliked the muddles of the customary law and the restraints imposed by critical and incompetent assemblies.

However, these failures of personal sympathy need not have seriously affected Pollard's interpretation of Wolsey, for he was after all also a very able historian with a sound understanding of the sixteenth century. He was an experienced biographer who had learned his trade in seven years' drudgery on the staff of the *Dictionary of National Biography* (for which he wrote the equivalent of a whole volume) and

---

[1] J. D. Mackie, *The Earlier Tudors 1485–1558* (Oxford, 1952), 333–4.
[2] For the best account of Pollard see V. H. Galbraith in *Proceedings of the British Academy* 35 (1954), 257 ff.; also J. E. Neale in *EHR* 64 (1949), 198 ff.

had made his name with notable studies of great men. His life of Henry VIII, first published in 1902, still remains the only serious book on the king.[1] But in dealing with Wolsey, Pollard faced a further personal difficulty. He admired, almost worshipped, Henry VIII. In the king he saw a statesman of superb judgment, great subtlety, long vision and deep insight, and virtually invariable success. He believed him to be a devoted constitutionalist, capable of fulfilling the nation's destiny because he felt profoundly at one with it. How just this bemused opinion was is not here at issue;[2] but it matters that exaltation of the king was bound to lead to a corresponding depreciation of the minister. Pollard was too good an historian to overlook the frequent errors and often ill-considered policies which are no less noticeable in the first half of Henry VIII's reign than in any other period of history, or the more particular sterility which seemed to him to afflict that age. He also probably overestimated the degree to which the Wolsey era deviated from the line of constitutional development which he held to be characteristic of England. Since he thought the king to be a paragon and a constitutionalist, he naturally placed the blame for whatever went wrong on the minister. Of course, Wolsey's overriding influence was a historical fact. But there thus emerged the picture of a man equipped with remarkable skill and intelligence who perversely pursued a foreign policy of no advantage to his country, and who failed to attend to the urgent domestic problems of Church government and finance because he was too busy with dreams of glory for himself. Pollard thus reversed Creighton's Bismarck-Wolsey, seeing in him a non-Bismarck whose policy was wrong because, unlike that of Henry VIII later, it did not advance the cause of the national state. In fact, his standards of judgment were as closely bound up with nineteenth-century ideas as those he criticized in Creighton: he was always liable to see Henrician England simply as the prototype of early twentieth-century England.[3] What he praised in Henry VIII was really his own vision of English history after the Reformation; and he therefore condemned in Wolsey his failure to recognize a *Zeitgeist* only visible to the preconditioned historian. He compounded an error characteristic of the so-called whig view of history by making an unjustifiably clear-cut distinction between the far-seeing king and the short-sighted

---

[1] [Until the appearance of J. J. Scarisbrick's book in 1968, for which cf. above, no. 5.]
[2] Cf. my *Henry VIII: an Essay in Revision* (Historical Association pamphlet, 1962).
[3] For a valuable, though in parts extreme, critique of Pollard's silent assumptions, see J. H. Hexter, 'Factors in Modern History,' *Reappraisals in History* (1961), 26 ff.

minister, a distinction not based on the facts but on his long-standing service to the memory of Henry VIII.[1]

If the axiom of Henry's political greatness caused Pollard to be rather unfair to the cardinal, the circumstances of his book and the materials on which it rests further circumscribed his vision. The book grew out of the lectures which Pollard gave as Ford's lecturer at Oxford, and its organization bears the marks of that genesis. This is not strictly a life of Wolsey so much as an analysis of various aspects of his work, surrounded by a brief statement of the main biographical data and concluded with a thoughtful, lengthy assessment of Wolsey's 'place in English history', itself a phrase which reveals the 'whig' approach. This structure gives the book its value, which lies in the mature discussion of a system of government and the making of policy rather than in the analysis of personality: Pollard, the constitutional historian, the man soaked in certain aspects of the Tudor constitution, never did anything better, though *Henry VIII* remains his masterpiece as biographer. However, if there is something less than satisfactory about the picture of Wolsey as a human being in this book, this is even more the product of Pollard's choice of materials than of his method. Pollard's history rested, to a quite extraordinary degree, on one great record publication. Of course, he knew just about everything that in his day had been printed on his chosen period, but his great Bible was the fine calendar of *Letters and Papers, Foreign and Domestic, of the Reign of Henry VIII* which appeared between 1860 and 1932, and which he knew inside out, better even perhaps than its editors themselves. This calendar was assuredly a splendid aid to historical study, and it enabled Pollard to revolutionize the standard accounts of Henry VIII's reign. But the calendar is also, like all abstracts of record material, a trap and occasionally a positive disaster; its very excellence, by seeming to render recourse to the manuscripts unnecessary, hides its inevitable and at times serious shortcomings; and despite an air of comprehensiveness, it leaves a great deal of material untouched. As Pollard recognized, Wolsey's supposed work in the Council and conciliar courts, or the reality of his supposed social policy, could not be studied without

[1] In my view, Wolsey was in fact responsible for such ideas as the government of those years lived on. That is to say, he designed both its successes and its failures. But Henry not only approved but as a rule could consider alternatives; when he had notions of his own, they prevailed; and he carries as much responsibility for this part of the reign as for the rest. Needless to say, he never played the conscious architect of later greatness that he seems to be in Pollard's imagination; even long-term views in the sixteenth century could not envisage the British empire, talk in terms of manifest destiny, or forecast parliamentary democracy.

using public records not yet in print; but he does not seem to have admitted to himself that his account of such central aspects of his subject's career was therefore not so much tentative as barely existent. Pollard, to put it bluntly, did not use manuscripts; he did not even trace back the more vital phrases in documents to their original form, unless they happened to have been printed in full. He had to hand a very good calendar and he performed excellently with it, but he could not expect on these terms to rival a Ranke or a Maitland, who read originals. This may seem a petty matter, of interest only to professional historians and professional jealousy-mongers, but in truth it lies at the heart of both Pollard and his *Wolsey*. His work formed a great improvement on what went before, and marked a necessary stage in the development of Tudor historiography; but simply because the recesses of the Public Record Office remained to him foreign territory, he could never achieve lasting authority. To take an obvious example: how can one judge the tone of a letter or the spirit of the man who wrote it from the neutered phrases of an abstract? This technical fact really matters more than Pollard's natural inability to free himself from his own, very strong, personality, or his own time with its teleological view of history. These are shortcomings he shares with all historians, but reliance on printed calendars is an avoidable weakness.[1]

Lastly, Pollard handicapped himself by a strange form of self-denial. This is a book about Wolsey, and portraits of Wolsey exist; yet they are not mentioned. They may not be very good, but they do show things about him – his corpulence, his youthful (even babyish) appearance, his definitely clerical aspect – which surely are not irrelevant. No doubt Pollard was right to avoid psychological speculation of the dreadful kind familiar enough in biographies about whose subjects we know little except the public *persona*, but there are legitimate ways

---

[1] I am bound to record also my unease concerning Pollard's accuracy because I have found him too often basing striking opinions on insupportable interpretations of the evidence (see e.g. *Tudor Constitution*, 162 n. 4, 234 n. 2). A spot-check reveals disturbing things in his *Wolsey*. Thus the statement that Henry VIII restored abbots deprived by Wolsey (p. 342), highly improbable in itself, is not supported by the document cited; one reference in p. 356 n. 3 has nothing to the point; the references in p. 359 n. 4 have nothing to do with the statement in the text; of the citations in p. 364 n. 3, one has nothing to do with Cromwell and none support the assertion that Cromwell had learned the 'methods' in question (in reality, routine operations of the king's patronage and in-fluence) from Wolsey; the discovery of a use of the phrase 'ship of state' in 1534 (p. 367) is unhappy because it suggests its appearance in English whereas it was really given in Latin and in that language is an ancient tag. The reader is free to regard such criticisms as pedantic; but all assertions are only as good as the evidence on which they are stated to rest.

of using such evidence. In any case, Wolsey commanded the post-humous services of a biographer who knew him – literally – in undress. George Cavendish, one of his personal attendants, left an unforgettable picture of both Wolsey and his society in the little book which he wrote twenty-five years after his old master's death.[1] Pollard disposed of the book with a withering phrase about 'the classic example of history as it appears to a gentleman-usher' (p. 2), a phrase which once again places this very nineteenth-century scholar in his own time; but he does not see or remark that the Wolsey who emerges from Cavendish's memory is a much more attractive man than the statesman described by himself, largely with the help of the charges made after his fall. Cavendish's Wolsey is not the whole of the story or of the man, but it is hard to see why Pollard's Wolsey should not be allowed to include him. There is other scattered evidence to cast light. The Wolsey who put accused heretics at their ease and listened sympathetically to men whose opinions he abhorred; who lived an enjoyable private life in the luxury he had earned by hard work; who, exasperated by the pigheadedness of certain litigants, himself paid for the hedge and ditch that were to mark the disputed boundary; who built because he liked building, and built beautifully because he had naturally good taste; even the Wolsey who could not bear to refuse a petitioner when he knew that he could never fulfil the promise – of these there is no trace in Pollard's book. The cardinal was really a much more pleasant, sensible and balanced man than he appears here.

These are criticisms which I advance in full consciousness of my effrontery in attacking a great professor and notable historian. I am also aware that they must raise the question whether Pollard's *Wolsey* is in fact worth reading. However, Pollard is worth searching criticism only because he was justly eminent and justly continues to carry weight among historians and readers alike. And the criticism is justified only against the supposition that his book is worthy to be read, is indeed very necessary reading for anyone who wishes to understand the reign of Henry VIII. Not only is it the best book on Wolsey so far written; it is also (despite its shortcomings) one of the best books on the period and Pollard's mature masterpiece. In assessing Wolsey and his place (not in English history but in his own time) one must start from Pollard; but it is also necessary to free the mind of the hold which

[1] George Cavendish, *The Life and Death of Cardinal Wolsey*, written in 1556–8. The best edition now is in *Two Early Tudor Lives*, ed. R. S. Sylvester and David P. Harding (New Haven, 1962).

Pollard has established by considering the question-marks which must be set against his methods and achievements.

Pollard analysed Wolsey's work into four main sections: the provision of equitable justice, reorganization of the king's government and control of the nation's economy, a foreign policy dominated by the interests of the papacy, and centralization in the Church. Though it will not be possible here to do full justice to all this, it is worth looking at these points again. Not a great deal of work has been done on the age of Wolsey since Pollard wrote; but there is some, and the periods surrounding his ascendancy – the work of Henry VII and Thomas Cromwell – are now very much better known than they were in his day. These more recent researches have left Wolsey's foreign policy virtually untouched, for present-day scholarship has little interest in diplomacy and international relations.[1] Pollard's view that Wolsey, so far from pursuing a nationalist policy or one guided by some principle of the balance of power, simply placed such influence as England possessed at the disposal of the papacy has not been seriously challenged, though certain new insights make one think that a challenge is overdue. Thus Pollard showed little recognition of what was probably the most powerful motive in sixteenth-century politics, the motive of dynasticism. As Hexter has said,[2] he overestimated the force of nationalism which he interpreted virtually in a nineteenth-century sense, though Hexter, it seems to me, underestimates the recognizable form which that passion took in the sixteenth century. But it is quite true that the foreign policies of monarchies turned in the main on their family relationships and their concept of honour; marriages, involving territorial gain, and prestige were the main considerations. It is thus disconcerting to be told (Pollard, p. 222) that 'matrimony was a fleeting foundation for a permanent policy'; on the contrary, at the time it was certainly the chief, sometimes the only, foundation of policy. It is therefore in itself not very probable that Wolsey should have been either willing or able to adjust his policy so exclusively to the whims of the papacy. Here Henry VIII is for once rather overlooked in Pollard's story.[3] At the same time, the king himself certainly regarded the holy father at Rome as entitled to his services, provided these did

[1] [But cf. now R. B. Wernham, *Before the Armada* (1966), chs. VII and VIII, which initiates a revision of Pollard's interpretation.]

[2] *Reappraisals*, 30–1.

[3] [These doubts now receive support from D. S. Chambers, 'Cardinal Wolsey and the Papal Tiara,' *BIHR* 38 (1965), 20–30.]

not conflict with his personal concerns, and harmony prevailed until about 1527. When dynasticism and papalism could go hand in hand, Wolsey could maintain his difficult position between the two sources of his power; in serving the king he served the pope, and in assisting the pope he did not cross the king. And the policy he pursued was in fact Henry's too: despite Pollard, no one after 1530 discovered 'nationalist' principles different from those upon which Wolsey had acted: in a different situation, the same ends – dynastic aggrandisement treated as an issue of national concern – were pursued in a different way.

With respect to Wolsey's work in state and Church, however, something can now be said in amplification and correction of Pollard's picture. In the first place, Wolsey appears as much less original than once he did. The machinery which he operated remained traditional, and such improvements as had been made in it were the work of the Yorkist kings and of Henry VII, who in particular revived the royal Household as an agency of national finance.[1] At best, Wolsey provided the more formal arrangement of officers appointed by acts of Parliament which replaced Henry VII's entirely personal dealings with his trusted councillors; but it is probable that even here he only took over what had been done by Henry VIII's councillors from the first, and it is reasonably certain that the existence of the organized office hindered rather than advanced Wolsey's direct control of the finances.[2] Indeed, it is difficult to see where Wolsey's often-stressed excellence as an administrator lay. Unlike Thomas Cromwell, he held no offices in the bureaucracy; apart from the lord chancellorship, he held no Crown office at all, and this, in a sufficiently sophisticated machine, meant that he could act only through orders to others.[3] This would not preclude efficiency and effectiveness, but it has to be said that there are precious few signs of influence or activity in the record; most of what

[1] *Tudor Revolution*, and nos. 3 and 4 above; W. C. Richardson, *Tudor Chamber Administration* (Baton Rouge, 1952); B. P. Wolffe, 'The Management of Royal Estates under the Yorkist Kings,' *EHR* 71 (1956), 1 ff., and 'Henry VII's Land Revenue and Chamber Finance,' *EHR* 79 (1964), 225 ff.

[2] Pollard treated the 1512 act for the general surveyors of Crown lands as the work of Wolsey and believed that he was thus able 'to dispense . . of the greater part of the revenues of the crown' (p. 130). There is no sign in the record that Wolsey managed the finances in person, while the need to secure the signatures and warrants of others is very manifest. The act in fact merely recorded an already existing situation.

[3] The importance of departmental office occasionally appears in unexpected ways. Thus the widow of a Household official, having for years tried to get payment of a debt out of the Exchequer, finally appealed to Cromwell, already lord privy seal, to order payment 'by virtue of your office as chancellor of the Exchequer' (PRO, St Ch 2, bundle 18, unnumbered fragments).

we think we know of Wolsey's government comes from the catalogues of sins of omission and commission compiled by his enemies at the time of his fall. At times it would appear that Wolsey's greatness as an administrator, especially after he had passed through his apprenticeship with the king, lay purely in his ability to monopolize the credit while leaving the work to others. Even if one supposed that the record hides his true personal activity – and this is possible – one would still come to the conclusion that he was that familiar figure, the expedient-monger in a time of crisis. All the solutions provided for problems of government and especially finance were short-term – with one exception. Wolsey's administration witnessed the invention of a new and efficient direct tax, the subsidy, a levy on income properly and freshly assessed which for a time succeeded in mobilizing the wealth of the country in a way not achieved since the early thirteenth century.[1] But again one must wonder if the credit should be Wolsey's, for he no sooner had an efficient tax to hand than he tried to make it the basis of short-sighted experiments in anticipated revenue and illegal exactions (Pollard, pp. 131 ff.). Occasionally he drew up grandiose schemes – reform of the Household, reform of the courts, reform of the Council – but not one of them ever produced practical effect. Ingenuity rather than principle, quick rather than fundamental solutions, mark Wolsey's work in the state. However one may assess Thomas Cromwell's reforming activity,[2] it is quite apparent that his attention was required not only by the strains which the Reformation put on the machinery, but also by the virtual neglect that had lain behind Wolsey's sometimes careless manipulation of insufficient machinery.

The central administrative problem of Wolsey's day concerned the Council and the institutions and activities associated with it. This is much too big a topic to be worked out properly here, but it must be said that Pollard's views have in great part been rendered untenable by the study of manuscript material.[3] Pollard had convinced himself that the clue to the mysteries of the Tudor Council lay in the fact that

---

[1] This is fully brought out in R. S. Schofield's unprinted doctoral dissertation, 'Direct lay taxation under the early Tudors' (Cambridge, 1963). [J. J. Goring has drawn attention to one enterprise of Wolsey's displaying determined and fundamental attacks on administrative problems: 'The General Proscription of 1522,' *EHR* 86 (1971), 681–705.]

[2] For the debate whether it constituted a revolution, see the article by P. Williams and G. L. Harriss in *Past and Present*, no. 25 (1963), and my reply in no. 29 (1964).

[3] Esp. W. H. Dunham, 'Henry VIII's Whole Council and its Parts,' *Huntington Library Quarterly*, 7 (1943), 7 ff., and the book reviewed in no. 16 below. See also my summary of preliminary conclusions in *Tudor Constitution*, 87 ff., 158 ff., and my analysis of some of the problems in no. 18 below.

what was spoken of as 'the king's Council' should really be described as 'king's counsel', a loose body of advisers which only on occasion formed an institution. The first time he argued this case he made some valid points and cleared away some error,[1] but the notion became an obsession, and the way in which it runs through this book can be very misleading. We now know that the institutional Council certainly existed and worked in Wolsey's day; while the cardinal frequently ignored its advisory function, he did not allow it to decay as a body. Its size, formality and regularity (at least in term time) increased rather than diminished, and it is probable that it also gained weight, as an institution, in the affairs of the kingdom: for Wolsey, not being king, was after all only the leading councillor. However much he monopolized power under the Crown, he neither would nor could force the king to listen to no voice but his. His continued jealousy of the influence of others is proof enough that he himself at least did not believe in that sole control over Henry's mind which historians have ascribed to him. Wolsey never forgot that in his day power depended on the ability to speak straight into the ears of princes, or that he himself was very often away from Court. The king's Council might not be a Cabinet, even a Cabinet under a prime minister; certainly no councillor could rival Wolsey or, before 1527, hope to get away with an independent line. But neither could Wolsey ignore the Howards and Brandons, Fitzwilliams and Lovells and Marneys, who sat in Council and spoke to the king. His control over both king and Council was never absolutist, always political: never assured, always to be worked for. It does, however, look as though Wolsey came gradually to surrender to impatience and arrogance, and Henry's growing emancipation from the cardinal's influence owed much to the existence of other councillors and other influences.

It is generally supposed that in his treatment of the Council Wolsey concerned himself mainly with its work as a court. To Pollard, his one unequivocal claim to respect lay in his determination to bring justice to the unprivileged, to enforce the law upon the strong, to assist its inadequacies and temper its harshnesses with the balm of common sense and equity. Unfortunately the evidence for all this is quite slight, and Pollard, of course, thought that a full understanding of Wolsey's work required an analysis of the unexplored records of Chancery, Star Chamber and Requests. No work has yet been done on the first, and that on the other two has not progressed very far. But

[1] *EHR* 37 (1922), 33 ff., 516 ff.; 38 (1923), 42 ff.

some things can already be said. That Wolsey meant to offer justice to the people is true; though, as the king's chief councillor, he could not in any case have escaped that task, we may believe that he made a special show of it. But show it was: Wolsey the great judge is almost certainly a myth. The really striking thing about the courts of the early Tudors is not the determination of government to provide justice, but the determination of litigants to seek it, or rather to seek that success at law which among the victorious passes for justice. The pressure of suitors was enormous and quite sufficiently accounts for the proliferation of courts. Litigation was a major enterprise in the nation; even without the probable effects of economic changes (a rising population, new ways of exploiting land, expanding commercial activities) the state of the land law and a century of confused inheritances laid up plenty of work for lawyers and clients alike. Wolsey's part in all this is not easy to assess. Quite possibly he was responsible for the increased activity of the Council in the Star Chamber at Westminster which made it into a court dealing with criminal or near-criminal matters.[1] Under Henry VII, the enforcement of the law on those whose private power too often enabled them to flout it seems to have been mainly carried out in the regular courts of the common law, assisted not so much by the Star Chamber (though it did some work there) as by a special committee of the Council, the council learned in the law, which was set up to pursue breaches of regulatory legislation, not riot or crime.[2] The evidence assembled by Pollard (pp. 77 ff.) which does suggest that the reorganization of Star Chamber into a regular court owed much to Wolsey is modestly supported by the patchy evidence of the record: activity in the court seems certainly to have increased quite dramatically from about 1515 onwards. Wolsey did not create the court, and he did not even complete its organization: until the making of the Privy Council in the 1530s, it was less a true court than still a body of councillors who at intervals turned from affairs of state to the affairs of the subject. But he was probably instrumental in confining its regular attention to such business, in making it an initiating rather than a responding tribunal, and in concentrating there those cases which involved peace and order and obedience to the law.

On the other hand, he cannot be credited with as much of a share in

---

[1] Pollard's view that Wolsey was mainly responsible for developing the peace-enforcing functions of the Star Chamber is almost certainly correct.

[2] R. Somerville, 'Henry VII's "Council learned in the Law",' *EHR* 54 (1939), 427 ff.

the creation of the court of Requests as Pollard supposed (pp. 82 ff.). The history of that court remains to be unravelled, but it may already be said that until the 1530s it did not really exist as a single, separate institution. Rather there were several and fluctuating committees engaged in hearing cases. Under Henry VII, the councillors travelling with the king began to hear petitions out of term: from this there developed term-time sessions of selected councillors; particular individuals came to specialize in attending the small pleas of (sometimes) poor men. The dean of the Chapel Royal (at Windsor) and the king's almoner were the leading specialists in this work, and as almoner Wolsey took some part in it, early in Henry VIII's reign. In 1518 he attempted a major reform of the system by setting up a series of equitable tribunals, but other councillors continued to do similar work, and the cardinal himself seems very occasionally to have presided at such sessions. But little endured of these experiments; it was not until the two traditions of councillors attending on the king and special commissioners, hitherto overlapping in their activities, coalesced into a settled court, that the court of Requests proper was born in the 1530s.

Altogether, Wolsey's share in the shaping of conciliar jurisdiction bears the marks of that moderately inspired amateurishness which is found in so much of his work. He had instincts both generous and self-aggrandizing, and therefore he experimented in various ways with the provision of justice for those who came to seek it; but he could never bear any sound solution which – since he knew no law – would of necessity have moved the limelight from him. He had little grasp of organization; his predilection for seeing in all government merely an extension of himself inhibited true reform. There is, to our present knowledge, no sign that he contributed anything to developments in the principles of law and equity. Wolsey, the judge in the Council courts, was simply the common arbitrator *in excelsis*. All the king's councillors were always likely to find themselves informally deciding between disputants who came to seek their aid, but such arbitration could only put forward a commonsense interpretation of contested facts and claims, without in any way affecting the legal position or the ultimate exclusive jurisdiction of the common law, and without in any way assisting that law to develop in new directions. This, as his surviving decrees suggest, was Wolsey's place: to assess a weight of facts and urge an arbitrament upon the parties. Of course, Wolsey was willing enough to impose his amateurish authority upon the agencies of the law, and his readiness to restrain powerful men or interests must on occasion have assisted justice. The fact during his ascendancy the arbitrating activities of Star Chamber and Requests grew frequent and formidable enough to equip these bodies with the curial character which the institutional reforms of the 1530s turned into practical routine gives Wolsey an important place in the history of the courts; he has none in the history of law.[1] Decades of work by professionals were required before the conciliar courts could stand by the side of the common-law courts as makers and interpreters of law. During those decades the men in charge were trained common lawyers. From 1529 the office of lord chancellor was nearly always held by a lawyer, so that in both Chancery and Star Chamber the 'new' law looked only to follow the principles of the old and thereby to fill in its gaps; in Star Chamber, the leading part played by the two chief justices underlined the fact; and in Requests, the earlier predominance of clergy (canon and civil lawyers) made way for control by regular lay judges of whom one at least was always a common lawyer. Common lawyers may have disliked Wolsey's unprofessional, though often very sensible, interference with their preserves, but the cardinal was neither learned nor systematic enough to offer the slightest threat to the ascendancy of the common law itself which, despite all that has been alleged on the point, was never in danger.

As an administrator and reformer, then, Wolsey was a true amateur, eager to do the right thing, full of personal activity and driving energy, but unsystematic, lacking direction and follow-through, and therefore ultimately sterile. The same qualities stand out more starkly still in his dealings with what the age called the commonwealth, with the national economy. There is really no sign that Wolsey ever truly understood any part of it. Notoriously he could make nothing of the commercial and industrial interests concentrated around wool on which English prosperity really depended. His foreign policy took no account of them, as his last venture, involving a breach with the Netherlands and disaster to the vital export of cloth, so clearly showed. But he did little better over another problem, that of enclosures and rural unemployment, though in this matter he has usually received praise from historians little more aware than himself of what was actually involved. He was certainly entitled to enforce the law, and it was not his fault

[1] [It is beginning to look as though Wolsey's lord chancellorship witnessed a crucial stage in the development of both the subpoena summons and injunctions, the two procedural weapons of the Chancery court.]

that the enclosure legislation of the time, especially the depopulation act of 1489, mistook the problem. In fact, the distinction there made between enclosure for arable and depopulating enclosure for sheep-runs and parks was a valid one (though by no means all sheep-runs led to depopulation); and given the limitations of Tudor administration, the law was sensible in proposing to control the phenomenon by means of total prohibition modified by individual licensing. However, Wolsey's much advertised concern for social justice produced nothing because he made the two fatal mistakes of the eager amateur. First with a great deal of noise, he attacked indiscriminately and put valuable enclosures to as much hazard as dangerous ones; and secondly, confronted with the complexities of reality, he lost interest and washed his hands of the business. Conversion of arable to pasture could and did cause hardship, as old-fashioned moralists like Thomas More were not slow to stress; it also, in an age of rapidly expanding cloth exports, provided the one true element of growth in the economy, led to fruitful capital accumulation (in selected pockets), improved industrial employment, and genuinely augmented national prosperity. It needed more refined weapons than those of the penal laws, and a better understanding of economic facts than that possessed by Wolsey, to tackle the abuses without damaging the growth. As it was, Wolsey did less damage than he might have done because he confined himself to collecting evidence of enclosing without following this up beyond a few prosecutions.[1] The inquest of 1517–18 left things pretty much as before. What even Tudor governments might attempt was later demonstrated by Thomas Cromwell who combined encouragement of the cloth trade with a more careful depopulation statute, some control over the use of land, and the beginnings of serious welfare legislation for the poor. By comparison, Wolsey's well-advertised concern for the rural commons looks pitiful indeed.

A late-medieval churchman, even an ex-bursar of an Oxford College, may be forgiven for not understanding the problems of a complex economy. It is more surprising to find that the king's minister really showed little grasp even of the resources of the monarchy he served. He began well: his new tax was a creditable piece of administrative reform and helped the king greatly in his early wars. But it looks as though Wolsey allowed the success of 1512–14 to go to his head; for the rest of his time, the Crown was never out of financial difficul-

---

[1] See Joan Thirsk, *Tudor Enclosures* (1959); to her bibliography, add E. Kerridge, 'The Return of the Inquisitions of Depopulation,' *EHR* 70 (1955), 212 ff.

ties. His inability, or unwillingness, to deal through the House of Commons had much to do with this; he seemed to take it for granted that, since the money to pay relatively high taxation existed, it would also be forthcoming. The real trouble, however, was that Wolsey never thought the problem through. Spendthrift himself, he made no attempt to correlate expenditure and income. He was the last man to curb Henry VIII's haphazard lavishness: king and minister shared an inability to think of money as something that has to be earned by hard work. The main indictment, on this count, is that Wolsey never set himself to analyse the available resources or to keep more than an accountant's eye on their use. In this matter, as in others, he lacked the creativeness of the true statesman. Unlike his predecessors in Henry VII's reign, unlike his successor Cromwell, he did not enquire into the resources of the Crown but took what seemed to be ready to hand and found that when more was needed (a need which his foreign policy of wars and subsidies to allies constantly increased) he did not know where to look for it. The true buoyancy of the English economy is best vouched for by the fact that even Wolsey never reduced it, or the king, to actual bankruptcy.[1]

However, in fairness to him it might be said that the solution adopted by Cromwell was not open to him. He could not spoil the Church. Or to be more precise, he could not spoil it in the king's interest, though he raided it sufficiently in his own. It will not, after all, do to forget that he was himself a cleric; his relations with the Church require attention. In this respect it is happily necessary to modify the dark picture painted by Pollard. For it remains an important clue to any understanding of Wolsey that he was a priest and a cardinal; the view which sees in him a layman inadequately disguised under a red hat is a dull and false one. His order meant much to him, and it meant not only the power embodied in his legacy but also the faith to which he ministered. He said mass frequently, which was more than his contemporary, the archbishop of Cologne, could do; he believed both in God and in the teaching of the Church; he valued learning and enjoyed the company of spiritual men. Of course, all this is readily overlooked in a man to whom the Church was a main source of patronage and wealth, a pluralist, simoniac and begetter of bastards; but it is

[1] [This paragraph is too harsh: cf. the article by J. J. Goring, cited above, p. 117, n. 1, which shows that Wolsey in fact attempted, or contemplated, a major review of national resources. The concept was characteristically grandiose – and impracticable, and was abandoned unfinished.]

too simple to suppose that personal failings and occupational delicts can occur only in a secularist hypocrite. Wolsey was quite as confused in his approach to matters spiritual and ecclesiastical as was the Church of which he stands as a concentrated embodiment. Certainly he was no very spiritual man himself; few bishops were. Certainly, unlike Fisher or Cranmer, he was no theologian; this saved him from over-estimating the importance of doctrinal squabbles. Unlike Nix of Norwich or Fitzjames of London, he was no bigot; he did not smell heresy everywhere, and few things reported of him are more attractive than his dealings with men denounced for heterodox views (whom he summoned to his presence, quaking, by ringing a little bell he kept on his table). His humorous and gentlemanly temperament shows to full advantage there. Even so, he assuredly believed in the distinction between orthodoxy and heresy: he was no sceptic out of his time. Wolsey's religion could do with a little more specific study; simply to assume that it was purely formal will not do, though very likely it was highly conventional.

Pollard maintained very firmly that the cardinal did nothing but harm to the Church and prepared it for the disasters which befell it when Henry VIII broke with the pope. With much of his case no one will disagree. Wolsey did weaken the bishops' independence, and he did tie the *Ecclesia Anglicana* too obviously to the fate of Rome. He demonstrated the possibilities open to one who controlled both the English provinces, and above all, by the example of his practice and his own fall, demonstrated the possibilities inherent in the law of praemunire. But two important reservations, which remove much of the case, must be made. In the first place, it needed no Wolsey to teach the English Church, and especially its bishops, to serve the king. Wolsey was only the most notable member of an episcopate nearly all of whom had reached their places by working for the Crown. Indeed, he differed from them by a much more obvious dependence on his second source of power: no other bishop was as papalist as he. Obedience to the Crown was not something either imposed by him or provoked by reaction to his highhandedness; it was ingrained. And secondly, the Church was not left in quite such a state of disarray and non-resistance as Pollard supposed; it took skill, hard work and much bearing-down before the Church gave way to Henry VIII. Recent research has underlined the powers of conservative resistance and prin-cipled opposition which some bishops and lesser clergy retained as late as 1532: immediately, the removal of Wolsey refreshed the self-confidence and renewed the vigour of the old Church.[1] Henry VIII and Thomas Cromwell had to do the work of subjugation themselves; they did not simply step into Wolsey's shoes. It is true enough that the cardinal failed to make much of his frequent protestations that he meant to reform the Church, though even in this he did better at times than he has been given credit for.[2] Europe was full of churchmen, from the pope down, who deplored the state of the Church, promised to amend it, and left as they had begun. Reform from within never got going until attack from outside rendered the situation desperate. And it should be noted that while the Henrician Reformation revolutionized the Church it did not succeed in reforming its abuses; only long labours were to achieve this, perhaps not before the second half of the seventeenth century. To the moralist, Wolsey's failure may seem discreditable; the historian must think it virtually inevitable, though he remains entitled to draw attention to the distance between pretensions and performance, and to Wolsey's notable share in lowering the tone of ecclesiastical life.

It must now look as though even Pollard's verdict on Wolsey may still err on the generous side; though he was unkind to the man, he thought more highly of the statesman than I seem to have done here. Responsible for an often mistaken and ultimately disastrous foreign policy, amateurish and uncreative in the government of the realm committed to his care, only moderately successful in ruling its Church: does Wolsey then stand before us as a true failure? Superficially this is certainly so. Within a few years, all that he represented was to vanish in England; coming at the end of an age, he could hardly avoid the appearance of failure. But for this he was not responsible: it was neither his fault nor his doing that in the 1530s the world should change so drastically, at home and abroad, that only ten years after his death the age of Wolsey would seem to have belonged to a remote past – a past which had included a universal Church, the scholarly amenities of the Renaissance and Christian humanism, an international scene determined by balanced rivalries in Italy, a realm ruled by prelatical councillors and superficially at least firmly anchored to the customs of

[1] This is especially brought out in two unprinted Cambridge dissertations: J. J. Scarisbrick, 'The Conservative Episcopate in England 1529–35' (1955) and M. J. Kelly, 'Canterbury Jurisdiction and Influence during the Episcopate of William Warham 1503–32' (1963). See also Scarisbrick in *CHJ* 12 (1956), 22 ff.

[2] The case of the abbess of Wilton speaks less ill for him and less well for Henry VIII than Pollard supposed (*Wolsey*, 202–4): see D. Knowles in *BIHR* 31 (1958), 92 ff.

five hundred years. Now there were national and regional Churches; doctrinal chasms had opened in the pleasant fields tilled by the intellectuals; the sudden prominence of the Habsburg complex and of Spain transformed the European stage; at home a revolution had taken place and all seemed different. The very world viewed by the statesmen of Europe underwent a disconcerting enlargement as both the Turk and the Indies suddenly became a very pressing part of it. However much the historian may note that all these new things were rooted in earlier times and events, he should also grasp that the men of the time experienced a series of very real shocks and had to think of themselves as living through an era of destruction and re-creation.[1] Some liked it, more hated it; that is the nature of man. Pope Clement VII died in 1534 and was succeeded by the first pope who grasped what the Reformation was about. By that time, the Emperor Charles V had won his place in Europe and lost his place in Germany; by that time Thomas Cromwell had set England on a path so divergent from the old that revolution is the proper term to apply to his activities. By that time, Wolsey would have been marvellously out of date. Perhaps he was happy in the time of his fall, but to call him nothing but a failure is to judge him by what happened after he ceased to be.

Yet not entirely: he had also failed (this has been shown) in too much of what he himself regarded as his proper task and ambition. He left behind no achievement of great note, for to have been remembered as quite influential in the establishment of the court of Star Chamber would not have seemed to him, as it need not seem to us, enough to result from fifteen years' violent activity in affairs. No doubt the survival of his college at Oxford would have struck him as a worthier memorial, but it, too, hardly represents a sufficient product of so much energy. In the last resort his work must be judged by another criterion: by his relationship with Henry VIII. Though at the end he may have recognized that he ought to have served his God at least as well as he had served the king, in the days of his greatness the distinction would have seemed meaningless to him. What is more, it would have seemed meaningless to his contemporaries, even to his enemies, who inclined to blame him for harming both God's cause and Henry's. He was the king's servant, and his God-given duty lay in that service, which in the circumstances meant also service to the nation. Assuredly he ham-

---

[1] Compare, e.g., Wolsey's dissolution of a few decayed religious houses with Cromwell's wholesale destruction. The first broke no custom, the second regarded none. Is it really sensible to think (with Pollard and others) of the first as 'leading to' the second?

pered himself by also taking service under the papacy, but until 1527 there was no reason to suppose that a man could not serve those particular two masters. Christ's vicar and the defender of the faith smiled jointly upon their servant's useful labours, and it was Wolsey's misfortune, in no sense his fault, to run into the quite unpredictable circumstances which made that position untenable. Even then all was not lost, for he could always remember his first duty (which he recognized) to the king. But quite apart from the personal elements in the story – the violent hostility of Anne Boleyn, the resentments of the nobility, the ruthless selfrighteousness of Henry VIII – both his whole frame of mind and his experience of politics disqualified him for the new age. Wolsey could not have run a revolution.

Yet Pollard in effect maintained that he taught that revolution to Henry VIII: that by precept he showed him the way to control the Church and by default instructed him in the use of Parliament and nation. I cannot follow Pollard in this. Henry was not the sort of man who 'learns' in this fashion at all. His basic notions were always rooted in his egocentricity and permanent conviction of supreme power; they could not and did not alter. In so far as he changed policy and method, he did so by allowing men of greater originality and application to organize success for him. He did not learn the facts of the royal supremacy from Wolsey, for he had never seriously doubted that he controlled his clergy, while he needed Cromwell to construct the new form which this control took after 1533. He did not learn from Wolsey to turn to his Parliament. Like every king of England, and most in Europe, he called the assembly when he thought it could be of use; there had been Parliaments in Wolsey's time, and the special character of the Reformation Parliament, unforeseeable in 1529, developed in the course of the revolution. Henry needed Cromwell to show him the part that Parliament could play and, up to a point, also how to manage it, though, since his own contribution to affairs was above all a remarkable instinct for handling men, this side of the work came natural to him. But the fact that in all essential respects – what was done and thought, how it was done and worked out – the age of Cromwell differed profoundly from the age of Wolsey seems to me to make it impossible to regard the cardinal in any significant way as his king's teacher. Naturally, the memory of what happened in those fifteen years contributed to the experience, and therefore the practice, of Henry VIII and Cromwell, and of others as well; but that is not to say that in some way they worked out the lessons of Wolsey's career and applied them as his pupils. If there was a lesson to be learned, it was a very elementary one: to do better than the man who had failed. Anyone with eyes in his head could see that Wolsey had tried to do the impossible, to rule as king when he was not king, to ignore the legal and constitutional traditions of England and substitute for them his own self-confident judgment, to do a highly professional job in a very amateur manner. He had lasted so long because in two things he was not amateur at all: he knew how to promote himself, and for most of the time he knew how to keep Henry satisfied. But there was really not much to be learned from that.

Thus the last word must remain that Wolsey's long period of ascendancy proved essentially sterile, nor do the many links between the before and the after alter that verdict at all. And why should this surprise? Wolsey was not a creative or reflective man, but an uncomplicated activist, a magnificent if often extravagant manipulator of what was available. And here lies some measure of redemption. To recognize that Wolsey contributed virtually nothing to the future is not to discard his present. For fifteen years he impressed England and Europe with his grandeur, his hard work, his skill and intelligence, and his very positive action in the affairs of this world. He often achieved what he set out to do, even if subsequent events showed his aims to have been mistaken and his solutions to have been patchwork. He made a great and deserved name, and his age would have been very different without him. And surely, this is something; surely it is enough.

7

THOMAS MORE, COUNCILLOR*

'The king's good servant, but God's first.' Few of Thomas More's words are more familiar than this valediction on the scaffold. It is therefore rather strange that the many historians who have concerned themselves with his life should have paid so little attention to the first part of this self-assessment, however justified they may have been, being moved by zeal, in writing glosses on the second. Even before he became lord chancellor, More had been a member of King Henry's government for some twelve years – a third of all his adult life. Yet in Chambers's biography, typical in this as in so much else, these years occupy seventy-nine out of four hundred pages, and even of these seventy-nine at least twenty-two are concerned with More's private life. Chambers was only following the pattern set by the early biographers, from Roper onwards, who all inserted their description of More's family and friends into those years. This imbalance, produced by the desire to get on to the dramatic last phase, has left us with some important and difficult questions – just why, for instance, did Henry choose More to succeed Wolsey? – and has obscured our view of some of Sir Thomas's most active years.

Between them, More and Erasmus have succeeded in creating a firm impression that More entered the king's service with the greatest reluctance and performed his distasteful duties in a constant spirit of nostalgic regret for the joys of uncommitted scholarship. Yet he was a councillor, held several offices, served as Speaker in the Commons, and made a good deal of money out of office; he was several times involved in diplomatic negotiations; and his name appears frequently in the official correspondence of the time. If the unforeseeable disasters of the divorce and the break with Rome had not supervened, he would have lived out his days as a respected senior minister, one of the statesmen of the age of Wolsey and Gattinara. There must at least be some doubt about accounts which pay so little heed to this side of him and so manifestly arrange events with an eye to the future.

* [*St Thomas More: Action and Contemplation*, ed. R. S. Sylvester (New Haven, 1972), 86–122. Copyright © 1972 by Yale University.]

The improbabilities and errors begin right at the start of the story, with More's entry into the royal service and his appointment to the Council. There is here a conflict between ascertainable fact and contemporary comment, the second having predictably been preferred to the first. In July 1518 Erasmus told Bombasius that More had been made a councillor, and in September that year Giustiniani spoke of the appointment as though it was recent.[1] Both were aware that entry into service had preceded entry into the Council, for the Venetian knew in February that More was commissioned to act in a dispute, while Erasmus in April lamented to More himself his desertion of letters for the royal service.[2] When More visited Calais in the autumn of 1517, Erasmus clearly supposed that he was not yet of the Council; and Professor Hexter therefore dates the entry into service into the first quarter of 1518.[3] All this is much too late, as the commissions for More's embassies testify. Two were issued for the one to Flanders which produced *Utopia*. The first is unhelpful, but the second, of 2 October, 1515, distinguishes between Cuthbert Tunstall and William Knight, called 'our councillors', and Sir Thomas Spinelli, John Clifford (governor of the merchant adventurers) and Thomas More, who are not so described. On the other hand, the commission for Calais, dated 26 August 1517, gives the councillor's title to all the commissioners – Sir Richard Wingfield, Knight, and More.[4] By this date, therefore, More was sworn of the Council. Whether he was at some earlier date already formally in the king's service, it is impossible to say. Envoys were normally in that position, which was formal, not casual, but exceptions certainly occurred. The 'dialogue of counsel' in *Utopia* (to use Hexter's description), between More and Hythloday, written in the late summer of 1516, has always been read as describing his inner debate whether to accept the call. Hexter has also noted, very perceptively, that in his defence of entry into the Council the fictional More for once gets the better of his humanist self,[5] which suggests the possibility that the decision may already have been taken. At any rate, by August 1517 More was a councillor. Yet Erasmus, whose correspondence with More remained frequent and regular, clearly stayed ignorant of this fact for the best part of a year. The record leaves no doubt of this, and it calls for a reassessment of More's behaviour.

---

[1] Allen, iii. 356 f.; *LP* ii. 4438.   [2] *LP* ii. 3976, 4110.

[3] J. H. Hexter, *More's Utopia: the Biography of an Idea* (Princeton, 1952), 133 f. I disagree, however, with his Appendix A, which denies that More could have been in Henry's service very much earlier than this.

[4] Rogers, nos. 10, 14, 42 (p. 94).   [5] Hexter, *Utopia*, 131 f.

The story of More's councillor's fee bears out these implications. In the end he got an annuity of £100, the usual retainer for the king's Council. The first mention of a pension occurs in a letter from More to Erasmus of 17 February 1516, in which he described his financial difficulties, 'even though', he says, 'on my return the king granted me an annuity, and this is manifestly not to be despised, whether one looks to the honour or the profit.'[1] But he added that he would probably refuse the money because it would conflict with his office as undersheriff of London: if he were feed by the king, he might not be thought impartial in defending the privileges of the City. Although this annuity was seemingly never paid, the one that was casts doubt upon the general supposition that his reasons for refusing in 1516 were not those he gave but rather a wider reluctance to enter the king's service. On 21 June 1518, he was granted £100 a year, backdated to Michaelmas 1517 and payable partly out of the Exchequer of Receipt and partly in assignments on the petty custom of London.[2] In practice, he was to receive half from each source, and the payments were made fairly regularly thereafter, on the authority of a patent enrolled in the Exchequer in the Michaelmas Term 1518. He never had long to wait for his money, at least half of which he got in cash, not tallies, and he was especially favoured on occasion by receiving tallies on sources of revenue different from those specified in the patent.[3]

The really surprising thing is the document which authorized the patent under which he was paid. If More had been as reluctant to accept the fee as is commonly stated, giving way only to pressure from the king, one would have expected a signet letter, the usual instrument for expressing the king's initiative. Instead one finds a signed bill, that is a petition from the grantee, in standard form, which the king's signature turned into a warrant for the great seal. The king signed on 21 June, and the bill was at once delivered into Chancery: in this speed, and in the bypassing of the lesser seals, there is a measure of favour. But the document makes it plain that the initiative came from More, and there is really no reason to question it. I have never found

[1] Allen, ii. 196: 'Quamquam mihi revertenti pensio annua ab Rege decreta est, eaque plane, seu quis honorem spectet seu fructum, neutiquam contemnenda.'

[2] PRO, C 82/463. The common statement that the annuity was wholly charged on the petty custom is wrong (e.g. E. M. G. Routh, *Sir Thomas More and his Friends 1477–1535* [Oxford, 1934], 92 f.).

[3] In 1521–2 More was paid only £50 (PRO, E 407/67[3]), but this was made up by a cash payment of £150 for the following year (PRO, E 405/193). Thereafter payments reverted to half cash, half assignment, though in 1525 the assignment itself was divided between the petty custom and the parliamentary subsidy (PRO, E 405/195).

cause to doubt that such signed petitions meant exactly what they said, and since Henry had other often-used instruments at his disposal if he was really engaged in forcing a fee upon More in order to tie him to his service, I am compelled to accept that, on the contrary, More had to petition for the money. The backdating of payment by nine months supports this view. It looks as though More was promised his fee in mid-1517, when he was first appointed to the Council, but then waited patiently and in vain for the king to act, until in the end he had to draw Henry's attention to the fact that nothing had been done.

Thus More was a councillor long before he allowed Erasmus to know as much, and had to take steps to get the money attached to the place. This hardly suggests the reluctance to enter office which has always been ascribed to him. Indeed, what evidence is there for all this reluctance? In *Utopia* he discusses the pros and cons, but, as we have seen, he puts up a very good case for accepting. His own stated reasons for refusing a pension had nothing to do with doubts about office. He had been a judicial officer of London since 1510. He was trained as a common lawyer, a man in close contact with government – incidentally, a background very different from that of all his humanist friends. The most explicit evidence for his distaste for office comes not from himself but from Erasmus who told Hutten in 1519 that the king had had to drag More into Court since 'no one ever strove more energetically to get court appointment than More endeavoured to avoid it', a point repeated a year later in a letter to Brixius in which More's exceptional qualities are said to have forced the king not to rest until he had dragged him (*pertraxerit*) into his inmost counsels.[1] More's own occasional comments on the horrors of court life and his preference for books or the company of his family are no more than the conventional – and conventionally sincere – talk of the intellectual involved in the absurdities of a public existence. These feelings got into the early biographies, as in Roper's pleasant story of More hiding his wit in order to get away from Henry's drawn-out supper parties.[2] When More told Fisher, soon after the decisive step had been taken, that everybody knew his unwillingness to attend Court (and that Henry himself was in the habit of twitting him about it),[3] he was no doubt telling the truth, but not all the truth, for his place at Court (as we shall see) was soon absorbing enough. There really is no evidence at all that he lived twelve years against the grain, and he followed Henry's call at so early a date that he cannot have hesitated long.

[1] Allen, iv. 20, 294.   [2] Roper, 11–12.   [3] Rogers, no. 57.

But he did not like to admit all this to Erasmus, so much so that he allowed him to suppose that no decision had been taken even while, as king's councillor, he was negotiating at Calais and expecting Erasmus to visit. More, it would seem, respected Erasmus's known opposition to a scholar's involvement in affairs sufficiently to prevaricate about his own contrary view. Yet despite Erasmus's occasional disgust at the loss to letters, he did to some extent take his friend's point: better a More in attendance upon that good humanist monarch, King Henry VIII, than the common run of councillors.[1] On the other hand, he soon reverted to a more normal attitude when in June 1521 he regretted, to Pace, More's advance in service: 'he is doing so well at court that I am sorry for him'.[2] More's earlier silence rested on a correct apprehension – in both senses of that word – of the great man's feelings about princely courts.

At any rate, in trying to understand More's place in government, we should abandon the conventional talk about his reluctance to enter it. He went with his eyes open; he meant to make a career; the story of his fee suggests that he was not stupidly averse to gaining some profit. In short, his entry into the Council was a serious matter, not the act of a man pulling faces privately at those with whom he worked publicly.

The official record of More's activities as councillor is not impressive. Of the twenty-five Council meetings of which evidence survives during the time of his membership, he attended only five;[3] even his father, the judge, did better with seven. In part, no doubt, this reflects the bias of the evidence which consists of transcripts concentrating on the Council's judicial activities, but the fact also suggests something important about the real meaning of More's part in government. Routine Council sessions were not for him. It is not even clear whether he was present in the Star Chamber as late as February 1528 when a dispute was committed to him, the chief baron and two lawyers: his fellow commissioners were certainly not there.[4] On the other hand, he from the first undertook work which suggests an inferior place in the official hierarchy but a meaningful place in the personal entourage, as when, in April 1518, he was seeing to the medical precautions for the court as it moved to Woodstock.[5] He took his share in the familiar legal councillor's work of putting Crown debtors under bond.[6] None

---

[1] R. W. Chambers, *Sir Thomas More* (1935), 175.   [2] Allen, iv. 506.
[3] Huntington Library, MS El. 2655. More attended on 29 October 1518, 27 October and 21 November 1519, 20 January 1521, and 15 May 1526.
[4] *LP* iv. 3926.   [5] *LP* ii. 4125.
[6] *LP* v. 1610, referring to a bond of 16 Nov. 1519.

of this signifies much or indicates what the king might have wanted him for. Roper says that he was made master of requests because nothing better was available at first.[1] No such office formally existed at the time, but More was certainly among the councillors detailed to hear poor men's complaints in one of the committees from which the real court was to spring, though the extant signs of his work are few. In January 1519 he signed a commission out of the court, and at some unknown date he personally endorsed on a bill the order for a privy seal of appearance.[2] He seems, in fact, to have been joined with one of the really active Requests councillors, Dr John Clerk, then dean of the Chapel Royal, an officer who at this time specialized in hearing these kinds of pleas. In October 1519 they shared a mess in the Household and worked together on some obscure business. A little later More shared a breakfast allowance with John Stokesley, the almoner and the other leading judge in Requests matters.[3] It almost looks as though the later practice of linking civilians in Requests with at least one common lawyer had already started, and as though More filled that place for some two years. It all amounts to saying that his was a very lowly start in the Council; clearly, his assurance to Fisher that he stood 'a long way from the king's close favour' was true enough.[4]

The moment of prosperity, which called forth Erasmus's dark suspicions, came with his knighthood and appointment as undertreasurer of the Exchequer. This happened in May 1521, nearly four years after his first entry into the Council.[5] According to Erasmus, he neither sought nor petitioned for the office, and the king preferred him to another good candidate who was willing to pay for it.[6] Perhaps: at any rate, if More was ever to make a career, it was high time for him to get something of value. The undertreasurer deputized for the lord treasurer in the Lower Exchequer. He supervised and co-ordinated the officials responsible for receiving and disbursing money and those engaged in the Lower Exchequer's chief formal activity, the production of tallies. In addition he had custody of the Treasury of the Receipt, the government's chief archive for treaties and other diplomatic documents. He possessed neither place nor authority in the Upper Exchequer, where the accounts were taken, or in the Exchequer of Pleas where revenue cases were heard; the office thus fell somewhat short of the splendour which Erasmus, who confused it with the lord

[1] Roper, 11.
[2] PRO, Req 2/2/76, 7/53.
[3] *LP* ii. 4025, 4055; iii. 491, 577.
[4] Rogers, no. 57.
[5] Routh, *More and his Friends*, 107.
[6] Allen, iv. 576.

treasurership proper, supposed to attach to it.[1] Nevertheless, it was a very real step up. How heavy its duties were cannot be estimated. The undertreasurer put his name to the annual 'Declarations of the State of the Treasury' rendered by the Receipt, but the work of preparing them naturally fell to the officers under his control.[2] No doubt he checked the statements, for which he was responsible, before letting them go forward. On one occasion, Henry had to do without More's attendance because some settling of accounts required his presence at the Exchequer.[3] He was personally involved on several occasions when documents in the Treasury were signed out in the course of diplomatic negotiations.[4] Manifestly, he attended to the routine duties of the office. To all appearance, these were not overwhelming; and there is not the slightest sign that his tenure included anything of interest in the history of either Thomas More or the Exchequer.

Perhaps another of Erasmus's remarks explains why More was offered and accepted an office for which nothing in his previous career had qualified him. Erasmus told both Pace and Budé, in identical words, that More's new appointment carried a 'far from disagreeable salary'.[5] The salary was £173 6s. 8d., easily the second highest paid in the whole of the Exchequer. Only the lord treasurer's £365 exceeded it; even the chief baron got only £100. More's principal subordinate in the Receipt, the writer of the tallies who as auditor of the Receipt was from about 1554 onwards to take over the undertreasurer's functions, had to be satisfied with £41 13s. 4d.[6] The undertreasurership was thus an exceptionally valuable office – light duties, and a remarkably high salary. The stipend probably reflects the fact that, unlike the active officers of the Receipt, the undertreasurer was not in the way of earning additional regular fees. He performed no services for individual clients of the Exchequer, and the chances are that More got just his official salary from the office. But that was a real plum.

On 30 September 1525,[7] More exchanged the office for the chancellorship of the Duchy of Lancaster, an appointment much more suited

---

[1] Ibid. An unduly suspicious mind might suggest that Erasmus must have had his exaggerated information from More himself.

[2] More's first Declaration belongs to 1521–2, as was to be expected (PRO, E 407/67[3]). *Deputy Keeper's Reports*, ii, App. II, 196–7, errs in assigning this to the following year. It is a draft book which shows that the sections of the Declaration were supplied by sub-departments before being copied fair into the final version.

[3] *LP* iii. 3563 (26 November 1523). [4] *LP* iv. 345, 1245, 1526; Rogers, p. 249.

[5] Allen, iv. 506, 576. [6] E.g. *LP* iv, p. 870.

[7] The date of the patent under the Duchy seal (PRO, DL 28/6/23, which recites the document).

to his training and abilities since its main function was that of an equity judge. His predecessor, Sir Richard Wingfield, who on 22 July had died at Toledo, on embassy to Spain, had been one of the king's most trusted councillors.[1] The chancellor of the Duchy received a salary of £66 13s. 4d. and, in addition,'wages' at 6s. 8d. a day for the time spent attending the court of Duchy Chamber. This time had become conventionalized at eighty-four days in the year, making a further payment of £28.[2] In the year ending Michaelmas 1525, the salary – or rather, since he died in the middle of the year, £50 of it – went to Wingfield; More had none of it, and it was presumably deliberate economy that delayed his appointment to the beginning of the financial year. On the other hand, More got the £28 wages for the year preceding his entry upon office, which suggests that he possibly already carried out its duties during Wingfield's absence. From Michaelmas 1525 till he vacated the office in October 1529 he was paid the full £94 13s. 4d., a markedly smaller income than that which the undertreasurership had yielded. However, it is quite certain that the chancellor was entitled to a share in the Duchy's sealing fees; for these, no account survives. More's tenure of this office is at present being studied by Miss Margaret Hastings, and I will not therefore pursue the point here any further; but it is already clear that he attended to what for a change were quite arduous duties with his customary conscientiousness.

More obtained one other office in this decade when, in 1523, he was elected Speaker of the House of Commons, at this time effectively a government appointment. The truth is underlined by the well-known story of Wolsey's exasperation which, Roper tells us, made him regret the day that he had More made Speaker. As usual, he did his duty by securing the much-needed subsidy against strong opposition, and he made his mark in parliamentary history by the striking plea for freedom of speech which he included in his petition for privileges. The story is too familiar to need re-telling here.[3] In itself, however, the Speakership testifies only to his favour with king and cardinal, and to his general standing among the gentlemen of England. Like the rest of his offices, it makes no particular sense in terms of an official career. More acquired places as they happened to fall vacant and were be-

---

[1] R. Somerville, *History of the Duchy of Lancaster* (1953), i. 393. The date there given of More's appointment is out by a day.

[2] All this is based on the Duchy accounts for More's time: PRO, DL 28/6/23–5. That for 1525–6 is missing.

[3] Cf. Chambers, *More*, 200 f.

stowed on him, it seems, as marks of respect and by way of gradual elevation. None of them gave him administrative responsibilities of the first order, none bestowed political power, and he never held more than one at a time.

More's incoherent career in office underlines another strange aspect of his service to the Crown. He fits none of the standard categories of royal officers. There were essentially three ways in which men trained for such careers – the ways of the courtier, the bureaucrat and the lawyer. A man might rise either through the hierarchy of the king's personal entourage, or by working in the executive agencies, or as legal counsel (lay or spiritual) involved in protecting the king's rights in the courts. Of course, the three roads were not always perfectly separate: Sir Reginald Bray, for instance, who had been primarily an administrator, also attended to the work of a Crown lawyer and, at the dull Court of Henry VII, counted for something of a courtier too. Nevertheless, it is usually possible to assign the servants of Tudor kings to one of these three categories. With Thomas More this cannot be done. Henry liked to have him around, in which sense he was a courtier: on one occasion he could be listed in the establishment of the Chamber.[1] His work in Council and Exchequer placed him with the administrators. His training and previous experience, on the other hand, cast him most obviously for the role of legal counsel. If the courtier careerist may be exemplified (as indeed he may) by the likes of Sir William Compton or Sir Nicholas Carew, the highly unmilitary and subfusc Sir Thomas More hardly fits the stereotype. The greatest of the administrators to reach high office was Thomas Cromwell, as different from More in background and use of office as can be imagined, but quite typical of his category of royal servant. And as legal counsel, More was not even a patch on his father who ended up as a judge (the proper culmination of that career) and frequently sat in the king's Council in that capacity. 'Office' thus hardly describes Sir Thomas's place in the government of England.

On the other hand, office gave him a necessary income. The legend endows More with a total indifference to cash; the facts, more sensibly, show that he made a reasonable thing out of his service. If Roper is right in saying that on entering the king's service More gave up £400 a year from private practice, he needed some recompense. From Michaelmas 1517 to his arrest, at Easter 1534, he received the £100 annuity attached to his councillorship. He did very well to obtain the

[1] *LP* iv. 2972.

highly paid undertreasurership, and he is not likely to have lost much, if anything, by exchanging it for the Duchy. Unlike some, he recovered the costs of his embassies.[1] He does not figure largely as a recipient of patronage, but he is not absent from the list. Lands he never went after, though in May 1522 he did acquire the manor of South, in Kent, out of the Buckingham forfeiture,[2] and he obtained two wardships – the valuable one of Sir John Heron's heir Giles (whom he married to one of his daughters) and that of John Moreton, a lunatic.[3] His most valuable grant was a licence of June 1526 to export 1,000 woollen cloths, a characteristic gift to a courtier who was expected to exploit it by selling it on to an actual cloth-exporter, as More no doubt did.[4] These are not large pickings, but neither are they negligible. There are also signs that he got the windfalls and private pensions which came to men of influence. As soon as his standing at court was assured, he found himself 'retained of council' by Westminster Abbey, a body good at spotting winners; this notional employment was worth 20s. a year to him.[5] As one of the negotiators of the Treaty of the More (1525), he shared in the pensions bestowed by Francis I to the tune of 150 crowns (about £35) a year,[6] and once he was chancellor of the Duchy he got on the gravy train supplied by men of substance who wished to buy favour through regular retainers. In December 1527, Bishop West bestowed on him the keepership of Hatfield Park, a sinecure worth 40s. a year plus customary dues.[7] Lord Darcy also paid him 40s. a year, and the earl of Northumberland, desperate for friends, gave him the very large annual fee of £21.[8] Since none of More's private accounts survive, we cannot tell how many more people acted similarly. The system of attaching interest at the centre by modest annuities was general – Darcy and Northumberland happen to have left private record of their purposeful munificence. It is more likely that this represents a minimum than that no one else recognized More's standing in the usual way.

More's total income cannot be calculated, but he clearly did well enough. A subsidy assessment of 1527 puts him very high among those

---

[1] *LP* iii. 1775, a warrant of 18 Nov. 1521, to pay him a backlog of £80 arising out of two embassies abroad.   [2] *LP* iii. 2239.

[3] *LP* iii. 2900; iv. 314, 2817.   [4] *LP* iv. 2248.

[5] Westminster Abbey Muniments, Miscellany, Treasurer's Accounts, MS 23021, 23023 (1520–2). I owe this information to Dr D. J. Guth.

[6] *LP* iv. 3619.

[7] Ely Diocesan Records, Register West G/1/7, fo. 43. I owe this reference to Mrs Felicity Heal.   [8] *LP* iv. 2527, 3380.

included in the king's Chamber, a repository of acquisitive wealth. At £340 a year in lands and fees (in his case, of course, mostly fees since the councillor's annuity and the duchy stipend amounted to nearly £200 a year) he was topped only by such notoriously greedy courtiers as Compton, Sir Francis Bryan and Richard Weston.[1] No one wants to suggest that More was secretly avaricious: the fact that he evidently did not use his position to exploit the king's bounty more frequently testifies to his essential restraint. However, he was by no means above the rewards of office, a point he proved in connection with the Speakership. Wolsey may have worked off some annoyance on him, but immediately after the end of the session he wrote to the king, suggesting that More had deserved the customary reward of £100 paid in the past over and above the Speaker's fee, which amounted to the same sum. The cardinal added a touch of personal kindness: he was taking the initiative because Sir Thomas 'is not the most ready to speake and solicit his own cause'.[2] Sir Thomas was very properly grateful when the king complied, but he knew the situation well enough to urge Wolsey to write specially to the treasurer of the Chamber so that the money, allocated there, would actually be paid when he sent for it.[3] The Parliament had been a hard one, but £200 was not a bad reward for some seventeen weeks' work.[4]

Service to the king provided a good living, but that had not been More's purpose in entering it. The history of More's offices, and of his activities in them, shows that neither the good living nor the routine administration involved reflect his intentions in entering the Council – or the king's intentions in placing him there. What then was he doing, at court, in Council, and day by day? An analysis of the surviving evidence shows that two types of activity occupied him most fully. He was much engaged in diplomatic negotiations, and he spent a great deal of time acting as a kind of secretary to Henry.

Diplomacy had first revealed his capacity to the king, and he remained one of the men whom Wolsey employed in the conduct of his foreign policy. It is not, in fact, too easy to sort out More's various negotiations from the accounts given by his biographers, ancient or modern, but it seems clear that in this matter, as in his holding of office, he worked his way up from a relatively lowly position to one of modest prominence. At the start, he took part only in commercial

[1] *LP* iv. 2972.   [2] *StP* i. 124.
[3] *StP* ii. 127.
[4] [More also held a sinecurist share in the keepership of the exchanges (*Reform and Renewal*, 117–18), an office of unquestionable profit, though we do not know how much it yielded.]

negotiations, as became a citizen and official of London. His visit to Calais in August–November 1517, when he was very much the junior envoy by the side of Wingfield and Knight, was mainly concerned with a dispute between English and French merchants there.[1] In February 1518 an obscure business over wines, involving the Venetian ambassador, was about to be committed to Pace and himself, though it does not look as though anything came of this.[2] In 1520 he was of the company that went with the king to the Field of Cloth of Gold, an experience which surprisingly seems to have left no echo among the reminiscences of his public life which he scattered through his various writings; on this occasion, too, matters of commerce provided his only employment when he was in a commission appointed to negotiate with the merchants of the German Hanse.[3] The discussions adjourned to Bruges where he followed Wolsey as the cardinal moved from the serious business of the Calais junketings to the frivolities of alliance-making with Charles V. On the first occasion he was the third of four commissioners, on the second the second of six; on both he talked more than anyone else and clearly acted as spokesman – as the Germans noted, the Englishmen replied 'Moro verbum faciente'.[4] He impressed the other side by his use of 'the soft speech and calm demeanour customary among the English'.[5] But the commissioners were not very high-powered – men of business rather than men of ambassadorial rank – and so far, at least, More occupied a distinctly minor place in the diplomatic service. At the same time, the Hanseatic reports leave a clear impression of skill and reasonable success.

When his chance came he turned it down, begging to be excused from the embassy to Spain in 1525. There is no reason to believe Roper, who thought the offer a plot of Wolsey's to get rid of a displeasing critic;[6] if More had been interested in a normal diplomatic career, the appointment would have marked a genuine promotion and been welcome. As it was, his luck held at this time. His replacement, Sir Richard Wingfield, died incontinently upon arrival in Spain, and More not only inherited the chancellorship of the Duchy but stepped

---

[1] *LP* ii. 3371, 3634, 3639, 3743, 3750, 3772, App. 38.

[2] Ibid. 3976.

[3] *Hanserecesse von 1477–1500*, ed. D. Schäfer (Leipzig, 1905–), Docs. 332, 448, 452. The negotiations filled the days 19 July–12 Aug. 1520 and 12 Sept.–30 Nov. 1521; the commission for the second phase was dated 22 July 1521. Since this paper was written, J. M. Headley, in his introduction to his edition of More's *Responsio ad Lutherum* (New Haven, 1969) has noted the importance of this record for the history of Sir Thomas More.

[4] *Hanserecesse*, Doc. 448, para. 55.

[5] Ibid. Doc. 332, para. 33.   [6] Roper, 19–20.

into the vacancy among the king's ambassadorial personnel. His first major employment followed close upon his refusal of Spain when, with Nicholas West, bishop of Ely, he engaged in the discussions which resulted in the important Treaty of the More (August 1525) – the treaty by which Wolsey announced his shift from an imperial to a French alliance after the emperor's triumph at Pavia.[1] More alone signed the draft of the treaty, but when the formal instrument came to be signed his name appears last of a list of nine, to testify to his continued inferiority in the official hierarchy.[2] Henceforth he remained reasonably active in such matters, engaged in an agreement with the French envoy de Vaux in August 1525, as one of the English commissioners for the treaty of April 1527 which preceded Wolsey's embassy to France in July that year (an embassy which included More),[3] and finally joined with Tunstall as envoys to the negotiations at Cambrai in mid-1529 when the peace between Charles V and Francis I destroyed Wolsey's foreign policy and in effect the cardinal as well.[4] Cambrai was a diplomatic disaster for England and for Henry VIII, but the blame fell on Wolsey, not on the two diplomatists who had been appointed over his head. They fared well: Tunstall was, in 1530, promoted from London to Durham, and More, of course, returned from Cambrai to find himself pressed to accept the great seal. Roper reckoned that this offer of the highest office in the land in part reflected the king's satisfaction with Sir Thomas's skill in his recent embassy.[5] Perhaps: though no one, not even More, could or did save anything from the wreck of the Ladies' Peace, and (as we shall see) there may have been better reasons for this striking promotion.

Thus, from 1525 More came to be one of the leading experts in foreign policy, though never until the last occasion (when Wolsey no longer controlled appointments) given first-class standing. He achieved some prominence in the king's entourage when Henry received ambassadors: in November 1526 he welcomed the new orator of Venice with a prepared speech in reply to an address of which Wolsey had thoughtfully obtained a copy three days in advance, and six months later he was again in attendance when Secretary Dodieu had an audience with the king.[6] His knowledge of languages and of

---

[1] *LP* iv. 1525, 1470.
[2] Ibid. 1600(3), 1601. He was preceded not only by the two archbishops, two dukes, a marquess, and a bishop, but also by two professional politicians in Sir Henry Guildford and Sir William Fitzwilliam.
[3] Ibid. 3080, 3138, 3216, 3337.
[4] Ibid. 5732, 5744.
[5] Roper, 36–7.
[6] *LP* iv. 2638, p. 1399.

Europe, his reputation for uprightness and fair dealing,[1] his notorious ability to keep his own counsel, all seemed to cast him for the diplomatic service. It looks as though he was treated as something of a specialist in French affairs. But in all this activity he was never anything but an agent, and there is no sign at all that he influenced policy. Since most of his activities took place in England and none took him far afield, he never achieved that distance from Wolsey which forced policy-making decisions upon so many ambassadors at this time of slow communications. No doubt the king was pleased with him, but could he himself be pleased with this tedious and uninfluential position? His work in foreign affairs explains neither his continued service nor his sudden elevation, nor does it justify his reputation. Many others looked far more important. The real secret of More's career lies closer to the heart of government than this.

As the record makes very plain, from first entering the king's service More remained very near to the king's person. Erasmus's constant use of 'court' as equivalent to 'office' is in More's case absolutely correct. In fact, though he never held the principal secretaryship, he was effectively a second or substitute secretary.[2] Wolsey recognized this as early as August 1518 when he used Pace (principal secretary) and More indifferently and jointly to communicate the latest news to Henry.[3] Henry himself played a variant on this theme in the following February: wishing to bestow a preferment in Tunstal's gift on Pace, he told More, in the beneficiary's presence, to write the necessary letter of request.[4] From the middle of 1519 onwards, there survives a regular series of letters showing More as intermediary between cardinal and king. More, accompanying the king's progress, reports Henry's special favour to the city of Waterford (always loyal), relates Henry's pleasure at Wolsey's good health (which his highness is pleased to ascribe to his own advice to avoid medicine), conveys instructions for diplomatic despatches to be written by Wolsey, possibly with a sense of pleasure passes on Henry's smug reminder that he had always distrusted the cardinal of Sion and told Wolsey so – whereby 'he thinketh your Grace

[1] As early as 1518, Giustiniani commented on More's reputation for justice (*LP* ii. 3976).

[2] The only time that More was described as 'secretary' was during the Calais negotiations of 1520 when the Hanseatic envoys called him 'secretarius regius' (*Hanserecesse*, vii. 580). The official record of the final agreement called him only 'armiger', and the secretary of Danzig even at this time knew that Pace was secretary: to him More was, significantly, 'comes' [i.e. sheriff?] et civis Londinensis' (ibid. Docs. 336, 348). His promotion to the undertreasurership did not go unnoticed when the two sides met twelve months later (ibid. Doc. 448, para. 7).

[3] *LP* ii, App. 51.   [4] *LP* ii. 76.

will the bettre truste his coniecture hereafter'.[1] At this time, Secretary
Pace was in Germany and More had taken his place. The continental
travels of 1520–1 intervened, and More's standing with the king
grew, till in July 1521 Pace found himself writing to Wolsey:

The Kynge signifieth Your Grace that where as old men doith nowe decaye
gretly within thys Hys realme, hys mynde is to aqwaynte other yonge men
wyth hys grette affayris, and therfore he desyrith Your Grace to make Sir
Wyllyam Sandys, and Syr Thomas More, priveye to all such matiers as
your Grace schall treate at Calice.[2]

More was forty-three, Sandys at least thirty-five (and Wolsey
forty-six) – but still: Sir Thomas's star seemed ascendant.

Yet so far as the evidence goes, his standing remained much the same,
or at any rate, such growth of influence and importance as one can
discern was no quicker than would be justified by the familiarity and
experience which the years were bound to bring. The correspondence
with Wolsey resumes in 1521 and continues steadily for some three
years. All of it is distinctly official but intimate. More gets involved
in searching the rolls (in company with his father and Serjeant Brooke)
to find precedents for the appointment of the Deputy of Ireland;
fortunately, he can agree with Wolsey's view of the matter.[3] The
minute Pace is off again on diplomatic missions, More acts in effect
as secretary, getting the king's signature on papers, reading Wolsey's
letters to him, conveying his instructions. He apologizes for his failure
to send a copy of Henry's letter to the lord steward, being forced to
summarize it from memory because Henry had had it despatched
before it could be copied.[4] He takes the opportunity to flatter Wolsey
on his 'moost politiquely and moste prudently devised' letters,[5] and
gets even more expansive when conveying the king's deep appreciation of Wolsey's 'labor, studie, payn and travaile' in dealing so speedily
with matters 'whan the onely redyng therof held hym aboue twoo
howris'.[6] The letters frequently record effusive thanks: More knew
how Wolsey, always jealous and suspicious of the king's secretaries,
should be written to. Between August and November 1523, when
Wolsey was at Westminster, the king on progress, and Pace in Italy
about the succession to Pope Adrian VI, there survive thirteen
letters which display More as intermediary between the king and
his minister. But not one shows him doing anything more than

---

[1] Rogers, nos. 77–9.
[2] *StP* i. 20.
[3] *LP* iii. 1675, 1709, 1774 (Oct. 1521).
[4] Rogers, no. 109.
[5] Ibid. no. 110.
[6] Ibid. no. 117.

receive and transmit orders and information in both directions: there is no single note of independent intervention. He had shown more of that (in a very small matter) in October 1522 when ordered to write a sharp letter to the earl of Arundel on Sir Arthur Pole's behalf, he successfully suggested that a loving letter be tried first.[1]

After 1523 few such letters of More's survive, but Wolsey certainly continued to use him as his link with the king. More's constant attendance upon his sovereign was manifest, and Vives thought that thanks to it it would be easy to arrange a visit from Erasmus.[2] After all, as early as June 1522, thinking himself insufficiently attended, Henry had asked that others besides Sir Thomas be detached from Wolsey's entourage and attached to his own.[3] Nor did the elevation to the chancellorship of the Duchy make any immediate difference: More was still employed in reading Wolsey's letters to the king.[4] His standing, however, improved somewhat. In September 1526, Pace's successor William Knight (who eight years earlier had clearly outranked More) dared not presume to open letters addressed to Sir Thomas in the latter's temporary absence on the king's business, though More kindly returned the despatch and asked Knight to act for him.[5] He was now a man of weight whose opinion was required to execute Wolsey's design of a proclamation, though if he were not to return in time Sir William Fitzwilliam would do instead, as the only other 'of the hed officers' present.[6] But business had to go on, and a few days later Knight overcame his diffidence sufficiently to open a letter addressed to More so as to read it to the king.[7]

From 1519 to late 1526, More was in effect the king's spare secretary; thereafter he rarely acted in this capacity, and since the date roughly coincides with his promotion in office the evidence of the extant correspondence is likely to be correct, not the product of accidental survival. Certainly all this put him at the centre of affairs, in the secret activities of government. For instance, he got involved in one of Wolsey's more dubious manoeuvres when, in February 1525, the cardinal decided to intercept the imperial ambassador's despatches. The way Wolsey told it to Richard Sampson, then in Spain, a messenger had been arrested on suspicion by the ordinary watch at Brentford; the letters found on him were taken to the solicitor general, who passed them to More, who sent them next morning to Wolsey, then

---

[1] *LP* iii. 2636.   [2] *LP* iv. 1828.   [3] *LP* iii. 2317.
[4] *LP* iv. 2526.   [5] *StP* i. 176.   [6] Ibid. 178.
[7] Ibid. 181 f.

sitting in court in the Chancery. In Spain they said that More had been responsible for the illegal arrest, though in Brussels they affected to believe Wolsey's story of an accident.[1] On another occasion, More was accused by Knight of responsibility for a muddle: More told Knight that he was to attend on the Burgundian ambassadors but failed to add that they had already arrived, so that they had unsatisfactory entertainment.[2] It looks, in fact, as though Knight himself had been at fault and was passing the buck.

More was certainly one of the important cogs in the less formal sector of government – the circle round Henry and Wolsey involved in the execution of inner policy – and he was still, by the mid-twenties, one of the most regular attenders at court. His peculiar position, which owed nothing to office, was summed up in Wolsey's great Household ordinance of January 1526, the Eltham Ordinance, in which four persons were made permanent attenders upon his majesty (or at least two of them at any time): John Clerk, the bishop of Bath who had earlier been dean of the Chapel, the present dean (Richard Sampson), the secretary (William Knight), and Sir Thomas More.[3] These men formed the upper royal secretariat of the 1520s. The first three were clerics and official careerists, men specifically trained for the job and holding appropriate offices. More stood among them as a freak. Neither experience, nor appointment, nor ambition made him a natural among the king's secretaries. But there he was; and he must have owed a position, which cannot be called elevated or obviously agreeable to his cast of mind, to his personal qualities and the king's special desires. Yet, whether he liked the place or not, and whether in the eyes of the world it stood high or not, inevitably such proximity to the king and such constant involvement in great affairs carried influence.

How much influence? His friends thought from the first that it was great. Erasmus spoke of him as 'totus . . . aulicus, Regi semper assistens, cui est a secretis', as early as April 1518,[4] and Fisher in 1521, seeking his help in the interests of the University of Cambridge, was sure that someone 'Regi tam intimus effectus' would be able to do a lot.[5] In reply, More questioned his influence with the king with whom, he said, he could assuredly do little.[6] So far as the evidence goes, this assessment of the situation continued to be true right down to 1529.

---

[1] *LP* iv. 1083, 1154, 1237.   [2] Ibid. 2397.
[3] *Household Ordinances* (Soc. of Antiquaries, 1792), 160.
[4] Allen, iii. 286.   [5] Rogers, no. 104.
[6] Ibid. no. 105.

In all those exchanges between Henry, Wolsey and More, there is no sign whatsoever that Sir Thomas ever contributed to the making of policy or tried to get his views heard. As secretary and as diplomatist he was an executor, or a channel of communication, no more. He never even offered advice to Wolsey, and the only personal touches (his formal thanks to the cardinal apart) occurred when he was transmitting explicit instructions from the king. Even in matters of patronage, a sound barometer, his voice was rarely heard and more rarely effective. Perhaps he was too straightforward for such things. In 1528, as chancellor of the Duchy, he was about to lease some property to Roger Wigston which the king wanted to go to Sir John Russell. Although Wolsey was asked to intervene on Russell's behalf, More adhered to his first intention, and the king was displeased.[1]

Why, indeed, was the king ever pleased to have More so constantly near him? What did he want from him? We know from Roper that he enjoyed More's wit and conversation. But in 1529 he made him lord chancellor: that is, he demonstrated that he had gained a high opinion of More's sense, wisdom and competence. No doubt he had observed these qualities in More's discharge of his daily secretarial tasks, and no doubt he received advice from him in the course of their intimacy of which the record shows nothing. Yet it remains true that no sort of significant influence can be traced in the decade; there is not the slightest sign that policy, firmly in the hands of Wolsey and Henry, was ever affected by anything that More did or said, nor has anyone ever suggested that it was. He may have spoken in Council, but in those years the Council rarely met to discuss policy, and More's record of attendance (so far as the pitiful evidence goes) is not, as we have seen, impressive. The only tale remembered of words spoken in Council is of no importance: how he opposed Wolsey's plan to create a permanent office of constable in England and drew the cardinal's rude annoyance upon himself.[2] Ten years 'a secretis' to Henry VIII, and so little to show for it. Just what did More mean to his king?

The only specific thing in which More assisted Henry in a more than routine capacity touched the controversy with Luther. Henry certainly discussed his book on the sacraments with More, though there need no longer be any doubt that he wrote it himself; and it is possibly true that More – as he related later – tried to warn the king against too

---

[1] *LP* iv. 4562, 4604.
[2] T. Stapleton, *The Life and Illustrious Martyrdom of Sir Thomas More*, trans. P. E. Hallett (1928), 136 f.

unquestioning a support of papal claims.[1] Nevertheless, More was specifically commissioned to reply to Luther's answer, a task which enabled him to display unexpected powers of vituperation. These engagements underline what seems to me the outstanding and revealing fact: More was to be Henry's tame humanist. The king enjoyed his company and conversation, kept him close to his person, and when the occasion offered exploited his intellectual gifts and his pen. Henry liked to have intellectuals around him; he took pleasure in talking about their concerns, and his interest in books and writers was genuine, though haphazard. For obvious reasons he distrusted politicians and men on the make, however freely he employed them; when he wished to relax he turned to men like More and Cranmer who were not forever watching opportunities or plotting personal advancement. With such men, his relationship was more personal than usual: one may speak of friendship. But all the signs indicate that he rarely gave them political power or relied on their advice in affairs. The fact is notorious about Cranmer, and we have not been able to discover any evidence that More's close relations with Henry in the 1520s ever permitted him to influence policy. More was Henry's pledge of Renaissance excellence, his intellectual courtier.

That this position did not satisfy Sir Thomas is hardly surprising. He had accepted office, with all the time-consuming attendance at court and the likely corruption of public life which he let Hythloday describe in *Utopia*, because he had become convinced that the scholar must, if pressed, take his learning and wisdom into the service of princes. His career was very far from meteoric, and his offices remained unspectacular. And though he was always near the king, his tasks there seemed to be confined to reading and writing the royal correspondence; and however much he talked things over with Henry, he could not see that he produced any effect upon events. While Wolsey ruled, and with a man as devious as Henry VIII, little political profit could derive from such intimacy, and More's well-known assessment of the king's friendship shows how fully he understood the position. And clearly he fretted against these pointless occupations, until his energies found more congenial employment in his concern for what was happening in the Church. So far as I know, More showed no special interest in Luther and the new heresies until Henry asked him to write the refutation of Luther's attack on himself, but More's involvement thereafter is plainly documented. About 1525 he struggled

[1] J. J. Scarisbrick, *Henry VIII* (1968), 112; Rogers, no. 199 (p. 498).

for William Roper's soul during its temporary apostasy, his mind turned more and more to the threat of heresy, and in March 1528 he got Tunstall's licence to study heretical books.[1] Even before this, in January 1527, he conducted a most surprising police raid on the Steelyard in search of vernacular bibles and Lutheran writings; he led the large company which broke in upon the Germans after supper, allegedly by Wolsey's orders, and when nothing incriminating was found he took the trouble to return next day to issue ominously worded demands for the surrender of anything hidden.[2] He was turning to new tasks and equipping himself for them. The humanist scholar had been frustrated by his decision to enter the royal service; the royal servant by his master's manifest refusal to go beyond personal friendship to political dependence. A man of More's stature could hardly rest content with secretarying for the king, talking to second-rank envoys, giving judgment in the Duchy court, and amusing Henry's leisure hours. Heresy, as it were, came to the rescue, and from late 1528 onwards More presented himself to the world as England's leading controversialist against Luther and Luther's English followers.

Of course, Moore's horror of heresy and his conviction that it needed to be exterminated were perfectly genuine. But so was his need for employment. He had sacrificed much in 1517 when he had accepted the king's invitation to become a councillor, as the fame and the disapproval of Erasmus were ever present to remind him. Was he to have given up the pleasures of scholarship and the family life he loved for the dust and ashes of a favourite's place without influence? Perhaps the More of tradition would not have worried over this sort of thing, or would simply have sought better uses for his time. The More of tradition bore all the accidents of fortune with a balanced, stoical amusement and prepared himself for the sainthood which posterity was to bestow. But this More of tradition seems to me some distance from the real More of the 1520s.

What do we really know about Thomas More, at least before those last years when everything, including the man, had changed? We have the testimony of his circle of learned friends, which is obviously perfectly sound so far as it goes; and we have the testimony of William Roper, manifestly in awe of his formidable father-in-law even while he loved him, who wrote his book late in life and with both eyes

[1] Chambers, *More*, 186 f., 254.

[2] *Hanserecesse*, ix. 402 f. The episode is discussed, not very satisfactorily, by M. E. Kronenberg, 'A printed letter of the London Hanse Merchants, 3 March 1526,' *Publications of the Oxford Bibliog. Soc.* new series, I (1947), 25–32. For the investigation see *LP* iv. 1962.

fixed firmly on the need to present the figure of human perfection which More's terrible end demanded. Yet there is also evidence that does not fit the conventional picture too well. That More had the instincts of a scholar and loved the company of scholars is surely true, but it does not seem to me that he was one with Erasmus and Budé, Reuchlin and Lefèvre; at least, not until the needs of controversy turned him into a competent theologian. Rather was he that familiar figure, the man of affairs who was also a man of letters, though unlike most of his kind he produced one work of genius. Very likely he was aware of the distinction, for his reaction to attacks by better scholars and worse men was characteristically petulant and fierce. The amount of touchy vanity which he displayed in his quarrel with Germain de Brie astonished Miss Routh and – more important – distressed Erasmus.[1] As William Ross, defending Henry VIII against Luther, he matched Dr Martin in violence of abuse, a remarkable achievement. His controversial manners were bad: in his exchanges with Tyndale, he generally proved the more scurrilous of the two, and he was savage to St German who had not been savage at all.[2] The tone of his writing changed only at the end: the *Apology* suggests that he was recovering his balance, and the *Dialogue of Comfort* testifies to the serenity which came to him in his last adversity. But during his career as a controversialist he was one of the most intolerant and unfair of writers. Nor will it do to pass this off with remarks about the customs of the age; More did not introduce this sort of thing into the disputes of the day, but he displayed more of it than most and at no time troubled himself about such things as scholarly caution, chivalrous moderation, or (as his treatment of the Hunne case shows) even elementary truthfulness.

Moreover, these excesses seem to reflect traits not often remarked upon. Centuries of adulation have accustomed us to regard his treatment of Dame Alice as affectionate, and so, up to a point, it was. But it was also mildly contemptuous, and he did not scruple to print tales about women which everybody knew were aimed at her. He did not disguise his conviction that his second wife was a bit of a fool. The manner in which he singled out his daughters for examples of female intelligence cannot have been anything but galling to their stepmother, especially when his opinion of her was not expressed only by implication. Yet, in truth, every time that we learn of an argument between

[1] Routh, *More and his Friends*, 101.
[2] For More's controversial writings cf. Rainer Pineas, *Thomas More and Tudor Polemics* (Bloomington, Ind., 1968).

them, it seems to me that she had sense and unselfishness on her side. Or take the stories of More's wit, More the jester. In this it is certainly hard to separate truth from invention, and much may well have been ascribed to him that he never said. Yet what his early biographers reported of him was, presumably, what they thought was his and wished people to believe of one they admired – and some of the tales are disconcerting. The well-known story of the cutpurse and the justice, More's comment on a bad book turned from prose to verse ('now it hath at least some rime, no reason'), his remarks about small women, and the lesson he taught Ann Cresacre when he thought her too fond of jewels, all have in common a rather unpleasing superiority to the weaknesses of lesser mortals and a touch of hard severity.[1] Perhaps none of these are authentic, though it is hard to see why the last (and worst) should not be, but it should be remembered that More's jests annoyed his contemporaries, as Hall testified.[2] Witty persons make enemies, and not without reason. There is one odd touch about Sir Thomas's wit: a preference for the rather crude in the 'merry tales' with which he tried to leaven the lump of controversy.[3] On two hardly apposite occasions, his similes reveal a preoccupation with virginity and defloration which is a little strange and recalls his insistence (in *Utopia*) that young men and women must inspect one another naked before venturing on marriage. When he rebuked the three bishops who tried to persuade him to attend Anne Boleyn's coronation More was right, but by what twist did the story of Sejanus's daughter (to be deflowered so that her virginity should not stand in the way of her execution for a capital offence) jump to his mind?[4] It does not really make the point he was after. And why, in explaining his failure to dedicate *Utopia* to Wolsey, should he have described Peter Giles's action in getting the work published at Louvain as a ravishing of the book's maidenhead?[5] I am not, I hope, being prissy: I am trying to get at the More inside the plaster statue. The point is that his humour ran readily upon such themes, and only those who tend to equate the early sixteenth century with Rabelais would suppose that in this he was typical rather than exceptional.

There is no question here of writing Sir Thomas down. It is so

[1] Ro. Ba., *The Lyfe of Syr Thomas More, Sometymes Chancellor of England*, ed. E. B. Hitchcock and P. E. Hallett (E.E.T.S. 1950), 107 f., 129.

[2] Hall, *Chronicle*, 817: 'it semed to them that best knew him, that he thought nothing to be wel spoken except he had ministered some mocke in the communication'.

[3] Pineas, *Polemics*, 92 f.

[4] Roper, 57–9.   [5] Rogers, no. 32.

difficult to see past the image erected by familial and devotional piety that every scrap of evidence needs to be carefully considered. And I wish to suggest that the More of the 1520s, More the councillor, was a man aware of his powers, anxious to put them to practical use, capable of vanity and not always able to conceal his justified sense of intellectual superiority, ready enough to ride opponents down. To so outstanding a mind – possibly a poor politician but unquestionably capable of first-class statesmanship – the decade must have been most frustrating. He had office, he had profit, he had the ear and friendship of the king, and his ambitions did sufficiently tend that way to make such things not disagreeable. People respected his standing and envied him Henry's favour. But that he saw through the hollowness of friendship without influence, we know; nor would he forget Erasmus's severe regret that he was lost to letters. On top of this came his growing obsession with the dangers to the Church and the faith which was forcing him to defend an institution that in his younger days he had been ready enough to criticize. And through it all he saw Wolsey pursue policies of war and empty grandeur which went counter to everything he believed in, while aware that the public and his friends were bound to associate him with these distasteful proceedings just because he seemed so much more influential than he was. Surely, More was throughout in a very false position, and he may well have re-read Hythloday's warnings against service to princes with a deepening regret derived from growing experience.

Yet in the end one more chance offered, all of a sudden. It, too, was flawed. Wolsey's fall, which led to More's elevation, arose from events in which More took his stand against the king's desires. Wolsey was removed not because he had failed in the sense in which More thought he had failed, but because he had not succeeded in the one thing that More did not want to see successfully accomplished. Once again his position was false. He owed the chancellorship to no previous power in Council but rather, ironically, his very lack of power: the king simply did not associate him with the fallen regime. No one seems ever to have commented on the very odd scene at the beginning of his tenure of office when the Duke of Norfolk, by special command, publicly presented him with much commendation as worthy of his new station.[1] This was so far from being common form that I know of no other single instance; clearly More's appointment was thought to be surprising, and the new chancellor needed introducing to a public

[1] Roper, 39.

barely aware of him. Henry thought of him as a skilful diplomat, an agreeable companion, a competent secretary, and possibly as a wise councillor whose instincts had now proven accurate. Above all, he clearly respected his abilities and regarded him as a friend, so much so that he was willing, for the time being, to let him contract out of the whole business of the divorce. No doubt he hoped in course of time to bring his obstinate friend round, but chiefly he, who prided himself on his knowledge of men, wanted this great man in high office. As he often did, he misjudged his man; himself so passionately convinced of the rightness of the divorce, he had lost the capacity to see that others might as firmly in conscience regard it as wrong. And he appears to have forgotten that part of More's charm for him was the very fact that he had never played the politician.

More, no doubt, accepted the great seal in part because it was difficult to resist Henry's pressure, but there is more to it than that. It is hagiography, not history or biography, to suppose that he must have been totally immune to the sensation of satisfied ambition which elevation of this kind would call forth in most people. More to the point, the offer came really as the culmination of the career on which he had entered – less reluctantly than is commonly thought – some twelve years earlier. To have refused now would not only have offended one who claimed to be a friend but would surely also have stultified that dozen years. If he had endured so long in the teeth of all the frustration and regret which the Wolsey regime imposed on him, was he to retire at the very moment when the years of waiting seemed about to pay off after all, when power and influence were suddenly and unexpectedly offered? Or, to put it another way, what right had he to consider his private comfort and the probability of a very difficult time when issues existed (the king's marriage, the future of the Church, heresy) on which he felt strongly and in which he must at least attempt to avert disaster? How disastrous the outcome would be for him personally he could not have fully foreseen; for one thing, he had a promise that the pressure of the last two years to underwrite the king's proceedings would not continue, and for another, the lengths to which Henry was capable of going when he found himself opposed by one whom he had honoured with his friendship had not so far become apparent.

More explained his reasons for taking office in the speech with which he opened the Parliament of 1529.[1] He has often offended his partisans

---

[1] Hall, *Chronicle*, 764.

by the tone he used about Wolsey, the 'great wether' who had led the king's flock astray, though in fact he was only following through, in the rhetorician's fashion, a metaphor on which he had embarked when he used the hackneyed description of King Henry as shepherd of his people. The essential point in his speech came at the start when he announced a reform programme. He declared the existing laws insufficient and out of date, and he alluded to the human frailty which had produced 'new enormities . . . amongest the people' for which laws did not yet exist. Though we must remember that we have only Hall's summary of the speech, it is quite clear that reform of the realm was foremost in the chancellor's mind, and from his mouth these were more than platitudes. The author of *Utopia*, the enemy of heretics who had witnessed Wolsey's negligent failure to arrest the decline of the Church, had arrived at a point where he might think himself able to carry some of his ideas into practice. His answer to Hythloday might yet be justified. After all, one of the burgesses who listened to him from beyond the bar of the House was before very long to use the position of Henry's chief minister to reform state and Church and reconstruct the commonwealth.

More, as we know, never got his chance. The humanist in power was to be as frustrated by events as the humanist working his way up had been by the cardinal's monopoly of power. In a way, of course, it was no fault of his that he so regularly found himself out of step and in a false position. The time was, for him, as thoroughly out of joint as it was convenient to Thomas Cromwell. Nor was More ever the conventional scholar unable to understand the reality of politics and power. He never made Reginald Pole's mistake of supposing that book-learning enables a man to teach the princes of this world their business. Indeed, if the analysis here put forward is anything like correct, More was not at all the scholar foolishly venturing into affairs. He was the trained common lawyer – possessed, that is, of a usual training for public life – with the ambitions and experiences of his kind and his station in life, fully aware (as his business letters to Wolsey show) what public service meant. If we knew nothing of *Utopia* or Erasmus, we should think More perfectly well placed in the company of such men as Dr William Knight or Sir Brian Tuke. He was a thoroughly competent civil servant and councillor: let there be no mistake about this. But he was trying to serve at a time when his fundamental ideas stood in opposition to the fundamental desires of those in power. We may well prefer the *pax christiana* to the effects of Wolsey's foreign policy.

In the struggle between the chancellor's conscience and the king's we may well award the palm to the first. But none of this alters the falsity of More's situation. The king's good servant throughout made the mistake of supposing that Henry wanted the service he was anxious to give, and not the service which would suit the king's very different purpose. In the last analysis, Hythloday was right.

SIR THOMAS MORE AND THE
OPPOSITION TO HENRY VIII*

In considering Thomas More, few historians seem able to forget
the end of the story. That More died a victim of Henry VIII, a martyr
to his conscience and a defender of the papal supremacy, is, of course,
perfectly true, but it is exceedingly rash to suppose that his whole life,
or even the last few years of it, was simply a preparation for the tragic
outcome.

From about the middle of 1532 More certainly lived in a retirement in which he meant to prepare himself for his death, though
not necessarily for one by violence; and from April 1534 he was in
the Tower and knew what the end must be. But before that he had
spent two and a half years of his life as lord chancellor, the king's
highest officer and a leading member of the royal Council, at a time
when Henry was manifestly striving for purposes that More detested.
How could he justify holding office at all? What line did he take over
the politics of those years? This part of his life occupies amazingly little
space in the standard accounts.

More's acceptance of the chancellorship has been a stumbling block
to his biographers. On Wolsey's fall it was clear to all men in high
places that the king's infatuation for Anne Boleyn was about to
unleash drastic events, full of danger for the Church and likely to
produce bitter clashes between the *regnum* and the *sacerdotium*.[1] More
had already made it plain that he thought the Aragon marriage valid
and would not be able to support Henry's endeavours to have it
annulled. Yet he took office. Bridgett supposed that he did not do so
until he had made sure of respect for his scruples of conscience,[2] and
even Chambers suggested that he obtained some sort of promise before
the appointment.[3] However, according to More himself, the king did
not explicitly grant him liberty to dissent on the issue of the Divorce

---

* [*BIHR* 41 (1968), pp. 19–34] reprinted with slight editorial changes from *Moreana:
Bulletin Thomas More*, 15–16 (Festschrift E. F. Rogers), 285 ff., by kind permission of the
editor, Father Germain Marc'hadour.
[1] Chambers, *More*, 236, is right to say: 'More knew quite well what was coming.'
[2] T. E. Bridgett, *Life and Writings of Sir Thomas More* (1891), 225.
[3] Chambers, *More*, 236.

until after he had made him chancellor,[1] and this is also what Roper understood to be the truth.[2] There is no evidence at all that More had such a promise in his pocket when he became chancellor; as far as we know, he entered office aware that he would still be called upon to involve himself in the burning question of the day.

That the decision to accept was not an easy one seems likely. Harpsfield, from whom the tradition of More's reluctance to take the great seal derives, offers no evidence, and Roper gives no hint of it.[3] Since Roper was living in More's household at the time, his silence should perhaps carry more weight than William Rastell's later recollection that More refused, made the king angry, and then was much laboured to; still, the story may be true, being not improbable in itself, though one should be a little more careful of Rastell's fragmentary notes than scholars have been.[4] From More himself we have only the short letter in which he told Erasmus what had happened; this does contain a possible hint that he was submitting to pressure.[5] But, as we shall see, other phrases in the letter are more interesting. Hall knew that the succession to Wolsey caused a good deal of difficulty; long discussions in Council turned on the choice of a layman, and in the end More was appointed.[6] But if there were difficulties it is too simple and hardly necessary to suppose that they were caused by More's inclination to refuse. If the great seal was on no account to go to a spiritual man, as Hall heard, More was the obvious man to choose: a trained lawyer, a man of European reputation and wide experience of affairs, chancellor of the Duchy and for several years one of the king's most intimate councillors. Erasmus understood that even Wolsey, who feared and hated More, regarded him as the only man in the kingdom fit for the office.[7] Yet to appoint at this juncture a man who had already declared his opposition to the Divorce must surely have given Henry pause and troubled the Council. The obviously qualified man was also politically one of the least suitable, whether he wanted the appointment or not.

In the end, the king decided to take the risk, and More decided to

[1] *St Thomas More: Selected Letters*, ed. E. F. Rogers (New Haven, 1961), 209.
[2] Roper, 224.
[3] Nicholas Harpsfield, *The Life and Death of Sir Thomas More*, ed. E. V. Hitchcock and R. W. Chambers (E.E.T.S., 1932), 51. Roper (p. 219) mentions only More's formal disabling speech, after the appointment was in effect settled.
[4] 'The Rastell Fragments' (printed in Harpsfield), 222. The material in the fragments was collected for a life of Fisher and deals only incidentally with More.
[5] Allen, viii. 294: 'Ego me rebus accommodo . . ..'
[6] Hall, *Chronicle*, 761.   [7] Allen, x. 136, 180.

submit to the royal pressure. What had either of them in mind? Very likely, as has often enough been suggested, Henry hoped to convert an opponent into a very useful ally; the king had a high opinion of his powers of persuasion and a low one of people's consciences, a subject on which he was something of an expert. As for More, historians have produced various conjectures: he thought he could be useful to the causes he valued;[1] he came in on a wave of Erasmian rejoicing at the prospect of serious reform in the Church;[2] he meant to confine himself to the professional judicial duties of a lord chancellor;[3] he had no choice because, once he had entered the royal service, he was bound to accept whatever was offered.[4] This last is not true; from Erasmus and More himself downward, contemporaries clearly supposed that though actual refusal might be difficult it was not impossible. The third explanation reveals some misunderstanding of what the professional duties of the king's leading officer and councillor were; no Tudor lord chancellor, presiding in Chancery, Star Chamber and House of Lords, and prominent at the Council table, could have thought of confining himself to the hearing of pleas. Incidentally, it is worth notice that except for a few anecdotes of Roper's nothing is so far known about More's much-praised work in the Chancery.

That leaves the first two explanations. Dr McConica rather over-states his case for an 'Erasmian' domination of Henry VIII's policy in the years after Wolsey's fall; writings are not the same thing as actions, and the things done rather than dreamed of reflect a popular anti-clericalism diplomatically exploited by the king's policy much more than they embody a humanist reform programme. But that Erasmus himself was pleased to see his friend in the place of power is true enough, and it would indeed have been odd if More had not expected the office to enable him to exercise some influence on the course of events. It is worth remembering that Chapuys' first reaction to the news of the appointment was to rejoice because this 'upright and learned man' was also reckoned 'a good servant of the Queen' (Catherine).[5] And what did More tell Erasmus? That he would energetically endeavour to fulfil the excessive hopes entertained by the king of his unworthy self, with all the faith and readiness at his disposal.[6] Common form perhaps, or else a hint essentially ironic, in the More

---

[1] E.g. A. Cecil, *A Portrait of Thomas More, Scholar, Statesman, Saint* (1937), 201.
[2] J. K. McConica, *English Humanists and Reformation Politics* (Oxford, 1965), ch. 5.
[3] C. Hollis, *Sir Thomas More* (1934), 157.
[4] Chambers, *More*, 236.
[5] *LP* iv. 6026.   [6] Allen, viii. 294.

manner, in its implications: the king was not the only man to entertain hopes of More.

If More's part in the years 1529–32 is to be understood, two particular problems need to be investigated: his attitude to heresy and his relations with the Reformation Parliament. Between them, they illumine More's own view of the political circumstances of the day – the action these demanded and the way in which they could be exploited.

It is necessary to be very clear about More's reaction to the changes in religion which he saw all around him. No doubt, the more scurrilous stories of his personal ill-treatment of accused heretics have been properly buried,[1] but that is not to make him into a tolerant liberal. Tolerance he would have abominated as treason to God; it was one of his objections to Wolsey that the cardinal had ignored the dangers to the faith.[2] All the evidence goes to show that More hated heresy with a real, even an exceptional, passion. 'Odit ille', wrote Erasmus in 1532, explaining More to one who did not know him, 'seditiosa dogmata'; of that he had never made any secret.[3] To Hall's parenthetical disgust, he 'leaned much to the spiritual men's part in all causes'.[4] Even the letter in which More told Erasmus of his resignation goes out of its way to lament the spread of the new sects.[5] Rastell recalled, perhaps correctly, that the more energetic pursuit of heretical teaching after 1531 resulted from representations made by More and the bishops.[6] While Dr McConica's Erasmian humanists were busy bringing out works calling for reform in the Church, More got ever more deeply into his controversy with Tyndale in which he increasingly defended a total orthodoxy. The More of the early 1530s can hardly any longer be called an Erasmian, and Dr McConica cannot in fact link him with the activities of the 'party' he has tried to document. The More of the *Confutation* may still be able to see, as the author of *Utopia* so clearly did, that not all is well with the old Church, but he is desperately certain that, as things are, reform can lead only to destruction and must be resisted. The only humanist in high places disappointed not only the king's hopes but also those of the Christian humanists.

It would surely have been strange if a man so aware of the pressing

---

[1] E.g. Chambers, *More*, 274 ff.
[2] More's attack on Wolsey (Hall, *Chronicle*, 764) included references to 'new enormities' among the people for which no law had been made, a conventional term of the time for divagations in religion.
[3] Allen, x. 138.
[4] Hall, *Chronicle*, 771.
[5] Allen, x. 33–4.
[6] Harpsfield, *More*, 223.

dangers of heresy had not used his high office to prevent disaster. Of course, he could not himself try heretics, a matter for the courts Christian; Chambers's argument that no heretics were burned in the diocese of London while More had influence appears to me irrelevant to an assessment of More's actions, and Erasmus was even more off the beam when he praised More for not condemning anyone to death for religion.[1] No lord chancellor [as such] has ever had the opportunity of pronouncing the death sentence on anyone.[2] However, he could arrest men, investigate their opinions, and hold them for trial by the spiritual arm; and this he seems to have done, even by his own admission, to a degree quite unknown among the king's lay councillors before or after. Perhaps a little more credence should be given than has of late been fashionable to the reports which reached Erasmus that More's successor was releasing numbers of 'Lutherans' imprisoned by his predecessor.[3] The numbers varied – forty perhaps, or only twenty – and rumours are not evidence. Yet there is evidence of More's determined persecution of heretics which has been too lightly written off. Thus a London merchant, Thomas Patmer, was in 1531 imprisoned by the bishop of London, and when his servant, John Stanton, tried to raise the matter in Parliament, More (he claimed) intervened to attack him with false accusations as a favourer of heresy.[4] Patmer, no doubt, was no victim of More's; Stanton did not assert anything like that, and if Audley released imprisoned heretics in 1532 Patmer would not appear to have been among them.[5] What matters is that More automatically sprang to the defence of the bishop's action and assumed the petitioner to be a tainted heretic.

There is also the case of John Field whose petition to Audley and the Council was first unearthed and used by Froude.[6] Field claimed to have been detained by More at Chelsea for eighteen days from 7 January 1530, securing his release only after he had bound himself to appear in the Star Chamber on Candlemas next. The outcome of that appearance was more than two years in the Fleet, in conditions of special hardship, without trial or knowledge of why he was held. On Palm Sunday (24 March) 1532 he was 'under our said sovereign's command-

---

[1] Chambers, *More*, 279 ff.; Allen, x. 138.

[2] 'Quum habeat ius occidendi', said Erasmus; but More had no such right.

[3] Allen, x. 116, 135, 180.

[4] *LP* v. 982.   [5] *LP* vi. 573.

[6] PRO, SP 1/78/246-7: cf. J. A. Froude, *History of England from the Fall of Wolsey to the Defeat of the Spanish Armada* (12 vols., 1872), i. 556-9. Froude's transcript contains his usual quota of unimportant errors.

ment and Sir Thomas More's' transferred to the Marshalsea, the officers of the Fleet having first robbed him of his money – as they said, to obtain their fees. In the Marshalsea he 'fell sick of the house sickness' and on Whit Monday (20 May) was 'carried out on[1] four men's backs' with more loss of money to the keeper there. However, he recovered, which fact came to More's ears. Although More 'went out of his said office of the chancellorship about the time your bedeman was carried out of prison', he made it his business through the services of the bishops of Winchester and London ('as your bedeman heard say') to persuade the duke of Norfolk to have Field put back in gaol. He was again released in October, on sureties, and for a year had been giving attendance every day of every term, as his bond demanded. Now he asked for his discharge and the restoration of his lost property. As happens so often in the records of this time, nothing else is known of this case.[2] But the ease with which it has been brushed aside will hardly do. The circumstantial detail, the absence of any explicit animus against More (a fallen minister and easy target), the accurate dating of More's resignation, and the care taken to qualify one detail which the petitioner could know only by hearsay, all carry a good deal of conviction.

Against this, it has been urged that More himself answered all such charges when he spoke, in the *Apology*, of accusers who had been investigated by the king's Council and found to be liars.[3] But should More's word be taken without question on points like these? However truthful a man he may have been, he could surely have been mistaken. Unfortunately there is no evidence except his work that charges of this kind were after his fall dismissed in the manner related

---

[1] MS: of.

[2] Both *LP* and A. I. Taft, in his edition of the *Apologye of Syr Thomas More Knyght* (E.E.T.S., 1930), 328 ff., identify this John Field with one who petitioned Cromwell in Nov. 1536 (or a later year) for his release (*LP* xi. 1164). But even if the two Fields are the same man, the later imprisonment cannot be linked with the former. Field then spoke of having spent nearly three years in the Counter: i.e. at some point he must have been newly jailed, and in a different prison, since on the earlier occasion he was certainly free for a year from Oct. 1532. The second petition deals manifestly with some non-religious offence; the first, despite Taft's unconvincing doubts, concerned a point of the faith since Field's books were investigated. The tone of the second petition, acknowledging that 'such grievous complaint is made against me that they to whom God has given authority to punish offences may no less do of justice than keep me in prison until the time of judgment', is very different from that of the first. If only one John Field (a common enough name) is involved in these two cases he may be thought accident-prone, but his later troubles are quite clearly distinct from his earlier and cannot be used, as Taft tries to do, to explain them away.

[3] Bridgett, *More*, 270; Chambers, *More*, 277.

by him, and what he himself has to say is less straightforward than his apologists have supposed. He mentions one accuser by name, Thomas Phillips, and what he offers in his own defence is surely a trifle peculiar. Phillips, he says, had strongly reminded him of Richard Hunne (some sixteen years earlier), and because he feared another suicide in the bishop's prison with all the consequences that he remembered from 1514 he had transferred him to the Tower, not the proper place for suspected heretics.[1] At its best, such action was irregular and unwise. But, More claims, the king had investigated the charge and absolved his late chancellor, telling Phillips he had been lucky to get away with so little. If this is true, it is a case of hard words breaking no bones: Phillips did well for himself thereafter and is found in 1538 as a gaoler in the Tower who converted Sir Nicholas Carew on the eve of his execution by introducing him to the Bible in English.[2] Clearly he was a heretic; clearly he was troubled by More's personal intervention; clearly he was liberated after More's departure from the scene. As for Field, the supposition that More had dealt with his accusation, too, will not do. More does not mention him by name, and what he has to say about unnamed accusers does not fit the case. The investigations of this clamour which, he says, resulted in sharp rebukes for the accusers dealt (according to More's explicit assertion) with complaints against the bishops and not against himself. But Field said nothing of bishops and confined his attack to the late lord chancellor. John Foxe may have collected too many exaggerated stories of More's doings, but he was right enough in his assessment of the chancellor's share in the seeking out of heresy.

Indeed, it would be quite wrong to 'acquit' More of action against heresy: he thought it his duty to use his place in the defence of the true religion. If Field may be trusted – and the weight of probability is in his favour – More went a very long way in his pursuit of suspects. All this agrees well with his known beliefs and his frequent bitter words. There is every reason to think that among the purposes he hoped to fulfil when he accepted office he put high the protection of the Church against its heretical enemies.

In this, however, he was not at all out of step with the official policy of those years. At the time, in fact, both king and Commons repeatedly

---

[1] *The Workes of Sir Thomas More, Knyght . . . written by him in the Englysh tonge* (London, 1557), 905–6. The danger of suicide was the greater because a cousin of Phillips's called Holy John had drowned himself in a well when accused of heresy!

[2] Hall, *Chronicle*, 827. Taft, who discussed Phillips's case in his edition of the *Apologye* (pp. 320 ff.), missed this revealing point.

demonstrated their orthodoxy in order to rebut the charge that their actions against clergy and pope were equal to heresy.[1] More was more zealous and almost certainly more sincere than most, but as an enemy of heresy he had, during his years as chancellor, nothing to apprehend from king or Council. Matters stood differently when it came to the defence of the Church against political attack, to the cause of the Divorce and the powers of the papacy. On all these, we know, Thomas More entirely disliked the progress of Henry's policy; but did he confine his disagreement to the privacy of his own mind or even to mere expressions of views?

More's recorded official actions in the Parliament, where events took place, are both few and unexceptionable: not so few as to hide his standing in the government, but sufficiently unexceptionable to have troubled the hagiographers. Thus he opened the proceedings of the 1529 session with his notorious attack on Wolsey, and whether one thinks (improbably) that he was here 'preaching to Henry VIII',[2] or (as is much more likely) 'that he spoke for all who were sympathetic with the need for reform',[3] it is clear that he was crossing official t's, not official lines. Attacking Wolsey in November 1529 would come well to his successor who had long regarded the cardinal as a major disaster; it would be agreeable to the king who wanted to justify to himself his rejection of a faithful old friend and servant; and it would delight most of the lords assembled to hear the speech. More's next known appearance in Parliament presents greater difficulties. In 1531 it was decided to silence rumour and press the king's views by presenting to both Houses of Parliament the opinions in favour of Henry's case that had been gathered from various universities. The day chosen was 30 March, and the man made responsible was the lord chancellor.[4] He started in the Lords, explaining how untrue it was that the king was seeking his divorce for the love of some woman and not out of a scruple of conscience; then he asked the clerk to read the opinions. Catherine's partisans protested, and Norfolk intervened to the effect that the king had sent the papers for information, not debate. Nevertheless, someone managed to ask More what he himself thought, to

---

[1] E.g. the defence of orthodoxy by an attack on heretical books had to wait until the king's policy had begun to turn against Rome (*Tudor Royal Proclamations*, i. 193 ff. The correct date of ibid. no. 122 is also 1530). Or cf. the Commons' reaction in 1529 to Fisher's charges of heresy (Hall, *Chronicle*, 766).

[2] Chambers, *More*, 242.

[3] McConica, *English Humanists*, 107.

[4] Chapuys (*LP* v. 171) and Hall (*Chronicle*, 775 ff.) report in very similar terms.

which the chancellor allegedly replied only that he had often enough told the king his views. He then led a deputation of peers to the Commons where he repeated the performance. After the reading of the opinions he added:

Now you of this Common House may report what you have seen and heard, and then all men shall openly perceive that the King hath not attempted this matter of will or pleasure, as some strangers report, but only for the discharge of his conscience and surety of the succession of his realm. This is the cause of our repair hither to you, and now we will depart.

Chapuys heard that the bishops of London and Lincoln (both well known as conservatives) also spoke in the king's defence, and that the Commons received everything in silence.

Roper must be right in saying that More did all this 'at the King's request', but how true is it that he 'was not showing of what mind himself was therein'?[1] As reported, his words were chosen with care. He did not commit himself on the justice of the king's cause; the only thing he himself supported was the king's claim to be acting for serious reasons of conscience and policy. He may have believed this, as indeed Henry himself believed it. No one could have used his remarks against him. But his omissions must surely have been noted: not a word from him to suggest that the opinions to be read out were in fact the truth. Yet as far as the less subtle were concerned, he had unquestionably associated himself with the king's policy, and while his careful abstention from any expression of personal views may have reassured his friends (and alerted his enemies) it cannot have satisfied More himself. He was in an impossible position, and it is no wonder that rumours about his intention to resign had circulated at the beginning of the session.[2] While he held the highest office in the state he was bound to come into contact with great affairs, in Council and publicly in Parliament, and no gracious concession, sincere or not,[3] to his conscience could insulate him against the contagion. By 1531 he could not really both serve Henry as lord chancellor and also maintain his

[1] Roper, 225.　　　　　　　　　　[2] *LP* v. 112.

[3] It seems to have been sincere – at least at first. As is well-known, More did not sign the appeal from the nobility to the pope which Henry VIII arranged in 1530. But this was not a courageous refusal, as Chambers (p. 249) in probable reliance on Rastell's dubious notes (Harpsfield, *More*, 223) supposed. Chapuys knew that More, together with Catherine's supporters among the bishops, was not called to the meeting which prepared that document (*Calendar of State Papers Spanish*, iv. I. 599), and while he ascribed the selection to suspicion it looks like a concession to the sort of promise that Henry had made to More.

conscience clear; and this carefully staged business of 30 March proved it. Thomas More, Catherine's and Chapuys' hope and a determined opponent of the Divorce, had had to take the lead in presenting to the nation the alleged evidence that the Divorce was just. How did he feel: determined to resign? No doubt, but he stayed another year.

On only one more occasion did More address the Commons, in April 1532, when he urged them to make a grant for the defence of the northern border.[1] It is possible that the occasion was not so politically innocent as it appears. We know that about this time Thomas Temse, burgess for Westbury (Wilts.), moved for a petition to the king to take back his wife; and James Gairdner linked this motion with the lord chancellor's request for money.[2] Certainly, Temse's move was answered by Henry with yet another explanation of the justice of his case, this time to a Commons' deputation summoned to meet him. However, Hall, who supplies the only evidence,[3] and who ascribed both events to the prorogued session that began on 10 April 1532, put More's visit into the end of 23 Henry VIII and Temse's speech in the beginning of 24 Henry VIII, the dividing date being 21 April. There is no evidence for Gairdner's allegation that Temse touched on Scotland; the troubles he wished to prevent were, according to Hall, the bastardization of Princess Mary 'and diverse other inconveniences'. Nevertheless Gairdner may have been right in linking the two events; as we shall see, the possibility of pre-arrangement even cannot be excluded. It is just possible that More provided the setting for Temse's motion. However, it is more certain that at this time the manoeuvres were going forward which resulted in the Submission of the Clergy and that in these More played no public part. Whether the king had ever again tried to involve him publicly in the defence of his proceedings we do not know; at any rate, More had not allowed himself to be so trapped again. At the end of this session he did resign, but the circumstances of that resignation and the evidence for his less public activities in his years of office need to be entirely reassessed.

[1] Hall, *Chronicle*, 785.
[2] J. Gairdner, *The English Church in the Sixteenth Century from the Accession of Henry VIII to the Death of Mary* (1903), 116–17.
[3] Hall, *Chronicle*, 788. Harpsfield's note in his *Pretended Divorce between Henry VIII and Catharine of Aragon*, ed. N. Pocock (Camden Soc., 1878), 197 is clearly taken straight from Hall. The editor of *Cal. S.P. Spanish*, iv. II. 994 confused Temse's intervention with the motion of a member for the city of London reported by Chapuys a year later, which in any case was quite different (cf. *LP* vi. 324).

After More's execution, Thomas Cromwell wrote a long letter to Gregory da Casale, the man used until 1535 to maintain a tenuous contact with Rome.[1] In it he explained the reasons for which, he alleged, Fisher and More had died. This, of course, was a piece of propaganda, and diplomatic propaganda intended for the pope at that; nevertheless, the letter does not deserve the neglect which More scholars have bestowed upon it.[2] One passage in it, which refers to a nameless opposition group, must be quoted at length:

And when the public council of the realm, which we call Parliament, was called to meet at stated times to see to the good order of the realm, they began everywhere to enquire secretly with busy diligence what matter should be in hand and what should in that Parliament fall to be done for the benefit of the commonwealth. And whatever they managed to gather, by the report of others, from their experience of past usage, and by conjecture, that they at once considered in their policy meetings, arriving at conclusions very different from what the peace and interest of the realm required.[3]

Having devised such contrary policies, they then buttressed them with much skill of argument, producing a point of view which could easily have deceived the rude people. And when after a bit they realized that the king was getting annoyed at this organizing of opposition, they stepped up their campaign by arranging for select speakers and preachers to spread the arguments that had been worked out. Investigations initiated by the king showed that More and Fisher stood at the heart of this conspiracy.

If Cromwell was telling the truth, he was describing methods of unexpected political maturity. According to his story, the summoning of the Reformation Parliament caused the opponents of the Divorce and defenders of the clergy to form a kind of defence committee which set out to counter everything said and done in Parliament by reasoned arguments designed to meet the exact steps taken, steps of which, since proceedings were secret, they should have been ignorant. What Cromwell called a conspiracy we may more properly call an organized

---

[1] Merriman, i. 427 ff. Also printed in *StP*, vii. 633 ff.

[2] The only historian to use it was, inevitably, Froude (ii. 283–6); he quoted it in a mock-Tudor translation of his own which is at times excessively free, though it does not pervert the essential sense.

[3] 'Et ubi publicum Regni concilium (quod parliamentum uocant) pro Regni quiete stabilienda, ut ad certa tempora haberetur, indictum foret, ceperunt undecunque sollicita cum sedulitate clanculum exquirere, qua de re tractari, quidque in hoc parliamento, ut expediens rei publicae agi oporteret, quicquid uero aliorum delatu ex re praeterita rerum usu, uel coniectura usque collegissent id statim communibus consiliis trutinabant, omnia secus interpretantes que Regni quies ac utilitas exposcebat.'

opposition outside Parliament but able to obtain information from within it, sufficiently coherent to prepare counter-efforts to the king's propaganda, and able to arrange for its members to speak publicly against the king's proceedings. The sermons of Peto, for instance, or of Forest might well have resulted from such a concerted programme.[1]

Even if Cromwell was telling the truth, it is still possible that he was unfairly involving More. More's discretion was and is notorious. In the spring of 1531 he even refused to receive a friendly letter from the emperor because such contacts might arouse suspicion, even though he felt that the proofs he had given of his loyalty should have assured his freedom from any such hostility.[2] But what matters is whether this discretion hid inaction or some deeper activity, and even More could not keep the record entirely clear of hints of the true position. In the same breath as he refused Charles V's letter he also told Chapuys that if he were suspected of any contact with the imperial cause he would lose his freedom to speak as frankly in Council as he had hitherto done on all that touched the emperor and his aunt. Chapuys, who had earlier identified both More and the earl of Shrewsbury as friends to Catherine, also thought that the chancellor had gone out of his way to show favour to the emperor and his servants.[3] More stood at any rate close enough to the Aragon faction to open his mouth on occasion, as when he reassured one of the ambassador's men that the emperor's preoccupation with the Turkish danger could not enable the English to take any action: 'there was no order nor power'.[4]

Thus it seems that More not only made no secret of his views but maintained some contact with the centre of intrigue, the emperor's ambassador, and contributed frank opinions in policy debates with king and Council. This is not quite the aloof More of tradition, but such action falls well short of what Cromwell later alleged against him. However, there is further evidence which seems to bear Cromwell out in essentials, and in particulars too.

Sir George Throckmorton, a man who in 1536-7 repeatedly ran into political trouble, used one of his confessional statements to tell a fascinating story which again has been quite unjustly neg-

---

[1] Cf. D. Knowles, *The Religious Orders in England* (Cambridge, 1948–59), iii. 201; H. Maynard Smith, *Henry VIII and the Reformation* (1948), 442.

[2] *LP* v. 171. Charles's letter has now been printed by H. Schulte Herbrüggen, *Sir Thomas More: Neue Briefe* (Münster, 1966), 97.

[3] *LP* v. 120. Earlier, Chapuys had heard that More's frequent defence of Catherine had put him in danger of dismissal (*Cal. S.P. Spanish*, iv. I. 727).

[4] *LP* v. 187.

lected.[1] In 1529 Throckmorton had been elected knight for the shire of Warwick and, according to his own account, acted in the House as a frequent and persistent opponent of the king's policy. Now, in 1537, he wished to explain to Henry his 'proud, lewd and undiscreet handling of myself to you ward . . . since the beginning of your Parliament anno vicesimo primo or thereabouts'. A little before the Parliament opened, Throckmorton was sent for to Lambeth by Friar Peto, the best known of Catherine's unswerving supporters. Peto told him what he had allegedly already told the king, both in sermons and in private audience, that since Prince Arthur's marriage was never consummated (concerning which point he insisted on believing Catherine's sworn statement) the queen's marriage with Henry could be dissolved only by death. There could in any case be no marriage with Anne Boleyn since Henry had 'meddled' with both mother and daughter. Having thus defined the line of argument, Peto went on to advise Sir George 'if I were in the Parliament House, to stick to that matter as I would have my soul saved'. Throckmorton took this advice and spoke against all the important acts – Annates, Appeals, Supremacy. He had many conversations with Fisher about the proposed legislation and the question of the pope's authority, and Fisher referred him to Nicholas Wilson, another very active supporter of Catherine, with whom also he had several talks. He went to be confessed by yet another well known opponent, Father Reynolds, who influenced him in the same direction: if he did not stick to his opinions he would surely be damned, 'and also if I did speak or do anything in the Parliament House contrary to my conscience for fear of any earthly power or punishment, I should stand in a very hard case at the day of judgment'. Reynolds was even more uncompromising than the others, telling him to speak out even if he was certain that he could not win; Fisher and Wilson had conceded that if he were sure that his speaking 'could do no good, that then I might hold my peace and not offend'. Reynolds argued that no one could know 'what comfort I should be to many men in the House to see me stick in the right way, which should cause many more to do the same'. Blinded by their pressure and by long habit, he had ignored many warnings from Cromwell against their influence, till now of late he had come to see the error of his ways.

Here, then, is proof of an organized opposition group which not

[1] PRO, SP 1/125/247–41; cf. *LP* xii. II. 552. His account contains some dating problems: writing up to eight years after the event, he was liable to telescope several parliamentary sessions. In re-telling the story I have adopted the most likely way out of several confusions.

only attempted to counteract the doings of the Reformation Parliament but succeeded in attracting at least one member of the House to itself, instructed him in parliamentary tactics and the arguments to be used, and used his freedom of speech in the Commons to gain a hearing for the opposition point of view. This is what Cromwell told Casale had existed since November 1529, and his letter was written some two years before Throckmorton's confession. His management of the House included endeavours to talk the opposition round and break their dependence on this non-parliamentary policy committee, as Throckmorton's reference to the warnings received clearly proves. Though we know for certain of no other members who took their orders from the Peto group, it is, of course, possible that Throckmorton was not the only one. Speeches in favour of Queen Catherine were reported on several occasions: they must now all be suspect as somewhat less than spontaneous.[1]

Yet what of More? Throckmorton tied him, too, into the story. Shortly after the opening of the Parliament (and apparently soon after Peto's first approach)[2] More, still chancellor, sent for Sir George to meet him in the Parliament Chamber. The scene is described in detail: More awaited his caller in a little room off the chamber which had an altar or something like it in it on which the chancellor leant throughout the interview. Throckmorton thought he remembered that the bishop of Bath was talking to More when he arrived, but More disengaged himself to speak to Sir George words of great comfort:

I am very glad to have the good report that goeth of you and that you be so good a catholic man as ye be; if ye do continue in the same way that you began and be not afraid to say your conscience, ye shall deserve great reward of God and thanks of the King's grace at length, and much worship to yourself – or words much like to these.

More's kindness and encouragement sent Throckmorton into ecstasies and greatly encouraged him to seek out the other counsellors already mentioned. There is really no reason to doubt that More spoke to the effect remembered by Throckmorton, but if he did so he must be considered one of the organized group. Peto had picked the right man in a political innocent like Throckmorton who could be threatened with hellfire first and flattered by a kind word from the lord chancellor

---

[1] E.g. Temse could have been a client, as suggested above, p. 164.

[2] Throckmorton says it happened shortly after the Parliament opened and when he had been arguing to the Act of Appeals (1533): both cannot be correct. Since he speaks of More as chancellor, I prefer the earlier date.

after, to such good purpose that he maintained opposition in the House for at least five of the Parliament's seven sessions.

Admittedly, More once again practised that care and discretion which distinguish his handling of himself in the tricky situation that his acceptance of the chancellorship had forced upon him. It might be argued that he had just happened to hear about Throckmorton's useful attitude and quite independently wished to offer his commendations; unlike Peto, Fisher, Wilson and Reynolds he held no long indoctrination sessions with Sir George. But the first is a good deal harder to credit than that More knew of Peto's schemes and helped them along; and as for the second, there was neither reason nor occasion why the lord chancellor should converse at length or frequently with a knight for Warwickshire. What really matters is the remark that support of the catholic cause would in the end earn favour from the king. This shows More well aware that for the present the king's attitude to Throckmorton was likely to be very different, that the present policy was hostile to the catholic cause, and that he himself was involved in trying to change that policy. Throckmorton's testimony supports Cromwell's allegations, and between them they place More firmly with one of the political groups of the time, that organized to oppose the king's Great Matter and to support the cause of Catherine and Rome. There is no doubt that the king and others were well enough aware of More's opinions and heard them expressed; it is another question whether at this early date they knew of his share in the 'conspiracy'. As More told Chapuys in 1531, he wished to retain his usefulness as a proponent of the organization's policy by avoiding all suspicion of contact with the group. Until 1532 he succeeded sufficiently in retaining the king's trust to make his continued stay in office, however distasteful, worth while.

That this is an accurate reconstruction is borne out by the story of his resignation – that moment when the old tie with Henry VIII finally broke and the old love turned to the new hatred that was in the end to bring More to the scaffold. There is no doubt that More resigned; Harpsfield was certainly right to reject the rumours spread by 'adversaries and evil willers' that More had been 'against his will thrust out of the chancellorship'.[1] He had at intervals been pressing for his release, using the friendship of the duke of Norfolk to persuade the king; one wonders just how good a friend he found that devious

---

[1] Harpsfield, *More*, 59–62. Continental reformers, too, spoke of More as 'iure depositum' (Allen, x. 116).

second-rater.[1] Thus, at least, Roper; but since More in the end resigned quite easily and with assurances of future kindness from Henry, one might ask just how hard he had tried before. In 1532 More pleaded ill health to get free of office,[2] but though no doubt he was at fifty-four no fitter than might be expected in the sixteenth century, he cannot have been really ill, for he was to survive an increasingly rigorous imprisonment with his health unaffected. Erasmus conjectured that 'perhaps he feared the unpopularity of that Divorce against which he had always advised',[3] and there may be something in this; however, no one even at the time supposed More guilty of promoting that particular piece of policy. It would possibly be more accurate to say that he did not wish any longer to stand by the side of those that advocated the Divorce, whether it was unpopular or not.

This is the usual view, but it will not quite do. Once again it would be wrong to suppose that More had been watching in an inactive despair. The main issue in the spring of 1532 was the attack on the clergy's independence which emerged from the Supplication against the Ordinaries promoted in and by the Commons. There has been some debate about these events. Years ago I suggested that the whole operation was from the first planned by Cromwell: that he took over genuine grievances well ventilated in the Commons in order to compel the clergy's submission to the king's authority. Mr J. P. Cooper in reply stressed more heavily the Commons' independent concern in these issues, and Dr M. Kelly has more lately made a good case for supposing that the sequence of events reflects not prearrangement but the playing out of conflicting policies and day-to-day developments.[4] The present reassessment of More's activities in part supports and in part casts doubt on Dr Kelly's views. For More played his part in this crisis, obscure though that part may once again be. It has long been noted that he resigned on the very day after the Convocation had finally surrendered, and Chapuys knew that in Council More had joined the bishops in opposing the king. Henry was said to be particularly angry with More and Gardiner.[5] Gardiner, of course, who had drafted the tough early replies of Convocation, had throughout

---

[1] E.g. Roper, 225; Harpsfield, *More*, 58–9 is curiously condensed on the whole of More's chancellorship on which, quite contrary to his usual practice, he does not quote Roper.

[2] As he explained to Erasmus (Allen, x. 31–2).

[3] Ibid. 124: 'fortasse metuebat invidiam repudii, quod semper dissuasit'.

[4] Below, no. 25; J. P. Cooper, 'The Supplication against the Ordinaries reconsidered', *EHR* 72 (1957), 616 ff.; M. J. Kelly, 'The Submission of the Clergy,' *TRHS* (1965), 97 ff.   [5] *LP* v. 1013.

stood forth as the champion of clerical liberties. But why More, unless he too had resisted more strenuously than the rest? The Submission was extorted after much public and private struggling in Convocation and Council; if Dr Kelly is right in thinking that it was 'an unexpected and precipitate development' of May 1532,[1] there is no need to doubt that More, with the bishops, would right to the end have supposed the issue insufficiently settled and could justly have continued argument and opposition for as long as a shadow of hope remained. On the other hand, in the light of the evidence assembled in all the articles cited, it looks as though the anticlericals on the Council, guided by Cromwell, had all along intended to obtain drastic concessions by means of the Supplication. The Submission may have come as a sudden and unwelcome development to More, but that is not to say that his opponents were not looking for something like it from the first.

Thus More resigned, after a last battle in which he had finally jeopardized what remained of the king's favour. The first chapter of Magna Carta was wiped off the book; the liberties of the English Church were destroyed. Surely the whole of More's career as chancellor now hangs together. He had taken office when Wolsey's removal opened some prospect of rational reform, but also at a time when the king's determination to get rid of Catherine showed to all thinking men that Church and clergy were likely to be in much danger. He dreaded heresy with a hatred that in so reasonable and balanced a man strikes one as a trifle abnormal.[2] Thus he hoped to use his office, as best he might, to stand guard over the things in which he believed: the orthodox faith and the liberties of the Church. In so far as he opposed the Divorce, he did so because he thought the king's legal case bad and because he dreaded the larger consequences; it is not easy to see simply a defender of Queen Catherine in the man who 'would not deny to swear to the succession' of Anne Boleyn's issue but could not take the oath tendered in April 1534, because it implied denial of the pope's supremacy.[3] So he employed himself in the detection of heresy, and he lent his aid and authority to that group of dissentients who hoped to organize opposition and seem to have had some success in the House of Commons. At the same time, of course, he tried to apply the brake in the Council and may have been partly responsible for the absence of any clear-cut policy in those years.[4] But he was never either

[1] Kelly, *TRHS* (1965), 105.
[2] Had More in his younger days experienced doubt about catholic orthodoxy?
[3] *More: Selected Letters*, 217.   [4] Cf. below, no. 9.

a reckless man or a really subtle politician, and the role he had chosen did not suit him too well. From early in 1531 at the latest, by which time Thomas Cromwell was increasing his influence at Court More realized that he was losing the battle. Nevertheless he stayed at his post; the cause of the Church demanded one last effort from him. The victory of the anticlerical policy in May 1532 and the destruction of the Church's independence in England closed a chapter. His usefulness at an end, his preferred policy irremediably destroyed, More could and must go. Is it any wonder that he now resolved to spend the remainder of his life away from the great affairs and in contemplation of 'the immortality of the life to come'?[1]

One may be sure that More sincerely meant this. Once he had broken with public life he would never in any form engage in it again. And yet, in the circumstances this was an unreal stance. For nearly three years he had been right at the centre of affairs and had not kept silent; as he had told the Lords in 1531, the king knew his views well enough. He had backed a losing policy, and when that policy was lost he had taken himself off out of sight: at least, this is the way in which things must have appeared to Cromwell and the king. Some suspicion of his relations with known opponents must have existed already, as the later charges concerning the Nun of Kent and Bishop Fisher indicate. What reason had the government to suppose that a man who had actively engaged in such controversial politics would now abandon them altogether? Being the men they were, neither Henry nor Cromwell would have really believed such a turning away to be possible; and even if, knowing their More, they supposed him capable of it,[2] they could well decide that the risk was too great for them to take. Here was a man of stature and ability and European renown who had already done much to discredit their policy both at home and abroad. Left at large, he must have seemed like a time-bomb to them. And so the tragedy was staged: more pressure upon the now inflexible man to accept the new order, the king's increasing hatred, the rigged trial and the condemnation on a charge which rested on perjured evidence. But though the charge was false in fact, it was (as More's speech to his judges showed) true in spirit, and by his part in the events of 1529–32 More had made certain that his conscience could not in the end be left private to himself.

[1] Quoted by Chambers, *More*, 287.
[2] In More's ultimate troubles, Cromwell's considerate treatment and his regret at More's 'obstinacy' became very plain (e.g. *More: Selected Letters*, 222, 236). It looks almost as though Cromwell would have left More alone if it had not been for the king.

KING OR MINISTER?
THE MAN BEHIND THE HENRICIAN
REFORMATION*

The question whether Henry VIII or Thomas Cromwell supplied the ideas and the policy which underlay the break with Rome is of more interest than may be imagined. Until it is answered neither the men nor the event can really be understood. The English Reformation gave to England, the English monarchy, and the English Church a character quite their own: this makes it important to know just how and why and through whom it happened. It may perhaps be thought strange that so well-worked a part of English history should be supposed to retain some mysteries still. Yet the last full-scale accounts of it are, on the Protestant side, Froude's great but partisan work published in 1862–70;[1] on the Anglo-Catholic side, Canon Dixon's weighty, condemnatory, and sometimes misleading volumes (1878–1902),[2] or James Gairdner's even more hostile and unreliable writings (1902–13);[3] and on the Catholic side the much briefer recent book by Dr Hughes.[4] To take the accounts more commonly used, there is Fisher's, written in 1913,[5] Professor Mackie's which after forty years adds nothing in interpretation,[6] and the overpraised work of Constant, now also some twenty years old.[7] The standard lives of Henry VIII and Thomas Cromwell appeared in 1902.[8] On the face of it, a new study of those critical years in the 1530s might, to say the least, not be without reward. Here I shall attempt only to elucidate the true relationship between the two leading personalities of that age, for the prevailing notions seem to me to do scant justice to the genius of the minister and vastly to

* [*History*, N.S. 39 (1954), 216–32.]

[1] J. A. Froude, *History of England from the Fall of Wolsey to the Defeat of the Spanish Armada* 12 vols. (1862–70).

[2] R. W. Dixon, *History of the Church of England from the Abolition of the Roman Jurisdiction*, 6 vols. (Oxford, 1878–1902).

[3] J. Gairdner, *The English Church from the Accession of Henry VIII to the Death of Mary* (1902); *Lollardy and the Reformation*, 4 vols. (1908–13).

[4] P. Hughes, *The Reformation in England: The King's Proceedings* (1950).

[5] H. A. L. Fisher, *The Political History of England*: vol. v, *1485–1547* (1906).

[6] J. D. Mackie, *The Earlier Tudors, 1485–1558* (1952).

[7] G. Constant, *La Réforme en Angleterre: Le Schisme Anglican* (Paris, 1930; English translation 1934).

[8] A. F. Pollard, *Henry VIII* (first published 1902, new edition 1905); Merriman.

overrate the genius of the king. One's opinion of Henry VIII must stand by one's view of his part in the Reformation. The positive achievements of his long reign were crowded into its middle years; if he deserves the high opinion of his skill and understanding which so many moderns seem to hold it must be because he was 'the architect of the Reformation'. But whether he was that remains to be seen.

Since it is the purpose of this paper to set up Thomas Cromwell as the moving spirit in the early Reformation, it will be of assistance to recall that this view is far from original. It was held, to begin with, by some of Cromwell's contemporaries – by Cardinal Pole, for instance, by the imperial ambassador Eustace Chapuys, and by John Foxe.[1] It was adopted outright – mainly in reliance on Pole and without proper investigation – by many nineteenth-century historians.[2] But then came Pollard, who held that the Reformation was a natural development from discoverable causes which was given its particular direction by the king himself;[3] and he had the support of the other early-Tudor pundit of the day, Gairdner, who ascribed to Cromwell at best outstanding executive skill with perhaps some independent advice.[4] Not everybody, however, has been completely convinced by Pollard's picture of the 'pilot who weathered the storm'.[5] Both Fisher and Dr Hughes have sat judiciously on the fence,[6] while Dr Parker has recently suggested in general terms that the plan for the Reformation may have come from Cromwell.[7] A general re-interpretation of the period was attempted a few years ago in a book whose weaknesses of proof and argument have caused it to be too much neglected;[8] its general thesis is not dissimilar to the one which I had formed before I read it and which is the basis of this paper. In tilting at Pollard – with all the deference due to so great a historian and fully conscious of my temerity in attacking one of his fundamental tenets – I am not, therefore, altogether without company both past and present.

[1] Reginald Pole, 'Apologia ad Carolum Quintum Caesarem', *Epistolarum etc.: Pars Prima* (ed. Quirini, Brescia, 1744), 66 ff.; *LP* ix. 826; John Foxe, *Acts and Monuments* (ed. Pratt, 1870), v. 366.

[2] E.g. Dixon, i. 50 ff.; Merriman, i. 89 ff.; A. D. Innes, *Ten Tudor Statesmen* (1906), 127 ff. Similarly, Froude, i. 588; ii. 82 ff.

[3] This view underlies Pollard's general argument in his *Henry VIII, Thomas Cranmer and the English Reformation* (1905), and *Factors in Modern History* (first ed. 1907).

[4] In his *DNB* article on Cromwell, and in *Engl. Church*, 100 ff.

[5] *Factors in Modern History* (ed. 1926), 80.

[6] Fisher, 295 ff.; Hughes, 195.

[7] T. M. Parker, *The English Reformation to 1558* (1950), p. 56; cf. also, his 'Was Thomas Cromwell a Machiavellian?', *Journal of Ecclesiastical History*, I, esp. p. 63.

[8] A. Ogle, *The Tragedy of the Lollards' Tower* (1949).

It is time to turn from what has been said about Cromwell and Henry to what can be found in the evidence. Is it, in fact, possible to come to conclusions in this matter which are more than opinions? Can one decide with any degree of certainty whether Thomas Cromwell or Henry VIII evolved the plan which led to the schism and the establishment of the royal supremacy, especially since both men must have worked together and much of the story must lie for ever hidden in unrecorded conversations, Council meetings, and even private thoughts? I believe that despite these obstacles an answer is possible. In the first place, we can investigate the relations between king and minister to see whether they permit an insight into their position towards each other. Secondly, a re-interpretation of the course of the Henrician Reformation collated with Cromwell's career will, it is hoped, offer a solution of the problem.

No attempt to ignore or despise Henry VIII could ever be successful. Whatever may be thought of his character, he dominated the history of his time: he was a mighty king, no man's puppet, and never ignorant of what was done in his name. He took much active interest in the running of the realm, decided what policy was to be followed, made and unmade ministers and servants, and kept in his head and hand the strings of government. To suppose that Cromwell's was the real mind behind the great revolution is not to suppose that Henry had no mind at all. But the events of the reign – its confusion, its changing character, Henry's dependence on ministers, and so forth – all go to show that his was definitely an unoriginal and unproductive mind, intelligent indeed and capable of the swift assimilation of ideas, but unable to penetrate independently to the heart of a problem and its solution. Henry had the qualities of a first-rate politician – especially a remarkable opportunism – without the equipment of a first-rate statesman. Moreover, he was lazy; he took little part in the detailed business of government and surrendered the kind of prime-ministerial position which Henry VII had occupied.[1] Between them, his unoriginality and his laziness made him less really decisive than his personality and the deference of others would suggest. For the king's part in government is the harder to assess because his servants constantly protested that they were merely carrying out his orders. In theory the king determined everything: his pleasure was invariably vouched in warranty. How meaningless this could be is well illustrated by a case in which two rival claimants in some land dispute both pleaded the king's pleasure,[2]

[1] Cf. *Tudor Revolution*, 66 ff.   [2] *LP* xv. 36; cf. *Tudor Revolution*, 122.

or again by Cromwell's habit of obtaining royal warrants for expenditure he himself had authorized, long after the payments were made.[1] We must never be so simple as to accept unquestioningly some Tudor politician's statement that he had his sovereign's orders for his doings, even as we must not be so subtle as always to disbelieve him. Sixteenth-century ministers did not proclaim their independence of the Crown, but their prudent citation of authority is not proof that they were not after all acting on their own initiative.

Cromwell's relations with Henry are the more obscured by this difficulty because Cromwell was normally careful to give no grounds for such accusations of independent action as had helped to bring Wolsey low. Instead he cultivated a sedulous obsequiousness in his letters to the king which contrasts strongly with his upright and straightforward address to all others. Advice which would involve the king in doing some work he wrapped up in apologies for his 'bold audacite'.[2] Though he had the king's ear, he knew Henry well enough to disclaim all ability to rule the king's wishes. Gardiner, on embassy in France, blamed Cromwell's alleged interposition for every sign of disfavour to himself, thereby moving Cromwell several times to point out that Henry VIII was not that kind of ruler. In private matters, Cromwell wrote, he would never act without orders.[3] (He did not say what his practice was in public affairs!) Nor could he pretend to 'that which is not in me, that is that I shoulde be hable to doo what I wold'.[4] He had no illusions about a favour which could never be taken for granted; in April 1536 he commented to Chapuys with unusual frankness on the mutability of things of which, he said, he had had a recent 'domestic' example in the fall of Anne Boleyn.[5] Henry VIII was hard to manage, as Wolsey's successors discovered before they learned how to do business with him.[6] Great care was the more necessary because his reliance on others might at any moment give place to personal intervention. He surrendered his kingship to nobody.

However, that the whole truth does not lie in this picture of an active king to whom all things are deferred is sufficiently indicated in Cromwell's own correspondence. He summarized letters from abroad because they were too 'long and diffuse' to trouble the king with;[7] he habitually drafted the instructions and other state papers which the king simply accepted by signing them,[8] he interviewed ambassadors

---

[1] Ibid. 154 ff.
[2] Merriman, ii. 177.
[3] Ibid. 20.
[4] Ibid. 68.
[5] *LP* x. 601.
[6] *LP* iv. 6019.
[7] Merriman, ii. 190.
[8] Ibid. 216.

and conducted most of the negotiations.[1] He could act without specific
authority, as when he 'thought better' to send instructions 'by my
priuate letteres then to put your highnes to the payne to have writen
and troubled your self with thesame', a delicate way of excusing his
omission to apply for orders.[2] In April 1539, ill with fever, he recited
a long list of things done on his own responsibility which would
ordinarily exhaust the energies of a man in the best of health.[3] Writing
from the Tower after his fall, he summed up his essential liberty of
action:

I have medelyd in So many matyers vnder your Highnes that I am not
hable to answer them all . . . but harde it ys for me or any other medlyng as I
haue done to lyue vnder your grace and your lawse but we must daylye
offende.[4]

Unless we wish to suppose that Cromwell meant to accuse the king of
authorizing breaches of the law – and of course he did not – it follows
that he was accusing himself of often acting in affairs of state without
the king's knowledge or authority.

   The question here is whether it was Cromwell's mind or Henry's
that evolved the plan for breaking the deadlock created by Wolsey's
failure to get the king his divorce. What has been shown so far is that
there is no justification for the frequent assertion that Cromwell was
a mere 'instrument',[5] in government and affairs he followed his own
mind. But while this makes it possible to see in him the maker of the
Reformation if further proof is forthcoming, it does not do so by itself.
The answer can only be found in a re-interpretation of the meaning,
and especially of the chronology, of the Henrician Reformation.

   The whole interpretation depends on chronology because Cromwell
did not immediately succeed Wolsey as the king's chief minister.[6] If
he represented a policy of his own one might expect to see it appear
with his arrival in power in 1532; and this is what happened. It is
necessary to keep in mind what the 'Henrician Reformation' really
meant: the break with Rome – the withdrawal from the papal
obedience – the creation of a schismatic English church – the setting up
of the royal supremacy. All these are different, and in part tendentious,
descriptions of one thing: the definition of independent national
sovereignty achieved by the destruction of the papal jurisdiction in

[1] Ibid. 176; cf. *Tudor Revolution*, 327, n. 1.   [2] Merriman, ii. 102.
[3] Ibid. 216 ff.   [4] Ibid. 266.
[5] E.g. Pollard in his article on Cromwell in *Encycl. Brit.* (11th ed.), or C. H. Williams in
    his in *Chambers's Encyclopedia* (1950).   [6] *Tudor Revolution*, 76 ff.

England. There lay the supremely important constitutional achievement of the 1530s. It came about because of the king's desire for a divorce from his first wife; it was greatly facilitated by the dislike of clergy and papacy which prevailed among the English laity; it may even have been assisted by the supposed spread of new and reformist ideas, whether Lutheran or humanist, though here the present writer would advocate the utmost caution. But in none of these things lay the essence of the change. Henry's campaign to have his marriage annulled is one thing; his break with the pope is another. The break was the means by which in the end the marriage was annulled; but Henry tried other means, and the historical importance of the break did not consist even mainly in the accomplishment of the divorce. To understand the years 1527–34 one must indeed start from the divorce, but one must try to follow events without allowing one's knowledge of the outcome to influence interpretation. One must attempt to discover what the king was up to as time went on.

This goes counter to Pollard's view that 'the general course of the Reformation was a perfectly natural development from existing circumstances which it is idle to attribute to the influence of any one man'.[1] It was his opinion that Henry knew from the beginning where he was heading, though he had hopes that he would not be driven all the way but might compel the pope to surrender before the break came. In Pollard's own metaphor, the outworks were sapped and the fortress taken step by predetermined step.[2] Gairdner, too, thought that Henry from the first 'claimed spiritual as well as civil supremacy in his own kingdom' since he never intended 'to accept the jurisdiction of the Roman Curia', an extremely doubtful statement indeed.[3] This I believe to be now the accepted view: it credits the king both with farsighted plans and with an immediate ready radicalism of action. But it cannot be reconciled with those six long and tiresome years spent over the business. More than sixty years ago, Brewer rightly asked why Henry did not assert his own supremacy as early as 1529 but continued to prosecute the divorce at Rome even after Wolsey's failure.[4] He answered that Henry 'never, in the first instance, seriously contemplated separation from Rome'. This view makes better sense. Unable to see how he could legitimately marry Anne without the pope's connivance, and unaware of the possible implications of a royal

---

[1] *Thomas Cranmer*, 47. [2] *Henry VIII* (1905), 276 ff.
[3] *LP* v, introduction, p. xv.
[4] J. S. Brewer, *The Reign of Henry VIII* (1884), ii. 462 ff.

supremacy in the church, Henry did not at first plan anything as extreme as a break with Rome. The ideas on which the revolution rested only appeared in the course of time.

To make the disagreement plain: Pollard held that a policy which relied on bringing Clement VII to compliance was the natural preliminary to a policy which solved the problem by ignoring the pope altogether. Put like this, it surely looks as though there were two radically different lines of approach rather than one naturally developing single line. With dubious logic, Pollard argued that the ultimate outcome, being inevitable (which one may doubt), was therefore envisaged from the first. What proof is offered? The Reformation was 'so far dictated by circumstances that intelligent observers could predict its general tenor' even before November 1529.[1] 'General tenor' is a question-begging phrase; of course, intelligent observers could foresee some of the issues that were going to be raised, but did they forecast, and did Henry show signs of aiming at, something very like the royal supremacy and break with Rome ultimately established? The alleged evidence – commonly cited from a calendar which at times mistranslates tendentiously – will not bear this out. There is Campeggio's report in October 1529 of Wolsey's warning that failure to give the king his divorce would result in the ruin of the realm, of Wolsey, and of the reputation of the church in England.[2] He cited Germany to show what a cardinal's intransigence could do and repeatedly asserted that this would shatter the authority of the Apostolic See which he had served so well and with which all his greatness was linked.[3] These last words, omitted by the calendar, are the clue to the whole: Wolsey knew his own fate and in his desperation painted things as black as he could to make Rome take action. If he had any idea how the authority of Rome would be *spacciata* he seems to have thought it possible – quite wrongly – that Henry might turn Lutheran. He thought, in fact, only that ecclesiastical influence would decline; there is nothing to prove that he ever considered the likelihood of England breaking all ties with Rome.

Nor is the proof to be found in the reports of various French envoys, especially Jean du Bellay, Bishop of Bayonne, who was in England in 1529. He wrote in August that Parliament would meet in winter and

---

[1] *Thomas Cranmer*, 68.
[2] H. Laemmer, *Monumenta Vaticana Historiam Ecclesiasticam Saeculi XVI Illustrantia* (1861), 30: 'presta et total ruina del Regno, di Sua Sign. Rev. et della reputatione ecclesiastica in questo regno'.
[3] 'Perche con questa ha congiunta tutta sua grandezza.'

that then 'they would act of their own unfettered power' if the pope
failed to oblige.[1] Again the calendar misleads; it renders 'de leur
puysance absolue' as 'absolute power', a term too full of later shades
of specific constitutional meaning to be employed with safety.[2] Of
course, everyone knew that Parliament was called and everyone
rumoured that it was intended to get the king what he wanted; one
cannot fairly read into these vague phrases a foreknowledge of the
parliamentary history of the next seven years. In October, Du Bellay
wrote that the lay lords dreamed of accusing the clerical estate and of
sequestering its goods; instead of foreseeing how accurately these plans
would be realized he called them fantasies and added ironically, 'je
croy qu'ils feront de beaux miracles'.[3] The calendar's translation
replaces a contemptuous remark by an apprehensive forecast, and – by
translating the general 'ils defferent' as the specifically legal 'to
impeach' – suggests a foreknowledge of the *praemunire* charge of
1530–31; it turns Du Bellay's scepticism into accurate prophecy.[4] A
little later the envoy noted that no priest was likely to hold the great
seal again and that the clergy would have 'terrible alarms',[5] a correct
interpretation of the prevailing anticlericalism but not a forecast of the
break with Rome. That there was talk in government circles of settling
the divorce without the pope – even loose talk of 'provincial' independence – is not surprising and is vouched for by another French envoy,
De Vaux, who reported in April 1530 that Henry spoke of dealing
with the matter in his realm by the advice of his Council, and Parliament without recourse to Rome.[6] But it was only talk, even to the
king himself. When he tried, several months later, to find means of
turning words into deeds, he was told by a committee of canon and
common lawyers, which had investigated the question, that Parliament
could in no way circumvent the pope and order the divorce to be
decided by Canterbury.[7] As Chapuys added, Henry was continuously
threatening the pope with the power of Parliament; yet there was so
little genuine understanding or purpose in the threats that the solution
later adopted without question was in 1530 ruled out as quite impossible. One cannot ask for better proof that in 1530 the government
had not yet arrived at the policy of the break with Rome; the vigorous
language of the disappointed king and his ministers was backed by no

[1] J. Le Grand, *Histoire de Divorce du Henri 8* (Paris, 1693), iii. 342.
[2] *LP* iv. 5862. [3] Le Grand, iii. 374.
[4] *LP* iv. 6011. [5] Le Grand, iii. 378 (*LP* iv. 6019).
[6] Le Grand, iii. 418 (*LP* iv. 6309).
[7] *Cal. S. P. Spanish*, iv. I. 758 (Chapuys to Charles V, 15 Oct. 1530).

design or practical project. It is fair to say that no one can be shown to
have prophesied in 1529, or even in 1530, the complete separation of
England from the papacy, though many expected attacks on specific
forms of papal authority. Among them was the Venetian envoy, also
put in evidence by Pollard, who in December 1530 remarks that the
English government were trying so to arrange affairs that they no
longer needed the pope in administrative matters.[1] Charles V similarly
heard that Henry would 'degrade' the pope whom he allegedly called
heretic.[2] The king was thought to desire a reduction of English dependence on Rome such as had long been achieved in France, not the
overthrow of the pope's entire temporal and spiritual authority. After
all, England, having been the most papalist and pope-ridden of
countries in the fifteenth and early sixteenth centuries, had some way
to go to attain the relative independence of France or even Spain.
Henry's continued stand against Lutheran heresy made plain that he
was not following the German example, and no one as yet – including
Henry – could visualize a Catholic country without the pope.

What matters are not the words of observers, but the deeds and
intentions of Henry's government. Wolsey's failure to free Henry
from Catherine of Aragon by means of the legatine court at Black-
friars was followed by the revocation of the case to Rome (July 1529),
and for the three years after that everything turned on the issue whether
Henry could be compelled to attend a trial at Rome or persuade the
pope to let the case be decided in England. All the manoeuvres on the
king's part revolved around this central point. His intention was clear
throughout: he wished to impress on Clement VII how much more
comfortable it would be if he complied with the king's wishes. As a
first step he called Parliament. Left to themselves, the Commons could
be trusted to attack the Church; they had shown their temper in 1515
and had been restive in 1523. The anticlericalism of that first session
was neither king-imposed nor king-inspired; at most it was permitted
by the king. The Commons' spontaneous action put pressure on the
Church and supplied Henry with ammunition for his attack at Rome –
at Rome but not on Rome, for it is patent that Henry thought a
divorce not sanctioned by the papacy insufficient to secure a legitimate
succession. The real purpose of Parliament was to overawe the Church;
it is too readily forgotten that Henry could no more afford opposition
among his own clergy if the pope permitted them to try the case in
England than if he acted (as ultimately he did act) entirely without the

---

[1] *LP* iv. 6774.　　　　　　　　　[2] Ibid. 6142 (11 Jan. 1530).

pope. Attacks on the independence of the English Church were not synonymous with attacks on Rome: hitherto king and pope had more commonly joined hands against the liberties of the English Church.

To start with, therefore, Henry's policy was to bring the clergy to heel in anticipation of their being called upon to adjudicate in the divorce, and to put pressure on Clement to permit them to do so. It continued in 1530. Parliament stood adjourned and rumours abounded. The general threats which were reported back to France and Venice have already been noticed: in words Henry was certainly growing fiercer. In October 1530, repeating that by the customs of the realm an Englishman could not be compelled to stand trial outside England, he warned the pope that his continued refusal would raise the whole question of his authority; what right had he so to treat a prince of such dignity 'ut superiorem in terris non agnoscamus'?[1] Lest we think that Henry had at last found a way out of his difficulties, let us remember that he had claimed to have no superior on earth as early as 1515,[2] six years before he committed himself to exceedingly high views on papal authority in the *Assertio Septem Sacramentorum*. He was ready to make resounding claims, but he had no idea how to give effect to them. His only action, a proclamation forbidding the procuration of papal bulls designed to interfere with the reforming legislation of 1529, attacked the authority of papal legates only and not that of the Roman Curia at all;[3] it did not touch the divorce in the very least. Despite all his brave words, Henry could do no more than spend a profitless year pursuing Cranmer's donnish suggestion by collecting the opinions of the universities on the two points at issue – the rights of the divorce suit and the plea that Englishmen were privileged to have their cases tried in England – in the hope that the weight of authoritative pronouncements would change the pope's mind. When it did not, Henry contented himself with a vigorous protest and an appeal to general councils and unnamed English laws; there is no particle of a threat of schism.[4]

The session of 1531 was preceded by another crop of rumours that something would be done concerning the divorce; Chapuys, who in September 1530 had reported the duke of Norfolk's promise to the papal nuncio that the king would not bring the matter before Parliament if the pope did nothing,[5] had heard from a 'well-informed man'

---

[1] *StP* vii. 261 ff. [2] Fisher, *Pol. Hist.* 215.
[3] *Records of the Reformation*, ed. N. Pocock (Oxford, 1870), ii. 49 ff.
[4] *LP* iv. 6759 (6 Dec. 1530). [5] *Cal. S. P. Span.* iv. I. 719, 725.

in January that the divorce would 'undoubtedly' be accomplished in the next session.[1] Norfolk proved better informed than Chapuys' anonymous friend: 1531 brought the king no nearer his divorce than 1529 or 1530. Parliament discussed no single measure in any way designed to promote the king's great matter, a fact which reminds one that a few months earlier the experts had decided that Parliament could not help. The contrast with those busy later sessions needs no comment. Some four years had passed since Henry first determined to exchange Catherine for Anne, but there was still no sign that anything had occurred to him except the hopeless plan of forcing the pope to agree to a trial in England which Catherine and her Spanish supporters refused to contemplate. One thing 1531 did produce – the surrender of the clergy to the threat of *praemunire* and their recognition of Henry as 'their singular protector, only and supreme lord, and as far as the law of Christ allows also supreme head'. Unable to make Rome do his will, the king at least succeeded in his other ambition of bringing the English clergy firmly under his control. Contrary to the accepted view, this title of 1531 looked back to the earlier vague claim that the kings of England had no superior on earth, rather than forward to the precise and effective position of jurisdictional and political authority which the same title was to imply in 1534. Canon Dixon could see no point in a phrase which, as he rightly said, added no new authority to the Crown: 'it was a piece of folly to surprise the clergy and the country by strange language'.[2] Perhaps it was less folly than a reflection of the fact that the new adviser in whose hands the title was to assume a formidable reality was then busy with the management of the Convocations,[3] but as far as the king's own understanding of the matter went Dixon's view seems sound enough. The reservation which Fisher and Warham had inserted made nonsense of any claims more extreme than those which the English monarchy had steadily asserted over the Church for centuries. Certainly the words 'as far as the law of Christ allows' were not meaningless; Henry himself interpreted them as excluding all spiritual authority and with it the one thing that mattered to him, the divorce. Replying to Tunstall's protest against the title, the king wrote that the words *supremum caput* ought to be qualified by the addition of *in temporalibus*. That the king is the temporal head of spiritual persons in his realm, he continued, appears from history: in the temporal sphere of

---

[1] *LP* v. 24.   [2] Dixon, i. 67 ff.
[3] *LP* v. 224 (Dean of York to Cromwell, 2 May 1531).

the persons of priests, their laws, their acts, and order of living . . . we . . . be indeed in this realm 'Caput'; and because there is no man above us here, be indeed 'Supremum Caput'.[1]

It may seem, and probably is, a disingenuous defence, but it is clear on one point: the king's title does not expressly deny the pope's spiritual headship or justify the withdrawal of England from the papal jurisdiction. As yet there is no policy of a 'break with Rome'.

It would be tedious and pointless to follow the negotiations at Rome which throughout 1531–2 turned on the small technical point whether the Curia should hear Edward Carne, sent to Rome as *excusator* to plead that Henry should not be compelled to appear in a foreign court in person or by proxy.[2] For two more years the pope held off both parties, refusing to let the case proceed in England, but also refusing to decide against Henry in Rome as the Spaniards demanded. All this time Henry continued his policy of convincing the pope of the justice of his case, showing so little decision that hostile observers repeatedly concluded that he would give in, put Anne away, and return to Catherine.[3] Reginald Pole heard similar reports: he alleged that Cromwell's advice rescued Henry from a fit of depression induced by his inability to see any way out.[4] The king was bankrupt in ideas. He knew what he wanted; that neither he nor his ministers knew how to obtain it is proved by those years of bootless negotiations. Strong words having failed, he was less violent in language in 1531 than in 1530. In July he again suggested that Canterbury might be allowed to adjudicate;[5] so far from wishing to withdraw from the Roman obedience, he still hoped to get papal approval for a trial in England. New envoys were despatched, only to report the obvious fact that nothing could be hoped for from Rome.[6] By December 1531 Henry was so far reduced that he was ready to have the case tried in France, a safe enough compromise no doubt, but an astonishing surrender of his claims as a sovereign prince and greatly at variance with the high language of 1530.[7] The letter ended in threats so vague as to lack all import: if the king knew what he meant he carefully hid his knowledge. Early in

---

[1] Henry's answer is printed in D. Wilkins, *Concilia Magnae Britanniae* (1737), iii. 762 ff. The date there assigned to it (1533) is wrong. This letter differs from the one summarized in *LP* v. 820, but there is no real reason for supposing that the latter document was a reply to Tunstall (ibid. 819) or that it belongs to 1531.

[2] *LP* v, p. ix.   [3] Ibid. 70, 1448, 1459.

[4] 'Apologia', 116.   [5] *StP* vii. 310.

[6] Bryan and Foxe to Henry VIII, 22 Sept. 1531 (*LP* v. 427).

[7] Pocock, *Records*, ii. 148 ff.

1532, when the pope seemed at last about to pronounce, Henry was desperate to have the case deferred;[1] throughout 1531 and 1532 there run like a thread the silly machinations designed to bribe some cardinals to Henry's side and so prevent a decision in consistory.[2] As late as this Henry was so firmly stuck in the mental processes of the past that he hoped to obtain his ends by the bestowal of English sees on Italians. Small wonder that early in 1532 Norfolk and Gardiner allegedly counselled the king to give up; it was about the only piece of advice they had left.[3]

By this time, however, Norfolk and Gardiner were no longer the leading advisers, and diplomatic pressure at Rome was no longer the only policy. Late in 1531 Cromwell was at last admitted to that inner circle of councillors who really advised the king and governed the realm.[4] Possibly the use of the term 'empire' by Norfolk in conversation with Chapuys in January 1531 reflects the beginning of Cromwell's real influence;[5] it can be shown – though not here – that it was he who introduced the notion of empire (= sovereignty) into the controversy. There are signs from that time onwards that the doomed policy of forcing Rome to act as England wished her to was being accompanied by steps of another kind. The clergy's surrender to the *praemunire* charge gave the king some positive gains, in particular the subsidies voted in an effort to propitiate the royal wrath; this was more than had resulted from all the energy spent in beating at the gates of Rome. However, the king's ultimate aims remained as unrealizable as before. If a new policy is to be discerned in the imposition of the title of supreme head, it is also clear that it was a policy pursued but half-heartedly and without a true understanding of where it might lead. In 1532 the undercurrent usurped the lead. At last Parliament was turned against the pope. However harshly the sessions of 1529 and 1531 had dealt with the English clergy, they had not touched the papacy. But in 1532 Parliament passed the first Act of Annates by which an important source of papal revenues was cut off[6] and promoted the 'Supplication against the Ordinaries' which enabled Henry to follow up his nominal triumph of 1531 with a real triumph over the English clergy by forcing it to accept his control of ecclesiastical legislation. Since – as Maitland has taught us – the English Church had no legislative in-

---

[1] *LP* v. 691–2.
[2] Pocock, *Records*, ii. 144 ff., 213 ff., 241 ff., 252 ff., 339.
[3] *LP* v. 834.   [4] *Tudor Revolution*, 90 ff.
[5] *LP* v. 45.   [6] 23 Henry VIII, c. 20.

dependence in the later middle ages, this meant that its dependence was transferred from pope to king; the manoeuvre based on the Supplication – the 'Submission of the Clergy' – was a real though a masked attack on the pope's authority in England.

Thus 1532 saw the inauguration of the policy which was to culminate in the complete destruction of the Roman jurisdiction in England and England's complete withdrawal from the Roman obedience. It also saw the first use for that purpose of the instrument by means of which the revolution was to be accomplished, a point of great significance which can only be hinted at here: there is good reason for supposing that Cromwell, who deliberately made a career in Parliament, introduced the king to the potentialities of statute. In the sudden eruption of a new policy, Cromwell's hand is manifest. It was he who brought the Supplication – first started by the Commons in 1529 but then not driven home – to the attention of the government, who prepared the final draft, and who managed the manoeuvre involved in its employment.[1] He drafted the famous clause in the first Act of Annates which postponed its effect until the king should have tried further negotiations with Rome.[2] In itself that clause marked a defeat for the new policy; it may be conjectured, on the basis of the developments already described, that Cromwell's act proved as yet too drastic for Henry, so that his first anti-papal measure had to be adapted to the purposes of that other policy which had relied for some three years on finding means to coerce the pope into compliance.

Like all its predecessors, this means also failed: Clement was not to be persuaded by the distant power of England while the neighbouring power of the emperor remained hostile. And so, a year later, in the session of February–April 1533, the Act in Restraint of Appeals to Rome, with its great proclamation of national sovereignty, signalled the triumph of the radical policy – the break with Rome. The prehistory of this act provides the last proof of the two separate policies which have been traced in this paper, and of the fact that Cromwell sponsored the one that proved successful. There survive two drafts for acts of Parliament in the hand of Sir Thomas Audley, who had succeeded More as keeper of the great seal in May 1532, which indicate that even late in 1532 some doubt remained as to the best way of getting the divorce legalized in the realm. One of them would have given parliamentary endorsement to a divorce pronounced by the

[1] Cf. below, no. 25.
[2] Cf. my 'Note on the First Act of Annates', *BIHR* 23 (1950), 203 ff.

archbishop of Canterbury;[1] this represented only an *ex post facto* sanction and not a parliamentary policy. The other intended to give to the archbishops parliamentary authority to act in the divorce in the pope's place;[2] it is the climax of that policy which had persistently endeavoured to get Rome to remit the case to England – the culmination of all those complaints, recitals of privileges, and vague threats of hostile action in which Henry had indulged ever since Wolsey's failure in the summer of 1529. It used Parliament, but only to permit Canterbury for once to stand in Rome's stead: not based on any profound principle, it was the half-hearted sort of thing that the lawyers' decision had held up in 1530. Its preamble recites the divine law against a man marrying his brother's wife, laments the long delays, and accuses the pope of aspiring to usurp the rights of princes; it is throughout full of apologies, self-justification, and polite references to 'the popes holynes'.

The statute actually passed, on the other hand, not only provided for a general prohibition of appeals to Rome – that is, it dealt with a wide issue of general significance instead of confining itself to the particular matter of the divorce – but also included a preamble which described in unequivocal language a theory of England as a sovereign state in which no other potentate might interfere. That it was Cromwell who evolved this measure, and how he overcame some remaining fears and doubts which proclaimed themselves in apologetic and justificatory phrases, has been described elsewhere.[3] Right to the end of the long-drawn conflict the two policies – one pursued since 1529, the other introduced by Cromwell in 1532 – vied with each other for the king's approval. So reluctant was Henry to take the decisive step that even towards the end of 1532 he could still toy with a partial measure designed to keep the door open at least an inch or two, even while a simple and thorough policy based on a devastating principle was offered to him. Cromwell's grandiose conceptions triumphed, but it seems to have been a near thing.

The Reformation, then, was not the inevitable development of the text-books. Whether it would have come anyway it is idle to speculate; but it came in the 1530s simply because Henry's desire for his divorce was baulked by an international situation which made co-operation with the papacy impossible, and it came as it did because Thomas Cromwell produced a plan which achieved Henry's ends by destroying

[1] PRO, SP 2/N, fos. 163–4.   [2] Ibid. fos. 155–62.
[3] Cf. below, no. 24.

the papal power and jurisdiction in England and by creating in England an independent sovereign state. This policy was not present from the start; it had to overcome much caution and conservatism as well as fear of the consequences before its bold simplicity was permitted to develop. The Henrician Reformation reflects the ideas – one may say, the political philosophy – of Thomas Cromwell.

THOMAS CROMWELL'S DECLINE AND FALL*

Even in the uncertain and tempestuous times of Henry VIII, Cromwell's fall from power was unusually sudden and precipitate. On 18 April 1540 he was created earl of Essex and great chamberlain of England, thus confounding his enemies and those onlookers who had seen him tottering for some time; for the next two months he appeared to be enjoying his master's confidence as much as ever; but on 10 June he was suddenly arrested at the Council table, hustled to the Tower, condemned without a hearing, and kept alive until a belated execution on 28 July only because Henry still wanted his testimony against Anne of Cleves. It is alleged that he foresaw his fall some two years earlier,[1] and indeed it is probable that he was always aware of the dangerous insecurity of a position which so entirely depended on the royal favour; nevertheless, when the knife actually fell it seems to have taken him by surprise. How and why it all happened are questions that have often been considered, but may never find a completely satisfactory answer because the principal actors in the drama did not commit themselves on paper. Burnet pointed out long ago that Henry's dissatisfaction with Anne of Cleves cannot have been the sole or even chief reason, because Cromwell obtained his last and greatest honours after that storm broke; he saw the decisive factors in the accusations of heresy which were brought against Cromwell.[2] Merriman agreed that these had something to do with alienating the king, but, ridiculing the idea of Cromwell having any real kind of religion, he thought that Cromwell ironically fell for an entirely unjust reason, though he deserved his fate on general grounds. He found the clue to the riddle in the foreign policy of those months.[3] No one has doubted that the machinations of Cromwell's enemies, with Norfolk and Gardiner at their head, were decisive in turning the king against his minister. However, the internal history of 1539–40 has never been fully explored

---

* [CHJ 10 (1951), 150–85.]
[1] Lord Herbert of Cherbury, *The Life and Raigne of King Henry the Eighth* (1672), 520.
[2] G. Burnet, *History of the Reformation*, ed. N. Pocock, 7 vols. (Oxford, 1865), i. 439, 442 (hereafter cited as 'Burnet').
[3] Merriman, i. 286 ff.

and, some important factors – such as, for instance, the act of attainder which condemned Cromwell – have been too much neglected: the story will bear re-investigation, especially as it will appear that developments were even more sudden and catastrophic than has been supposed.

I

Despite his pleasant conversation and capacity for friendship,[1] it cannot be said that Cromwell succeeded at any time in attaching any member of the king's Council firmly to himself. While he was in power other councillors naturally thought it best to be on good terms with him, and there are signs that such men as the earl of Wiltshire and Lord Russell were very much on his side as late as 1539.[2] But Wiltshire, whose days of power were over in any case since his daughter's disgrace and death, himself died in March 1539, and Russell was a careerist who easily survived Cromwell's end despite their long-standing friendship. Audley, the chancellor, acted generally as though he was a creature of Cromwell's, but if the lord privy seal ever hoped for much support in a crisis from that quarter, he was bound to be disappointed. That ostensible friend, Fitzwilliam, earl of Southampton, was one of the first to turn against him.[3] The troubles of the last year – the Act of Six Articles and the consequent split in the episcopate – provoked Cromwell into active hostility to the majority of the bishops: he tried very hard to get convincing evidence against Tunstall whose age, standing, and conservatism made him a constant thorn in the radical minister's side,[4] and after he had succeeded in laying Sampson by the heels he had, it was rumoured, his eye on five other bishops whom he wished to accommodate in the Tower.[5] Not only were ecclesiastics like Tunstall and Sampson enemies on the Privy Council, but a Council group of laymen was supposed to be behind a move, reported in 1539, to replace Cromwell by Tunstall – Kingston, Browne, Southampton, good catholics all.[6] One man whose time was yet to come kept remarkably aloof from the troubles of 1540: there is no sign that Hertford, the future Protector Somerset, took any part on either side. Cranmer, as is well known, stood firmly behind Cromwell, and he had a strange influence with the king; alone of

---

[1] Cf. P. Van Dyke, *Renascence Portraits* (New York, 1905), 237 ff.
[2] *LP* xiii. II. 511, 673.   [3] *LP* xv. 804.
[4] *LP* xiv. II. 750.   [5] *LP* xv. 737; cf. below, p. 219.
[6] *LP* xiv. II. 750.

Henry's servants he never lost his master's favour, and Cromwell once told him so with a mixture of affection and envy.[1] But though Henry looked after his archbishop, he never allowed him much say in lay affairs, and Cranmer was little use in a political struggle. If it is true, as partly it probably is, that Cromwell promoted Sadler and Wriothesley to be secretaries in April 1540 because he wanted to strengthen his hand in the Council, it cannot be said that he was very successful. Sadler, to quote his only biographer, 'was cautious enough to give his enemies not even the shadow of an accusation against him' on Cromwell's fall,[2] and calmly continued in office; his constant association with Henry for some five years before must have helped to take away the sting of his old master's and protector's disgrace. Wriothesley did better: he soon discovered catholic sympathies within himself, rejoined his earlier patron, Gardiner, and put himself forward so well that he succeeded as chancellor on Audley's death, an appointment so extraordinary for one who was neither a lawyer nor a churchman that one may justifiably suspect a promise of reward. Indeed, his change of front in June 1540 was so complete that it is quite possible that he had been secretly betraying Cromwell. This suspicion was entertained by the anonymous author of a poem on Gardiner who is accused of trying to find someone 'that Crumwell trustyd and of his councell were'. The writer alleged that Gardiner found this spy in his 'secrete ffrende and of old acqueyntaunce' whom yet Cromwell thought to be his friend 'as brother to brother', all of which fits no one so well as Wriothesley who, though he had begun his career under Cromwell, had as a clerk of the signet been intimate with Gardiner during the bishop's tenure of the secretaryship.[3]

Cromwell, then, had no reliable friend on the Council except Cranmer, and it would be false to speak of his party there. On the other hand, however, there was no organized party opposing him, either. We must not think of the Council factions of Henry's reign as similar to those of the time of Elizabeth. Leicester, Walsingham, Burghley, differed on fundamental matters of policy and generally

---

[1] *Narratives of the Reformation*, ed. J. G. Nichols (Camden Soc. 1859), 258 f.

[2] F. Sadleir Stoney, *Life and Times of the Right Honourable Sir Ralph Sadleir* (1877), 68.

[3] For the 'poem' cf. *BIHR* 6 (1933), 22. For Wriothesley's early career cf. *DNB* xxi. 1063a; *LP* iv. 6600 (11), v. 723. He may have become known to Gardiner, at Cambridge, in the early 1520s. Cromwell seems to have kept in touch with him even at a time when Wriothesley was Gardiner's servant; in Jan. 1531 he secured him an annuity the gift of which was in his hands since he was administering the vacant see of York (*LP* v. 80 [25]). Throughout Cromwell's ministry Wriothesley was his confidential chief clerk. [Cf. *Tudor Revolution*, 307–12.]

managed to attract other councillors to their way of thinking, thus truly splitting the Council along party lines. In the earlier period, men like Cromwell and Gardiner might take their stand on diametrically opposed principles, but the remainder of the Council followed whatever star was in the ascendant, and were careful of nothing but themselves. It was no time for party manoeuvres: winner took all, and to be on his side was therefore exceptionally important. Therefore men like Southampton, Wriothesley, Russell, and the rest stood behind Cromwell while he held power and opposed him when the tide turned, and in doing so they could even claim to be acting from principle. Their service and allegiance were to the king, and as the king decided so they veered. It was all perfectly comprehensible, and we may be sure that Cromwell comprehended it; Wriothesley may have been the only one about whom he cherished illusions.

But if there were no true parties on the Council, there certainly were divisions. Men like Southampton did not feel happy about the changes in religion; they were ready enough to follow when the arrogance of the Church was attacked and when property which they coveted was wrested from the monasteries, but that was not the same thing as favouring these newfangled 'Lutheran' ideas. Others combined with this feeling a strong dislike of the upstart minister; the Tudors' policy of 'equal opportunity' was never much appreciated by those whose ancestors had already managed to reach the heights. It is possible to think that Henry deserted Cromwell not because the minister was working contrary to the king's desires in religion but because backing him further would have meant forfeiting that support of the new aristocracy, the gentry, and the middle classes on which the dynasty instinctively rested; the point is not material because, if Henry had really felt this, the motive would have been transmuted by the alchemy of his conscience into the fear that Cromwell was a heretic. What matters is that Cromwell could never rely on any members of the Council beyond the point where the king's hand was withdrawn from him. His position towards the councillors can best be illustrated from his relations with the two leaders of the revolt against him – the duke of Norfolk, and Stephen Gardiner, bishop of Winchester.

Thomas Howard, third duke of Norfolk, was one of the most unpleasant characters in an age which abounded in them. If he had a principle beyond self-advancement, it was loyal service to 'whatsoever king shall reign', but he did not allow this to stand in the way of personal and family ambition. Two of his nieces married the king – Anne Boleyn and Catherine Howard – but both proved broken reeds as far as power at court for their uncle was concerned.[1] The supreme irony of his life was his arrest in the last months of Henry's reign: it was as if the king were trying to prove that no amount of suppleness, of – in Sir William Paulet's words – being of the willow and not of the oak, could save a man from disaster at his court. On the other hand, Norfolk's escape under sentence of death through the king's earlier demise put the finishing touch to a life spent in crawling out of danger into favour. At the same time, he was an able soldier who shared in the resounding victory of Flodden and showed considerable skill in suppressing the pilgrimage of grace; he served Henry faithfully enough as a minister at home and ambassador abroad, though his was never more than a second-rate brain, incapable of living up to the high place in the state to which he believed his ancestry and dukedom entitled him. In consequence he was always at heart the enemy of the upstarts whom the king promoted to power, and both Wolsey and Cromwell found him at the end leading the assault against them.

Norfolk had become, to all appearance, the king's chief minister after Wolsey's fall, and though he never stood in the cardinal's place he was an obstacle in Cromwell's way. It seems that their relations were at first friendly enough, at least on the surface, but – if Chapuys, the emperor's ambassador, may be trusted – late in 1534 the troubles in Ireland caused a split in the Council which showed up their latent hostility.[2] This seems to have decided Cromwell to make a determined effort against his rival; by February 1535 the duke had retired to his country house at Kenninghall in Norfolk to nurse his grievances.[3] In effect he had been driven from the Council and from proximity to the king, and there can be little doubt that Cromwell had done the driving. Norfolk did not, it is true, stay away for good, but his visits became rarer and rarer, and throughout 1535 and the better part of 1536 he had to leave the field clear for Cromwell. In this predicament he displayed those powers of duplicity against which his wife, who suffered much from a husband who put her away in order to live with his mistress, warned Cromwell when she wrote that she would never trust the duke who 'can speak fair to his enemy as to his friend'.[4] Throughout those eighteen months between his retirement to Norfolk

---

[1] Also as wives, of course; the two failures went together.
[2] *LP* vii. 1141.
[3] *LP* viii. 263 (p. 104).   [4] *LP* xii. II. 1049.

and the outbreak of the northern rising, the duke did his best to persuade Cromwell of his friendly feelings, using him as a channel to the king, reporting on his activities in the country, assuring him of eternal friendship ('grudge who will').[1] After the fall of Anne Boleyn he was in a worse position than ever, and in the autumn of 1536 he seemed to see the Tower near. Once more he turned to Cromwell. On 5 August he had heard from several friends 'that the kynges highnes shuld be in gret displesure with me because my lord of richmond was not caried honorably and So buryed'.[2] He made his excuses, but 'A gret brewte doth ron that I should be In the towre of london; when I shall deserue to be there, totynhaum shall torne frenche.' He offered to fight the inventor of the tale on Shooter's Hill. All these rumours made him desire to come to court and put himself straight. He finished with a few friendly words about Cromwell's son Gregory, then his guest, who was 'not sparyng no horse fleshe to ron after the dere and howndes'.

The friendly terms on which the two ostensibly were are manifest from this letter, but the reference to his coming to court is interesting. 'Iff I had not be mynded affore to haue come to the court, these newse wold have spurred me A pase.' What was holding him back? For next day, a Sunday, he was again writing to Cromwell, telling of further rumours of disgrace, and this time begging straight out to be told the plain truth – by the man whom he probably suspected of being behind the rumours. On Thursday he could be at court, but he would see Cromwell first, 'for sory I should be to come to the court before I spake with you'.[3] But on Thursday, the 10th, he was still at Kenninghall and again writing to Cromwell, this time about a new worry: he wanted his share of the monastic lands. He had had a letter from Cromwell which, we must conclude, was the cause of his not fulfilling his intention of going to London, though it also must have reassured him on the point of those hostile rumours, for there is no further mention of them. But – will Cromwell please look to his, Norfolk's, interest, 'for the tyme of Sowyng is at hande, and every other noble man hath all redy his porcion'.[4] A few days later he was offering

---

[1] *LP* viii. 532, 673; ix. 308, 398.

[2] PRO, SP 1/105, fo. 245 (*LP* xi. 233). Norfolk had been put in charge of the funeral of Henry's illegitimate son who had married the duke's daughter.

[3] PRO, SP 1/105, fo. 247 (*LP* xi. 236).

[4] SP 1/106, fol. 157 (*LP* xi. 434). Similarly ibid. fo. 173v (ibid. 458), on 16 August, acknowledging Cromwell's letter of the 15th: 'I know no noble man but hath ther desires, and if I shall now dawnse Alone my bak frendes shall reIoyse therat.'

thanks all round, humble thanks to the king 'for his most kynd handlyng me. . . . And A myllion of thankes to you, my gode lord, for your paynes taken In all my affayres.'[1]

Before the correspondence was resumed, Norfolk's fortunes had taken a turn for the better in circumstances which hardly merited a million thanks to Cromwell, and which came near to bringing that minister low. The Lincolnshire rising broke out on 1 October, and a week later Chapuys reported that Henry had recalled Norfolk – reluctantly, because Cromwell had poisoned his mind against the duke, so much so that Norfolk was supposed to be half banished from court. Now, however, the duke had come down in high glee, become reconciled to the king, and had left again for Norfolk to raise troops and go against the rebels.[2] In fact, the rebellion had certainly saved him from mouldering in retirement, but his military reputation forced him again to leave the king's person, and though he may have hoped for Cromwell's fall, as Chapuys hints he did, that resourceful man was yet very far from done for. His rival was still unable to bring direct pressure to bear at court, and in the meantime he saw to it that Norfolk should regard him as his chief hope and link with the favours of court life. The correspondence resumed in November with the first of a series of letters from the duke begging Cromwell to see to the interests of his daughter, Richmond's widow;[3] at his departure for the north Norfolk asked Cromwell to be 'his buckler',[4] and throughout the next year he wrote to him for help and protection.[5] He appointed Cromwell executor of his will,[6] and told him stories of the punishment he had meted out to men who had spoken ill of the lord privy seal;[7] to judge from these letters, they were the best of friends and allies.

In March 1537, however, there was again a small cloud. It is the same old story: the duke wants to return, ostensibly to look after his interests, but repeated requests for permission only result in a refusal from Henry whose letter, drafted by Wriothesley, suggests Cromwell's hand at work.[8] Norfolk in the north was one thing, and one could afford to be friendly with him – even do him some service to keep him sweet; but Norfolk near the king was quite a different matter. The duke appeared to bear no malice, and his protestations of friendship continued: he will be Cromwell's friend for life, and this letter may be

[1] SP 1/106, fol. 183 (*LP* xi. 470).
[2] *LP* xi. 576.
[3] *LP* xi. 1138; xii. I. 42, 381, 469, 1157.
[4] Ibid. 216.
[5] Ibid. 318, 416, 439, 469, 499, 991, 1157, 1173.
[6] Ibid. 252.
[7] Ibid. 318, 381.
[8] Ibid. 777, 809, 810, 863.

7-2

kept to be used in evidence against him 'if ever fault of promise shall be found in me hereafter'.[1] But in July 1537 Cromwell seems to have tried too hard to keep him in the north; Norfolk wrote in his usual manner, but added that he could not take the lord privy seal's advice to stay because he had 'back friends' who would do him harm.[2] When advice failed, stronger measures were resorted to; on 8 August 1537, Norfolk, still in the field, complained that he had been prevented from seeing the king when he came north to Ampthill.[3]

Probably he did see the king soon after, and – his work north accomplished – soon found himself again retired to Kenninghall. The hectic year had done nothing to alter the position; Cromwell was as firmly in the saddle as ever, and a wise man kept on as good terms with him as he might, especially when there were rumours and suspicions of popery.[4] Thus, from March 1538 onwards when Norfolk had certainly returned to his country seat, we once more find him corresponding in a most friendly and submissive manner with Cromwell, letting him know when he was coming up to see the king, asking his advice and reassurance about Henry's feelings towards himself, assuring him of his hatred of the old 'mumpsimus and superstitions'.[5] In March 1539, at a time when things were already beginning to turn the other way, he wrote to Cromwell perhaps the most friendly of all his letters: 'My lord, I require you to grace me no more in your letters, for surely it is not convenient that one of your sort should do so'.[6] From 1534, therefore, when Cromwell politely but definitely shouldered Norfolk out of office, until the middle of 1539, the duke had lived in virtual retirement, only broken by his active service against the pilgrims; he had established ostensibly friendly relations, and Cromwell had been willing enough to bind him to himself by

---

[1] *LP* xii. II. 101.   [2] Ibid. 229.   [3] Ibid. 479.

[4] Norfolk had to defend himself constantly against accusations of lukewarmness and sympathy with the rebels (*LP* xii. I. 416, 439, 469, 1157, 1162, 1173). Cf. also a letter to him in March 1537 (ibid. 778), in which a Carthusian monk, later to be martyred, asked him to help the king back to the true path and away from the supreme headship. That was dangerous stuff to write to a man anxious to keep his head. On the other hand, Henry had to administer a gentle rebuke because Norfolk had believed 'light tales' and fretted without cause (ibid. 1192).

[5] *LP* xiii. I. 504, 690, 691, 741, 784; II. 365, 554.

[6] *LP* xiv. I. 541. Of the three letters marked by Merriman as written by Cromwell to Norfolk (nos. 107, 188, 219), the first two are rather formal instructions; the last was almost certainly written to someone else. Norfolk's very personal and rather chatty letters must have elicited some similar replies which are unfortunately lost (Cromwell would not have kept drafts of unimportant personal notes); he would hardly have gone on for years writing in that style if he had got nothing but formality in return.

services and kindnesses which ought to have turned these relations into real friendship. All the same, it may be doubted if Cromwell really needed the duchess's warning; he must have known how untrustworthy Norfolk was, if only from memories of Wolsey's fate, and he was probably content enough to keep him from court and Council throughout those years. As for pretended friendship, two could play at that game, and so far at least Cromwell had shown himself much the more skilful player.

Cromwell's relations with his other leading enemy, Stephen Gardiner, was more frankly hostile. The bishop of Winchester had been well on the road to power after Wolsey's disgrace, a road he had hoped to smooth by his ostentatious desertion of the fallen cardinal; but his absence in France early in 1532, at a time when Cromwell was gaining the king's ear, undermined his position, and he risked everything when on his return he took upon himself the defence of Convocation against the onslaught of the Commons' Supplication. From the first, therefore, he and Cromwell clashed on matters of policy and principle. From the first, also, they were personal enemies, for Cromwell signalled his victory by depriving Gardiner of his office of secretary. Hostility based on two such pillars was likely to endure. Cromwell's triumph came soon after Gardiner's opposition to Cromwell's policy had burst out in the session of 1534 and resulted in his disgrace and retirement to Winchester for nearly a year and a half.[1] In that time, the bishop made at least one effort at establishing better relations with the man in power,[2] but gentle humility sat ill on those proud prelatical shoulders, and unlike the pliant duke of Norfolk Gardiner wrote no fulsome letters to the man who had supplanted him.

Cromwell, on the other hand, seems to have borne Gardiner little grudge for his opposition, and he was too wise to triumph over him, or to consider so able a man permanently removed from the scene by anything short of death. He assisted the bishop when the registrar of Winchester tried to exploit Gardiner's disgrace in one of those cathedral city squabbles, and in 1535 he sounded him on his views on the royal supremacy in the hope of enlisting his pen on the king's side.[3] The

---

[1] J. A. Muller, *Stephen Gardiner and the Tudor Reaction* (New York, 1926), 55 ff.

[2] In a letter of 6 July 1534 (*The Letters of Stephen Gardiner*, ed. J. A. Muller [Cambridge, 1934], no. 45) Gardiner thanked Cromwell for the 'frendly handeling' of his affairs, hoped for a 'continuance of your amitie', referred to him as his 'especial frende', and even included a little joke in the only informal letter extant he wrote to him after Cromwell's arrival to power. The other letters in those years (ibid. nos. 41–2, 47–51) are formal business letters.

[3] Muller, *Gardiner*, 55, 57 f.

product of these enquiries was the treatise *De vera obedientia* which in the autumn of 1535 restored Gardiner to favour and employment, but – as was thought at the time[1] – Cromwell saw to it that his rival should not be near the king. For nearly three years, from September 1535 to July 1538, Gardiner resided as ambassador in France, filling an important and responsible post but unable to make his views felt at home or take a hand in the shaping of policy. His own extant letters to Cromwell during that time are cool enough and deal only with business and affairs, but Cromwell's letters allow a glimpse of the reality underlying their superficially amicable relations. Early in 1536 Henry had granted to Sir Francis Bryan an annuity forfeited by Henry Norris's attainder; Gardiner, who was in debt and anxious for money, wrote a letter of protest to the minister which drew from Cromwell one of the two most dignified rebukes to be found in his correspondence.[2] He censured Gardiner's 'contencion' over the annuity and his 'fantazie' that its disposal was due to Cromwell's personal hostility; the action had been the king's. 'Truly, my lord, though my talent be not soo precious as yours, yet I trust, with his helpe that gave it me, to vse it soo as it shall doo his office without gathering suche suspitions vppon freendeship. I repete that worde again bicause I ment freendely in the writing of it.' He then turned to Gardiner's complaints of penury, pointed out that he had previously warned him not to squander his money while debts remained to be paid, and then reproved him for arguing that he ought to have had the annuity either for his past service as of grace, or because in any case it was due to him at law.

Whiche whenne I perceyved that his Maiestie toke not in very good parte, ne determyned vppon that gentle dilemma to leave his determynacion imperfite, I wrote vnto youe, freendely aduising youe rather frankly and with an apparance of good will to satisfie his grace thenne soo to contende in it ... And now for that aduise, whiche I toke to be freendly, ye take greate payne to make me beleve that I haue neyther freendeship in me nor honestie; wherin howe freendely ye procede with me, But that ye be moche given to your oune iudgement, I durst make yourself the Iudge.

The rebuke cannot have been any more palatable for being justified; certainly, arrogance and suspicion of other men's motives were among Gardiner's chief characteristics.

However, while he was in France the bishop of Winchester was to all appearance harmless, and once again the two men returned to a

---

[1] *LP* xii. I. 960.
[2] Merriman, ii. 19 ff. The other was addressed to Nicholas Shaxton, ibid. 128 ff.

show of comparative amity.[1] At one point in 1537 Henry showed some inclination to recall Gardiner, but he changed his mind because of the difficult times; it is possible though far from certain that Cromwell was behind this.[2] Gardiner himself, as one might expect, seems to have been trying for his recall.[3] The worsening of Anglo-French relations early in 1538 naturally reflected on the ambassador whom Cromwell took his share in blaming for irritability and clumsiness;[4] but Cromwell went out of his way to soften an official censure sent to Gardiner in February that year, assuring him that the king's letter was not meant to imply so much displeasure or blame as its words might be thought to convey; it was merely meant as a spur. 'I Pray you to take his graces meanyng non otherwyse thenne soo, Nothing doubting of the contynuaunce of his favour towardes you, with no less Respect and consyderatyon to be had thereof to your comfort and consolacion in tyme cummyng thenne your good merytes doo deserue.'[5] Such kindness had to be its own reward, for Gardiner continued hostile and tried Cromwell's patience high. In April 1538, the lord privy seal had again occasion to complain of unworthy suspicions, though he was ready to forgive and forget:

Bicause the repeticion of suche contencyous matier as hathe been writen betwene vs shuld be but displeasant and noysome to bothe parties, I shall laye the same aparte and . . . only aduertise youe that howesoeuer you haue taken me, I haue shewed myself your freende whenne the tyme and occasion hathe serued . . . And therfor I thought meself the more touched that for my gentlenes I shuld receyve suche vnkinde answers. But as I haue nowe given place to your courage, soo I shall put those matiers in obliuion that haue thus passed betwene vs.[6]

It is only fair to add that as far as we know Cromwell's protestations were borne out by his actions. He was never a man to treasure grievances. On the other hand, he may have had a special reason for trying to keep Gardiner friendly at this juncture; a few months later the bishop was back in the country, and the problem of his opposition became again acute. At first, however, he could do nothing; once again he retired to his diocese where he vented his spleen against Cromwell in a necessarily rather petty manner, ejecting one of the lord privy seal's

---

[1] In May 1537, Gardiner's nephew Germain, in a letter to his friend Wriothesley, expressed pleasure at hearing that the old strife between their respective masters was laid by (*LP* xii. I. 1209).
[2] *LP* xii. II. 78 (12 June 1537).   [3] Ibid. 586 (27 Aug. 1537).
[4] Report of the French ambassador Castillon, 21 Jan. 1538 (*LP* xiii. I. 117).
[5] Merriman, ii. 115 f.   [6] Ibid. 136.

nominees from a benefice.[1] His chance of active opposition came with the parliamentary elections of 1539, but of those we shall have to speak in detail later.

It will be seen, therefore, that from his arrival to power until the first half of 1539 – six or seven years – Cromwell succeeded in dominating the king's counsels to the exclusion of all rivals. He did his best to keep on good terms with the potential leaders of the opposition; though he was successful with the deceitful Norfolk, he could not permanently persuade Gardiner to even the appearance of amicable relations. At the same time he took practical steps to draw their teeth by keeping them away from the court and out of the Council. It may remain a moot point whether he was sincere in his professions of friendship, or whether he was simply out-Norfolking Norfolk in his protestations, but this much can be said: his letters to Gardiner do not read like false pretence, and though he did not allow either the duke or the bishop any say in the making of policy he also made no attempt to persecute them. His attitude to them in the years of his power contrasts powerfully with their vindictive and violent proceedings in the early months of 1540 which were to lead to his fall. As far as we can tell, Cromwell had no personal feelings in the matter and preferred to stay friends all round; his policy, of course, must not be hampered, but that could be achieved by merely keeping his opponents where they could do no harm. Norfolk and Gardiner, on the other hand, hated Cromwell personally, the latter especially making no secret of the matter at any time and the former coming out with it when it was safe to do so; it was a mistake to treat them as Cromwell treated them, though a mistake which goes strangely counter to the accepted view of the minister's character. Can we doubt that Cromwell would have had no difficulty in trumping up the necessary charges to convince Henry and despatch his enemies? That he was insufficiently ruthless in the years of his greatness, the events of the twelve months in which the king was won away from him were soon to show.

II

In the spring of 1539, preparations went forward for the election of a new Parliament, and these preparations have provided material for some fine displays of moral indignation at Cromwell's expense. There is no question that he endeavoured to influence elections, but the

---

[1] Muller, *Gardiner*, 79; *LP* xiv. I. 412.

views commonly expressed on this fact are singularly unhistorical.[1] The methods employed were those familiar to us from Professor Neale's study of Elizabethan elections, and even from Professor Namier's analysis of the distant parliamentary scene of the eighteenth century.[2] They may have been new in 1539, though it is likely that they had at least a few years of tradition behind them, and Cromwell may have been their inventor; the evidence is slender, and in any case we must not stray into subjects too far off our present road. Cromwell used his influence and that of other leading men in the kingdom in the various constituencies where they had such influence; with the rise of Parliament to its new position, with the growth of government pro-grammes, with the new ambition for seats on the part of the gentry, the methods which were to combine a strong executive, parliamentary representation, and the weight of the great men of the country into a workable conglomerate naturally came to the fore. Whether, with Neale, we speak of clientage, or with Namier of interest, the thing is much the same; it is the product of a peculiar political machinery superimposed on a complicated social structure, and it was to endure – understood by all and approved of by most – until the society which demanded it passed away in the nineteenth century. Small wonder that the political reforms of the Puritan interregnum did not take root until after 1832; the Commonwealth and Protectorate were based on a social structure very different from that which prevailed both before and after, and therefore they saw only abuse in what was necessary and suitable under Thomas Cromwell, Burghley, Danby, Walpole, and Newcastle.

One other error about this Parliament of 1539 may be disposed of. Cromwell, it is alleged, packed the House in his personal interest;[3] it is therefore possible to point a suitable moral by recalling that this Parliament passed the Act of Six Articles and Cromwell's own attainder without any difficulty. The truth is that Cromwell did not attempt what

---

[1] Cf. Merriman, i. 253 ('the Parliament of 1539 was undoubtedly his masterpiece'); Fisher, *Political History of England*, v. 434. Dr Pickthorn is the exception: he realized that there was nothing scandalous in election or management (*Henry VIII*, 405 f.). Froude, after concluding that the examples he records show nothing very improper, yet added that 'more extensive interference was . . . indisputably practised' (*Hist. of Eng.* iii. 191); as he took his example from the 1536 election, the point hangs in mid-air. For a modern appraisal, cf. J. E. Neale, *The Elizabethan House of Commons*, 284 f.

[2] J. E. Neale, *The Elizabethan House of Commons* (1949); L. B. Namier, *The Structure o, Politics at the Accession of George III* (1929).

[3] Even Pollard thought so: *Henry VIII*, 261; *Factors in Modern History*, 120 f. The view appears in most of the textbooks in one form or other. Cf. Froude, *Hist. of Eng.* iii. 193.

was obviously impossible. When he told Henry that 'I and other your dedicate counseillers be aboutes to bring all thinges so to passe that your Maiestie had never more tractable parliament',[1] he was saying as clearly as could be that the elections were being influenced in the king's interest; and indeed the Parliament proved tractable enough in the twists and turns of Henry's policy. There was no question of packing the House in the minister's cause, nor can we really speak of any packing at all: 'influence' was exercised to see some reliable government men returned, an indispensable step in the days before government parties. In this very letter Cromwell explained his appointment of his servant Richard Morison, the pamphleteer, to a seat in the House (he does not mention where he found him one) by saying that 'no doubte he shalbe redy to answer and tak vp such as wold crake or face with literatur of lernyng or by Indirecte Wayes If any such shalbe, as I thinke there shalbe few or none'. Morison was to be used as spokesman in accordance with his special qualifications, a most sensible precaution in days when debates mattered.[2]

Let us now consider such evidence as there is of Cromwell's machina-tions. The earl of Southampton was employed to secure suitable returns in Surrey and Sussex. He failed to get Sir Richard Weston, undertreasurer of the Exchequer, to stand for the shire because that government official was too ill; consequently he trusted that his own brother and Sir Mathew Browne 'according to the kinges pleasure . . . shalbe chosen for Surr' withouzt difficulty'. At Guildford he used the familiar argument that the borough might save itself expense by taking his advice and the men he 'wold provide . . . to supplie the rome'; the mayor and burgesses had already promised one seat to a local man (who happily turned out to be related to Cromwell's receiver), but gave Southampton the other nomination. For this place the earl asked the king's desire – perhaps he had someone of his Chamber in mind; if not, Southampton would appoint a servant of his own. As for the knights for Sussex, he was doing his best for the men already picked by the government – Sir William Goring, a leading local gentleman, and Sir John Gage, the vice-chamberlain. Petworth and Godalming 'make no burgesses; ffarnham dooth'. But he had not touched Farn-ham which belonged to the bishop of Winchester and had the lord

---

[1] BM, Tit.B.i., fo. 257 (*LP* xiv. I. 538): 17 March 1539.
[2] That he was certainly employed once in this fashion is known from a draft speech in his hand, corrected by Cromwell, in favour of the subsidy bill of 1539 (*LP* xiv. I. 869). [This speech belongs to the session of 1540.]

chamberlain for its steward. He was also arranging for the burgesses of Portsmouth and Midhurst (?). In short, he was using his local influence for what it was worth, but not where there were prior claims to patronage.[1]

There is the less need to go in detail into most of the other known cases because this is no history of Parliament, and because they all prove clearly that Cromwell was simply trying to use the connections of men near the throne to influence elections in favour of suitable candidates. At Gatton, later famous as a rotten borough and already, by our standards, as rotten as could be, an agent wished to have Cromwell's nomination so that the 'owner', Sir Roger Copley, could have the indenture drawn up with the sheriff; the nominee was to take no wages, the agent having promised Copley as much.[2] The election of the knights of the shire for Norfolk makes a more complicated story, because here a local gentleman, Sir Edmund Knyvett, tried to oppose Cromwell's official candidates (backed incidentally by the duke of Norfolk), but he did not get very far.[3] Whatever the circumstances. and whatever the total of elections that Cromwell influenced either directly or through some other councillor, it all obviously went to the creation not of a personal party but a 'safe' Parliament in the king's interests. It was government influence, not personal influence, that he brought to bear; the men appointed were either worthy local men or king's servants, not his own. In Cornwall he attempted to place the sheriff's own son, and his servant, Godolphin, but had to face the strong opposition of local gentlemen who had made their plans before his wishes became known; it is not known how things worked out.[4] Certainly Cromwell's requests were far from being commands, another similarity with the experiences of later managers of elections down to the great reform bill.

However, there was one area where Cromwell encountered more than purely local opposition. The elections of March–April 1539 were

---

[1] BM, Cleo. E. iv, fos. 209–10 (*LP* xiv. I. 520). The last borough appears as Middnest or Midduest in Southampton's very shaky orthography.

[2] SP 1/144, fos. 257–8 (*LP* xiv. I. 645). The writer, Christopher More, continued: 'And further, if it be your lordeshippes plesure to haue any moo of your frendes to be appoynted in any other lyke place, I suppose your lordeshipp may spede therein . . .'.

[3] Knyvett, a headstrong man who, according to his uncle Norfolk, was 'only Rewled by his owne sensuall will and iij or iiij Light naughtie knaves of Walshemen', applied for the position to Cromwell, was politely turned down, and then started a rumpus at the election which resulted in his being bound to keep the peace and answer in the Star Chamber (SP 1/146, fos. 242, 274–5; 150, fos. 155–6, 160–1; *LP* xiv. I. 672, 706, 800, 808). [4] SP 1/144, fos. 69–70 (*LP* xiv. I. 598).

the first occasion since the debates of 1534 on which Cromwell found Gardiner active against him. The bishop of Winchester chose to make an issue out of Farnham and the Hampshire county elections; in both borough and shire Winchester influence was normally paramount, and Cromwell's attempts to insinuate his own candidates must have seemed to Gardiner the rankest impertinence. At Farnham the minister was rather late; Southampton and St John reported that Gardiner had already made his arrangements, though they hoped they might still be able to do something. The real test came in the county where Cromwell put forward Wriothesley and John Kingsmill, a local gentleman with Court connections; the latter, however, was the sheriff that year and therefore ineligible (though Cromwell promised to get him in somewhere else)[1] and this muddle forced Southampton to postpone the election until Cromwell had found another candidate! Both Wriothesley and his new colleague, Worseley, were elected by large majorities, despite the opposition of Gardiner which greatly amazed Kingsmill: 'I maruylle natt a lytylle the grett Intendyd Inderance off the byschopp off Winchester', which however failed of its purpose, for 'there whas never Seen . . . So many Jentyllmen ne ther other ffreholders that had So many voyces to be theyre knyght off theyre sher as you fyrste and master Worsley to be tother'.[2] Kingsmill thought the reason for Gardiner's attitude was either personal animosity against Wriothesley for his share in the spoliation of St Swithin's, Winchester, or fear that Wriothesley would 'purge the Cankerde and Rusty herttes ffrome theyre wolde Superstytutyes'; we may believe, rather, that hatred of and opposition to Cromwell in the only place where at that time he could show it were Gardiner's motives. He tried to thwart the lord privy seal at least in Hampshire which was the bishop's home ground. The struggle was the first sign of that ever increasing onslaught on Cromwell's position which was to bring him down in a little over a year. For the moment Cromwell had triumphed again, but Gardiner had at least shown where he stood. Nevertheless,

[1] He hoped for Ludgershall (Wilts.) where he thought Cromwell had 'a place' since the 'resident' member, Sir Richard Bridges, whose family had usually sat for the borough, was now knight for Berkshire (SP 1/146, fos. 237–40; *LP* xiv. I. 662). Details like these make one realize how completely Prof. Neale's picture of the Elizabethan Parliament may be projected backwards; even the invasion of the boroughs by the gentry had clearly begun. An important difference is that Cromwell found it much easier than later ministers to manage *county* elections.

[2] SP 1/140, fo. 197 (*LP* xiv. I. 634), Kingsmill to Wriothesley, 31 March 1539. For other letters on this election cf. BM, Vesp. F. xiii, fo. 230; Otho, E. ix. fos. 77 ff. (*LP* xiv. I. 564, 573).

it must be said once more that there is no question of either protagonist trying to build a personal party in the Commons; Cromwell was interested in influencing as many elections as possible, he had good cause to distrust Gardiner's use of his influence, and the bishop was not unnaturally provoked by this unprecedented interference with private patronage. The fact that Cromwell succeeded so easily is an interesting illustration of the power of the Crown; we cannot doubt that if the fight had been between Cromwell and Gardiner only, the bishop would at least have made a better showing. But the minister represented the king, and government persuasion was very powerful.

III

Cromwell thus went into the Parliament of 1539 with strength renewed and in good heart. But as far as he was concerned the calling of Parliament had one distinct disadvantage: it enabled his enemies to come to Court. Gardiner hastened up from Winchester, and Norfolk down from Kenninghall, and the issue was joined almost the first day of the session. This is the famous Parliament which passed the Act of Six Articles and thereby signalled the end of reformist leanings in the Henrician church; it is the Parliament of the so-called 'catholic reaction'. The story has been told before, but it will be advisable to go over it again in order to disentangle the ups and downs in the personal battle between Cromwell and his opponents; one or two new points will also emerge which throw rather a different light from that normally seen on Cromwell's position and skill at this time.[1]

The first thing to note is that Cromwell was well aware of the chief business to be discussed in the forthcoming Parliament, long before that body met. His remembrances for the drafting of bills for this session were jotted down in early March, one of them reading 'A device in the Parliament for the unity in religion'.[2] He was therefore certainly not taken by surprise; whether he also knew which way Henry was inclining is another matter. It seems, indeed, very probable

---

[1] The longest and perhaps best account of the passing of the act is in Burnet, i. 410 ff. Cf. also Froude, *Hist. of Eng.* iii. 194 ff.; Merriman (i. 253 f.) spent remarkably little time in discussing one of the critical turning points in his subject's life.

[2] *LP* xiv. I. 655. The date of this note is given by the entry 'for the appointing of Sir Edward Baynton and his wife to my lady Mary and lady Elizabeth, and of the revoking of the lady Kingston'. On 14 March, Cromwell reported to the king that he had seen a very penitent and submissive Lady Kingston (her offence was connected with the Pole troubles), and that Baynton and his wife 'have wyllyngly accepted the charge by your grace appoincted vnto them' (Merriman, ii. 193).

that the king did not know himself;[1] he may well have been trying to discover where majority opinion lay and what would be most acceptable all round, for however despotic in these matters Henry VIII appeared, he never, in fact, went counter to the inclinations of the people on whom his power rested. As for Cromwell, he had recently told the Saxon envoys in a surprisingly frank phrase that 'the world being at this time what it was, he would believe even as his master, the king, believed', though he seems to have hinted at Lutheran leanings at the same time.[2] Once and for all it ought to be said that Cromwell was not an atheist, and certainly not an agnostic, that virtual impossibility in a pre-scientific age; all the evidence goes to show that he had his faith, though it was not very ardent (was he so different in this from ninety-nine out of a hundred of his fellows?), and this unguarded statement probably represents the truth. He held that Lutheranism or something like it was the form of religion best suited to an anti-papal state, but the basis of his creed was a firm, and in all likelihood sincere, belief in the doctrinal supremacy of the king, a logical erastianism only more complete than that of most of his contemporaries. It follows that he could approach the coming struggle over 'unity' without excessive qualms, except inasmuch as it reflected on his foreign policy; with the principle of unity he had, we may be sure, no quarrel at all. However, it does not appear that he succeeded in drawing up the 'device' projected in his notes; the problem was shelved by a proclamation enjoining peace and charity on the parties until Parliament should have spoken,[3] and the government went into the session without its mind made up or a bill prepared, in itself proof to anyone familiar with Cromwell's mind and practice that the lord privy seal was no longer in full control.

This momentous Parliament opened on 28 April 1539, to round off the Henrician Reformation by adding a definition of dogma to the political and jurisdictional revolution carried out in the 1529 Parliament. Cromwell was handicapped from the start by a fever which had troubled him for a fortnight before the session opened and had not left him by 4 May.[4] There were parties, or perhaps they had better be

---

[1] Cf. Froude's convincing argument, *Hist. of Eng.* iii. 195 f., borne out by the course of events in Parliament.

[2] Merriman, i. 279: 'er siehe vnser maynunge den glauben betreffen aber wie die welt iczt stehet wesz sich sin her der konnig halte desz wolle er sich auch halten vnd solte er darumb sterben'.

[3] Printed by J. Strype, *Ecclesiastical Memorials*, i. Records, cx.

[4] *LP* xiv. I. 877, 921, 922.

described as streams of opinion – one conservative and looking to orthodoxy, and one reformist and intent on introducing Lutheran ideas – and Gardiner and Cranmer were undoubtedly the respective ecclesiastical leaders. Among laymen, Norfolk and Cromwell may be said to have represented the two factions, but both, it must be remembered, were generally ready to sink personal views in obedience to the king: and the king had not yet made up his mind. To help him to this end he asked for a Lords' committee to be appointed, under the presidency of his vicegerent; he also asked for a speedy report.[1] The committee was chosen, but its composition was fatal to speed, or in fact to any decision. Cranmer, Capon of Bangor, Goodrich of Ely, and Latimer of Worcester represented the reformist element; opposed to them stood Lee of York, Tunstall of Durham, Clerk of Bath and Wells, and Aldridge of Carlisle.[2] Cromwell, it may be noted, had not only succeeded in asserting his personal claims as vicegerent in spirituals, but had also managed to keep Gardiner away from the discussion; so far there was no sign of weakening power.

Perhaps, however, that very success was a mistake, for in the next ten days, while the committee pursued its bootless wrangles, the king made up his mind. On 16 May Norfolk rose in the House, declared that the committee had done nothing and was never likely to do anything, and offered six points or articles to be examined in full session, round which the doctrinal definitions would take shape, the result to be established by a penal statute against 'illos qui eandem aut aliquam parcellam violabunt aut infringent'.[3] These were the famous six articles, cast in the form of questions; we need not discuss them as the problem of religion does not concern us. What is important is the inner history of this move. It is so unlikely as to be impossible that Norfolk should have acted off his own bat. Contemporaries saw the hand of Gardiner in the shadows;[4] as he did not appear in public as head of the faction whose leader he really was, they must have had other sound reasons for suspecting him. The first extant draft of the act was revised by the king himself,[5] and it may be taken for certain that Henry had authorized Norfolk to act

---

[1] *LJ* i. 105. The speech was made by Audley on 5 May, the third meeting of the Parliament.

[2] For the views and standing of bishops mentioned in this and subsequent sections, cf. *DNB*.

[3] *LJ* i. 109. [4] *LP* xiv. II. 186, 379, 423.

[5] *LP* xiv. I. 868 (9); printed by Wilkins, *Concilia*, iii. 848. The draft is so much shorter and less detailed than the act that it was almost certainly at a very early stage.

as he did; it may be suggested that the duke and the bishop of Winchester, free while Cromwell's committee debated and absorbed his time, managed to swing the king to their way of thinking, with which in any case he was in sympathy. The fact that Norfolk was chosen to make the proposal was ominous enough; the common practice of this Parliament was for the chancellor to introduce all ordinary bills, while Cromwell handled those concerned with religion. In this case, Cromwell was left out completely, in the preparing and proposing of the measure. He had lost the second round.

Four days later Norfolk was on his feet again to propose a move which is not easily explicable. He put forward the peculiar plea that all members would like to recompense the king for his expenses and trouble incurred in the guiding and reforming of the realm, but that time did not serve (Whitsunday, 25 May, necessitating a recess); the king should therefore be asked to grant a prorogation.[1] The absurdity of the pretext makes the whole business obscure; however, on the 21st the king, present in Parliament as he often was in this session, granted the request, and on the 23rd – having rapidly disposed of the bill for the making of bishoprics – the House was prorogued for a week.[2] Perhaps the idea was simply to give time for further study; when Parliament reassembled Audley declared that the bishops and the king had much studied the questions in the meantime, that they had come to an agreement, and that the king now wanted a penal statute passed to enforce the newly discovered truth.[3] It seems therefore, that Gardiner and Norfolk had failed to rush Henry, and the delay imposed by his desire to feel his way proved Cromwell's salvation. As far as can be seen, he quietly withdrew into his prepared position of following the king's desires; as one catholic member of the Lords wrote afterwards, 'we of the temporalty have be all of one opinion, and my lord chancellor and my lord privy seal as good as we can devise'.[4] He was not prepared to defend the indefensible and hastened to re-establish his alliance with Henry, so seriously undermined by the surprise move of 16 May. Now that he knew where Henry stood he knew how to act, and there need be no serious doubt

[1] *LJ* i. III.
[2] Ibid. 112. The bill, introduced by Cromwell, was read three times and despatched to the Commons where it immediately received its first reading – all in one morning.
[3] Ibid. 113. It was probably during this recess that a record was made of the bishops' reaction to the articles (*LP* xiv. I. 1065, 2). On the basis of this information Henry then went ahead to establish orthodoxy.
[4] Burnet, vi. 233 (dated about 30 May by *LP* xiv. I. 1040, but probably a little later).

that he hoped from the first to use his position to soften the blow to his supporters among the reformers.[1]

The act now rapidly took shape: on Friday, 30 May, two committees were appointed to draft their versions – one reformist and one conservative.[2] The absence from the former of out-and-out reformers like Shaxton and Latimer, and the presence on the latter of Gardiner, now for the first time openly active in the affair, probably indicate that Cromwell had not yet succeeded in recovering the ground lost. He cannot have been pleased, either, when a bill concerning the ordination of priests, introduced by him, was committed for revision to Tunstall and Gardiner.[3] But soon after that the balance began to be restored. The two committees had reported to the king on Sunday, 1 June; on the 7th, Cromwell's associate Audley brought in the bill; on the 10th it was read a third time and sent to the Commons.[4] Norfolk had lost the initiative which he had gained so unexpectedly. Four days later the bill came back with a proviso which was assented to, and on the 16th the act seemed to be complete.[5] However, two further moves took place, and as both had the effect of softening some of the harshness of the act they must be considered as mild triumphs of the reformist party; they help to mark Cromwell's return to the position from which Gardiner had so nearly succeeded in dislodging him. On 24 June both Houses came to an agreement to postpone the date fixed in the act by which married clergy had to put away their wives; this had at first been midsummer's day but was now more reasonably put at 12 July. The bill was amended accordingly.[6] Three days later Audley introduced a further schedule to be annexed to the act; this was quickly passed through all stages in both Houses, to be ready for the royal assent and prorogation of Parliament on the 28th.[7] It is as certain as can be that the schedule mentioned was that embodying sec. xxii of the act by which the duty of observing vows of chastity was limited to persons who had taken them freely and at the age of twenty-one or

[1] Cf. Burnet, i. 427.
[2] *LJ* i. 113. Cranmer, Goodrich, Barlow and Dr Petre; Lee, Tunstall, Gardiner and Dr Tregonwell.
[3] *LJ* i. 115.   [4] Ibid. 116–17.
[5] Ibid. 118. The proviso was almost certainly the first of the two schedules attached to the act (cf. *Stat. Realm*, iii. 743, n.); secs. xx–xxi, concerned with the punishment of priests keeping concubines and of the women involved. The Commons showed no reluctance in passing this orthodox and savage act (they seem to have read it once each on three successive days, 11–13 June), thus proving that once more Henry knew how to fit his convictions to the prevailing trend.
[6] *LJ* i. 122.   [7] Ibid. 123–5.

over;[1] the iniquity of vows taken by children who did not understand their meaning had been one of the chief points put forward by the reformers at the dissolution of the monasteries, and the proviso took away much of the string of the third of the six articles by which ex-religious were tied to their vows despite the dissolution.

The immediate consequence of the act was that Shaxton and Latimer, the only two bishops not prepared to subscribe to it, resigned their sees;[2] however, their successors, John Capon and John Bell, though far from being radicals, were also far from conservative orthodoxy. Another vacancy occurred with the death of Stokesley of London;[3] the appointment of Bonner was at that time a move so hostile to Gardiner, who had violently quarrelled with him on handing over the embassy to France, that it must without question be ascribed to Cromwell's influence.[4] Bonner, who was still in France, had taken no part in the debates of the summer; it may not have been known that he would turn out to be so stout a pillar of orthodoxy, and in any case he was thought of as a Cromwellian until the minister's fall.[5] These replacements are sufficient proof that Cromwell was not seriously shaken. Ardent reformers like Bucer and Luther might fear the worst and lament the fall of Cromwell and power of Gardiner,[6] but Franz Burckhardt, vice-chancellor of Saxony, who had earlier in the year been on an embassy to England and knew what he was talking about, thought differently. In October 1539 he wrote to Melanchthon, to reassure him: the six articles had been the work of Stokesley and Gardiner of whom one was dead and the other excluded from the Court and all public business; the king was already showing signs of displeasure with the orthodox party.[7] Cromwell survived the attack; what was more, he once again succeeded in keeping Gardiner away from the king. Perhaps fear of the bishop's reappearance was behind the double prorogation of Parliament on 3 November and 14 January;[8] the assembly of Parliament had given Gardiner his chance in May 1539, and Cromwell cannot have relished the thought of another such

---

[1] *Stat. Realm*, iii. 743 and note.
[2] They had done so by 6 July (*LP* xiv. I. 1219).
[3] About September–October 1539 (*LP* xiv. II. 423).
[4] Foxe, *Acts and Monuments* (ed. Platt), v. 154 ff.
[5] Foxe, who hated both Gardiner and Bonner, alleged that 'so long as Cromwell remained in authority, so long was Bonner at his beck, and friend to his friends, and enemy to his enemies'. He says that Bonner and Gardiner were reconciled immediately after Cromwell's fall and tells a story of Grafton's to prove his case which sounds true (ibid. 413).   [6] *LP* xiv. II. 186, 379.
[7] Ibid. 423.   [8] *LJ* i. 126–7.

opportunity. It was a new position for the master-manager of Parliament to be in, but, with the king in his present mood and half weaned from dependence on his lord privy seal, no risks could be taken. The events of 1539 had shown Cromwell how determined his enemies were, and how precarious was his position; and both sides went into the new year, knowing that a decision could not be long delayed. For the moment Cromwell was again firmly in the saddle, and his opponents must have wondered what was in store for them.

IV

At this point it would become necessary to study in detail the foreign and matrimonial policy of 1539, but that has been done, and done exhaustively and well.[1] It will already have become plain that we cannot agree with the view which sees the clue to the whole story in these diplomatic negotiations and the international situation; on the other hand, it would be folly to suppose that they played no part at all. In the summer of 1539 it appeared likely that the rapprochement between the empire and France might be broken, and Cromwell's policy of allying with the German princes (not necessarily Lutheran – the duke of Cleves was a catholic) had little to recommend it; in the autumn, Charles and Francis were seen to be still good friends, and on 4 October Henry was tied down to an alliance by the signing of the marriage treaty between him and Anne of Cleves. The foreign situation only helped to restore Cromwell to full power; as has been seen, the attack on him had failed before the end of the parliamentary session in June, and he certainly did not depend for his security simply on the continued amity between the empire and France, though this enabled him, for the moment, to bind Henry more firmly to his side. That this temporary success was a sad delusion is well known: Henry followed his minister with grave misgivings about the advisability of any foreign entanglements (one lesson he appears to have learned from Wolsey's mistakes), and as the cause of the step, the combined hostility of the great continental powers, did not last, Cromwell was to find himself, early in 1540, in the position which Wolsey had so dolefully occupied in the summer of 1529: by means of his foreign policy he had placed the king in an awkward position, and Henry's easiest way out was likely to prove the overthrow of the minister. The situation

---

[1] Cf. Merriman, i. 242 ff., for a painstaking account of a singularly involved episode; a brief summary will be found in Fisher, *Pol. Hist.* v. 439 f.

was aggravated by Henry's personal dislike of the new queen forced upon him by Cromwell, and from the day of the marriage, undertaken with great reluctance after the first meeting, Cromwell knew that his position was desperate. By dint of circumstances he had so handled the king that Henry had been forced to do what he abhorred; for the first time he had actively thwarted the man whom hitherto he had managed so delicately.

What had driven him to so serious a mistake is a doubtful point. Perhaps, as is usually supposed, he was only sincerely afraid of the potential alliance against England; perhaps the chance of at last putting through a policy of which he had dreamed almost from the beginning of his ministry proved too attractive; perhaps his reformist and Lutheran tendencies were stronger than posterity has believed; perhaps he was so put out by the handling he had had in the summer that he determined to prevent any recurrence by forcing the king to his side. All these motives may have played their part; the result, anyhow, was that Cromwell deserted the principle of six years and for the first time took the lead in foreign policy instead of, as hitherto, following the king. It was a field in which he was less master than in most, and for which his logical mind and preference for speedy and decisive action were less well suited than Henry's opportunism.

The question is whether the mistake, once made, was bound to prove fatal, and surely the answer must be that it was not. The marriage took place on 6 January 1540; relations with France were good by March;[1] yet Cromwell was to reach still greater heights in April, to look like triumphing late in May (after the passage of those money bills the need for which, it is alleged, alone kept him in power), only to be felled suddenly in early June. There can be no doubt that Henry wanted to be rid of Anne; who was better qualified to achieve this end than the lord privy seal? Cromwell had shown the way in the first divorce; he had displayed no scruples when it came to the overthrow of Anne Boleyn who had been his ally; there was no reason to suppose that he would prove more difficult or less skilful now, especially as he was well aware of what was at stake for himself. As late as 6 June (or on the 7th), Cromwell was revolving ways and means for ending the marriage; it is true that he was also at a loss how to proceed, but the reason for that was not that he felt himself bound to Anne or the Cleves alliance.[2] If he was really attached to that alliance, he must have

---

[1] Merriman, i. 283 f.
[2] *LP* xv. 850 (11). For the cause of his hesitation, cf. below, p. 213.

possessed a degree of independence in religious matters which is quite at variance with his views as he expressed them to Burckhardt and Baumbach.[1] Certainly, there were no conclusive signs that his power was weakening. Marillac, who found him in charge on arriving in September 1539, still thought him 'the first councillor in credit and authority' on 2 February 1540;[2] he continued without interruption in his work of administrative reform and we shall show that even after February he still remained the king's first minister, until he was so suddenly struck down. It may be that Henry had lost confidence in him before, but the evidence is all the other way; undoubtedly the failure of his foreign policy and the king's dislike of Anne of Cleves made things much more difficult for him, but they did not unhorse him. That was achieved by his enemies who exploited this and other errors.

When Cromwell recovered his power in the second half of 1539, Gardiner once more retired to Winchester, but Norfolk was less easily disposed of. There is a story that he and Cromwell quarrelled openly and furiously at Cranmer's house on 29 June 1539, the trouble being started by Norfolk.[3] The tale, which is vouched for by an eyewitness, rings true, and it is likely that at that point – with everything achieved that he had set out to do except his foremost aim, the overthrow of Cromwell – Norfolk was in a savage mood and forgot his usual caution. Cranmer pacified his troublesome guests as best he might, but, as Burnet says, 'the two great ministers . . . were never afterwards hearty friends'.[4] However, Norfolk's chance did not come until February 1540 when he was sent as special ambassador to France. Cromwell may have been gratified by his rival's removal, but on the other hand any restoration of good relations with France was bound to work against the Cleves alliance and make him expendable. It is also likely that the French Court was something of a centre of anti-Cromwellian opinion. For three years Gardiner had resided there and his view of Cromwell must have coloured the local view; in any case, throughout the 1530s Cromwell had been rather imperialist than otherwise, while Norfolk had done something to earn the pension which he had from France;[5] and when Cromwell's fall was reported, Francis rejoiced as at the overthrow of a personal enemy.[6] He also

[1] Above, p. 206.
[2] *LP* xiv. II. 223; xv. 154.
[3] Burnet, i. 425.
[4] Ibid.
[5] The view was held by Chapuys (*LP* x. 351, 688; xi. 40), the bishop of Tarbes (ibid. 238), and Castillon (*LP* xiii. I. 995, 1101–2, 1135).
[6] *LP* xv. 785.

hinted that he had taken the opportunity of Norfolk's visit in February to discuss Cromwell; it is probable that Norfolk received much encouragement and may even have brought back a promise of French amity if only Cromwell were removed. Though on his return[1] he maintained superficially good relations with Cromwell, the die was cast. Cromwell knew it: he went out of his way to warn Richard Pate against the duke, a fact later used by Pate to ingratiate himself with the victor.[2] Norfolk knew it: when Cromwell tried the old trick of keeping his rival from the Court, this time on the pretext that a case of plague in his household made the duke a dangerous visitor, Norfolk replied that there was no danger as the sick man had not been near him for long and asked to know the king's opinion; if he was not to come to Court he would stay in London.[3] No more Kenninghall for him.

In March, the folly and arrogance of one of his reformist protégés added the last measure to Cromwell's cup by bringing the more dangerous of his rivals also back into the arena. This was the famous case of Bishop Gardiner and Friar Barnes. The details may be read elsewhere;[4] the point to note is that the controversy gave Gardiner a chance he did not neglect. He had no reason to love Barnes, for an earlier attempt of his to suppress the cocksure Lutheran had resulted in his own dismissal from the Council and a prolongation of his unwelcome exile.[5] On 12 March Barnes recanted his first sermon, on the 30th he withdrew his recantation publicly in another.[6] In the first days of April the king, scandalized by this example of the disunity which he had hoped to end by the Act of Six Articles, came down heavily on Gardiner's side, Cromwell's influence proved insufficient (if indeed it was ever exercised), and Barnes with two other Lutherans found himself in the Tower.[7] The city was full of rumours: on 10 April Marillac, the French ambassador whose none too well-informed despatches are almost the only comment we possess on the events of these months, reported that Cromwell and Cranmer 'do not know where they are'. He prophesied a great change within a few days; the king had recalled Gardiner, Tunstall and Clerk to the Council whence

---

[1] He arrived at the French Court on 15 Feb. (*LP* xv. 222) and was back in England by 11 March (ibid. 329).

[2] *LP* xv. 812.   [3] Ibid. 442 (1 April 1540).

[4] Froude, *Hist. of Eng.* iii. 281 ff.; Merriman, i. 287 f.

[5] *LP* xiv. II. 750 (p. 279). Sampson of Chichester was apparently coupled with Gardiner on that occasion. The date of the event is doubtful – perhaps early 1539, as Froude suggests (iii. 259), perhaps after the close of the 1539 session.

[6] *LP* xv. 334, 425.   [7] Ibid. 485.

Cromwell had excluded them; Tunstall was to be vicegerent and Clerk lord privy seal.[1] Marillac was probably reporting the hopes of the Norfolk faction with which he was likely to be in touch, but he added that Cromwell's own supporters did not expect him to retain the title of vicar-general. Very interesting is his further statement that if Cromwell remained at all it would be because he was 'very assiduous in affairs' – because of his outstanding administrative ability, that is. The matter cannot here be worked out in detail, but that important factor was rendered null by the newly organized Privy Council, supposedly capable of equal 'assiduity' in affairs;[2] Norfolk and Gardiner, who must have remembered the year of fear between Wolsey's fall and Wolsey's death, had no intention of leaving their enemy alive and of risking another change of mind on the king's part.

As a matter of fact, Marillac, or his informant, was rather premature. It was no doubt reasonable to expect Cromwell to fall with Barnes, but it does not seem that the minister allowed himself to be involved in the business. He made no known effort to save the preacher whose fate was due to his own foolish self-confidence, and though the advancement of Gardiner, which was the chief result of the affair, cannot but have been highly unpleasant to him, he did his best to save something from the wreck. Once again he beat a strategic retreat. On 30 March, on the day that Barnes quite ruined himself by recanting his recantation, Cromwell had Gardiner dine with him and spent four hours in restoring friendly relations, with apparent success.[3] In view of the fact that Henry was about to recall Gardiner to the Council, this was a wise step: at least it saved Cromwell from putting himself in the wrong at the Council Board, and it effectively countered any suggestion that he had been behind Barnes's impertinence. Once more he had managed at the last moment to block a most promising move against his position, and Gardiner was once more baffled, except that Cromwell had not been so far successful as to keep his rival away from the king. The shock tactics had proved a partial failure only.[4] It was at this point, too, that Cromwell gave up the secretaryship, in part at

---

[1] Ibid. 486. If Clerk was a privy councillor, he had succeeded Foxe of Hereford on that bishop's death in 1538.

[2] The Privy Council was organized as a board of government by 1536.

[3] *LP* xv. 429. Merriman's supposition that Cromwell was 'forced to grovel' before Gardiner (i. 289) depends on the view that Cromwell was actively involved in the Barnes affair; but there is nothing to show that he was.

[4] How little Cromwell's control of affairs and standing with the king were as yet affected is clear from an exchange of letters between him and Sadler on 7 April (*LP* xv. 468–9).

least in order to strengthen himself in the Council by the appointment of two of his supporters.

With things so uneasily balanced, the Parliament reassembled on 12 April. It was opened in a short speech by the chancellor; then Cromwell got up and, having applauded Audley's 'preface', spoke at length and in deadly earnest on the subject of religious unity.[1] He professed to speak in the name of the king, and no doubt he was representing his master's views correctly; the fact that he made the speech indicates how far he was as yet from disgrace, and the words and sentiments were his.

The king's majesty [he said] desires nothing more than concord . . .; he knows there are those who would stir up strife, and that in many places in his field tares have sprongen[2] to harm the wheat. The forwardness and carnal lust of some, the inveterate corruption and superstitious tenacity of opinion of others, excite disputation and quarrels most horrible to good Christian men; one side calls the other papists, and the other again calls them heretics, both naughty and not to be borne; and that the less so because they miserably abuse the Holy Word of God and the Scriptures which the same most noble prince of his gentleness and for the salvation and consolation of his people has permitted them to read in the vulgar tongue. They twist God's sacred gift, now into heresy and now into superstition.

The king, who 'favours nor one side nor the other but, as becometh a Christian prince, professes the true Christian faith', therefore desires three things. First, the 'true doctrine and rule of the Gospel shall be published clear and established'. Secondly, 'the pious observation of ceremonies shall be distinguished from the impious, their use taught and their abuse abolished'. Lastly, the penal laws already made must be enforced, and further steps taken to root out disunity by punishments. To these ends two committees are to be set up of bishops and divines, one to formulate true dogma and the other to devise the book of ceremonies. 'They shall not lack his majesty's voice and his true and accurate judgment.'

The king's anxiety for unity in religion was, thus, as strong as ever. In 1539 a basic test had been imposed by the six articles; now, in 1540, the work was to be rounded off by an authoritative statement of

---

[1] *LJ* i. 128–9. Cromwell's speech, undoubtedly made in English, is preserved in the stilted humanistic Latin of the underclerk of the parliament, Thomas Soulemont, who was also Cromwell's secretary; we may be sure, therefore, that it is an essentially exact rendering.

[2] Perhaps the archaism in the translation may be forgiven on the plea that this was a favourite word with Cromwell.

doctrine and ceremonial. Cromwell might well echo the cry, for in the king's orthodox mood and linked as he himself inevitably was, do what he might, with the aims of the reformers, he could only lose if the squabbles continued. So far he was still vicegerent in spirituals and addressed the House as the king's mouthpiece; but the two committees showed that the radical party was losing ground, though Henry still did not quite know his mind and Gardiner had not mastered it. The committee for doctrine contained, indeed, Cranmer, Barlow and Richard Cox, but on the other side were ranged solid conservative ranks: Lee, Tunstall, Gardiner, Heath, Thirlby, Nicholas Wilson, Owen Oglethorpe, William Tresham, Roger Edgeworth, and, we may add, Bonner who probably proved to be conservative already, as well as some whose opinions were less clear. The other body was more equally balanced, with Goodrich and Holgate opposed to the out-and-out orthodox Clerk and Sampson, while Capon and Bell must have led a doubtful sort of life in the middle.

However, Cromwell's own business in this session was rather the confiscation of the property of the order of St John and the passage of the subsidy bill, the two measures which it is generally supposed induced Henry to leave him in peace for the moment. So to argue supposes a deep duplicity on the king's part for which there seems little reason; it may be doubted whether Henry really thought his other councillors incapable of achieving a similar result with this very 'tractable' Parliament. The interpretation also leaves out of account the points already adduced which show Cromwell to be undisputed 'manager' certainly until the first days of the session, and entirely fails to explain the astonishing promotion which took place on 18 April, Cromwell being created earl of Essex and great chamberlain.[1] He thus succeeded to the inheritance of two ancient lines – the Bourchiers of Essex and the Veres of Oxford – a fact which must have galled Norfolk in particular, and he stood in a position where no subject could approach him. Apparently as powerful as ever, he piloted the financial measures through Parliament; all this time, however, the three Lutherans remained in the Tower, and the problem of Anne of Cleves hung over his head. While the evidence is clear that Henry was not yet ready to throw in his lot with Gardiner and the anti-Cromwellians, Cromwell's apparent power was built on appallingly insecure foundations.

On 1 May the bill annexing to the Crown the property of the knights of Jerusalem was sent down to the Commons; on the 8th the

[1] *LP* xv. 541.

subsidy bill had passed through all its stages.[1] One part of the business
of the session was largely concluded, but as Audley said on the 11th,
in proroguing Parliament to the 25th, the major task had proved too
big for solution. Neither episcopal committee had got much further,
and the respite was apparently intended to give them a chance of
preparing something that Parliament might discuss.[2] The recess also
brought to a head the struggle for power which was going on behind
the scenes. About this time at the latest, Cromwell must have become
aware of the new threat to his position contained in Henry's growing
infatuation for Catherine Howard, so considerately put in the king's
way by that pander, her uncle of Norfolk.[3] Within a fortnight of
Cromwell's fall, Henry was still putting his trust in him to bring off
another miracle in the royal matrimonial affairs, but Cromwell found
it impossible to think well of the king's plan.[4] It is probable that his
depression on 6 or 7 June, recorded by Wriothesley, and his apparent
indecision regarding the steps to be taken in the matter of Anne of
Cleves, had their origin in the fact that the obvious solution was no
longer available to him. He might now secure Henry a divorce, and
nothing (as Wriothesley pointed out to him) could be easier if Cromwell's fear that 'she be yet as good a Mayd for hym as she was when
she came to England' was well founded.[5] But in the circumstances
re-marriage could only result in the triumph of Catherine Howard
and the Norfolk faction, and for Cromwell to help Henry to his
divorce was tantamount to putting his enemies in the saddle. The result
of all these difficulties was that soon after the prorogation of Parliament the lord privy seal suddenly threw off the restraint which had
hitherto marked his treatment of the opposition, and began to thresh
about, much as a whale does in his 'flurry' of approaching death and
with similar peril to his assailants. On 19 May Lord Lisle, deputy of
Calais and hitherto considered a friend of Cromwell's, was arrested on
a charge – intelligence with Cardinal Pole and popish leanings – which
proves the attack to have come from Cromwell;[6] another 'great

[1] *LJ* i. 133, 135. [2] Ibid. 137.
[3] She received a small gift – the goods of two outlawed felons – on 24 April, and a present
from the king's Wardrobe on 18 May (*LP* xv. 613 [12], 686).
[4] Merriman, ii. 266, where Cromwell recalls his conversation with Henry and permits
a certain amount of reading between the lines.
[5] These facts emerge from Wriothesley's deposition made after Cromwell's fall (*LP* xv.
850 [11], printed by Strype, *Eccl. Mem.*, i, Records, CXIV, no. 9).
[6] Lisle had been on the 'wrong' side in the religious discussions of 1539; cf. his disapproval of one of the Calais burgesses, Thomas Brooke, who had tried to uphold
reformist views in the Commons (*LP* xiv. I. 1108, 1152, 1166).

personage' was rumoured to be in similar danger, and a leading London merchant was in trouble because he had kept a popish chaplain.[1] A day or two after Parliament reassembled, Cromwell brought off his last big stroke with the arrest of Richard Sampson, bishop of Chichester, who had been Gardiner's most active lieutenant in the struggle with the lord privy seal.[2] With him went Dr Nicholas Wilson, staunch conservative in religion and, like the bishop, a member of the committees set up in April. Cromwell was reported as saying that he had his eye on five other bishops; though no names were mentioned, it may be supposed that they were Gardiner, Clerk, Tunstall, Lee, and Heath, the solid core of the orthodox party. Rumours flew about – Barnes was to be released, Wallop had fled to Rome from the French court and Cromwell was trying to seek him out.[3] Sampson's arrest seems to have been designed to give Cromwell a chance of getting at his leading enemies rather than at the immediate victim to whom he wrote words of comfort, 'signifying that his Highnes was & is my most gracious Lord'; he succeeded at least in throwing the opposition into confusion and Sampson recklessly hurled accusations about to save himself.[4]

For a few days more, Cromwell seemed to be completely successful in the one quarter where it mattered – with the king; early in June, Sadler reported – in a letter which suggests that Sampson's arrest was made on Cromwell's own responsibility[5] – that the king was far from liking the bishop's denial of accusations so patently proved; also he would further consider Latimer, then under house arrest, when he could have word with Cromwell.[6] Cromwell, it seems, was trying to liberate his partisan, and the king's reaction was not unfavourable. On the other hand, it may be considered ominous that Henry insisted that Cromwell should not for the moment confiscate the bishop's property; when Cromwell himself was arrested, the immediate seizure of his house and goods indicated to people in the know that he was as good as dead already.[7] Indeed, it is probable that even at this moment

---

[1] Marillac to Montmorency, 21 May 1540 (*LP* xv. 697).

[2] Marillac to Francis I, 1 June 1540 (ibid. 736). Sampson was in Parliament on 25 May but absent from the 28th onwards (*LJ* i. 138).

[3] All this was reported by Marillac (*LP* xv. 373). Though the French ambassador is not the most reliable of sources, he has to be believed to some extent, and in any case there is little other information.

[4] *LP* xv. 758, printed by Strype, *Eccl. Mem.* i., Records, xciii.

[5] 'After I declared to the Kinges Majestee how the Bishop of Chichester was commytted to warde to the Tower . . ..'

[6] *StP* i. 627–8.   [7] *LP* xv. 766.

Cromwell's enemies were getting the upper hand. Cromwell had not been to Court for some time;[1] busy in Parliament and handling affairs with the assistance of a part of the Council permanently in London,[2] he had had to leave the king to other influences, keeping Sadler as his link, representative, and source of information. Very soon it was seen that the party of Gardiner and Norfolk had after all succeeded in winning the king over; suddenly, out of the blue, the long drawn out struggle was decided when, at three o'clock on Thursday, 10 June 1540, the captain of the guard entered the Council Chamber to arrest the lord privy seal.[3] The scene which followed has been described for all time by Marillac: how Cromwell threw his bonnet down in a rage, calling on his enemies' consciences to say if he was a traitor, and how – despairing of all hope – he only asked not to have long to linger. Norfolk and Southampton amused themselves by stripping him of his decorations, and every one reviled him, and so he passed through a postern into the boat which took him to the Tower.[4]

Until certainly the day of Sampson's arrest (26 or 27 May), and apparently for some days afterwards, the king had not yet decided against his minister. The change occurred in the week before Cromwell's arrest when his enemies must at last have succeeded in gaining Henry's ear; what the arguments were that they used must now be told if Cromwell's fall is to be made comprehensible.

v

The ostensible reasons for Cromwell's arrest were given to the world as heresy and secret working against the king's purpose in religion;[5] that the case was not complete on 10 June appears from an enquiry in France for details of an earlier report that Cromwell declared in 1538 he would make himself king and marry the princess Mary.[6] This enquiry also illustrates the king's readiness to believe anything; a more absurd report could hardly be imagined. Even if Cromwell had aimed at the crown (and of course he did not), would he have told the French ambassador? Even if he hoped to ally himself with the Tudors (and again, of course, he did not), would he have chosen Mary whom he had himself brought to bastardy? The story, of which nothing more is

---

[1] He was in London certainly from 11 May onwards (Merriman, ii., nos. 345–7), while the king stayed at Greenwich from Whitsunday, 16 May (*LP* xv. 697).
[2] Cf. e.g. ibid. 468.   [3] *LJ* i. 143; *LP* xv. 765–7.
[4] *LP* xv. 804.   [5] Ibid. 765–6.
[6] Ibid. 801.

heard, is useful, however, in showing that once Henry had turned
against his minister nothing was too ridiculous or far-fetched to be
believed and used; it helps us to understand how Cromwell's enemies
could succeed in one short week in overthrowing the minister who
appeared to have just restored his supremacy after tottering for some
time. If they managed to feed the king, whose mind grew ever more
suspicious and bloodthirsty as he grew older, with stories of Cromwell's treason and heresy, if they could produce one or two pieces of
evidence which, however absurd to the outsider, would convince
Henry, then Cromwell's fate would be quickly sealed, and once he
was down it would be easy to prevent his getting up again.

The best statement of the stories and proofs brought forward is in
Cromwell's attainder which Burnet alone of all the historians concerned with the event seems to have studied.[1] Its history in Parliament
is peculiar: introduced in the Lords on 17 June, a bare week after the
arrest, it was despatched to the Commons on the 19th; ten days later a
bill of attainder 'de Crimine Heresis et Lese Maiestatis per Communes
de novo concepta' was sent up with a proviso regarding the deanery of
Wells;[2] this was passed by the Lords on the same day 'et simul cum
ea referebatur Billa Attincture que prius missa erat in Domum Com-
munem'.[3] It appears, therefore, that the Commons, dissatisfied with
the Lords' bill, drew up one of their own to which the proviso for
Wells was attached before both bills were returned, or more probably
that the government introduced a second and later bill in the Commons; the Lords then agreed to the Commons' bill and shelved their
own. The purpose of these manoeuvres is difficult to discover since
only the final form of the act has survived; it can be said, at any rate,
that there is no sign of weakening or generosity in the attainder as it
stands, and that the Commons clearly made no attempt to save
Cromwell. Perhaps it may be supposed that the government collected
further 'evidence' after 17 June and wished to incorporate this in the
bill, using the Commons for the purposes; this would also account for
the calm acceptance of the new bill by the Lords.

[1] Burnet, i. 443 f. Merriman's account of the act (i. 295 f.) is perfunctory and inaccurate
in several details: e.g. Cromwell forfeited all his property, of course, and not only that
held since March 1538 (in any case the date should be 1539). The only accusation not
brought forward in it was that Cromwell had betrayed the king's confidences about
Anne of Cleves (partly refuted and partly acknowledged as true by Cromwell in the
Tower: Merriman, ii. 266); that was not suitable for publication.
[2] Cromwell was dean of Wells, and the proviso excepted the deanery from the penalties
of the act.   [3] *LJ* i. 145b, 146b, 149b.

The preamble of the act,[1] which in effect quotes all the more extreme assertions about the royal supremacy both lay and ecclesiastical which Cromwell himself had published in his Reformation legislation, is more byzantine in its adulation of the king than even Cromwell's preambles had been. It lamented the fact that Thomas Cromwell, earl of Essex, whom the king had raised from a 'very base and low degree' to be one of his 'most trusty counsellors, as well concerning your grace's supreme jurisdiction ecclesiastical, as your most high secret affairs temporal', had proved a false and corrupt traitor, and then recited the charges. These were:

(1) That Cromwell had taken it upon himself to set at liberty people convicted and attainted of misprision of high treason and 'suspicion of high treason'.

(2) That he had sold to aliens and subjects, contrary to the proclamations, licences to export money, corn, grain, beans, beer, leather, tallow, bell-metal, horses, and other commodities.

(3) That, 'elated and full of pride', he had of his own authority constituted commissions in many 'great, urgent, and weighty causes and affairs' without the king's knowledge.

(4) That being a person of poor and low degree, 'as few be within this your realm',[2] he pretended to great power over the king and said he was sure of him, a thing no subject should say of his king.

(5) That of his own authority and without the king's consent he granted passports to aliens and subjects to pass without search.

(6) That, furthermore, 'being a detestable heretic and ... utterly disposed to set and sow common sedition and variance among your true and loving subjects', he had spread heretical literature, caused heretical writings to be translated into English (assuring the translator, who protested, that the stuff was sound doctrine), and asserted that 'it was as lawful for every Christian man to be a minister of the said sacrament, as well as a priest'.

(7) That as the king's vicegerent in spirituals he abused his position to license heretics to preach and teach.

(8) That by the same authority, and falsely pretending the king's consent, he caused heretics to be set at liberty and refused to listen to accusations of heresy, rebuking the accusers, 'the particularities and specialties of which said abominable heresies, errors, and offences ... been over tedious, long, and of too great number here to be expressed, declared, or written'.

[1] The version printed by Burnet (iv. 415 ff.) from the parliament roll has here been used. The act is not in *Stat. Realm*.

[2] The almost pathological hatred shown in these repeated references to Cromwell's low origin is interesting. It suggests the hand of Norfolk rather than the king's in the drafting of the act.

(9) That, to the intent of more firmly establishing these heresies, he drew to himself 'by retainours' many whom he infected.

(10) That, 'supposing himself to be fully able, by force and strength, to maintain and defend his said abominable treasons heresies and errors', he declared on 31 March 1539, in the parish of St Peter the Poor in the city of London, that the teaching of Barnes and others accused of heresy was good, saying, 'if the king would turn from it yet I would not turn; and if the king did turn, and all his people, I would fight in the field in mine own person, with my sword in my hand against him and all other'; that then he drew his dagger, saying, 'or else this dagger thrust me to the heart, if I would not die in that quarrel against them all: and I trust, if I live a year or two, it shall not lie in the king's power to resist or let if he would', with further oaths and affirmations.

(11) That 'by oppression, bribery, extort power, and false promises made by him' he had obtained much wealth, and that, being so enriched, he had derided the nobles of this realm; that when reminded of his low origin he said traitorously (on 31 January 1540, in the parish of St Martin in the Fields), 'if the lords would handle him so, that he would give them such a breakfast as never was made in England, and that the proudest should know'.

For these reasons, Thomas Cromwell, earl of Essex, was to stand convicted of high treason and heresy, to suffer the pain[1] and loss of goods as was usual, at the king's pleasure.

Not all these charges were of equal value. Points 2, 3, and 5 accused Cromwell of abusing his power in the administration. It is possible, of course, that the king merely desired to dissociate himself from the sale of licences and passports which so much Tudor legislation made necessary, and which was no doubt obnoxious to the mercantile interest represented in the Commons, but it was nonsense to pretend that Cromwell, left to handle these matters himself, had acted without general warrant and against the king's desire. In particular cases, no doubt, he had despatched such business without bothering about special warrant, and there can be no surprise that out of eight years' virtual autocracy in administrative matters enough material could be quarried for an accusation or two. Cromwell himself admitted that 'I haue medelyd in So many matyers vnder your Highnes that I am not able to answer them all', adding that any offence was unwitting, though 'harde it ys for me or any other medlyng as I haue done to lyue vnder your grace and your lawse but we must daylye

---

[1] In fact the act only states that Cromwell was to be 'adjudged an abominable and detestable heretic and traitor', going on to his goods and chattels (Burnet, iv. 421); the death penalty involved was, however, clear in the law and did not have to be specifically mentioned in the attainder. There may also have been some doubt, as the penalties for heresy and treason were not the same.

offende'.[1] Henry had even better reason for putting the blame on Cromwell for the many commissions of enquiry and action which had harried the country since 1534; on the other hand, we know of no case where Cromwell's creation of such bodies was not covered by his powers or by acts of Parliament, and the accusation was wild. Equally absurd, though superficially more convincing, was point 9: that he kept retainers. He had indeed kept a great household and had employed reformist writers (though it could hardly be claimed that he had 'infected' a Starkey or Morison or Taverner), but he had offended neither technically nor in the spirit against the law. To quote his own defence:

If euer I retaynyd any man but suche onlye as were my Howsholde seruaunttes . . . god Conffound me but, most gracyous souerayng, I haue bene so Called on and Sewyd to by them that Sayd they were my Frendes that Constraynyd therunto I resayuyd thayr Chyldren and Freendes, not as Retaynours, For thayr Fathers & parentes dyd promyce me to Fynde them, and so toke I theme not as retaynours to my great Charge and For none evyll, as god best knowythe; interpret to the Contrarye who will.[2]

These were not the charges which persuaded Henry to throw his minister to the wolves.

More serious is point 1, though it was phrased generally, and it is impossible to imagine what case could have been made to prove that Cromwell had set at liberty persons convicted of misprision of treason. The real weight of the attack was concentrated in points 6–8 which contained the accusation of heresy. Whether Cromwell was a convinced Lutheran or not (and let us remind ourselves that he told the Saxon envoys he was, at the same time as he revealed his fundamental – and in the circumstances highly contradictory – erastianism), it is certain that the reformers saw in him their patron, and that, as Burnet says,[3] Henry himself had advanced a good way towards reform, so that his sudden reversal in 1539 left Cromwell isolated. We have seen how hard he tried to recover: how he came to terms with the Act of Six Articles and carefully avoided being implicated in Barnes's follies in March 1540; nevertheless he could hardly hope to live down his past and his partisan associations – the English Bible and the translations from advanced continental authors which he had authorized – though right until the end the king seems to have been convinced of

---

[1] Merriman, ii. 266. Burnet states that 'when he fell, no bribery, nor cheating of the king could be fastened on him' (i. 454), which appears to be true and is both remarkable and significant.   [2] Merriman, ii. 267.   [3] Op. cit. i. 445.

his essential loyalty. The charges were again very vague and un-supported, and even the heretical words he is supposed to have spoken are given neither time nor place; the most particular of them – that he had not listened when men were denounced as heretics – is not im-proved by the refusal to elaborate because to do so would be too tedious and long. The vagueness of the act makes one suspect that Cromwell was not permitted to stand his trial, not so much because he had set a precedent in the countess of Salisbury's case or because his enemies feared his skill in defence, but simply because they had no case against him that would have stood up to a moment's judicial scrutiny. And though Norfolk might get a conviction in the Lords he could hardly take the chance of showing up to the king the flimsiness of the tissue of half-truths and lies he had constructed.

However, though Henry was credulous when matters of heresy were concerned and though he was growing ever more wildly suspicious of treason in the most unlikely places, something more specific was needed to turn him against Cromwell; those details were supplied by points 4, 10 and 11. The first is the least convincingly put, for there is neither time nor place; if Cromwell did say that he was sure of the king, it was either on some particular occasion when he had the king's warrant to do something, or he was a fool. Altogether, the statements attributed to him more than justify Burnet's caustic com-ment that if he had been guilty of such rude talk 'Bedlam was thought a fitter place for his restraint than the Tower'.[1] The last two points served to provide the necessary proof at law under the act of 1534 which had made words treasonable; the alleged action with the dagger could hardly constitute a treasonable deed since, if anything, it was directed against himself rather than the king,[2] but the words reported are chosen with extraordinary care to provide clear proof of treason – the levying of war on the king and the stress on 'my own person'. That was the meaning of the triumphant sneer that 'he should be judged according to the laws he had made', for as Marillac commented, these were 'so sanguinary that often words spoken inadvertently with good intention had been constituted high treason'.[3] Norfolk and

[1] Ibid. i. 446.

[2] Burnet (loc. cit.) points out, however, that the drawing of his dagger, as an overt act of some kind, might be thought to clinch matters. The aptness made him rightly suspicious.

[3] *LP* xv. 803. That was – and is – the common view; for a more precise and less sensa-tional estimate of Cromwell and 'treason by words' cf. I. D. Thornely, in *TRHS* (1917), 106 ff. One would also like to see a list of cases where words spoken 'with good intention' had been twisted into treason by Cromwell.

Gardiner had managed to produce 'evidence' usable in a trial and also sufficiently precise to underline the general and vague accusations of treason and heresy which had already undermined the king's trust in Cromwell. Now they gave him proof – could he hesitate any longer? He did not hesitate.

The value of the proof lies partly disclosed in the statements themselves, so wild as to be incredible in a man of Cromwell's stamp: they do not fit either his rigid circumspection or his unhesitating subservience to the interests of state and king. A much more probable picture is painted by Cromwell's own protestations in defending himself against the charge of treason, too long to quote here;[1] the words are quite noble and ring true. Furthermore, the persons on whose word the charges were based destroy any lingering belief one might have had in their truth. It appears from Cromwell's first letter to the king after his arrest that these were Sir George Throckmorton and Sir Richard Riche;[2] probably they swore at least to point 10, for 11 by itself – though aggravating – could not have constituted a decisive charge. The former was an old enemy who had run foul of Cromwell during the Pole troubles in 1538; the other had once before, in the case of Sir Thomas More, burdened his soul with perjury in order to produce the verbal details of treason which would secure a conviction at law.[3] As Cromwell said: 'Your grace knowythe what manner of man throgmerton has euer bene euer towardes your grace and your procedinges; and what Maister Chauncelour [of the augmentations] hathe bene towardes me, god and he best knowyth – I will ne Can accuse hym; what I haue bene towardes hym your Magestye right well knowyth.' Moreover, he could not recall that he ever spoke with the two of them together; and if he did he was sure (as we may be sure) 'that I neuer spake of anye Suche matyer'. Bedlam indeed, rather than the Tower.

No, Cromwell was condemned on false witness, and the king turned against him so violently and swiftly at the end because he believed these lies. He must have honestly believed them, or he would not have come down so suddenly and completely on the side of Gardiner and Norfolk. At the same time, he found belief easy because to some extent Cromwell's behaviour had given him grounds for faith. Cromwell did

---

[1] Merriman, ii. 264 f.   [2] Ibid. 265.

[3] Cf. e.g. Chambers, *More*, 337 ff. The fact is used to point another moral against Cromwell. At the same time, it should be noted that Riche's companions who denied having heard More's alleged treasonable statement were Cromwell's servants; it is at least possible that Riche improved the occasion on his own initiative.

soften the Act of Six Articles in the application, he had linked his fate –
and attempted to link the king's – with the Cleves alliance and a
rapprochement with the Lutheran princes, he had got dangerously out
of step. As he put it after his fall – 'I woolde to Crist I hadde obbeyed
your often most gracyous graue Counsayles . . . then it hadde not bene
with me as now it ys'.[1] He had certainly gambled in his last year or
two of power, and the skilful machinations of his enemies, assisted by
Henry's growing reluctance to go further along the road entered upon
in 1532, had steadily manoeuvred him into a false position. The
creation and existence of the Privy Council had given Gardiner and
Norfolk their chance, though they had had to fight for their rightful
places on it; even as one 'assiduous in affairs', in Marillac's phrase,
Cromwell was now no longer necessary, and the tightly organized
board could be turned against him as easily as he had kept it under
his control for five years. There was no chance of forming a genuine
party on it, even if Cromwell had ever contemplated a thing so alien
to his conception of the royal power and supremacy. His enemies
were less scrupulous; they organized their supporters – Tunstall,
Kingston, Southampton, Browne and others; and when Cromwell at
last turned against them it was too late. Henry VIII was persuaded to
destroy the 'best servant he ever had' by lies and false accusations
which had a superficial appearance of truth;[2] in fact, the king, who
appeared to control everything, was being manipulated by a few men
who cleverly exploited his orthodoxy and the minister's essential lack
of it. What they failed to realize was that one could easily cheat
Henry into a rash action, but that it was much more difficult to control
him over a number of years; neither Gardiner, nor Norfolk, nor
anyone else, was to be a true successor to Cromwell. There were no
more prime ministers while Henry lived.

VI

This is no biography of Cromwell, and we cannot here describe those
weary weeks of waiting between the condemnation and the execution,
dragged out by the divorce from Anne of Cleves for which the king
required his cast-off minister's testimony. But there are two points
which deserve brief attention because they appear in almost every

[1] Merriman, ii. 265. The comparison with the biblical Susannah, which follows, is
however more than far-fetched.
[2] As he himself realized: *LP* xvi. 590.

account of the matter and are usually put in a way that goes sadly astray.

The first is this: on 30 June 1540 it was the case that his attainder had passed but the king was still undecided when, or even whether, to carry it out; and because on that day Cromwell concluded a long letter to the king with an appeal for 'mercye, mercye, mercye',[1] he is charged, in effect, with abject weakness, lack of dignity, and similar distressing symptoms.[2] Cromwell's first reaction on his arrest was to renounce all hope of pardon and ask for a quick end;[3] small wonder that imprisonment, callously prolonged until the king should be safely divorced (in case Cromwell's living testimony might be necessary, apart from the written affidavits he sent), wrought upon his mind, both weakening his resolution and raising false hopes. In this very letter he put his position clearly: 'I am a most wooffull prysoner, redye to take the dethe when it Shall please god and your majestye, and yet the Fraylle Fleshe incytythe me contynnewallye to Call to your grace ffor mercye and pardon. . . .' There was also some calculation in these appeals; Cromwell, we may well believe, was ready to try anything, and, if Foxe is to be credited, he did succeed in moving the sentimental king profoundly with one of his letters.[4] But Gardiner and Norfolk were at hand to stiffen Henry, if indeed he needed it; Cromwell was to go for good and all, and his pleas availed him nothing. But to pick them out of those last letters as sole evidence, when the rest of the same documents, however full of adulatory deference for the king, contains much that is dignified and steadfast, and to ignore the circumstances in which the appeals were made, is to give a singularly distorted picture of Cromwell's character.

The other point is the reiterated statement that Henry stripped Cromwell of all his honours and titles after his arrest, and ordered him to be thenceforth called nothing but 'Thomas Cromwell, shearman'. The statement rests solely on a report of Marillac's,[5] and it is simply not true. There are dozens of official references to Cromwell after his arrest and after his death, and in none of them is he ever called anything but earl, or late earl, of Essex, or the late lord privy seal. The very Act of Attainder, so full of contemptuous asides, employs no other description;[6] the Privy Council register invariably gives him his due

---

[1] Merriman, ii. 273.
[2] Merriman, i. 297; Fisher, *Pol. Hist.* v. 446 ('slavish and abject in the moment of danger'); Maynard-Smith, *Henry VIII and the Reformation*, 177 ('hysterical appeals').
[3] *LP* xv. 804. [4] Foxe, *Acts and Monuments*, v. 401–2.
[5] *LP* xv. 804. [6] Burnet, iv. 415 ff.

title;[1] Henry himself, or others writing to him, accord Cromwell full courtesy.[2] These examples, of which more could be cited, can leave no doubt that, whatever personal enemies might call Cromwell, and whatever rumours might float about London, no attempt was ever made to reduce him from the position to which the king had raised him. His offices, of course, were taken away, but his social rank was not touched. In this connection one must wonder whether Marillac's other report – that Cromwell would suffer the extremity of the law as a common felon – and his subsequent statement that the beheading actually carried out was an act of grace, are not equally misleading.[3] He asserts that Cromwell was condemned to a more painful and ignominious death, but that is not true, for the attainder makes no mention even of the death penalty itself, let alone the method. Perhaps its silence reflects Parliament's doubts as to the king's intentions, or the Norfolk party's desire to carry their vengeance even to the scaffold, in despite of Cromwell's peerage. If Cromwell never ceased to be a peer, he could only be beheaded, and the complications were merely introduced by a hostile foreigner ready to listen to rumour.

In any case, the execution was unusually cruel – on 28 July Cromwell mounted the scaffold, made a speech which may or may not be the one circulated afterwards in print and preserved by Hall and Foxe,[4] 'and so paciently suffered the stroke of the axe, by a ragged Boocherly miser whiche very vngoodly perfourmed the Office'.[5] The general feeling at his fall was set down by Edward Hall, who had worked under Cromwell in Parliament and who shared his enthusiasm for the Tudor Crown as well as much of his anticlerical passion. They are sober words from a contemporary and they rightly lay the stress on the true cause of Cromwell's fall. Not false policies or opposition to the king's religious desires really brought about his overthrow, but the personal enmity of the men whose power he had taken away. Whatever our views – whether we feel with those that rejoiced or those that lamented

---

[1] E.g. *LP* xv. 996; xvi. 14, 300, 349, 479 etc.

[2] *LP* xv. 801; xvi. 9.

[3] *LP* xv. 847, 926. Melanchthon also heard that Cromwell was hanged, quartered and burnt (ibid. 982). The rumour certainly got about.

[4] Cf. Merriman, i. 301. There is a version preserved among the papers of Bishop Cox of Ely at Corpus Christi College, Cambridge (MS 168, art. 25) which essentially corresponds with the version known from Foxe (the full version in ed. Platt, v. 402, after the 1563 ed.), though it adds a few odd touches whose authenticity it is difficult to be sure of. Thus according to the transcriber Cromwell ended his speech and prayer with the words (turning about): 'farewell, Wyat, & gentell Wiat, praye for me'.

[5] Hall, *Chronicle*, 839.

– Hall's words would be hard to better, and they may stand here, to conclude this matter:[1]

Many lamented but mo reioysed, and specially suche as either had been religious men, or fauored religious persons; for thei banqueted and triumphed together that night, many wisshyng that that daie had been seuen yere before; and some fearyng lest he should escape, although he were imprisoned, could not be mery. Others who knew nothyng but truth by hym bothe lamented hym and hartely praied for hym. But this is true that of certain of the Clergie he was detestably hated, & specially of suche as had borne swynge, and by his meanes was put from it; for in ded he was a man that in all his doynges semed not to fauor any kynde of Popery, nor could not abide the snoffyng pride of some prelates, wiche vndoubtedly, whatsoeuer els was the cause of his death, did shorten his life and procured the end that he was brought vnto.

[1] Ibid. 838 f. I have modernized the punctuation.

11

THE GOOD DUKE*

Professor Jordan never does things by halves. To his massive studies of toleration and philanthropy he is now adding a narrative history of the brief reign of Edward VI, of which the first part, covering thirty-three months, runs to 523 pages. The tale itself is told in all the detail possible, with a fair amount of personal comment, and the narrative is amplified by sections discussing the structure of power, the administration of the realm, and the economic crisis with its reflection in contemporary thought.

The method and the intention are admirable, as are the sheer effort involved and the fact that the book got done. Let no one underestimate these points. In a profession whose members too often rest content with small publication or none, Mr Jordan stands out as a major producer, a Krupp or Peugeot among historians. The reader of this volume will gain much knowledge of the two and a half years during which the Protector Somerset ruled England; he will be able to follow in detail the making of the Reformation; he will come to understand the details of the domestic scene, foreign affairs, the clash of personalities. Though the interesting marriage between analysis and narrative does not quite come off – much analytical detail would have better found accommodation in appendices – the book reads easily, and (as usual) Mr Jordan's engaging devotion to heaped and sometimes Homeric adjectives comes across as no more than an idiosyncrasy. Whether, however, the historical problems have been successfully solved is another question. Is this a really definitive and novel account? And here doubts must unfortunately arise, for there are rather too many dubious statements, and too many major points of interpretation cannot really convince.

Particular mistakes, of varying importance, do rather mount up. The 1542 edition of Hall's *Chronicle* was proved legendary some thirty-five years ago (p. 31 n.). The record of Stephen Gardiner's clashes with the governments to whom he was accredited hardly

* [Review of *Edward VI: the Young King. The Protectorship of the Duke of Somerset*, by W. K. Jordan (1968). *HJ* 12 (1969), 702–6.]

entitles one to speak of his 'unmatched skill as a diplomatist' (p. 47).
Sir John Russell was a peer before 1547 and should not, in another
place, be called Lord John Russell (pp. 81, 462). At least six members
of Edward's first Council, and possibly eight, were courtiers, which
invalidates the statement that 'almost without exception' these councillors' careers had been in offices of state rather than at Court (p. 82).
The fines entered in the Council register were not Star Chamber fines,
nor does Pollard, here quoted, say they were (p. 87). Mr Jordan says
that in the land sales 'the ancient crown lands, regathered by Henry
VII, were really left untouched' (p. 121): the parenthesis is wrong,
and the main statement unprovable and highly improbable. There is
no reason at all for supposing that the commission which investigated
the revenue courts in 1547 was 'probably' meant to supply councillors
with ammunition in Parliament (p. 170): this shows a serious misunderstanding of the administrative situation and of the relation of
government to Parliament. Riots not equal to levying war on the king
had never been treason (p. 173); altogether, the account of the treason
law here given is very unsatisfactory. Cecil cannot have been secretary
to the Council since no such office existed (p. 212). Heresy had a
perfectly precise meaning in the sixteenth century and not one identical
with opposition to the State (p. 225); adherence to Rome was never
called heresy, and the statement that parts of Roman Catholic worship
'were in legal fact heretical, though they were not in truth so to be
treated under the law' is as meaningless in fact as it is puzzling in sense.
Lay career diplomats were very far from 'new' under Edward VI
(p. 233). There was no Parliament in 1517 (p. 411). The Edwardian
'commonwealth-men' only followed in the footsteps of their Henrician
predecessor, as Professor A. B. Ferguson demonstrated in a book here
ignored in favour of an earlier article (p. 417). The 'life tenures' on
p. 428 should be leases.

This list suggests that there are aspects of his subject with which the
author is less familiar than with others, and the suspicion is reinforced
by more complex misunderstandings scattered through the book. The
account given of the court of Requests (pp. 359 ff.) is bedevilled by a
basic error: Somerset was not charged with transferring 'the' court
to his own house but with there setting up 'a' court of that name.[1]
'Court of Requests' was not, in fact, the technical name of any particular institution, but rather a technical term for any tribunal erected

---

[1] A. F. Pollard got this point right: *England under the Protector Somerset* (1900), 233, 243,
280.

to deal with the complaints of those unable to get justice at law; bodies so described existed, for instance, in a variety of towns. *The* court of Requests, properly known as the King's Council in the White Hall at Westminster, remained perfectly active in Somerset's day. Mr Jordan's long discussion of land sales is very obscure, in part because it does not start from the well-known fact that prices were calculated at so many years' purchase but arrives at this (calling it a rate of interest) in a very roundabout way (pp. 105 ff.). The statistics there are hard to follow, nor is there any mention of the burdens imposed on purchasers. On the other hand, Mr Jordan does well to bring out the lavish dispersal of Crown resources by gifts and preferential sales, and the manner in which, during the king's minority, the men in possession helped them-selves. The Council's concern with public order is hardly 'obsessive' (p. 351); this was one of its few specific duties, and the picture of violence is, in any case, overdrawn. To cite the words of patents appointing teachers or doctors as proof of a deep concern for social improvement is a surprising lapse in Mr Jordan's 'feel' for the sixteenth century (p. 357). In his accounts of the two parliamentary sessions of the period (pp. 179 ff.; 305 ff.) the problems posed and the answers presented seem somewhat off-key. Thus the tallies of bills failed mean nothing when no account is taken of the facts that the government had no monopoly in introducing 'public bills' (whatever they may have been at this time) and that every session in the century produced many abortive starts. The analysis of acts passed, on the other hand, applies unreal and twentieth-century categories. An unsolved mystery is created by the mention (no evidence cited) of three 'acts' which allegedly passed the Commons, did not receive the royal assent, and were yet treated as having the force of law 'though not being counted as statutes because of their limited or private nature'. What is all this?

Perhaps this sort of criticism is needlessly finicky; at least, if one could accept the general interpretation here given of Somerset's regime, the rest would fall into place. But can one? In essence, Mr Jordan adheres to Pollard's old view of the good duke, full of high idealism, done down by the selfishness of the upper classes and his own un-worldliness. There are some signs that Mr Jordan is reluctant to give up established opinions. Pollard is not the only elderly authority who commands his allegiance. The brief discussion of the Henrician Reformation rests firmly on Powicke's misleading little book, as though A. G. Dickens (and others) had never written. After Hexter (and others) it is strange to find an historian who so labours the notion that the Tudor 'new men' were 'middle-class'. The analysis of the mid-century's economic troubles remains at the stage at which Tawney left it, with the misconceptions of *The Agrarian Problem* still firmly repeated here. Edwin Gay's ancient and exploded article on enclosures is used; Eric Kerridge's important re-opening of the question is ignored. A casual remark on state intervention in the economy (p. 427) reveals that recent work on the subject has not been taken into consideration. Mr Jordan (p. 395 n.) cannot bring himself to accept Mrs Dewar's convincing revival of the supposition that the *Discourse of the Common Weal* was written by Sir Thomas Smith, though the book's contents point that way and Miss Lamond's argument for John Hales has even more holes in it than Mrs Dewar noticed.

Above all, however, there is the question of Somerset's policy which turns on three main points: his private character and ideas, the real meaning of the reaction against Henry VIII, and the methods which the duke employed in his government. Mr Jordan does recognize some of the Protector's unfortunate traits – his arrogance, impatience of criticism, imperious readiness to offend others. But he denies him ambition (p. 73), credits him with a belief in the goodness of man (p. 172), calls him lenient and pacific (p. 268), ascribes to him great talents and magnanimity of spirit (p. 348), and thinks 'this strange and complex man . . . one of the true architects of the modern world' (p. 436). Yet what evidence is there for all this? We know that Somerset favoured a paternalistic economic policy and encouraged complaints against the rapacity of the great. Yet no man had shown himself more greedy of wealth or ruthless to others than Somerset when he built up his fortune during Henry VIII's lifetime;[1] of all the Edwardian councillors, he was the most savage invader of the Church's rights, simply for the purpose of augmenting his estate.[2] The most one can say of him is that he preached well and practised dubiously. To deny personal ambition to a man who manoeuvred at length and successfully in the early days of the reign to gain that single-handed control which Henry VIII had hoped to prevent seems strange. Mr Jordan tries to show his hero coming to prominence by his own efforts and calls his rise at Court rapid (p. 34). But the truth is that he was a minor figure in Court circles for more than ten years, until his sister cast her inexplicable spell

[1] Cf. M. L. Bush, 'The Lisle–Seymour Land Disputes', *HJ* 9 (1966), 255 ff. Dr Bush's unpublished Cambridge dissertation on Somerset's early career establishes the case more fully.
[2] P. M. Hembry, *The Bishops of Bath and Wells 1540–1640* (1967), 105 ff.

over the susceptible king; thereafter, as the king's brother-in-law, he did indeed do well, and – to be just – proved in due course to have marked talents in war. But nothing in Somerset's career foretold any ability to rule the realm, and the outcome – not, of course, solely his fault – confirmed the shrewdness of the old king's refusal to appoint him to high political office. Somerset may well have had real sympathy for the poor, though the record of his actions needs more analysis than it gets here,[1] and he unquestionably had some fine ideals in religion and politics; but he was also an outstanding example of the self-aggrandizing *nouveaux riches* of the sixteenth century and personally so rude and disagreeable that the only wonder is how long the other councillors suffered him.

But did he not, right from the start, announce a policy of toleration and mild rule – a policy which, possibly rash, was nevertheless commendably high-minded? This is certainly Mr Jordan's view. He lays heavy stress on the striking preamble to the act repealing many of Henry VIII's treasons and felonies, a piece of writing which, even after one has made allowance (as Mr Jordan does not) for the propagandist purposes of Tudor preambles, still leaves a reasonable impression of sincerity. On the other hand, it must be remembered that new reigns always started with a relaxation of rigour and attempts to gain popularity for the new regime; Somerset said more than most, but many of the allegedly objectionable laws soon crept back. Mr Jordan finds it difficult to account for the 'hysterical and really vicious' act of 1547 against vagabonds; but he does so only because he regards Somerset's sympathy for the poor as 'steady' (what proof?) and his whole social policy as invariably magnanimous (p. 177). He altogether over-simplifies too much: neither was Somerset so plainly a twentieth-century welfare legislator out of his time, nor was he so solely responsible for every act passed.

The most suspicious circumstance surrounding the Protector's government is here treated with a mixture of inadequate exposition and misleading gloss. I refer to Somerset's remarkable liking for proclamations. In his two and a half years of power he issued seventy-five, almost the same number as had appeared in the preceding seven years.[2]

---

[1] The Protector's conversion of all tenures on his estates to copyhold (p. 306) may have been as generous as is here claimed, but the complications of copyhold law and practice were such as to make any simple identification of copyhold with generosity problematical. This needs more study. The disparking of Hampton Court may have sprung from consideration for the poor (p. 415), but the Council minute spoke also of loss of rents and the expenses of maintenance (*APC* ii. 190). [2] Cf. below, no. 17.

Contrary to recent practice, the bulk (more than two-thirds) were exercises of the prerogative, unconnected with authorization by statute, and this even though Parliament met twice during his rule. Well may Mr Jordan say that there is no evidence whatsoever of any timidity in the employment and expansion of royal power by the use of proclamations' at this time (p. 350), though why this should reflect credit on Somerset, the good duke, is less obvious. Mr Jordan does not seem entirely clear about the constitutional proprieties: he suggests that the repeal of Henry VIII's acts concerning proclamations may have been intended to 'posit the effective power of proclamations on more nearly acceptable constitutional grounds', as though there could have been better grounds than an authorizing statute.[1] Perhaps the real reason for the repeal should be sought in the fact that Somerset thereby freed himself from the necessity of getting the signatures of twelve other councillors to all his proclamations. At any rate, his use of proclamations based exclusively on the prerogative power to issue and embodying non-statutory regulations was distinctly autocratic. The implications of this may be read various ways, but the fact must be recognized.

It may be thought that we should approve the duke's practice because it enabled him to push through orders comfortable to the commonwealth which he could not have got through Parliament or manipulated through the Council. In fact, Somerset's proclamations exemplify far more a vigorous personal rule than any social concern; the occasional enforcement of existing statutes aside, and ignoring routine orders, one finds an odd assortment of strangely personal acts of government. This was not only rule by edict, but a rule less concerned about either the forms of law or public opinion than anything seen under Henry VIII. The Protector's edicts seem to stand well with his overbearing and impatient character, his contempt for others. Nor do the facts bear out the allegation that the repeal of 1547 was intended to mitigate the heavy penalties used in the previous reign; indeed, they cast doubt on the view that the generous preamble of the repeal statute represented a sincere change of heart. In the reign of Henry VIII, the sanctioning clauses of proclamations reserved the heaviest penalties – fine and imprisonment – to serious offences close to felony or heresy.[2]

[1] An interesting constitutional point is raised by the opinion (cited p. 168) that a treaty with France needed to be ratified by Parliament. The opinion was offered not by Somerset, as Mr Jordan alleges, but by the Council, a point correctly made by Pollard whom Mr Jordan says he here follows. Presumably parliamentary ratification was thought necessary during a minority.   [2] *Tudor Royal Proclamations*, i, no. 272.

The new reign opened with a spate of proclamations which, among other things, threatened imprisonment or 'pain' for repeating rumours, assaulting scholars, and private innovations in the services of religion.[1] Abettors of pirates were to be executed (a highly dubious extension of the powers of proclamations); deceitful cloth-making carried punishment at the Council's pleasure, while Somerset at his sole pleasure was to deal with those who killed the king's deer.[2] This list extends on either side of the session which repealed the Henrician acts; the policy was active and severe throughout.

The facts thus suggest a very different conclusion about Somerset and his policy from that put forward here, in agreement with A. F. Pollard. Both historians may have been influenced by their approval of a religious policy which was certainly in part the duke's (though Cranmer possibly does not get enough credit here) and by Somerset's attachment to the commonwealth party with its just complaints and its ill-thought-out remedies. Against these points, however, one should set others: the overbearing rule of a self-centred man, greedy for private gain while severe on the profits of others, incompetent at handling all personal relations and disastrously incompetent in politics, well-meaning but erratic, willing to employ drastic instruments and ignore the basic elements of the constitution – in the end the creator of nothing that endured and the architect only of his own ruin.

Mr Jordan has yet to give us a second volume on the reign, and some of the criticisms here made will possibly find an answer there. Some of them may be matters of opinion, but others do seem to be matters of fact. At the same time, it would be quite wrong to end this long review without once more stressing the virtues of this detailed and loving narrative. There are some good and solid accounts, as of the Scottish war or the making of the first Prayer Book. And even though it is hard to agree with him, Mr Jordan's enthusiasm for Somerset gives this long and crowded book a vigour and zest which make for compulsive reading.

[1] Ibid. nos. 281, 292, 299.   [2] Ibid. nos. 284, 286, 323, 328.

12

QUEEN ELIZABETH*

Queen Elizabeth, of Blessed Memory, ruled over her people for forty-five years, about half as long again as most of them had any cause to expect to live. When she herself died, nearly seventy years old, there were very few alive who could even recall that another sovereign had ever sat on the throne of England. And though towards the end she had been not only old but also somewhat out of touch with the attitudes and ambitions of a new generation, she retained to the last the love and worship of a nation accustomed to a monarchy clothed in the splendour of divine right but also embodied in palpably real people. Whatever else the Tudors may have been, they were aggressively alive, sculpted in the round, formidable personalities of the kind that create living legends in their own lifetime and do not lose their vitality even in death. The Queen's long reign accomplished the promise of her father's rule; the age of Elizabeth is rightly regarded, not only by historians but also in the popular memory, as a time of greatness breeding greater things still than it actually witnessed.

It is thus a little surprising that good biographies of Elizabeth should be so few in number. Here is a figure of history about whom it is easy to discover plenty of personal facts, known in detail from early childhood, heavily documented through sixty-nine years. Character is revealed in action, sayings, and writings. The interest of both person and period is undoubted and has never ceased. And if there are uncertainties, if the Queen could be an enigma to the observer, surely this should only stimulate the biographer and relieve him from feeling that the work has been done. Yet there are only two lives of Queen Elizabeth worthy of attention, both admittedly excellent: J. E. Neale's, published in 1934, which would now be generally regarded as the standard work, and this present book which first appeared in 1896 and still retains independent value after a time as long as the great Queen's own life. Neale's book owes its eminence to the employment of a professional historian's equipment, allied to literary skills of a high

---

* [Introduction to the reprint of M. Creighton's *Queen Elizabeth*, New York, Crowell, 1966.]

order; it embodies the research and understanding of a whole generation unknown to Creighton and benefits from solid interests in
government and society alien to him. If in the opinion of those
qualified to judge it has nevertheless not succeeded in relegating
Creighton's book to oblivion, this is in part because good studies of
Elizabeth are so few, but in greater part because the bishop of London
brought to his work special qualities which give a distinct and distinguished air to his life of Elizabeth.

Mandell Creighton was born on 3 July 1843, the son of a master
carpenter of Carlisle in Cumberland.[1] He made his way by his brain.
Educated at Durham Grammar School and Merton College, Oxford,
he obtained a first class in Greats and, after only six months' study, a
good second class in the honours school of law and history. Even
before he took his degree he had been elected a Fellow of his College,
and there he remained for nine years as the most influential of the
tutors. Marriage in 1872 was followed by ordination in 1873, and in
1875 he decided to leave Oxford in order to vary his experience. His
life as parson of Embleton in Northumberland was both pleasant and
successful, and his duties left him time to begin his career as an historian.
He had resolved to write the history of the Papacy from the Great
Schism in 1377 to the Sack of Rome in 1527, and the first two of the
work's ultimately six volumes were published when the Dixie chair of
ecclesiastical history, founded at Cambridge two years before, came to
be filled in 1884. Creighton's fame assured him of the appointment
which he held, writing and teaching with vigour and success, for six
years. In 1886 he joined with others in the foundation of the *English
Historical Review*, became its first editor, and set standards both of
content and typography which have altered little since. In 1890, the
world once more made its demands on one who at heart preferred the
academic existence, and he obeyed the call to become bishop of Peter-
borough. From there he was in 1897 translated to the see of London,
which at the time was convulsed by the ritualistic controversy provoked by Anglo-Catholic innovators and nourished by their bigotedly
low Protestant opponents. Creighton here found a new opportunity
for his great energy and his striking ability to use every minute of the
day. However, overwork inflicted an ill-treated ulcer upon him, and
he died, after a severe haemorrhage, in 1901, before the move to
Canterbury, confidently predicted for him, could come his way.

[1] For Creighton's life and person see *DNB; Life and Letters of Mandell Creighton*, by his
Wife (2 vols., 1904); and W. G. Fallows, *Mandell Creighton and the English Church* (1964).

In person, Creighton was tall, slender, with a big nose, long reddish beard, bald head, and formidable air. His mind exemplified the qualities commonly associated with men from the north country. He was plain, downright, determined, and though he quite liked the pomp and majesty of a bishop, he was entirely devoid of pretence and saw through himself as well as through others. In the solemn setting of the late-Victorian Church, his sardonic wit and a liking for plain truths expressed in paradox secured him a reputation for frivolity, and the fools that he did not suffer gladly were sure that the bishop did not regard serious things seriously. This was nonsense. Creighton had the brilliant teacher's instinctive gift for arresting attention, but pomposity too often saw in this only 'unsoundness'. It speaks well for Creighton's sweet temper and charm of manner that this reputation, which has proved fatal to many a man's career, did nothing to harm his. To his Church, Creighton stood in a simple enough relationship. His faith was commonplace; he did not favour the extravagances of either extreme party, and he admired the Church quite as much for the sake of its history and institutional authority as for its ministry. There was something almost aggressively uncomplicated about Creighton.

These same gifts of straight seeing and straight thinking, down-rightness and simplicity, mark him as an historian. Like most of his contemporaries, he regarded Ranke as the model to imitate, and his preoccupations were, therefore, with political history, diplomacy, and personality. He had some small interest in social problems, the facts of the national economy, instruments of government, but he knew little enough about them; it is quite strange to think of him as a contemporary of Maitland and a younger man than Stubbs. He refused to pass lofty judgments, a restraint for which Lord Acton severely censured him; but Creighton was right, and his notable freedom from the prejudices of his own time has allowed his work to survive, still readable and still read. His habit of taking down the scaffold when the building was finished and of putting a good coat of matt paint over the whole may disguise the great learning and wide reading that went to the making of his books. In his life of Elizabeth, for instance, he quotes constantly from the documents but gives not a single reference, and his quotations are not only apposite but also correct. In short, he wrote to be read; he wrote swift, plain, narrative history; he knew how to make events fascinating and people alive; and he did all this with a minimum of selfconscious art. But his equipment lacked an important professional dimension; he rarely, if ever, used manuscripts;

and he could not penetrate below the level of high politics. Curiously enough for a cleric writing on ecclesiastical institutions and religious centuries, he did not handle at all well the facts of religion or its impact on history, and his great work on the papacy palpably falters when he has to turn from the politics of Renaissance Italy to the eruption of Luther.[1]

This sober, unemphatic, undogmatic attitude to religious history, combined with his close attachment to the kind of liberal Churchmanship which dominated the Establishment of his day, mars his account of the Elizabethan Church. That he made serious mistakes about the history of Puritanism is no blame to him; a great deal of work has been and is being done for which he lived too soon. But it is a shortcoming that he could not really understand its spirit because he disapproved of its violent enthusiasm. On the other hand, his own attitudes enabled him to do full justice to Elizabeth herself; he understood her too well to suppose, with some now current opinion, that she had no religion, and his description, in this book, of her faith is in some ways his masterpiece. The *History of the Papacy*, for sheer size alone, must remain his chief work, but yet he never did anything better than this clear delineation and sympathetic analysis of a character he thought in many ways deplorable. Unlike more recent historians of the age, he could appreciate the skills, intelligence, and achievement of the Queen without having to gloss over her evasiveness, frequent indecisiveness, bad manners, and sillinesses. 'If Elizabeth had been capable of a bold policy . . . ,' says Creighton outright (p. 96) on an occasion when he finds her missing her opportunities. One would look in vain for a similar condemnation – calm, measured, perhaps a trifle condescending – in the pages of Neale or A. L. Rowse. Creighton managed to admire the Queen without especially liking her or falling for her posthumous charms. In consequence, his picture of Queen Elizabeth remains in many ways the most satisfying yet painted. If it lacks some of Neale's sparkle, as well as much of the broad historical coverage he provides, it scores by a powerful strain of distance and independence in the historian. Above all, there is Creighton's very fine sense of realities. He continually persuades the reader that he knows how things happen in the realms of high policy; the master carpenter's son has a splendid way of suggesting a lifetime spent among princes and potentates. The modern mitre at first hand, the medieval tiara at second, clearly did most to shape this historian.

[1] Owen Chadwick, *Creighton on Luther* (inaugural lecture, Cambridge, 1959).

However, it must be said that paradoxically Creighton's success in this book owes most to his greatest failing as an historian. He did not like Elizabeth, who seemed to him a tiresome woman of somewhat shaky morals and far too little scruple, and he said at one time that he did not really like the sixteenth century at all. This comes through clearly enough in the little moralizing that this uncensorious historian permitted himself. The men of Henry VIII's age were 'low-minded, sensual, self-seeking, hypocritical and unscrupulous' (p. 6). No doubt many were, by the standards of a Victorian don and bishop; so were many of those that he shared his own world with. This unfortunate judgment, which has found wide acceptance, has often prevented a real understanding of the earlier sixteenth century. When Elizabeth acts out a mild flirtation with a Scottish envoy (who knew how to play up to her), we are brought up standing by the comment: 'It is impossible to say what Elizabeth meant by this conduct' (p. 56). It is most certainly not impossible: she was amusing herself. And the words 'this conduct', straight from the mouth of the stern moral tutor, remind us that in his young days Creighton had been a remarkable prig. Francis Bacon is censured for his cynicism which shows 'that a political career was recognised as a form of personal adventure' (p. 180), a comment which shows that Creighton actually believed it to be something different in his own day. He should have known better. Those who in a democracy pursue power with the welfare of the people forever in their mouths have only adapted the principles of Tudor politicians who claimed to be devoted solely to the service of their prince. It is not clear whether Creighton ever really grasped the importance of royal pomp and patronage, the means by which political society was held together and managed. On the other hand, his robust view of the idiocies to which the famous love-cult of Elizabeth could descend in the hands of labouring courtiers is more convincing than the usual attempt to dignify them by reference to the need for queen-worship. No one denies that Gloriana found it easiest to attract loyalty by a species of elevated and formalized dalliance, but even contemporaries regarded some of the cult's manifestations with distaste, and Creighton's occasional contempt for it, modified by his understanding of its purpose, is just (for instance, pp. 175–8).

In any case, Creighton moralized very little and on the whole managed to keep the nineteenth century out of the sixteenth – much better than his friend and critic Acton. But if he did not labour his distaste for Elizabeth, he still had to overcome it, and this he achieved by a bad slip in historical understanding. What he approved was not the Queen's character, but what he persuaded himself was her true achievement. As the final pages of his book show, he believed that Elizabeth gave to England a new start in life, and that she did so because she possessed an inborn understanding of her people. Others have made much the same point, but with Creighton it ran away into a grey kind of mysticism. Elizabeth never acted 'unless she felt that her people were in hearty agreement with her'; when action was called for, she did not weigh the advice of her councillors but 'fell back upon her instinctive perception of what England wanted' (pp. 198–9). The 'people' and a personified England crop up much too readily in this book, and what England wanted in the reign of Elizabeth was, apparently, an imperial career culminating in the late-Victorian sense of mission. Elizabeth 'educated Englishmen to a perception of England's destiny' (p. 198). What destiny can she herself be shown to have been aware of? The question needs only to be asked to reveal the empty rhetoric of Creighton's assertion. In fact, Elizabeth pursued the only policy open to a sixteenth-century monarch: she promoted her country's interests by promoting her own, tried to avoid military or diplomatic defeat, tried to preserve unity at home, tried to adjust her resources to the sacred cause of public display. Certainly she sought 'greatness', but if she had had to define it she would have spoken of Henry V and Henry VIII rather than of unknown lands over the seas. In so far as she was aware what English seamen were doing, it is plain that she grudgingly admitted the usefulness of piratical treasure but otherwise showed little understanding and less liking for these adventurers. They, indeed, were often moved by zeal for Queen, country, and their religion; she was not inclined to serve any of these causes in the manner of Drake and Hawkins. The people whose assent she cultivated were hardly the nation: they were that small part of her subjects, perhaps one in twelve of them, who held wealth and power in the realm and had to be kept reasonably contented as well as ruled and controlled. Creighton's unexpected lapse into cloudiness is readily explained. He was himself a fervent patriot, with a true love of his nation and its achievements. As he once said: 'I am not ashamed to own that I am an Englishman first and a Churchman afterwards.'[1] He lived at the height of England's greatness and showed his feelings when he followed the Unionist wing of the Liberal party in the great split of

---

[1] It seems this remark shocked some people who, unlike Creighton, apparently supposed that Churchman equals Christian.

the 1880s. And so he read that greatness back to what he conceived to be its origins, implanted an absurd and anachronistic degree of foresight in Elizabeth, and spoke of the relations between Queen and people in terms more appropriate to a newspaper editorial than to a work of history.

Nevertheless, this lapse saved his book. He could, in consequence, come to study and to praise Elizabeth. Nor did he overdo the nonsense: most of the time he set her in the context of her real problems. The occasional errors corrected by later research do not matter much either, though the main ones should perhaps be briefly mentioned here. Creighton's account of the Elizabethan Church settlement of 1559 (pp. 32–3) needs to be revised in accordance with Neale's demonstration that the Queen had to make some fundamental concessions to a parliamentary lobby of extremer Protestants.[1] The theology absorbed by the English exiles during Mary's reign was Zwinglian rather than Calvinist (p. 82). Creighton was quite wrong to suppose that English wool was still being exported in quantity 'a few years before' 1578 (p. 106); manufactured cloth had gradually replaced raw wool as England's chief export from the later fourteenth century onwards. Secretary Davison, though sacrificed in public to the Queen's anger at the execution of Mary Queen of Scots, was in fact treated very differently in private (p. 150).[2] Creighton's account of the Armada campaign is marred by traditional error; the story has now been told fully and brilliantly by Garrett Mattingly.[3] On Puritanism and Parliament, Creighton's few words need to be vastly supplemented by much recent work.[4]

More important than the obvious detailed deficiencies of an older book are the points of interpretation on which it is not easy to agree with Creighton's views. That Elizabeth's definition of the royal supremacy over the Church 'reserved the freedom of the Church' in any way, that she deliberately avoided interference in its affairs (p. 34–5), is hard to credit when one remembers her use of ecclesiastical commissions, her suspension of Archbishop Grindal, and her personal activity against parliamentary intervention in matters spiritual. Creighton may have meant that the Queen was no pope – that she did not personally define doctrine or administer the Church – which is true;

[1] *EHR*, 65 (1950), 304–32.
[2] R. B. Wernham, *EHR*, 46 (1931), 632–6.
[3] *The Defeat of the Spanish Armada* (1959).
[4] Especially J. E. Neale, *Elizabeth I and her Parliaments* (2 vols., 1953 and 1957).

but what he actually said cannot be maintained. The Elizabethan Church was inexorably under the control of its supreme governor. The explanation, offered on p. 155, for Elizabeth's inability to act decisively grows out of Creighton's mystical concepts; there is absolutely no evidence that the Queen held that the country would 'grow into a new consciousness of its position if it had time for reflection and experiment', no probability that anyone thought along such lines or would have been well advised to do so, not the slightest sign that the Queen was even capable of that kind of thought. The whole of those two pages is sheer conjecture, and very unconvincing conjecture at that. As a rule, Elizabeth avoided action because the dilemmas were too formidable, because she was temperamentally inclined to procrastination, and because she had found by experience that her problems were often better solved by being left undecided for a while. Creighton's Elizabeth is at this point a highly unlikely mixture of minor prophet and mother hen. It may also be doubted whether the aftermath of the Armada campaign produced the confidence and release from fear which Creighton thought he saw (p. 156). He was seemingly not aware that the war never went so well again as at its beginning; and the 1590s, troubled by plague, bad harvests, and heavy taxation, were years of unrest and unease rather than this fine confident morning of Creighton's imagining. For myself, I also cannot accept his explanation of Elizabeth's very unpleasant and often hysterical reaction to marriage among her courtiers and entourage (p. 161). The truth is that she resented others marrying when she herself had not been able to follow her inclination by doing so, though it must be added that secret marriages, especially among people close to the Tudor family, were in the unsettled state of the succession a real political problem. But who had left it unsettled?

These are all, however, points of no overwhelming significance. One would hope that after seventy years of energetic historical research and writing a book's details would require revision, and that even its main interpretative approach might seem improbable. Creighton's life of Elizabeth comes remarkably well out of so searching a test. That is not to say that a new study of the Queen is not highly desirable. It is now over thirty years since Neale's book appeared, and these thirty years have added a large amount of knowledge and understanding, much of it owing to Neale himself. There are things about both Creighton's and Neale's Elizabeth that it is no longer easy to accept. The first has been sufficiently criticized here; as to the second, it might be said that that paragon of unfailing political skill arouses suspicion when time and again she is found in crises both internal and external into which she can be seen to have slipped either by her refusal to make up her mind or by her arrogant assertion of her prerogative. It looks, in fact, as though the next biographer of Elizabeth would do well to test Neale's Queen by the criteria and with the detachment used by Creighton. One can only hope that he will write as well as those two predecessors and contribute as lasting a work to English historical literature.

II

TUDOR GOVERNMENT

13

THE PROBLEMS AND SIGNIFICANCE OF ADMINISTRATIVE HISTORY IN THE TUDOR PERIOD*

During the past sixteen years 'administrative history' seems to have come and gone as a term of distinction in the historical study of Tudor England. In the later 1940s there were a number of scholars newly aware of the vast wealth of government records in the English archives and enormously impressed by the achievements of the medievalists – of Tout and his school – who deplored the absence of comparable studies for the post-medieval period and, for a time, came to seek salvation in an ever more stringent and particular investigation of the processes of government. But that phase did not last long. Now it can be said by Joel Hurstfield, himself a notable contributor to that flowering of administrative history, that 'we have passed beyond recall the stage when the machinery alone, however intimately understood, can answer the questions'.[1] The study of social history is all the rage now, by which is meant the history of a given society in its various aspects and manifestations – or rather, whatever may in fact emerge from that awesome ambition. Fashions change, and nowadays they change pretty rapidly; but one need not regret that not-so-distant dawn or believe that the evening has yet come. Let it be made clear, however, what is meant, or should be meant, by administrative history. Certainly this involves the analysis and description of past administrative processes, the discovery of principles implicit or explicit in the conduct of government, and an understanding of the manner in which the theoretical mechanism operated in practice. By itself this is enough to make one doubt whether the critic is just who speaks of understanding 'the machinery alone'. But beyond this, the study of government compels the historian to investigate ideas – ideas of law and legislation, ideas concerning the purpose of the state, ideas of opposition and resistance. It involves at least a sound comprehension of a society's economy and the conditions created by it for administrative action. Administrative history runs up against problems of social, family, and personal relationships which it can neither take for granted nor

* [*Journal of British Studies*, 4: 2 (1965), 18–28.]
[1] Joel Hurstfield, review of *Tudor Constitution*, EHR 77 (1962), 730.

ignore, but must investigate. In its concern for 'machinery' it can never forget personality; the historian of administration who overlooks the fact that it is people who administer is himself best overlooked. In short, administrative history is no more sectional or partial history than is any other of those convenient classifications with which scholars assist, and at times fetter, themselves. It has to consider everything, and the only things which distinguish it are its point of departure and the highroad it follows through country also over-run by other historical explorers. It begins from the machinery of government and keeps its main interest centred on that. In view of the fact that down to the death of Elizabeth, at least, the bulk of surviving records is supplied by the deposits of government action, this still seems a sensible approach; and when one considers the state of affairs in the history of more recent centuries (to speak of England alone), one cannot be at all sure that the growing abundance of more lively and less technically complicated records is pure gain. Has it not had some unfortunate effects on writers of history who too readily come to think that where so much can be told so easily, knowledge of the 'machinery' hardly matters?

In any case, to suppose that, for the sixteenth century, 'the machinery alone' is yet understood with sufficient intimacy is simply not correct. Not for one moment need it be suggested that the reconstruction of that machinery is all that should be attempted or that it will answer all questions; but it should be most emphatically asserted that questions answered without such intimate knowledge are questions spoiled and answers (to quote Queen Elizabeth) answerless. The experience of recent years shows this. Not so long ago few subjects in English history would have been thought better known and more fully studied than Tudor government, the constitution of the sixteenth century. Yet how many of the accepted generalizations of, say, 1940 stand today? Where are Tudor despotism, the packed Parliament, Star Chamber as an instrument of autocracy? What has become of Henry VII, the innovator, or of William Cecil, the incorruptible? Naturally, no one would suggest either that the whole story as told before the Second World War was wrong, or that some of the important work in revising the history of the century was not done by a previous generation of historians. But where earlier scholars like Newton and Pollard were responsible for initiating a new understanding, they did so by asking pertinent, if usually isolated, questions about the manner in which things were actually done – administrative questions[1] – and since the War the much more systematic and conscious assault on the realities of Tudor government has led to a recasting of the whole story in so fundamental a manner that, in truth, some have not yet realized the revolution that has taken place, others are digging in among the abandoned redoubts, and revolutionaries are inclined to be too cocky about their discoveries.

Although it may be arrogant to say so, it may nevertheless be asserted that the work of the last fifteen years, starting from a serious attempt to understand 'the machinery', has brought Tudor history out of the heroic into the scientific age. The embalming fluid has given way to the scalpel, the painter's brush to the draughtsman's pencil: not all of it gain, by any means, but how much gain there has been! It was the administrative approach more than any other which sub-jected historians of the sixteenth century to the fundamental – the elementary – demands of all true historiography; ask to know exactly how things were done, and ask this of all the available evidence. A case in point is the extraordinary change brought about in parliamentary studies by Sir John Neale's determination to find all the surviving material bearing on his concerns: and this is only the best known example of a genuine revolution in method which replaced reliance on calendars, on Tanner's *Tudor Constitutional Documents*, on what happened to be in print, by a broad-fronted attack on the vast resources of public and private archives. Of course, one still uses calendars and printed materials; the latter are perfectly legitimate, and as to the former, there is so much stuff that without some short cuts nothing at all would get done. But the practice is not safe – experience of even so excellent a calendar as *The Letters and Papers of Henry VIII* is chastening – and scholars are now aware of the dangers in ways that Pollard, for instance, never was. Pollard could write his books without ever enter-ing the Public Record Office. This is not to say that books on Tudor history are not still written with that same handicap, but it is doubtful if anything like Pollard's reputation could be made in that way today.

Laborious proof for these assertions is not in place here. But two small instances may be given of the sort of fundamental error easily dissipated by a real acquaintance with the governmental machinery. Take the well-known statement that the court of Star Chamber used

[1] For example, A. P. Newton, 'Tudor Reforms in the Royal Household,' *Tudor Studies*, ed. R. W. Seton-Watson (1924), 231–56; A. P. Newton, 'The King's Chamber under the Early Tudors,' *EHR* 32 (1917), 348–72; A. F. Pollard, 'The Growth of the Court of Requests,' *EHR* 56 (1941), 300–3.

torture. Holdsworth said this, and consequently it is found in several textbooks. Yet the briefest check on Holdsworth's evidence shows that he was relying on the Privy Council Register and confusing the Council's political and police activities with the exclusively judicial functions of the Star Chamber.[1] Behind this mistake which, despite the endeavours of better informed historians, has helped to maintain the court's bad reputation, lay, therefore, a real failure to understand the structure and nature of certain closely related but nevertheless distinct institutions: a serious misunderstanding of the machinery produced ramifying error. Or take another, very general, notion. Few statements are more regularly found in any general book on the sixteenth century than that the gentry's hold on the office of justice of the peace prevented the enforcement of legislation which was contrary to their interests. The examples usually given are the acts against enclosure and depopulation, sometimes in consequence called a dead letter. But it takes only a glance at the acts – admittedly a glance sharpened by an understanding of judicial procedure – to discover that the enclosure acts were not enforceable by the J.P.s at all: as was customary with penal statutes, cases arising from them were to be brought in the central courts and especially the Exchequer.[2] This is an interesting point because it touches on the whole difficult problem of the enforcement and effectiveness of legislation. Those who regard the study of machinery as inadequate for the answering of real questions – such questions as what being governed really meant to the Tudors' subjects – seem to think that the administrative historian cannot help with such issues or would even ignore them. Joel Hurstfield is justified in saying that hard work is still needed to solve these problems; but no one can in fact have any hope of solving them unless he is first quite clear about what was supposed to happen – about the administrative realities both in the blueprint of intention and in the mingle-mangle of execution.

Thus the place of administrative history in the study of Tudor

---

[1] Cf. *Tudor Constitution*, 170, n. 1.

[2] The acts in question are 4 Henry VII, c. 19 (1489), 7 Henry VIII, c. 1 (1515), 27 Henry VIII, c. 22 (1535), 5 Elizabeth I, c. 2 (1563). Two acts, abortive in their effect and rapidly repealed, experimented with special commissioners as enforcing agencies: 5 and 6 Edward VI, c. 5 (1551), and 2 and 3 Philip and Mary, c. 2 (1555). The new start was made in 1597, when all the previous acts were repealed; 35 Elizabeth I, c. 1 innovated as to enforcement only by empowering justices of assize to hear pleas on the statute. How far the gentry, through social pressure or political influence, might succeed in preventing successful enforcement is of course quite another question; but I incline to think that this, too, has been exaggerated.

England seems still well assured; the point of such confidence in understanding the machinery has not yet been reached that scholars might advance – if that is the right term – to other considerations and methods of enquiry. Constitutional history has often enough been laid to rest by impatient historians, only to rise up again in far from ghostly form to plague them as they ran their heads into unsuspected obstacles created by their insufficient knowledge of the way in which things actually happened – of the rules and mechanisms, the laws and institutions, which governed action. Hurstfield is correct in asserting that scholars should investigate such fascinating topics as 'the function of patronage' or 'the impact of the centre on the provinces', but these seem precisely the sort of questions for which a more refined knowledge of the machinery is indispensable. How does one properly evaluate patronage unless one knows who disposed of what patronage – that is to say, really grasps the facts of office-holding? How does one estimate the impact of the centre unless one knows the means available for the centre to assert itself and those available to the provinces for resistance? That these are major topics of study is incontestable; that they require more than a narrowly administrative treatment will be readily conceded; but that they can be managed on the assumption that the machinery is now known and some other, subtler, attack must be made may be regarded as highly dubious. If a good deal that at present passes for certainty in these problems of social relationships and the work of government at the grass roots is to be distrusted, it is because it too often seems to ignore even what little is known of the administrative and legal framework within which everything operated. How many of the interminable discussions of the gentry show themselves aware that the sixteenth-century village community continued really to live by manorial custom settled in the manorial court, thereby often depriving the lord of the manor of freedom to act in ways which his interests or sociological doctrine would seem to demand? Is one ever told, among the commonplaces concerning the restoration of law and order, of the extraordinary legal limitations set to royal action, or the equally extraordinary complications of the commission of oyer and terminer, or the practice of out-of-court arbitration? Or (to take an example working the other way round), how many people, confident that tax assessments made by taxpayers must be false and that tax commissioners from the gentry would, of course, weight the burden against the poor, know the administrative background which provides pretty conclusive evidence for fair assessment and collection, at least in the first half of the century?[1] The truth about the social questions of the day continues to depend on a better and deeper knowledge of government and administration.

Indeed, the problems of Tudor administrative history are not at present concerned with its allegedly restricted significance and range, with its having reached the limits of the useful contribution it can make. They arise rather from the formidable tasks still before it. There are, in the first place, the unsolved questions, the institutions yet unstudied. What is known of the Council? Any book on the Tudor period naturally gives some account of it, but it is really a little surprising to find on how little serious study such treatment must of necessity be based. Apart from a few attacks on pieces of the story, there are only the generalizations inherited from the past or derived from a quick survey of such master records as are in print. Yet the Council was the central institution of Tudor government, the one piece of machinery which must be thoroughly understood if justice is to be done to the whole complex of institutional and constitutional problems. Its history needs to be known: how it changed (if change it did) in function and composition. Its powers need to be known, its practice, its effectiveness – what it could do and what in fact it did. A very careful investigation of its relationship with other parts of the machinery is necessary, above all those other parts which had a recent formal connection with it, the courts of Star Chamber and Requests. Fortunately, systematic beginnings are at last being made: Thomas Barnes is working his way back from the Stuarts through the Star Chamber records; one of his pupils is engaged on ten years of the Elizabethan Privy Council;[2] the present writer is investigating the Councils of Henry VII and Henry VIII. This is not to ignore the work of C. G. Bayne and W. H. Dunham, but their notable monographs have left room for a really detailed and a really general study.[3]

If the Council enabled the Tudors to govern, the Exchequer supplied them with the machinery for raising and spending the money indispensable to government. Scholars are by now quite well informed about the financial organs of the early Tudors, but the Elizabethan

---

[1] This is emerging from R. S. Schofield's work. See his unpublished disseration, 'Direct Lay Taxation under the Early Tudors' (Cambridge, 1962).

[2] [This work has appeared: M. B. Pulman, *The Elizabethan Privy Council in the 1570's* (Berkeley, 1971).]

[3] C. G. Bayne and William H. Dunham, *Select Cases in the Council of Henry VII* (Selden Soc. 7, 1958); William H. Dunham, 'Henry VIII's Whole Council and Its Parts,' *Huntington Library Quarterly*, 7, (1943), 7–46.

Exchequer and Treasury have barely been touched. But until much more is revealed than is now known both about taxation and about borrowing, the most basic aspect of Tudor government remains in darkness. What can be really said, with or without confidence, about the law courts? And yet the ordinary contact between governors and governed – the common way in which government appeared to the people – was in the courts of law. Here is a field vast enough for several scholars of exceptional courage, stamina, and indifference to physical hardship; but unless they also possess notable imagination and that instinctive grasp for the condition of a past society which makes the true historian, they will do more harm than good. Here are a few of the questions which a study of the courts must seek to answer. What were the structure, interrelation, and separate competence of the courts, both common law and conciliar? What were the ordinary person's demands on the law and what was his experience of it? How far did the courts try to enforce the law and succeed in doing so? Who were the lawyers – can one speak of a legal profession? What influence did government exercise over the courts, or alternatively, how far was government tied by the courts? In respect to all these and other questions, did the situation change in the course of the century? Surely these are all points of fundamental importance, knowledge of which must be vital to a real understanding of the period. Once again, it should not be denied that beginnings have been made in these matters; but the known area consists of small and barely held clearings in the encroaching jungle. And this can be asserted with equal conviction of a part of government so obviously vital that one would suppose it to be well known – local government: the actual working of law and administration in the localities and at ground level. What passes for light in this field (always excepting the occasional ray of true sunshine usually hidden away in introductions to volumes in local records series) should not deceive a blind man. When Charles Beard, in 1904, published his book on the justice of the peace (still sometimes recommended in bibliographies), he did little more than rearrange the details of William Lambarde's *Eirenarcha*. On the national scale no one since then has attempted even so much. It seems improbable that progress beyond a handbook of 1581 should really be impossible. Recent work on local government under the Stuarts highlights the Tudor neglect,[1] and there is some danger that, for lack of specific studies, people may read the 1620s and 1630s back into the previous century.

[1] Notably Thomas G. Barnes, *Somerset 1625–1640* (Oxford, 1961).

All this may be regarded as special pleading, searching in nooks and crannies for something more to do. Is not the constitutional history of the Tudor period notoriously 'worked out'? (When Sir Lewis Namier embarked on his major studies, he was authoritatively informed that Lecky had done all that.) And even supposing that the examples given of gaps to be filled – gaps? vast empty deserts, rather – are in themselves just, is too much being made of them? Not if one remembers how often one can come up against blank walls in the course of an investigation, how often one sees scholars stopped in their tracks because the material on which they are working was produced by a system of which no one has more than imperfect knowledge. Furthermore, many assured assertions and received interpretations turn out to be simply impossible as knowledge of the machinery improves. The conclusion is inescapable that administrative history still has much work before it in the sixteenth century, and that until that work is done a great deal of what passes for Tudor history must remain provisional.

But if the foregoing analysis is correct, one would certainly like to know more about this unsatisfactory state of affairs: why the study of administrative history should not only be so short of perfection but should at the same time be decried as narrow and played out. There are two major and what might be called respectable reasons for this. One is the superior attraction of other lines of investigation. There is, of course, every reason why men should study the economics, art, literature, religion of the age, though they would do so more successfully if they understood the machinery better. But even in the specific context of the constitution, Parliament, the Church, and ideas have held the attention more than councils, courts, and Exchequer. English historical studies in the post-medieval period have still not quite lost the teleological conviction that what matters in the last resort about the sixteenth century is the establishment of constitutional monarchy and of a Protestant Church. Assuredly, these are important topics, though not the only ones of importance; and even they would benefit from being tackled more determinedly from the administrative rather than the constitutional end. To determine precisely how and why they worked in the way they did is now more pressing than study and restudy of their content of ideas – more analyses of parliamentary management and less hot air about constitutionalism, more understanding of the administrative structure of the archdeaconry and parish and fewer generalizations on Puritanism or the *via media*. Neale's analysis of the Elizabethan House of Commons, or the growing body of writings on Church courts may be cited as exemplary,[1] but on the whole historians of Parliament and Church remain more interested in the superstructure of politics, ideas, and personalities than in the under-structure of organization, procedure, and practice. Important as the first will always be, it cannot be well done until the second is out of the way.

The diversion of employable energies to other concerns is assisted by the second chief problem attendant upon administrative history: its difficulty. And this difficulty arises in great part, though not exclusively, from the materials from which it must be written. In particular, these suffer from two seemingly contradictory faults: there are far too many of them, and there are not nearly enough of them. W. C. Richardson's appendices to his books on *Tudor Chamber Administration* and the *Court of Augmentations* have demonstrated the wealth and variety of records available on certain sectors of the front; anyone who has ever looked at only the lists of surviving proceedings in Chancery or the conciliar courts will know why no proper study of these institutions has yet been made; the Exchequer records for the century baffle by their bulk quite as much as by their complexity; and as for the common law courts, there are not only the plea rolls (very little of which has been analysed so far) but, in King's Bench at least, also the writs returned, bundled up in sacks, stacked to the ceiling of a sizable room, and for all practical purposes totally inaccessible.[2] Yet at the same time, important parts of the record are missing, either lost or never kept. Where are the decree books of Council and Star Chamber, or most of the warrants to the privy seal, or the signet docket books before 1584? These lost materials pose the usual problem of patchy evidence; there are ways of getting over that, but the pitfalls and snares are naturally very serious. If desirable records were never kept (as for example regular annual statements of all the revenue, or full minutes of Council meetings), that in itself reveals important things about Tudor admini-stration but does not exactly ease the historian's path. The difficulties of the material for government at the centre are nothing compared with the insufficiencies of evidence for local government, in itself explanation

---

[1] I. J. Churchill, *Canterbury Administration* (1933); B. L. Woodcock, *Medieval Ecclesiastical Courts in the Diocese of Canterbury* (Oxford, 1952); R. A. Marchant, *The Puritans and the Church Courts in the Diocese of York 1560–1640* (1960); Robert Peters, *Oculus Episcopi: Administration in the Archdeaconry of St. Albans* (Manchester, 1963). Mrs Margaret Bowker of Girton College, Cambridge, is engaged in a study of the diocese of Lincoln in the sixteenth century. [Cf. her book, *The Secular Clergy in the Diocese of Lincoln 1495–1520* (Cambridge, 1968).]   [2] [In great part accessible now.]

enough for the pitiful state of that subject. At the very least a thorough search of all possible local and private archives is required; anyone who would publish the results of such a survey, together perhaps with a bibliographical note on materials for local government in the central archives, would at least enable that study to be undertaken in a serious way. He would in fact be taking up where Bertha Putnam left off, but he would be doing better because he would be presenting a more fundamental kind of evidence than that collected by her: evidence of what actually happened in the work of local commissions and local courts, rather than evidence of what was supposed to happen.[1]

Even when the materials have been more fully explored and made available, the problems of the administrative historian remain large. (So will be the rewards.) The meaning of the record is by no means always plain, and one often finds oneself running round a tiresome circle. The records are the product of administrative processes and should therefore illumine these. But often the records cannot be interpreted aright until the administrative processes are understood. This is not so impossible as it sounds. The rediscovery of the early Tudor Household system of finance is a good case in point, and an even better one is the work done recently, in an unpublished Cambridge dissertation, by R. S. Schofield on the Exchequer method of dealing with direct taxation. But assuredly, possible or not, it is difficult and uncertain work, with error always more than possible and perfection a long way off. The historiography of Tudor government is scarred by a long line of serious mistakes arising from failure to understand the meaning of the record, ranging from the elementary error of seeing significance in some piece of common form to some aspects of F. C. Dietz's studies of finance where figures are taken from apparent master records that were nothing of the kind. I speak as one who has made quite enough mistakes in his time and is sure he will make more. For instance, I now think that I accepted far too readily the apparent evidence for a restricted kind of Council in the first years of Henry VIII's reign, and it is no excuse – indeed this makes it worse – that I followed existing opinion in doing so.

These then are some of the problems which beset Tudor administrative history: large unexplored regions, stretches of scrub but partially surveyed so far, materials of great diversity and difficulty. It

---

[1] A limited beginning has been made: Thomas G. Barnes and A. Hassell Smith, 'Justices of the Peace from 1558 to 1668 – a revised list of sources', *BIHR* 32 (1959), 221–42. [J. H. Gleason's *The Justices of the Peace: England 1558–1640* (Oxford, 1969), is not the answer to these prayers.]

must, however, be emphatically stated that the work is perfectly possible; it needs neither a genius nor a magician; the ordinary historian can do it. And the gains are well worth the labour. The main point here asserted is that no one can hope to write about any aspect of Tudor history without the solid grasp of the realities and probabilities, without the deep understanding of the records before him, which administrative history – using the term in its wide and proper sense – alone can supply. Of course, there will never be an end to the search nor will advance be unattended by disputes and disagreements concerning the meaning of discoveries or the implications they may have for different and other facets of the period. Such quarrels over 'models' are not the subject of this paper, nor are they as a rule anything but barren. Certainly there can be no understanding of history without meaning, and no meaning without some measure of systematization and imposed arrangement. But these things are hypotheses, and, convinced as historians should be of their hypotheses, they should be much more concerned with the continuing and continuous process of discovery. Controversies there will always be: they might at least be based on a foundation of knowledge steadily and co-operatively augmented through the years.

14

THE RULE OF LAW IN
SIXTEENTH-CENTURY ENGLAND*

Interest has recently revived in a slightly old-fashioned problem, the essential character of the Tudor state. The problem is less artificial than might be supposed. Of course, there is always something artificial about any attempt to establish a generalized identity for over a hundred years of history; there is danger in any formulation which necessarily ignores the changes brought by time; and there may well be deficiencies in an analysis which turns away from the realities of social relationships to the abstractions of legal and political thought. Nevertheless, I believe that we are right to inquire by what title the system of government under the Tudors should be described. For one thing, in doing so we attend to matters about which a good many people who lived under that system were concerned to think and write. For another, we need to have a firm grasp of these concepts – the sixteenth century's concepts, not ours – if we are to see the events and personalities of the age aright. Just because it follows more closely the lines of thought that engaged the sixteenth century itself, the discussion is actually nearer the heart of any sound understanding than are even those important inquiries about social structure and mobility, economic transformation, or the role of education which have rightly attracted so much attention of late. What the true relation should be between power and law, by what right kings reigned, how far obedience was due to them, how a commonwealth should be – and how England was – governed: these are questions we should continue to debate if we want our minds to remain attuned to the age we study.

At the same time it is true that the sixteenth century has suffered more than most from historians' predilection for concise description and memorable labels. At one time (not so long ago) Tudors and despotism went unquestioningly hand in hand. The tally of headless victims and the violence of royal passions seemed to make no doubt of that. But Pollard argued powerfully that Henry VIII was a constitutionalist, happy in meetings of Parliament, and Neale demonstrated that Elizabethan governments had to take serious account of the House

* [*Tudor Men and Institutions*, ed. A. J. Slavin (Baton Ronge, La., 1972), 265-94.]

of Commons; Tudor rule was redefined as essentially constitutionalist and limited. Before this, I have endeavoured to clinch the point when I tried to persuade anyone who would listen that even that Machiavellian figure Thomas Cromwell was really the champion of law and Parliament and limited monarchy. However, a few years ago Professor Dunham discovered and raised a paradox in Tudor constitutional thinking: he discerned in it both a convinced deference to the sovereign law and a steady augmentation of a lawful regal power superior to the law. More recently still, Professor Hurstfield firmly reopened the whole question by reviving the notion of Tudor despotism. It therefore seems desirable to consider whether they have in fact succeeded in undermining the newer orthodoxy of Tudor constitutionalism.

Mr Dunham was troubled by what seemed to him like contradictions.[1] He recognized that Tudor theorists believed themselves to be living in a system in which law ordered each man's place, rights and duties, and that the theory, at least, put similar restrictions on rulers and ruled alike. But it seemed to him that the developments of the sixteenth century both reinforced an inherited respect for the rule of law, and by changing that law, constantly added to the power of the Crown, till a possible conflict existed between what he calls the *lex parliamenti* and the *lex coronae*. He thought that the problem was shelved by the Elizabethan jurists because in their pragmatic approach they felt no need to raise it, but that it remained to become the issue between the Stuarts and their Parliaments. In this, of course, he was sufficiently orthodox: that the Tudor failure to resolve the theoretical conflict between the rule of law (the rule of the common law) and the lawful powers of divine-right monarchy led to the confrontations between the Stuart kings and constitutionalist parliamentarians is one of the oldest of explanations for the breakdown of government in the seventeenth century. I also find it one of the least convincing, if only because at least down to 1640 the debates continued to be conducted precisely in Tudor terms. That is to say, all sides remained agreed that (to quote Mr Dunham) 'government according to procedures duly recognized as having validity of law' was the proper constitution of the realm of England.[2] If the Elizabethans failed to inquire which law it was that should authorize these procedures, then so, too, did the subjects of the first two Stuart kings. Actually, I think that they were

---

[1] William H. Dunham, Jr, 'Regal Power and the Rule of Law,' *Journal of British Studies*, 3 (1964), 24–56. Hereinafter cited as Dunham.

[2] Dunham, 56.

all quite clear about the law they had in mind and that Mr Dunham sees a distinction which is not there. Their arguments failed not because they advanced from different positions but because in fact they shared a common position by that time irrelevant to the real problems of the state. What put an end to the traditional discussion was the discovery that the rule of law, by itself, was no longer enough either in practice or by way of a concept.

Mr Dunham defines his paradox as arising from the fact that 'statutes strengthened both political law and regal authority; and many an act of Parliament expressly enlarged, but at the same time limited, the regal power'.[1] His point, it would seem, is that Tudor statutes often added to the personal power of kings, with the result, for instance, that Henry VIII in the end had a position close to 'that Free Monarchy whose True Law James I was to describe'.[2] Note that we are here dealing with innovation and addition, not with that 'regal power' which medieval jurists readily enough ascribed to the most constitutionalist of kings. Now it seems to me that Mr Dunham has tended to confuse things that should be kept apart. In the first place, he treats the extensive powers granted to the Crown by statute as though they in some way established a legislative authority in opposition to statute. But so long as the king's right to annul attainders, enforce or disallow acts of Parliament, or bequeath the Crown by will rested on statute, so long the exclusive legislative authority of Parliament was maintained and nothing was added to the free or prerogative powers of the Crown. One common and frequent purpose of all law-making is to encourage and promote action by adding powers to the executive, and the new laws of Henry VIII's day certainly did a lot of this, as indeed does much modern legislation. Yet none of this in any way detracts from the ultimate supremacy of the body which makes the law, or from the fact that such powers are defined and settled by law. To say that Henry VIII 'was not too proud to use the regal powers that statute had bestowed' is surely to mistake the ordinary relationship between legislature and executive.

Secondly, by a contrary confusion, Mr Dunham, in trying to depict a vastly growing power in the crown, fails to note how rarely these statute-granted powers were in fact used. They did not remain

---

[1] Ibid. 29. Mr Dunham never defines what he means by 'political law', but it would seem to mean the whole body of constitutional rules which determined the rights of government and subject. Unfortunately, no one in the sixteenth century had risen to any such concept, and the term remains somewhat unreal.   [2] Ibid. 30.

dormant, but their application was sparing. This underlines the basic fact behind the first point, behind the readiness of statute to delegate powers to the crown: an age of intermittent Parliaments, employing statute in a novel way to carry out large political programmes, simply had to leave a good deal of flexibility to the empowered agent. That is to say, royal power increased but it did not do so as regal power. So far from being liberated, the prerogative (necessarily the actor in any executive steps) was repeatedly placed upon parliamentary authority: and in theory (which is what matters here) this represents a form of restraint. The dominant doctrine was both consistent and uniform: England was ruled by law and law-determined processes; that law comprehended the powers of the Crown; those powers could be altered only by the action of the supreme legislator. If Elizabethan jurists failed to debate a conflict of laws it was not because they wilfully overlooked the reality but because they recognized and accepted the real truth. There was no conflict between *lex parliamenti* and *lex coronae*, two terms which I do not remember encountering in the Tudor authorities. Their use confuses the argument by putting on a par two very different aspects of the concept *lex*. The law of Parliament was the law made by Parliament; the law (or prerogative) of the Crown was the law-established power of the Crown. The first was sovereign in the act of legislation; the second comprised the special rights of the chief executive. The first was capable of adding to itself; the second could not breed. The first therefore controlled the second, even though that control may frequently have been used in a beneficial and pro-creative manner. That this was indeed the accepted relationship between the two shall be shown in a moment.

With Professor Hurstfield we are in a less rarified atmosphere, among some of the facts of power rather than among the theories.[1] Admittedly he offers a definition of despotism: an authoritarian rule in which government enforces its will, suppresses dissent, and rules a society whose members have few means of influencing major decisions.[2] But while he is right in saying that a really rigorous definition of despotism would – because men are not perfect even in their more evil intents – free even harsh regimes from that label, his own definition would seem to pull in the majority of regimes dead or living. A definition which could apply equally to the rule of Henry VIII and of Joseph Stalin, of Augustus Caesar, King Solomon, and the younger

---

[1] J. Hurstfield, 'Was there a Tudor Despotism after all?', *TRHS* (1967), 83–108. Here-inafter cited as Hurstfield. [2] Hurstfield, 86.

Pitt, and which occasionally looks accurate also for modern Britain and the United States, would seem to be altogether too generous. However, Dr Hurstfield's argument centres upon two more specific issues. First, he wishes to reassert the old view that Thomas Cromwell (and by implication Henry VIII as well) meant to create a monarchic rule free of traditional restraints; and second, he holds that the notion of parliamentary consent had so little reality in the sixteenth century that government by statute was simply a more efficient way of promoting despotism. The problem of considering these views is complicated by Dr Hurstfield's admission that he has 'not mentioned a single new document',[1] a claim which in itself constitutes no virtue when a good many old documents are also not mentioned, important additional ones could be found, and the ones used are treated as though they had not before this been thoroughly and frequently discussed. It will therefore be advisable to consider the fundamental issues involved before turning to Dr Hurstfield's particular arguments.

The issues raised in the debate are important though hardly novel. In essence they are three: the relationship between law and prerogative, the king's position with respect to the making of law, and the political question of consent (the reality of the parliamentary process).

The first problem – the prerogative and the law – comes first because it describes the manner in which these matters appeared to Tudor writers. What concerned them, and should therefore concern us, was not perhaps the freedom of parliamentary elections or the politics of consent, but the relationship of the royal prerogative to the ordinary processes of the law. Was the prerogative superior or additional to the law, or was it comprehended in the law?

On this central point the best opinion was quite clear. William Staunford wrote his treatise on the prerogative in 1548, but half a century later his authority was still supreme. Reviewing the theorists of the law in 1600 for the benefit of students, William Fulbecke described him thus: 'In Master *Staunford* there is force and weight, and no common kind of stile; in matter none hath gone beyonde him, in method, none hath ouertaken him; in the order of his writing hee is smoothe, yet sharpe, pleasant, but yet graue; famous both for Iudgement in matters of his profession, and for his great skill in forraigne learning, And surely his method may be a Law to the writers of the Law which succede him.'[2] What this paragon had to say about the

---

[1] Ibid. 107.
[2] William Fulbecke, *A Direction or Preparative to the Study of the Law* (1600), fo. 28.

prerogative was quite unequivocal. The term comprises privileges vested in a given person and more particularly in a 'soueraine gouernor of a realm'; it includes a variety of special rights at law (the holder of prerogative cannot be sued, or disseised, or dispossessed, his goods cannot be taxed or distrained, etc.). Prerogatives are many, but they are precise and have in part been summed up in a statute (the spurious act *de prerogativa regis*). 'Howbeit, this parlament maketh no part of the kinges prerogatif, but long time before it had his being by th'order of the common law.'[1]

This opinion was delivered at the end of Henry VIII's reign when, on the showing of both Mr Dunham and Dr Hurstfield, one might have expected a less 'common law' view of the prerogative. It was thoroughly borne out in judicial pronouncements in two cases in Elizabeth's reign, reported by Plowden. In *Williams* v. *Berkeley* (Trinity term, 4 Elizabeth I), Brown J. said: 'The King cannot do any Wrong, nor will his Prerogative be any Warrant to him to do an Injury to another . . . If he should take the whole, he would do a Wrong to the other, which his Prerogative will not suffer him to do . . . The Estate was the cause of the Act, and is restrained by the Act, which the King cannot enlarge by his Prerogative without another Act of Parliament, but in taking the Estate he is restrained along with the Estate.' In other words, the prerogative is subject both to the common law (which will so interpret it that, there being no legal remedy for wrong done by the king, no injury shall result from its exercise) and to statute which where it applies governs the actions of the king as much as of anyone else. And even in the *Case of Mines* (9 & 10 Elizabeth I), in which the existence of prerogatives not listed in the spurious statute was stressed, it was explicitly stated that all these are rights 'allowed to the King by the Law'.[2]

Tudor lawyers, therefore, regarded the royal prerogative as a department of the common law, definable but not establishable by statute. They seem to have held that no new prerogatives can be created, while all those known were 'allowed by the law'. Thus it would seem that the legislation of Henry VIII followed strict common-law principles (*modo Cromwelliano*) when it attempted to give statutory recognition to the prerogative power of issuing proclamations; it may even have gone a bit further, as Sir Roger Twysden saw, when another act of 1539 laid down the precedence of the lords in Parliament

---

[1] William Staunford, *An Exposicion of the Kinges Prerogative* (1567), fo. 5.
[2] *Plowden's Reports* (ed. 1779), 246–8, 322.

and thereby limited the undoubted prerogative of granting honours and establishing an order among them.[1] This is a very legal and legalistic concept of the prerogative, and one might perhaps expect it to weaken in the face of the Crown's expanding political power. Did opinion swerve from Staunford? Mr Dunham discovered in William Lambarde's *Archeion* an exposition of the potentialities of conflict between the ordinary positive law and the 'regality, prerogative or judicial power' of the Crown, together with an attempt to resolve the conflict by subjecting both to a third entity to be called 'the rule of law'.[2] Unfortunately, by quoting him out of context, Mr Dunham has misrepresented Lambarde's argument which is not about these issues at all. He ascribes to Lambarde a high view of the prerogative, in the manner of the later Stuarts; but so far from calling (as is alleged) the king's power 'absolute and unbridled' Lambarde supposed that others might mistakenly understand him to think of it in those terms.[3] For himself, he was concerned solely with a possible conflict between the ordinary courts and the prerogative courts over the provision of justice. His argument turned not on the prerogative as such but on the king's right to dispense justice outside the ordinary courts; he emphasized that it was pressure from suitors that called forth such action; what worried him was no conflict of laws but the prospect of excesses in practice – the readiness of the royal Council to go beyond the 'prefixed limits' of their power, and the impatience of 'the *Common Man* . . . to have his Causes determined either at the *Councell-board* without open hearing, or by absolute authoritie, without prescribed rule of ordinary proceeding'.[4] The '*Contrariety* of *Law*' of which he spoke consisted solely of a conflict of jurisdictions applying the same body of law; his resolution of this *Antinomia* does not demand the establishment of a separate and superior rule of law, but describes the existing practice by which extraordinary jurisdiction was reserved for cases in which the common-law courts, for one reason or another (and he lists them), could not settle matters.[5] Lambarde's 'Law absolute and ordinary' are not the prerogative and statutory authorities which Mr Dunham reads into them, but the two forms of procedure in court, one by the rules of process defined in the common law and the other

---

[1] 31 Henry VIII, c. 10; cf. Roger Twysden, *Certain Considerations upon the Government of England*, ed. J. M. Kemble (1849; Camden 1st ser., vol. 45), 21.
[2] Dunham, 53–4.
[3] William Lambarde, *Archeion*, ed. C. H. McIlwain and Paul L. Ward (Cambridge, Mass., 1957), 62.
[4] Ibid. 65.   [5] Ibid. 66–8.

without them (absolved from them). Nowhere in his treatise does he come within hailing distance of the problems which engage us here.[1]

On one occasion in the sixteenth century the possibility seems to have been mentioned that the absolute power of the Crown may not be subjected to adjudication by the law. The case is peculiarly documented but worth citing. At some time in the reign of Elizabeth, a dispute was argued in a court (probably Common Pleas) between the queen's printer, Christopher Barker, and the University of Cambridge, touching the former's claim to a monopoly of bible-printing.[2] On Barker's behalf it was argued: 'The privilege to appoint printers, and to allow what books they should print, is a matter of absolute prerogative and is not to be ordered by rule of law nor disputable by the same; therefore, her majesty making her special grant to Mr Barker, that only stands good and none else.' To this counsel for the University replied: 'It is true that the matter is a matter of prerogative; but when it has pleased her majesty's progenitors to interest any corporate body or natural person in the said prerogative, then is the same to be censured by the law and to be ordered by the rule of the same.' He was relying on the argument that Henry VIII's grant to the university of 20 July 1534, which empowered the chancellor, masters, and scholars to appoint printers and license books, created not an authority in the university but an interest because it implied 'a matter of profit or benefit'. We do not know the decision of the court. If the printer had won, it would have been held that a patent of monopoly might not be

[1] That Mr Dunham has perverted the sense of Lambarde's remarks by citing them out of context may be briefly shown. Lambarde speaks of the king's '*Regalitie, Prerogative, or Iudiciall Power*' used in summoning defendants into court and points out that it in no way offends 'the free course of the *Common Law*' (p. 73); Mr Dunham collects the first part of the sentence together with others equally mishandled to suggest a concept of prerogative law. When Lambarde mentions 'a certaine soveraigne and preheminent *Power*', he explicitly has in mind nothing but the power to remedy defects in the common law and modify its rigour (p. 43); Mr Dunham uses the phrase to underpin his contention that Lambarde regarded the king's prerogative as a power separate from the common law. Mr Dunham says that Lambarde 'paradoxically' made the law itself fall under the law; but the point made by Lambarde, no paradox at all, is the perfectly sound and sensible one that trial at law has the advantages of '*ruled law* and bounded *jurisdiction*', whereas trial in Star Chamber leaves the party without any certainties of procedure: even counsel will be bewildered.

[2] This is vouched for by a copy of a report, now preserved among the archives of the Cambridge University Press (deposited in the University Archives, Cambridge). The copy is undated and probably incomplete, but it reads like a proper account in translation. I have not tried to track the case in the uncharted wastes of the plea rolls, especially since the court that heard it has to be conjectured.

disputed in the courts because it derived from the 'absolute pre-rogative'. But as the university continued to print the bible it must be supposed that the court rejected this submission and accepted the view that by making a grant the prerogative subjected itself to the control of the law. This is equal to saying that the prerogative, however absolute, becomes law-governed when it embodies itself in action; or, to put it another way, that any prerogative to be called absolute is free of legal restraint only so long as it remains dormant. Such doctrine would ingeniously defeat the whole concept of an absolute (*legibus soluta*) power in the Crown and exclude the rule of law only from those operations of the monarch's authority which do not touch the subject's interest.

In fact, I know of no decision under the Tudors which contradicts Staunford's definition of the prerogative as governed by the law, indeed as a department of the law. For a different opinion we have to wait for the reign of James I, but even then it is suspect. Dr John Cowell, in his *Interpreter*, certainly put forward a totally opposed view, calling the prerogative 'that especiall power . . . that the King hath in any kind, ouer and aboue the ordinarie course of the common lawe, in the right of his crowne'. He agreed that some of the rights involved had been defined in the law, but maintained that most were not and that even the 'custom' of England, by which the king allowed Parlia-ment to participate in the making of laws, rests on his 'benignitie' only.[1] He derived his interpretation from the axiom 'that the king of England is an absolute king. And all learned politicians [writers on politics] doe range the power of making lawes *inter insignia summae & absolutae potestatis*'. A splendid piece of *a priori* reasoning influenced by Bodin. In passing, it is worth noting that Cowell ascribed no legislative authority at all to the king's proclamations which to him were only notices 'publikely giuen of any kind of thing, whereof the king thinketh good to aduertise his subjects'.

Cowell's absolutist views sprang from his learning as a civilian, and he quotes extensively from non-English laws and precedents. As is well known, both Parliament and James I agreed readily in condemning the book just because of his statements on the prerogative, a plain acknowledgment of what the right doctrine was thought to be. But in 1607, when Cowell wrote, he had a recent judicial pronouncement on his side. Chief Baron Fleming was a common lawyer who in his

---

[1] Cowell made the point several times, *sub verbis* king, Parliament, Prerogative (*The Interpreter*, Cambridge, 1607).

notorious judgment in Bate's case (1606) defined the prerogative as 'double, ordinary and absolute', asserting that only the former was 'guided by the rules of the common law', while the latter were better termed 'policy and government'.[1] Though in a way he was only echoing Bracton's distinction between *jurisdictio* and *gubernaculum*, the 350 years since Bracton's day had altered the meaning of many terms, and Fleming clearly opened a road to the discovery that the king's prerogative included powers superior to the law. That, however, Fleming and Cowell (if the former had any clear notion whither he was tending) were not typical even of early-Stuart opinion emerges plainly enough from the views of that rabid royalist, David Jenkins, one of Charles I's judges and a prisoner in Newgate when he wrote his treatise on the prerogative in 1647.[2] He was not perhaps trying to curry favour with his jailers: the book is a violent attack on the Parliament and a vigorous defence of the king. Yet the table of contents states simply: 'The King's Prerogative, and the Subject's Liberty, are determined and bounded by the Law'. And in the text he explains with perfect clarity that both these terms are defined ('admeasured') by the 'written law'. 'We do not hold,' he added, 'the King to have any more power . . . but what the Law gives him.'[3] As Twysden, a less determined royalist, put it about the same time: prerogatives 'are not numberlesse, but conteyne in themselves matter of prescription' – that is, are defined in law.[4]

Thus, in the crucial century between Staunford and Jenkins, authoritative opinion held that the royal prerogative was a set of rights defined in the law and subject to its rule, and that this rule is to be found in the common law and in explicatory acts of Parliament. It follows that the king was still, as in the thirteenth century, held to be under the law, though the growth of the law had resulted in producing more specific limitations to royal action than Bracton ever knew. The rules of law – observance of its substantive and procedural rules – governed both monarch and subject.

As the seventeenth century was to discover, there were two weaknesses in this apparently clear-cut and satisfactory position. It held good without difficulty only so long as the law was somehow regarded

[1] *The Stuart Constitution*, ed. J. P. Kenyon (Cambridge, 1966), 62–3.

[2] *The Works of the Eminent and Learned Judge Jenkins upon divers Statutes concerning the King's Prerogative and the Liberty of the Subject* (n.d.).

[3] Ibid. 61. This phrase almost exactly repeats the opinion of several judges and councillors given in 1610 (cited W. Notestein, *The House of Commons 1604–1610* [New Haven, 1971], 396).   [4] Twysden, *Certain Considerations*, 87.

as fixed: what was the king's position with reference to the making of new law? And it did not exclude the possibility that the lawful prerogatives of the Crown included powers which might affect the law itself. We turn to the second of our issues in debate.

The first point, in fact, posed no real problem until alien views of the need for a single, undivided legislative authority penetrated into England. Lawmaking was the province of Parliament, and the king alone could give to nothing the force of statute. Neither, of course, could the Commons or the Lords. The point, which is commonplace throughout the literature, was most neatly employed by John Aylmer in 1558. He was trying to counterblast John Knox's *First Blast of the Trumpet*, and he set himself to prove the innocuousness of a woman ruler in a constitutionalist regime like that of England. Even twenty years later he would no doubt have sung Eliza's praises, but at the start of her reign he could only maintain that the common harmfulness of a woman on the throne was in England exorcized by her inability to do anything on her own. 'She maketh no statutes or laws but the honourable court of Parliament.' What harm can she do? 'If . . . the regiment were such as all hanged upon the king's or queen's will and not upon the laws written; if she might decree and make laws alone, without her senate; if she judged offences according to her wisdom and not by limitation of statutes and laws; if she might dispense alone of war and peace; if, to be short, she were a mere monarch and not a mixed ruler, you might peradventure make me to fear the matter the more.'[1] An admirable description of the commonplaces of the rule of law, for once from a non-lawyer. Exactly the same kind of monarchy was still regarded as characteristic of England by Twysden, nearly a century later: English government rests entirely upon the common law, and the English monarchy is 'restrayned', that is limited in power. The king must govern by the laws he has sworn to maintain; he cannot by himself alter old law or make new: and he cannot proceed except in the established courts by the known law.[2]

All this is ordinary enough – in which fact lies its importance. I claim no special excellence or wisdom for any of these writers; the point is that they state the generally agreed assumptions. Their testimony is the more valuable, much more valuable than the words of deeper thinkers like Hooker, Bacon, or Hobbes. And all agreed that the rule of law under which they conceived themselves to be living extended also to the making of law. Equally, as I have shown before

---

[1] *Tudor Constitution*, 16.   [2] Twysden, *Certain Considerations*, 17, 87.

this, the royal prerogative to issue proclamations did not enfranchise any personal legislative authority in the Crown, before, under or after the Act of Proclamations. Proclamations were best defined in the words of the *Discourse upon the Statutes*, possibly written by Thomas Egerton in his student days: they were good if made 'in supplement or declaracion of a lawe', but 'for anie thinge that is in alteration or abrydgement they have no power'.[1] There is no prerogative power of making new laws or abrogating old; legislation is the function of the king in Parliament, the united action of the whole realm, and the rule of law is thus capable of being maintained in full, even in the process of changing that law. Such was the theory, and such (which is more) the practice.

Nevertheless, a further word is needed on the Act of Proclamations because it continues to trouble both Mr Dunham and Dr Hurstfield. The former reads the phrase in its preamble which mentions 'what a king by his royal power may do' as offering an explicit description of regal greatness. In fact, however, it has no such general meaning; rather it specifically refers to one aspect of prerogative action, recognized by the law – the issuing of proclamations and their just claim (ignored by wicked men) to be obeyed. So far was this much maligned act from wishing to augment the king's power that, rather surprisingly, it expressly asserted the opposite intention: one reason for legislative action on that occasion is stated to be the fear that in his eagerness to make people behave themselves the king might 'extend the liberty and supremacy of his royal power'. This expansion beyond the limits set by the law the statute treats as undesirable, and it therefore must be regarded as limiting. Dr Hurstfield, who (like all of us today) accepts that the act as passed did not increase the power of the Crown because it merely gave statutory expression to powers which the prerogative already possessed at common law,[2] nevertheless continues to think that the bill originally introduced was a different matter altogether. We do not know its terms, and he may be right in ignoring my attempt to reconstruct the bill's history in which I endeavoured to show that the Commons were probably responsible for forcing the restrictive second clause into the act, that the Lords showed themselves sensitive on the issue of parliamentary authority, and that the final outcome is unlikely to have been profoundly different from the original bill.[3] But how does he arrive at his own vision of that bill?

---

[1] *A Discourse upon the Exposicion & Understandinge of Statutes*, ed. S. E. Thorne (San Marino, Calif., 1942), 105, 107.

[2] Hurstfield, 93.   [3] Below, no. 19.

For his assessment of the government's extreme intentions – namely that it wanted an act which would make unlimited legislation by proclamation possible – Dr Hurstfield relies on the memories of opposition and the terms of the preamble. On the first, I have nothing much to add: I have before this shown that opposition existed and what it amounted to. I might just note that the replacement of one bit of paper or parchment by another in the passage of the bill, traditionally supposed (in this case) to demonstrate the violent changes needed (but really necessitated by the addition of an internal clause embodying the safeguards asked for and promised),[1] occurred quite commonly in Henrician Parliaments and proves nothing about the intensity of opposition or the character of the original bill.[2] The preamble, however, needs a further word. It does not deserve Dr Hurstfield's profound suspicions or his curious comparison with Hitler's enabling law. Those, to him, ominous phrases about 'unity and concord' or 'the good and quiet of his people' are not broad hints of enlarged ambition but explicitly refer to what the king in his government has done in the past; they are perfectly correct historical statements on the use of proclamations. The preamble is solemn and pompous, in the best Cromwellian manner, but it utters no novel claims or disturbing threats. All that it says is this: the king has been issuing proclamations

---

[1] Dr Hurstfield says (95–6) that Gardiner thought the government wanted more than they got. But what Gardiner said (*Tudor Constitution*, 24) was that after 'liberal words' a 'plain promise' was given that proclamations would not do 'anything contrary to an act of Parliament or common law', which – since it concerns the content and not the constitutional position of proclamations – offers no support for the view that the original bill meant to replace parliamentary by prerogative legislation.

[2] Mr J. I. Miklovich has kindly supplied me with a list of bills (1536–47) which the Commons amended so drastically that they drew a new version which they sent up together with the rejected old one. These are: the bill for Robert Sherborne's pension (28 Henry VIII, c. 23: *LJ* i. 93a), the bill enabling ex-religious to hold lands (31 Henry VIII, c. 6: *LJ* i. 121a), the bill for proclamations (31 Henry VIII, c. 9: *LJ* i. 122b); the bill protecting various forms of game (31 Henry VIII, c. 12: *LJ* i. 124b), the bill concerning tithes (32 Henry VIII, c. 7: *LJ* i. 155a), the bill for titles of nobility (32 Henry VIII, c. 9.: *LJ* i. 148a), the sanctuaries bill of 1540 (32 Henry VIII, c. 12: *LJ* i. 149b), the bill for the breed of horses (32 Henry VIII, c. 13: *LJ* i. 149b), the bill for the honor of Wallingford (32 Henry VIII, c. 53: *LJ* i. 161b), the attainder of Thomas Cromwell (32 Henry VIII, c. 62: *LJ* i. 149b), the abortive bill for customers' registers (*LJ* i. 227b). It is worth noting that the 'tractable' Commons of 1539–40 were far more active in this way than any other House. In addition, two bills were replaced by new drafts after committal in the Lords, as also happened to the proclamations act at one stage (those for Canterbury, 34 & 35 Henry VIII, c. 18 [*LJ* i. 232b], and for the preservation of woods, 35 Henry VIII, c. 7 [*LJ* i. 259b]). It would be hard to divine major political problems in most of these cases; manifestly, procedural consequences of routine disagreements and amendments are more likely to be the explanation.

which wicked people have disobeyed; the absence of statutory authority has made enforcement difficult; the needs of public affairs often demand regulations at short notice which it might be disastrous to have to put off to the next Parliament;[1] it is undesirable that the Crown should, by public misbehaviour, be driven to an arbitrary extension of its powers; the king, by the advice of his Council, should be able to issue proclamations; and an act of Parliament should be provided to supply means of enforcement. There is not one word in all this that conflicts with the act as passed, and it is not possible to argue from the preamble that the original bill would have replaced statute by proclamation or given 'the Crown in its own person' freedom to legislate – which, as Dr Hurstfield rightly says, would have been despotism.

But Cromwell in 1535, as we are once more reminded, told the duke of Norfolk how delighted he was to hear from the judges that the king could by proclamation stop the export of coin from the realm. The lord chief justice even said that such an order would be 'of as good effect as any law made by parlyament or otherwyse', a phrase to be echoed four years later in the act. Dr Hurstfield thinks that this shows Cromwell pleased at being able to use proclamations instead of statutes.[2] It shows only that he was unfamiliar with the power of proclamations at common law, with the massive precedents for the use of proclamations touching coin, and with a relevant statute of Richard II's. There were many gaps in Cromwell's legal education, but none in his constitutionalism. We have recently learned how his regime really used proclamations: in support and execution of statutes, not in replacement of them. To quote Dr Heinze's conclusion of his study of meat price proclamations:[3] 'The whole pattern documents Thomas Cromwell's preference for legislation by statute wherever possible. . . . When the Statute of Proclamations is viewed in this context, it is difficult to conclude that the governments had any surreptitious intent.'

[1] Dr Hurstfield's gloss on this passage really will not do. The phrase reads: 'considering also that sudden causes and occasions fortune many times which do require speedy remedies, and that by abiding for a Parliament in the mean time might happen great prejudice to ensue in the realm'. This was a commonplace experience in the sixteenth century. To suggest (Hurstfield, 97) that after all it took only a few weeks to get a Parliament together and that in reality the Crown wished to avoid the discussion of 'emergency – or controversial – measures' in Parliament is to apply suspicion rather than analysis and to suggest, absurdly, that every single emergency (a sudden need to attend to some prices, for instance) should have led to the calling of a Parliament.
[2] Hurstfield, 97–8.
[3] R. W. Heinze, 'The Pricing of Meat: A Study in the Use of Royal Proclamations in the Reign of Henry VIII', *HJ* 12 (1969), 583–95.

This is indeed so. Statutory authority was sought and found for the Crown's common-law prerogative of issuing proclamations, and the effect of this was restrictive rather than expansive. At any rate, Somerset, who repealed the act, issued far more and far more ominous proclamations than Henry VIII had done, with or without the act.[1] Cromwell's purposes are perhaps better deduced from the effect of his legislative programme and his known support for Thomas Starkey's constitutionalist views on government, than from his pleasure at being able to prohibit the export of coin without having to draft a new statute.[2]

It thus remains true that the Tudor Crown neither could make law in its own right nor ever wished to acquire the power to do so. Yet this still leaves the question whether the king could not perhaps control the law made by the mixed legislative sovereign in such a way as to render his theoretical subjection to that legislative sovereignty in effect meaningless. As is well known, the Crown had the power to exempt individuals from the operation of statutes by licences *non obstante*. Such licences could be authorized in the act or they could rest solely upon the prerogative. Mr Dunham may be right in saying that 'in politics' such action, even when based on statutory authority, 'subordinated statute law to regal power', but the distinction is essential: statute-authorized licences preserved the principle of the superiority of the king-in-Parliament over the king *solus*, while prerogative licences demonstrated the existence of an occasional power in the king to control statute. The problem has not been much discussed, and this is

[1] Dr Hurstfield (95) once more uses Somerset's repeal to suggest that 'this innocent piece of legislation' had left a nasty taste in the mouth. I must remind him once again that without the repeal Somerset would have needed the constant consent of twelve other councillors to make his lavish proclamations policy legal. On this policy, see above, no. II, esp. pp. 235-7.

[2] Cromwell wrote his letter to Norfolk in 1531, not 1535. This is proved not only by its extraordinarily deferential tone, very different from that which by 1535 he was using to the duke, but also by its contents. It is concerned with preventing the export of coin from the realm, and the committee of legal advisers wished to rest the necessary proclamation on an act of Richard II. The proclamation which resulted was published on 18 July 1531 (*Tudor Royal Proclamations*, ed. Paul L. Hughes and James F. Larkin, i, no. 133). There was no proclamation on the subject in 1535. This redating has some consequences. Cromwell's apparent ignorance of the power of proclamations is explained now that we know he expressed it early in his official career, while the eight years between this letter and the Act of Proclamations make quite sure that he did not, in consequence of what he had learned, lay up a thought of substituting proclamations for statutes throughout the time of his ministry. The date of 1531 makes the letter entirely useless for Dr Hurstfield's purposes. It may also be noted that the lord chancellor who presided when that allegedly dangerous opinion was given was not Thomas Audley, but Thomas More.

not the place to explore so large a topic fully. The one investigation so far made of it has shown that the prerogative was in this function as in others closely controlled by the law which admitted the power in the sphere of the king's administrative responsibility but denied it in cases where a subject's rights at law might be affected.[1] As is well known, the question was raised in the monopolies debate in 1601, because, as Francis Bacon said, these licences applied particularly to penal statutes of the kind proposed for the restraint of monopolists, so that any act made would remain subject to the Crown's power to grant exemptions from it.[2] He used this argument because he favoured an approach by petition which might be less offensive to the queen. Others who also wished to proceed in this fashion agreed with him on the liberty of the prerogative.[3] But all of them had a reason for pressing the point and may have exaggerated. In this same debate, Henry Montague pointed out that the queen's licence could 'not alter the law, which cannot be but by Act of Parliament'; the licence could only dispense a man from the penalty of the law.[4] As he explained, judicial opinion had held that 'a grant to the hurt of the subject is void' and also that 'law and prerogative are the same thing' – that is, as I have shown, that the prerogative was treated as part of the law; and from this he drew the conclusion that a bill could not be said to touch the prerogative because 'there is no rule of prerogative but the laws of the land'. In law, he seems to me to have been absolutely correct. Licences *non obstante* rested either on the authority of the statute to which they were applied or on the law-restrained prerogative. In either case they left the law untouched; in either case they were controlled by judicial inter-pretation; in neither case did they equip the Crown with powers superior to statute.

However, as Montague's arguments suggests, this theory could still have left the facts of the case quite different: what virtue is there in a law when in a given case its sole sanction can be rendered nonexistent? Did the prerogative of licensing exemptions from the law in practice enable the Tudor Crown to disallow statute? The example of James II comes to mind: the dispensing power could be used in very drastic

[1] Paul Birdsall, ' "Non Obstante" – a study of the dispensing power of English kings,' *Essays in History and Political Theory in Honor of Charles Howard McIlwain* (New York, 1936), 37–77.
[2] Simonds D'Ewes, *The Journals of all the Parliaments in the Reign of Queen Elizabeth* (London, 1682), 645.
[3] Francis Moore (ibid. 646), George Moore (ibid. 647), and Mr Spicer (ibid. 649).
[4] Cited in J. E. Neale, *Elizabeth I and her Parliaments 1584–1601* (1959), 382.

fashion. This is a question which requires massive research and lengthy exposition; at present I can only offer a provisional conclusion that the practice of the Tudors did not transgress the conventions of the law. We must take note of the real purpose of penal statutes. Intended to regulate, they could not be totally rigorous; flexibility was meant to be there from the first because absolute rigour would have been self-defeating. The acts stated general rules which, if enforced, would often have led to stagnation or else total evasion. The administrative structure (and the weaknesses) of the Tudor state made it necessary, on the occasion that some attempt was made to control an area of public or private life, to proceed by general prohibitory acts to be articulated by means of licensed exemptions. This means that one is bound to find some licensing; I am almost prepared to argue that acts never exempted from by *non obstante* patents were acts never enforced. But, secondly, we know far too little so far about the licensing policy of the Crown, and much of the little we have been told was said by scholars who erroneously supposed that every licence was an evasion of at least doubtful propriety. I once made a sample check in the reigns of Henry VII and Henry VIII: and there I found surprisingly few such licences. Of those found, the main bulk dealt with trading at the ports (sometimes under the Navigation Act which had to be so operated if it was to have any meaning at all, and sometimes under the prerogative power to control trade), or with dispensations for clerical pluralism and non-residence specially provided for in the relevant act. Potentially dangerous licences, exempting from penal statutes, amounted to one in the years 1495–1500 and to twenty-six in the years 1531–1538.[1] I therefore have my doubts about Henry VII's dozens and Henry VIII's hundreds alleged by Mr Dunham.[2] The situation would not appear to have changed markedly in the reign of Elizabeth, though an increasing population and additions to the statute book should have resulted in more lavish licensing. The index to the last published volume of the *Calendar of Patent Rolls* lists over six hundred licences for the four years 1569–1572, but the bulk of these touch alienation of lands and only twenty-one would appear to have been *non obstante*; and not one of these last turns out on inspection to be objectionable. Licences need a

[1] Below, pp. 291–2.
[2] Mr Dunham relies on E. F. Churchill's highly misleading discussion ('The Dispensing Power and the Defence of the Realm,' *Law Quarterly Review*, 37 [1921], 412–41) which is shot through with false assumptions but at this date hardly worth criticizing any longer. However, even Churchill mentions only one dozen for Henry VII and one hundred for Henry VIII.

lot of analysis, and a crude use of figures could mislead badly. When all the conditions are taken into account – the necessary principle of proceeding by statute-cum-licence, the licences authorized by statute, and the very small number of licences which actually put aside an act by the exercise of the prerogative – it may appear that the theoretical subordination of the prerogative to Parliament's legislation was supported by what actually happened.

Thus the conclusion must stand that Tudor thinking and practice on the law subordinated everybody, the king included, to the rule of law which defined rights and duties, and defined the processes by which these could be obtained or enforced. The law could be altered only by its own doing (judicial decision) or by legislation in which the whole realm was deemed to participate, and the whole Parliament certainly needed to act in harmony. This is the truth of the law: and it means that insofar as sixteenth-century England had a justifiable doctrine concerning its constitution this was neither despotic nor divided between the concepts of statutory authority and regal power. The doctrine – unitary, single, and conscious – spoke in terms of the rule of law and the lawmaking monopoly of Parliament.

Such was the general and effective theory, but it now becomes necessary to turn to the fundamental objection raised by Dr Hurstfield, namely that the political structure of Tudor England made nonsense of these theoretical positions. In his view, Thomas Cromwell in particular wanted nothing to do with a Parliament that might obstruct the free making of law by the king; he despised the institution. Dr Hurstfield once more uses Cromwell's well-known letter which wittily lambasts the futile labours of the 1523 Parliament:

I amongst other have endured a Parliament which continued by the space of seventeen whole weeks, where we commoned of war, peace, strife, contention, debate, murmur, grudge, riches, poverty, perjury, truth, falsehood, justice, equity, deceit, oppression, magnanimity, activity, force, attemprance, treason, murder, felony, conciliation, and also how a commonwealth might be edified and also continued within our realm. Howbeit, in conclusion we have done as our predecessors have been wont to do, that is to say, as well as we might and left where we began.[1]

Let me once more try to lay this ghost. Dr Hurstfield at least agrees that the letter is amusing, but he regards it as 'the comment of a bored, impatient, cynical man' to whom the whole session was a waste of time and who simply despised Parliaments.[2] Cromwell, who 'wanted

---

[1] Merriman, i, 313 (spelling modernized).   [2] Hurstfield, 92–3.

legislation, not deliberation', clearly saw nothing but nonsense in those assemblies; contrary to what I had once suggested, he did not here show himself fascinated by and involved in their often tedious processes. Is that so? I offer the following quotations:

The House of Commons has nothing to do and can scarce make a house to adjourn. The last money bill is before your lordships, and the Speaker will not let it pass, till the session is at an end, that he may have some pretence for the flourish about the Close.[1]

My lords, we have it from the highest authority that in the multitude of counsellors there is safety; but we in this nation may from experience say, that in the multitude of legislators there is confusion; ... every member of the other House takes upon him to be a legislator. ... The other House, by their being so numerous . . . are too apt to pass laws which are either unnecessary or ridiculous, and almost every law they pass stands in need of some new law for explaining and amending it.[2]

As we have got more members, and more space to put them in, we shall want more hours to talk in, more clerks to attend their business, and so to patch up the constitution of the Chair, and of the Table, that they may be able to go through twice the fatigue that was required of their predecessors.[3]

No more the disciplined array of traditional influences and hereditary opinions. . . . That is all past. For these the future is to provide us with a compensatory alternative in the conceits of the illiterate, the crotchets of the whimsical, the violent courses of the vulgar ambition that acknowledges no gratitude to antiquity – to posterity no duty.[4]

[He] spoke of the immense multiplication of details in public business and the enormous task imposed upon available time and strength by the work of attendance in the House of Commons. He agreed that it was extremely adverse to the growth of greatness among our public Men.[5]

A Parliament is nothing less than a big meeting of more or less idle people. In proportion as you give it power it will enquire into everything, settle everything, meddle in everything.[6]

[The virtue of patience] seems to me essential for one who has to undergo the tedium of long debates, much repetition, and many irrelevancies. I frequently

---

[1] *BM*, Add. MS 35423, fo. 23.   [2] *Parliamentary History*, xv. 724–39.
[3] Cited in O. C. Williams, *The Clerical Organization of the House of Commons 1660–1850* (Oxford, 1954), 206.
[4] Cited in W. F. Monypenny and G. E. Buckle, *The Life of Benjamin Disraeli* (1914), iii. 108.
[5] Cited in John Morley, *Life of Gladstone* (ed. 1905), i. 299.
[6] Walter Bagehot, *The English Constitution* (standard ed.), 180.

used to inculcate upon the clerks at the Table . . . that it was of no use repining, and that come weal, come woe, we would have to remain at our posts until the middle of August, with the additional prospect of an autumn session, and that we could do nothing towards a more rapid expedition of business.[1]

The session of 1887 was the most arduous of my recollection. . . . There was no limitation to the length of our sittings. . . . For those who, like myself and probably a majority, were busily engaged in their own affairs during the day, the stress was such that only youth, and an ironclad constitution, could withstand.[2]

And who were these 'bored, impatient, cynical' men who so despised the time-wasting, pointless and frustrating business of Parliament – men whose agonies surely persuaded them to seek other ways of making a career? Who were these agents of legislation who clearly would have wished to remove from the body politic an instrument of so little practical virtue? They were Henry Pelham, writing to Lord Chancellor Hardwicke in 1746; Hardwicke himself in the Lords a little later; John Hatsell, clerk of the House of Commons, in 1800; Disraeli, speaking in the House in 1848; Sir Robert Peel, in conversation with Gladstone in 1846; Bagehot writing his comments in the 1850s; Speaker Lowther recalling the first decade of the twentieth century; and H. H. Asquith who stayed in the Commons for some thirty-five years after his ironclad constitution had been first undermined by the absurdities of parliamentary business. This is the voice of the old House of Commons man – exasperated, resentful, this-is-the-last-time-y, but ever fascinated by the strange institution which brings him to the centre of affairs and determined to use it to rule the state or promote such lesser ambition as may move him.

In all this, Cromwell's letter differs from the rest only by being a good deal wittier and perhaps also a little more perceptive. I doubt whether there are many things said by Mr Gladstone which would have extracted a nod of agreement from Thomas Cromwell, but I think he would have applauded the G.O.M.'s reaction to an impertinent lecture from Thiers on representative institutions: 'When they talk to us about the House of Commons, there is a reply which but for the proprieties would be best: "Teach your grandmother to suck eggs." '[3] To the evidence collected elsewhere for Cromwell's activities

[1] J. W. Lowther, Viscount Ullswater, *A Speaker's Commentaries* (1925), ii. 298.
[2] H. H. Asquith, *Fifty Years of Parliament* (1926), i. 168–9.
[3] *The Political Correspondence of Mr. Gladstone and Lord Granville 1868–1876*, ed. Agatha Ramm (1963: Camden 3rd ser., vols. 81–2), i. 129.

as a parliamentary statesman,[1] I may add a small but revealing detail. In the Reformation Parliament, certain members opposed the government's policy, and one of them at least, Sir George Throckmorton, followed the guidance of a group of politicians out of Parliament, led by Fathers Peto and Reynolds. Their counsels and long custom maintained his views, and Cromwell, well aware of the situation, confined himself to frequent warnings not to listen to such advice.[2] Thus, in a matter of some delicacy, Cromwell's behaviour, far from displaying impatience with tiresome elected bodies or eagerness to bully troublesome men, was characteristic of a parliamentary manager, a 'leader of the House'.

Cromwell's supposed despotism, though worthy of refutation, is a relatively minor issue. The crux of Dr Hurstfield's argument lies more weightily in his discussion of the problem of consent. He agrees that Tudor government legislated by statute but holds that the evidence will not sustain the assumption 'that the use of statute is somehow hostile to despotism'.[3] A good point. Perfectly legal means have been used before this to produce an overthrow of the law. But what is in question here is not whether this or that tyrant (especially whether Dr Hurstfield's chosen example, Hitler) so used legal means, but whether the Tudor use of legislation by Parliament disguised despotic action. Here Dr Hurstfield leaves me bewildered. He reminds us at length that Tudor Parliaments were elected on a narrow franchise and under a system of patronage. If there was consent, it was therefore the consent 'of a minority of the minority of the population'.[4] (Surely it should be a majority of that minority?) True enough: the sixteenth century did not practise democracy or manhood suffrage. The universal consent, which all Tudor writers on the subject agree was represented in Parliament, concerned the consent of the members of the realm (shires, cities, boroughs), not of individuals who were, however, deemed to be present because their community was represented. In practice, it is fair to say that consent was a reality even for individuals (as much of a reality as in most modern democracies), provided they belonged to what we have learned to call the political nation, Sir Thomas Smith's 'them that beare office' – and let us remember that Smith included among them not only noblemen and gentlemen but also citizens, burgesses, and yeomen.[5] By sixteenth-century standards,

---

1 Below, no. 31.   2 *LP* xii. II. 952.
3 Hurstfield, 98.   4 Ibid. 102.
5 *De Republica Anglorum*, Book I.

the English political nation was exceptionally large, as indeed the House of Commons was far and away the biggest representative assembly in Europe, especially in proportion to population.[1]

But no, Dr Hurstfield continues, their free consent, too, is a double fiction. In the first place, Parliaments were packed. It is nice to see this skeleton brought out of its cupboard again. Dr Hurstfield still cites Edward Hall's remark that the 1529 House of Commons contained a majority of king's servants, though this charge was disproved over a hundred years ago by the discovery of a membership list of that Parliament. He once again treats the unique case of Cromwell's dictatorial handling of the 1536 Canterbury election as typical, without heeding the strong hint in the evidence that what we do not know in the story might very probably remove the odium from Cromwell's action.[2] And he makes much of Cromwell's promise to Henry that the 1539 Parliament, the elections for which involved much display of conciliar management, would produce a 'tractable' House ('tractable' being glossed as 'subservient', which is not the same thing) – even though it was this allegedly subservient body that allegedly forced the king to abandon his allegedly despotic intent to substitute proclamations for statutes. There are some misapprehensions here. Cromwell, I fear, as is the habit of electoral managers, overstated his achievement, but no doubt he had some success in organizing returns, while his very boast proves that tractability was not to be taken for granted in Henrician Parliaments. 'Good government,' says Dr Hurstfield, 'as he [Cromwell] indicated to Henry VIII, required a subservient parliament.'[3] No such thing: any system of government which involved the presence of a representative assembly with the taxing and lawmaking powers of the sixteenth-century Parliament required methods designed to make executive and assembly capable of working together, though the perfect machinery for this was not worked out till the emergence of true democracy and very modern parties.

Lastly, Dr Hurstfield denies the validity of consent in Tudor England by another of those modern parallels which he says he dislikes using. Searching for 'evidence that this was a free society in which men reached their decisions by the reasonable processes of free discussion', he remembers 'the emergence and misuse of a mass medium of communication of gigantic proportions' in our own lifetime. The consent allegedly present in Tudor Parliaments was similarly controlled, he

---

[1] These points are elaborated in vol. 2, no. 22, esp. pp. 40 ff.
[2] *Tudor Constitution*, 284. [3] Hurstfield, 101.

says, by active propaganda and the very active repression of all forms of dissent.[1] Thus government could pretend to rule by consent and make laws with the agreement of the realm, when in reality it did as it pleased and forced hostile voices into silence. Now, of course, censorship, control of press and pulpit, the exploitation of the majesty of the monarch – were all features of Tudor government. By the absolute standards apparently set here, sixteenth-century England was not 'a free society': what society is? But neither was it a despotism; there are stages between those extremes. One need do no more than remember that in every reign these supposedly tractable Parliaments, composed of men whose opinions had been manipulated by the pressures of government propaganda and repression, raised serious opposition to the Crown and often forced changes in action and policy. I agree that 'this was minority rule, an uneasy and unstable distribution of power between the Crown and a social *élite*', though the élite was larger and the power distribution more stable than Dr Hurstfield recognizes.[2] Tudor rule was certainly determined, hostile to political and religious dissent, equipped with formidable emergency powers – though it was also astonishingly incapable of creating that general habit of obedience for which it longed. We are asked to ignore legalism and look at the realities of the situation. Yet, seeing that these included an often painful legalism, a passionate deference to entrenched rights, unending disagreement, frequent resistance, and far more violent disobedience than is found in the following century, how can this system be called a despotism, even by the loose standards applied by Dr Hurstfield? In theory, monarchy was limited by law and consent; in practice, this strong Crown depended for the execution of all its notable powers on the willing co-operation of a large political nation (down to village constables) over whom it had very few physical means of control, and whom – its own readiness to obey the law apart – it could only hope to retain co-operative by observing the rules of the game. I cannot accept Dr Hurstfield's arguments for a despotism because I am forced to think the terms in which he has discussed the problem essentially wrong – imposed upon the sixteenth century rather than appropriate to it.

Yet it may be held that in stressing the rule of law I have overlooked too much. Anyone wishing to list acts of doubtful legality committed in the sixteenth century will have little difficulty in finding some; and the tally will be larger in Elizabeth's reign than in her father's, a fact

---

[1] Ibid. 103–4.   [2] Ibid. 104–5.

which may account for Dr Hurstfield's growing conviction that Tudor rule was despotic. Some of the state trials, however legal in form, were certainly rigged; wilful power at times asserted itself; the treatment of Mary Queen of Scots cannot be described as being according to the rule of law; Elizabeth showed an improper readiness to imprison people without trial by way of asserting her authority or working off her spleen. The fact that the judges in Darnell's Case (1627) were forced by the precedents to accept an order of king and Council as a bar to granting *habeas corpus* does not make those precedents any more reassuring. Many people may well feel that the Tudors were both ruthless and despotic in that area of which they themselves are exceptionally aware – in politics and the business of state. It is therefore necessary to define what is and what is not at issue in this discussion. In emphasizing the rule of law I am not condoning acts of brutality or wilfulness. But moral reprobation offers no clue to the inquirer who would understand the nature of the Tudor state, while understanding that nature must not be read as equal to discarding all moral judgment. The opinion is wrong which confuses a demonstration of the realities with simple approval of the abuses that occur in reality, as is that which supposes that breaches of the law or morally repulsive behaviour can occur only in a despotic system. Tudor law, like Tudor life, was often savage; and Tudor rulers, like all rulers, occasionally did things which were not lawful. In the sixteenth century, the rule of law in fact permitted quite enough horrors to make the politically conditioned rare evasions of that rule seem morally little worse than many of the actions taken in perfect observance of it. I insist only that it is possible to separate recognition and condemnation of vile behaviour from an enquiry into the true structure of the sixteenth-century political system, and I maintain that to describe that system from its occasional perversion of its own fundamental principles is to distort. No system, of course, has ever been absolutely perfect and consistent in political operation, least so when a society has become convinced (as that of Tudor England was with good reason convinced) that its very existence was frequently in danger. It is that system, not its moral virtues, that have here been discussed. The faults and lapses of Tudor governments do not disprove the existence of the rule of law under which they governed. Our question has been whether the Tudors governed as despots or as limited, law-controlled monarchs, not whether they would be acceptable in the houses of the gently nurtured.

The rule of law is not identical with either the rule of charity or the rule of good sense, though these two are perhaps more likely to prevail when law rules than when will is all. The revolution which we call the Reformation had its victims, none less deserved than Thomas Cromwell, who on the scaffold implied a pointed distinction between the law by which he came to die and the justice he had sought at the king's hands. Throughout his stage of the revolution, Cromwell saw to it that the rule of law applied, as I hope to show elsewhere at much greater length.[1] With the worst will in the world, and often their will was good, Henry VIII, Elizabeth, and their servants neither could nor would escape from the two great limitations upon their executive power: their dependence on a network of self-reliant men throughout the realm and throughout society, and the rule of law.

[1] [See now *Policy and Police*.]

15

STATE PLANNING IN EARLY-TUDOR ENGLAND*

It is a commonplace of our books that sixteenth-century England witnessed the creation of a paternal state; the early Tudors, in particular, are held to have pursued a discernible policy towards the social and economic life of their country. The point is more often assumed than argued; if one attempts to trace its origins and grounds, one ends up either with general references to the statute book or with Georg Schanz's impressive work – *Die englische Handelspolitik gegen Ende des Mittelalters* – published as long ago as 1881. Though Schanz dealt only with trade and industry, the usual notions seem to assume an even more universal programme for society.[1] Doubts have not been entirely silent. Schanz may have too readily identified Tudor policy and the national interest; there is the possibility that what to us looks like perspicacious paternalism was really fiscal opportunism; the example of Edward III is ever there to warn one.[2] Mr Stone has argued that 'security, not prosperity, was the main object of Tudor economic policy'.[3] Professor Fisher has denied that sixteenth-century economic history was in any way the product of planning; to him market conditions were paramount.[4] But these disputes all rest on a common assumption: it is supposed that we know what policy was and can confidently ascribe it to Crown and government. It is thought that we know enough to say that Henry VII did this or Henry VIII wanted that. Now I wish to suggest that, on the contrary, we are as yet in no position for any such confident assertions. The problem has not yet been studied with either rigour or depth; there are major pitfalls to

---

* Paper read to the XIth International Congress of Historical Sciences, held at Stockholm in August 1960 [and published in *Econ. Hist. Rev.* 2nd Series, 13 (1961), 433-9.]
[1] Cf. eg. the remarks of T. F. T. Plucknett, 'Some Proposed Legislation of Henry VIII,' *TRHS* (1936), 119 ff., or of L. Stone, 'The Political Programme of Thomas Cromwell,' *BIHR* 24 (1951), 1 ff.
[2] Cf. G. Unwin, 'The Economic Policy of Edward III,' *Studies in Economic History* (1927), 117 ff.
[3] L. Stone, 'State Control in Sixteenth-Century England', *Econ. Hist. Rev.* 17 (1947), 103 ff.; the quotation is at p. 111.
[4] F. J. Fisher, 'Commercial Trends and Policy in Sixteenth Century England', ibid. 10 (1940), 95 ff.

note and unexplored lines of research to indicate. I have at present no answer to offer; I merely want to draw attention to the problems and difficulties involved in any serious investigation of the relations between Tudor governments and their subjects.

In the first place, if we are to analyse government planning of the economy, where shall we find evidence of indisputable government action? The records involved are of three kinds. Royal proclamations may reasonably, and without further proof, be taken to testify to royal purposes; but they are on the whole the least revealing documents because they very often rested on statutes. In any case, proclamations remain a subject to be studied; we do not even yet possess a complete list, since R. R. Steele's well-known catalogue has gaps, nor has anyone yet attempted a systematic analysis of their content, enforcement, and general significance. At least, however, they do not raise problems concerning the mind behind them. The difficulty here is much greater with the other two categories of material – projects of reform, and statutes. For the period from about 1530 onwards there survive a good many schemes and treatises which, it is well known, come as a rule from the pens of private persons and should not be read as proof of government planning;[1] yet sometimes notions reappear in enacted legislation, and it is clear that an analytical problem exists in the relationship between such programmes and government planning. The one inadmissible thing is the tacit assumption that any early Tudor treatise may be used as proof of the overall plan; yet Schanz, for instance, treated the memorials printed by Pauli as though they proved something for official thinking.[2] That links sometimes existed between those writers and those who directed policy is not questioned, but our real knowledge in this field is very limited. It is beginning to look as though a group of writers associated with Thomas Cromwell may have formed something like a planning staff; not only were they employed in justificatory exercises for the king's policy in Church and state,[3] but a little has also been done to link their names with the economic legislation of the time.[4] However, we await a thorough and systematic investigation of the writers and pamphleteers, untrammelled by the search for anticipated conclusions.

[1] Cf. e.g. S. T. Bindoff, 'Clement Armstrong and his Treatises of the Commonwealth,' ibid. 14 (1944), 64 ff.

[2] R. Pauli, 'Drei volkswirtschaftliche Denkschriften aus der Zeit Heinrichs VIII. von England,' *Abhandlungen der k. Gesellschaft der Wissenschaften zu Göttingen* (1878); Schanz, *Handelspolitik*, e.g. i. 459.   [3] Zeeveld, *Foundations*.

[4] Cf. below, no. 26 [and *Reform and Renewal*, ch. 4].

Far and away the most important evidence for planning lies, of course, in the statute book. On the face of it, this should be straightforward enough: most historians would no doubt agree with Dr Pickthorn that under Henry VII important legislation reflected the will of the Crown,[1] and would be even more certain of this for Henry VIII. I would suggest that this attitude begs the question; such ready generalizations are no substitute for the real study of the manner in which legislation came to be drafted and enacted which as yet we lack. One cannot assume that appearance in statute-form proves the government provenance of a particular notion, though this assumption is often made. I have before this shown that men who had no part to play in government were perfectly capable of casting their proposals in the form of parliamentary statutes and that their unofficial dreams included some of the most strikingly planned and paternalistic schemes of the time.[2] No idea could be further from the truth than that which supposes that only the king's councillors thought of making law in Parliament, or, to quote Dr Pickthorn, that whatever the ostensible origin of an act 'the will of the crown was . . . the principal factor in the action of the commons'.[3] Much legislation, of course, was government legislation, but some was not, and the distinction must be studied. John Rastell, in 1534, asked that his private plans of reform should be put forth by authority of Parliament;[4] the weavers of Essex, dissatisfied with working conditions, drafted their own bill for the 1539 session and begged Cromwell to assist its passage;[5] in the same year, Cromwell was informed that many people in Lincolnshire wanted acts for the cleaner keeping of churchyards (priests were using them to pasture their cattle) and for the reduction of ecclesiastical exactions.[6] Everyone looked to Parliament.

An example of the dangers which beset these studies is found in those 'remembrances' or memoranda for acts to be devised which occur among the state papers and are always quoted as though they were bound to represent government intentions. The assumption, once again, is unsafe. Take a list of late 1534 of 'things necessary, as it seemeth, to be remembered before the breaking up of the Parliament'. It is mainly concerned to argue the authority of kings over that of bishops and therefore seems royal and 'official' enough; yet it also includes a note about the need to rebuild decayed towns which is

---

[1] Pickthorn, *Early Tudor Government*, i. 127 ff. [2] Below, no. 23.
[3] Pickthorn, i. 130. [4] *LP* vii. 1071.
[5] Ibid. xiv. I. 874. [6] Ibid. 1094.

surely reflected in an act of the next session for precisely this purpose which would appear to have resulted from a petition presented to Parliament.[1] Two lists more specifically foreshadowing acts of Parliament and drawn up probably only a few weeks apart demonstrate how careful one ought to be. Both are concerned with the session of early 1536. One contains twenty proposals for statutes of which nine are immediately identifiable as having been enacted that year; all nine are pretty certainly official statutes and four of them explicitly record the government's determination to act in certain matters.[2] The remaining eleven proposals are simple and practical; most of them concern ways in which government servants like sheriffs or customers might be compelled to do their duty better. The other document adumbrates seven acts of which one can be loosely linked with an act passed in 1536 but none can be firmly identified with enacted legislation.[3] In the main the proposals record some sweeping and utterly impractical suggestions: 'to prevent young men from marrying until they are of potent age and strong men from marrying old widows', 'for restraint and utter extinction of abuses of lawyers', 'that merchants employ their goods in traffic and not in buying lands'. While the first list is unquestionably official, there is nothing to prove the second so; the extravagance of some of its notions leaves little doubt that it embodies some unofficial and irresponsible projecting which can in no way be used to describe government planning. It would therefore seem unsound to follow Professor Plucknett in treating these particular notes as part of a general royal programme for the preservation of the existing social structure.[4]

Evidence of this sort causes difficulties enough, but the great unsolved questions cluster round the so-called penal statutes, that is acts which prohibited certain things or laid down certain rules under the sanction of a fine or forfeiture half of which accrued to the Crown and half to the informer who brought the alleged offender to court. These acts compose the main body of controls within the national economy; they deal with matters affecting international trade, industry, agriculture, individual behaviour (sumptuary laws), and so forth. In view of the royal interest in their enforcement it is no doubt natural that they should normally be regarded as evidence of government initiative. Yet

---

[1] Ibid. vii. 1383; 27 Henry VIII, c. 1 which asks that 'it may please the king' to take certain action. [But cf. *Reform and Renewal*, pp. 108–9.]

[2] *LP* x. 252. The acts are 27 Henry VIII, cc. 2, 4, 6, 19, 23, 24, 28, 60, 63.

[3] *LP* ix. 725 (ii).   [4] Plucknett, *TRHS* (1936), 124.

once again one may doubt if the assumption is valid in every case. The phrasing of the statutes deserves attention. In the period under review, acts declare that they are made on the initiative either of the king, or of a Commons' petition, or of a petition presented to the Commons from outside. Some of them complicate the issue by talking only of the Parliament or even only of Lords and Commons, omitting the king, but for reasons into which it is not now possible to go these should probably be assigned to government action. The king's will is professed to be behind only 15 of Henry VII's 36 penal statutes, while 14 rested on Commons' petitions and 7 grew out of requests put forward by sectional interests. Yet we are confidently assured by Professor Gray – on whom Dr Pickthorn, responsible for the general acceptance of the notion, rests his equally confident statements – that under Henry VII government-sponsored bills predominated and all important legislation came from the king.[1] Much, of course, depends on what one means by important; to Gray this signified mainly political and constitutional acts, often of such little practical consequence as the so-called Star Chamber Act of 1487. Yet there were acts of eminent interest to the Crown which seemingly owed their existence to the Commons, like that of 1485 forbidding hunting in disguise (a danger to peace)[2] or the Navigation Act of 1489.[3] Though Gray accepted the words of acts as defining their provenance, he applied a personal choice as to what mattered and misled others into overestimating Henry VII's initiative. Busch, too, who has had much influence on general accounts, used all statutes indiscriminately to support his thesis of 'monarchical policy', as he called it. Thus he speaks of Henry's treatment of usury embodied in an act which claimed to be the work of the Commons (11 Henry VII c. 8), and of his policy in limiting the export of cloth even though the act in question (3 Henry VII c. 12) consisted of a petition from the cloth interests.[4] On the face of it it looks as though in economic and social controls, at least, the policy was only in part the king's, and the evidence must raise doubts whether Henry VII had any consistent policy in these matters at all.

The position is even more obscure in Henry VIII's reign because the enacting clauses of statutes began to grow more stereotyped. The number of penal statutes increased enormously: 83 in the reign, and

[1] H. L. Gray, *The Influence of the Commons on Early Legislation* (Cambridge, Mass., 1932), 141 ff.
[2] 1 Henry VII, c. 7.   [3] 4 Henry VII, c. 10.
[4] W. Busch, *England under the Tudors* (1895), 241 ff., esp. 248, 255.

of these 44 were the product of those drastic ten years from 1529 to
1539. Of the total only three professed to originate with the Commons
and 16 embodied outside initiative. However, in this reign we occasionally know the sort of behind-the-scenes detail which we lack for the
other, and some of it throws doubt on the usefulness of enacting
clauses. Thus a 1534 act for pewterers, as manifest an outside petition
as one could wish to see, was preceded by a draft prepared by a
government clerk and corrected by Cromwell.[1] On the other hand,
the three anticlerical acts of 1529, which were certainly first drafted by
Commons' committees, look in their finished form like pure Crown
statutes.[2] Indeed, we know that the grievances concerning probate
and mortuary fees were listed, before the session opened, among the
matters which a committee of the Mercers' Company was preparing
for submission to the Parliament.[3] Whichever way these doubts are
taken, they underline the importance of establishing, as far as may be,
where in fact the initiative lay, before one uses all this grist to feed the
mill of 'Tudor policy'.[4] For what it is worth, I may perhaps record
my impression that the 1490s and 1530s marked two peaks in this
history of control by statute, and that in the latter period the initiative
did come from a government presided over by a self-conscious
reformer (Cromwell) assisted by a staff of advisers and planners. In the
earlier reign, I suspect, much has been put down to Henry VII that
was only accepted, not initiated, by him – and I think so in despite of
Bacon's views, for Bacon knew much less of the reign than we do.[5]

We may never be able to discover very much about the forces
behind statutes, but that does not absolve us from trying or entitle us
to beg the question. The problems of enforcement and effectiveness
seem more likely to yield to the kind of systematic enquiry which has

---

[1] 25 Henry VIII, c. 9; PRO, SP 2/P, fo. 23.

[2] 21 Henry VIII, cc. 5, 6, 13; Hall, *Chronicle*, 765 f.

[3] Mercers' Company, Acts of Court 1527–60, fo. 23 v. I owe this reference to Professor
S. T. Bindoff.

[4] The problem is not, of course, peculiar to the sixteenth century and even more difficult
in the later middle ages. To quote Professor Chrimes against Professor Gray: 'The
forces behind private or public bills cannot be presumed – they have to be ascertained'
(*English Constitutional Ideas in the XV Century* [Cambridge, 1936], 239). Miss H. M.
Cam, trying to do this, seems to me to have been unable to avoid here and there the
argument that an act proceeded from an interest it benefited, a dubious point ('The
Legislators of Medieval England,' *Proc. of the British Academy* 31 [1945], 127 ff.).

[5] Francis Bacon, *The History of King Henry VII*, ed. Lumby (Cambridge, 1885), 72 ff.,
repeatedly speaks of the king (not Parliament) 'making' laws for all sorts of purposes.
This uncritical summary has been accepted, consciously or not, by most writers on the
period.

not yet been attempted. The most obviously needed line of enquiry would follow up the endeavour to enforce penal acts in the courts, by studying informer actions in Exchequer, Common Pleas and the Council courts, and the collection of fines in the records of Exchequer and Chamber. So far the only detailed study of a penal statute is Mrs Davies's investigation of the 1563 act of artificers.[1] Professor Beresford's tentative start on the problem also leaves the early Tudors virtually untouched.[2] Mr Kerridge has shown how very unsatisfactory the usual treatment has been of even so familiar a problem as the policy on enclosures,[3] and I have used an individual instance to draw attention to the question of enforcement.[4] But that is all.

Another obscure aspect of the penal laws is their relation to the licensing system – the practice of exempting individuals from them by grants *non obstante* (notwithstanding any statute made on the subject). Schanz thought that planned policy was weakened by the use of licences,[5] but the patent rolls had not been much calendared in his day and he relied on vague contemporary statements. The only serious study of licensing – Mr Dunham's investigation of retainder and livery – also treats it as a sign of weakness and surrender on the part of the government, with the secondary purpose of revenue from licences thrown in.[6] Yet his own instances strongly suggest that licensing represented a deliberate part of the system. The law against retainers had to be phrased categorically; its application was then varied by allowing exceptions determined in the main by national military needs.[7] But can we take this to have been the usual practice? A spot-check for two sets of years following close upon the enactment of many penal laws (1495–1500 and 1531–8) does not suggest that licensing by grants *non obstante* was a major element in the early-Tudor system of control. In the first period I can find only five licences of which all but one – a grant to Empson to impark open land – deal with exports and imports.[8] Contrary to received opinion, it thus looks as

---

[1] M. G. Davies, *The Enforcement of English Apprenticeship 1563–1642* (Cambridge, Mass., 1956).

[2] M. W. Beresford, 'The Common Informer, the Penal Statutes, and Economic Regulation,' *Econ. Hist. Rev.* 2nd Series, 10 (1957–8), 221 ff.

[3] E. Kerridge, 'The returns of the Inquisition of Depopulation', *EHR* 70 (1955), 212 ff.

[4] G. R. Elton, 'Informing for Profit', *Star Chamber Stories* (1958), 78 ff.

[5] *Handelspolitik*, i. 453 f.

[6] W. H. Dunham, Jr, *Lord Hastings' Indentured Retainers* (New Haven, 1955).

[7] It seems that Henry VII and Henry VIII licensed freely only when war was threatening, and that the plentiful licences issued between 1547 and 1563 went to government servants (ibid. 108 ff.).   [8] *CPR, Henry VII*, ii. 21, 81, 125, 139, 163.

though Henry VII meant the laws to work and was little concerned to gain money from exemptions (though, of course, it remains to be established whether licences were usually enrolled). The era of Thomas Cromwell's administration yields many more instances but no very different conclusions. Thirty licences to export foodstuffs were issued;[1] and there were 34 import licences, practically all permitting the shipping of Gascon wine and Toulouse woad in contravention of the Navigation Act of 1489 (4 Henry VII c. 10).[2] It is apparent that in international trade licensing formed at this time a significant part of the control, but the same did not apply to acts controlling the internal life of the country. True, the Crown used its dispensing power 65 times between 1531 and 1538, but analysis deprives this figure of its weight. Forty-three licences were granted for exemption from the 1529 act against pluralism, non-residence and the taking of farms by the spiritualty, to those classes of clerics for whom special provision had been made in the act itself.[3] This is therefore an entirely untypical case. Five foreign craftsmen were licensed to employ foreign labour in excess of the number permitted by the act of 1523,[4] and twelve men got exemption from the 1534 act forbidding the use of the crossbow.[5] The remaining five are a licence to impark, one to keep retainers, and three to permit bowling and other prohibited games in London pubs.[6]

Evidently, then, certain specific penal laws were designed to be operated through a system of dispensations, but in view of the very large number of such acts passed in these years it does not look as though licences were a necessary part of the policy or as though fiscal purposes were uppermost in the minds of Tudor governments. Penal statutes could be temporarily suspended altogether: in 1536–8 protests

---

[1] *LP* v. 80 (12, 13), 119 (47, 59), 220 (21), 278 (11, 14), 364 (24), 457 (6), 627 (9, 13, 16), 766 (13), 838 (3), 909 (28), 978 (18); vii. 761 (36), 1217 (5), 1352 (4), 1498 (8, 19); viii. 632 (7); ix. 1063 (13); x. 775 (10); xi. 519 (15), 1217 (10); xii. I. 311 (17, 29), 795 (31), 1103 (7).

[2] *LP* v. 80 (16), 318 (13), 766 (16), 978 (27), 1065 (29), 1598 (1, 19, 21, 22, 23), 1693 (10, 11); vi. 196 (34), 300 (5), 737 (1), 1383 (26), 1481 (22), 1595 (10); vii. 262 (10), 1498 (2, 26); viii. 481 (27); ix. 236 (11), 729 (13), 914 (9); x. 392 (42), 775 (22), 1256 (49); xi. 1417 (8, 17, 21, 22, 24); xii. I. 795 (48).

[3] 21 Henry VIII, c. 13: *LP* v. 119 (32), 166 (58), 506 (13), 766 (36), 909 (4), 978 (25), 1207 (11), 1499 (6, 14); vi. 105 (21), 578 (14), 1060 (3), 1383 (16), 1595 (12); vii. 147 (8, 13), 589 (1), 1498 (23, 25), 1601 (3); viii. 149 (24), 291 (7), 481 (33), 632 (14, 29), 634 (4), 802 (31); ix. 729 (17), 914 (1, 40), 1063 (12); x. 226 (26), 597 (33), 775 (25), 1256 (15), xi. 202 (38), 385 (28), 1217 (11, 21); xii. I. 539 (30, 31), 1330 (60); xii. II. 1150 (39).

[4] 14 & 15 Henry VIII, c. 2: *LP* v. 278 (8), 1270 (4); vii. 922 (14); viii. 634 (3); xi. 519 (17).

[5] 25 Henry VIII, c. 17; *LP* vii. 1122 (2), 1217 (13), 1601 (17); viii. 149 (5, 6); ix. 914 (17); x. 392 (14); xi. 385 (31); xii. I. 311 (26), 1105 (4), 1330 (3); xii. II. 191 (25).

[6] *LP* vi. 105 (25); vii. 1026 (29); viii. 149 (11), 962 (29); xii. I. 1103 (14).

from the clothmakers of Essex and Suffolk against the standards enforced by the 1536 statute (27 Henry VIII c. 12) resulted in two proclamations postponing its effect until the local industry had retooled.[1] However, suspension was so rare as to be negligible and licensing was reserved for special cases; on the whole it seems that the statutes were meant to be applied and that from the government's point of view their value lay in social planning rather than in the prospect of revenue from the sale of dispensations. However, this can be only a provisional view, based on nothing like sufficient study.

I hope I have said enough to support my claim that we are some way yet from confident pronouncements on early-Tudor policy in the social and economic fields. Though I do not mean to belittle the study of economic phenomena, statistics and principles, I cannot help feeling that the problems on which I have touched here will never be solved by the standard methods of the economic historian. Nor, if I may say so, should we be wise to seek their solution, in the absence of evidence, through the short-cut of sociological theories, of whatever kind – theories which might, for instance, lead us to classify legislation as monarchical, capitalist or anti-feudal and thus once again blithely beg the question. If we are to get anywhere we need, in the first place, a much more systematic study of evidence which is commonly used selectively and by way of illustration only; and in the second, a fuller understanding of the personal, administrative and legal issues involved. We must get away from the impressionism too common in these matters – the method which garnishes statements taken from contemporaries with helpful bits of evidence handpicked from the mass. Only a comprehensive and critical attack on admittedly often difficult materials will stand a chance of discovering the truth. At the same time, let us remember that we have no hope at all of getting answers to all our questions.

[1] Ibid. xii. II. 737, 863. The clothmakers of Berkshire, Oxfordshire, Hampshire, Surrey, Sussex and Yorkshire, not satisfied with the suspension, petitioned for repeal of the statute (probably) in the summer Parliament of 1536 (PRO, St Ch 2/23/115).

16

HENRY VII'S COUNCIL*

This book has been a long time in the making. As Professor Plucknett tells us in an introductory note, Bayne had completed the monograph on the early Star Chamber, which forms the introduction to the present volume, as early as 1937, and though he worked on for ten years more, the completion of the edition by Mr Dunham has occupied yet another decade. It would appear from internal evidence that Mr Dunham did not think it right to alter the study in any way by taking note of more recent work. In consequence the book was in some respects behind the times before ever it appeared; in such matters as the career of Reginald Bray, the making of the Privy Council, or the nature of Henry VII's policy it should be treated as belonging to 1947 rather than 1958.[1] This necessarily detracts a little from its value, but Bayne's concerns were really so narrowly confined that the harm is not great. A second preliminary criticism, which can only be suggested here, concerns the value of publishing useful monographs as introductions to expensive collections of documents which tend to be difficult to obtain. Bayne's work originally consisted of a dissertation on Henry VII's Star Chamber, and essentially it has remained that. Yet he was persuaded to collect more of those cases of which Leadam had already published a selection, and the book was in the end called 'Cases in the Council'. It may be said at once that this is probably a better title than Leadam's 'Cases in Star Chamber', but Bayne's introduction habitually speaks of Star Chamber rather than Council (he makes a case of sorts for this on p. lxxvi) and bears all the marks of having been written in advance of the collection which it introduces.

It is quite true that some of the cases selected for publication have a special institutional interest, and one is of course always grateful for

---

* [Review of *Select Cases in the Council of Henry VII*, ed. C. G. Bayne and W. H. Dunham, Jr (Selden Society, 1958), in *EHR* 74 (1959), 686–90.]

[1] Cf. Richardson, 'Sir Reginald Bray,' *Tudor Chamber Administration*, 451 ff.; Robert Constable, *Prerogativa Regis*, ed. S. E. Thorne (New Haven, 1949); *Tudor Revolution*, esp. 316 ff.; and no. 3 above. More surprising is the absence of any reference to Mr Dunham's own articles on the Council of Henry VIII (esp. in *Huntington Library Quarterly*, 7) which appeared in 1943.

more of this material in print. Of even greater value is the inclusion of what Bayne and Dunham (following the Elizabethans) call the *Liber Intrationum*, a transcript of all that can be recovered of the Council Registers of Henry VII's time. Copies of these in the Harleian, Huntington and other collections have been known for long, but to have them conflated into something like a register again (with careful notes on the sources of the various entries) is most welcome. Yet here once more the genesis of the book makes itself disconcertingly felt. The introduction consists essentially of three parts. In the first place it discusses Henry VII's Council – establishment, personnel, committees, etc. Next it analyses the 1487 Act 'pro camera stellata'. The bulk of it is concerned with the Council as a court – with Star Chamber in all its details. This last point rests almost entirely on one kind of source, the surviving Star Chamber proceedings for Henry VII's reign which amount to no more than 194 cases (p. lxxiii). The publication of the *Liber* has assisted in the first part of the introduction but not in the last; neither the Council as an institution nor the court of Star Chamber receive sufficient, or sufficiently based, analysis. Only the second part of the introduction does work which need never be done again. Here Bayne not only elaborates the view established by Pollard that the tribunal created by the act and the Council as a court are two different things which have little to do with each other, but also produces hitherto unknown evidence of the tribunal's activity and makes a strong case for believing that the criminal jurisdiction later exercised by Star Chamber was in Henry VII's reign usually attended to by the special committee of the act. The discussion of the act supersedes, and in part nullifies, all earlier writing on the subject.

There is no room here to engage in a full examination of the many problems raised in this important book, but something must be said on the two big issues: the nature of the Council as a political body, and the kind of court the Star Chamber was in this period. Though Bayne has done a good deal to advance understanding of the first point, he has ultimately left it in the air. His analysis of Henry VII's councillors will provide a good starting-point for further study, and he may have done something to exorcise the legend of a purely 'middle-class' body of advisers; but he neither sufficiently investigates individuals nor even performs the elementary task of discovering how large the Council was at any given moment. Statements about the novelty of the institution (ascribing it to Edward IV: p. xxiii) raise doubts, and the so-called Council Attendant appears here as far too institutional. We are still left in doubt who it was travelled with the king, or what happened to the various groups of councillors in term time. Bayne makes the very interesting suggestion that the registers of the court of Requests (which survive almost complete from 1493) record business done before the king's councillors attendant 'wherever he might be'. He goes so far as to say (p. xxv) that 'all we know of the Council in attendance is that under the name of Court of Requests it was assiduous in the trial of civil suits', but this is both less and more than the facts warrant. We cannot be sure that the peripatetic 'court' was held by all the councillors in attendance; we need not doubt, as Bayne does, that councillors in attendance on the king acted (as those attending on him at Westminster in term time certainly did) as advisers; we cannot even at present make any serious distinction between the hearing of civil pleas on progress ('Requests') and the same work at Westminster ('Star Chamber'). Bayne was going to investigate the court of Requests; since he did not live to do this, we must consider the whole subject, and with it the out-of-term activities of the Council, as an open question.

However, the real concern of this book is with the Council sitting as a court at Westminster, and here Bayne's analysis not only entirely replaces Leadam's but in such matters as procedure, competence, and punishments provides some very welcome light. Bayne's chief contention is that Henry VII's Star Chamber was mainly a court for civil suits between private parties. Even its jurisdiction in riot was largely set in motion by private bills and only very rarely by the government. Contrary to received opinion, it was therefore not Henry VII's weapon for the enforcement of the law and the restoration of order. Bayne stresses its moderation, calling it 'the mildest-mannered tribunal that ever sentenced a criminal' (p. clxxii). Much of this new view must certainly be accepted. The presence of so many civil suits, on matters which the Elizabethan Star Chamber would have regarded as outside its competence, is striking, though their chief meaning is to underline how little the 'Star Chamber' had yet developed into a proper and separate court. More important is Bayne's demonstration that official prosecutions for the notorious retaining offences took place either before the 1487 tribunal or (very frequently) at common law. Indeed, there is here every indication that the Crown did not at this time deliberately abandon the traditional law-enforcing agencies, and that the growth of conciliar jurisdiction may in great part have been due to pressure from suitors. But the argument cannot carry entire conviction because it rests solely on the proceedings. To argue (as Bayne does) from the absence of evidence when only 194 cases survive for twenty-four years would seem dangerous in the extreme. Moreover, the proceedings can be helped out by other evidence, some of which Bayne himself here prints, though he makes no use of it in his discussion of the Council as a court. The *Liber Intrationum*, for instance, is prefaced by a note based upon the lost registers from which the *Liber* itself is drawn, and this note claims that under Henry VII the Star Chamber dealt with every sort of crime as well as civil disputes, and also with political matters (pp. 6 f.). Some of the extracts, too, suggest that the Council heard more criminal cases at the king's or a subject's suit than the surviving proceedings confirm. A case of riot dismissed to the king's own hearing (p. 8); Robin of Redesdale arrested at the Council's suit (ibid.); a man summoned by subpoena in a case of murder (p. 11); a general order referring rioters to punishment by king and Council (ibid.); enquiries into an alleged embracery (p. 17);[1] a case of false imprisonment (p. 20); not to mention a long list of matters dealt with in ten days in 1488 (p. 21) – the examples pile up.

The trouble would seem to be twofold. On the one hand, Bayne wrote his study of Star Chamber before he had a chance of seeing the important Huntington Library manuscripts on which the *Liber*, as here printed, so largely rests;[2] and Mr Dunham made no changes in the text. But more serious is the fact that, despite disavowals,[3] Bayne was prepared to treat the court of Star Chamber as established and distinct from the Council acting in other capacities at a time when this is probably erroneous. With great lucidity he shows how primitive and informal its procedure could be, how different its dealings and even its scope from those of the Elizabethan Star Chamber; he even demonstrates with some cogency (p. lxxvi) that to call the institution by the name of court of Star Chamber is an anachronism. Nevertheless he not only always uses the term but treats certain Council activities as specifically Star Chamber work and ignores the very real difficulties which this creates. Insofar as the 'Star Chamber' kept a record of transactions, it is plain from the words of those who saw the books and made extracts from them that the only record existed in an undifferentiated Council book. In this were entered all the doings of the Council sitting at

[1] On p. cxix it is stated that only one case of embracery survives. But this case in the *Liber* is a different one. [2] Cf. Professor Plucknett's memoir on p. vi.
[3] Bayne argues (p. lxxiv) that 'the Council as an executive board was indistinguishable from the Council as a court of law', yet refuses to use the records of the Council as evidence for its curial activities.

Westminster in term time, and it is quite possible that the so-called Registers of the court of Requests represent a similar book kept by the councillors on progress with the king. Important and sound as much of Bayne's work is, the basic flaw – a distinction between Council and Star Chamber which is nowhere justified and produces a misleading view of 'the Star Chamber's' work – cannot be overlooked.

A few particular difficulties should be noticed. The statement on p. xii which identifies a Council record of 1540–3 with the lost Star Chamber registers is wrong: the book in question is the first volume of the Privy Council Register kept by the clerk newly appointed in August 1540. On the same page, an argument is advanced that two registers must have been kept by the Council *temp. Hen. Sept.*; but the evidence only suggests that at some time in the sixteenth century someone made an abstract (index ?) of the proper book of entries. The Privy Council did not 'come into existence early in Henry VIII's reign' (p. xxii). On page xxxi the prior of St John of Jerusalem is included among the clerics on the Council; yet the presence lists always put him fairly low among the laity, and the appointment appears indeed to have usually gone to a layman. On the same page, the civilians on the Council are written off too readily as 'of little note in the field of civil government'. A curious and dubious distinction is made (pp. xxx and xxxv) between courtiers and officials among councillors; this sort of pigeon-holding has its notorious dangers. The statement quoted from the *Liber* that the Council sat 'in manner every day in the term' (p. xlii) probably meant not daily sittings but sittings on any day of the week. The assertion that the Star Chamber records are well preserved after 1509 (p. lxxiii) will cause surprise among those who have had to work on them. In the case quoted on page cvii, the committal of a vexatious plaintiff to await further punishment at the king's pleasure does not represent 'an adjournment' but the disposal of a case by somewhat arbitrary action, and it may be doubted whether it might have 'occurred at any period'. One hopes that 'dominum presidentum' (p. xxxviii) is a misprint; but why does a volume of this sort, published by a learned society, translate every bit of Latin in the documents? Moreover, one cannot always accept the translation. Thus 'Jurisperitos de Concilio Regis' (p. 15) surely means the lawyers (and probably the civilians) on the king's Council and not some new, obscure body, 'the legal advisers of the King's Council'; or – to take a simpler case – 'per ipsos defendentes' (p. 25) means 'by the same defendants' and not 'by the defendants themselves'.

One could continue with questions and doubts of a minor sort to which (it goes without saying) a work of this kind must give rise. These criticisms are not offered in a captious spirit. Like the larger observations, they are intended to assist and, perhaps, to warn. The history of the early-Tudor Council is still to be written, and Bayne has not discharged the task for the reign of Henry VII. So much premised, it should be stressed that he has greatly contributed to this fascinating and exacting problem. Above all, he has settled the act of 1487, has clarified the procedure of the Council in judicial matters, and has suggested several new lines of investigation.

17

GOVERNMENT BY EDICT?*

There has never been any doubt that Tudor monarchs used royal proclamations to announce their decisions and govern the realm. Until
recently, however, few of these documents have been available in
print; analysis of their scope, purpose and power has had to rely on
the list of bare abstracts prepared by R. R. Steele for the *Bibliotheca
Lindesiana*.[1] This situation has now been remedied by the devoted
labours of two American scholars who are planning to provide full
transcripts of all Tudor proclamations and have so far published the
first volume, covering the reigns of Henry VII, Henry VIII and
Edward VI. Since this review of their work will in part be critical, it
must first be stressed that the debt under which they have placed all
students of the period is very great. The mere fact that a large amount
of record material is here made easily accessible must cause rejoicing,
and the importance of these documents – the importance, especially, of
being able to study the precise wording of nearly 400 orders of the
central government – becomes very clear in the act of reading them.
Professors Hughes and Larkin have made possible a quite new and
immeasurably more accurate study of one of the central problems of
Tudor rule; they have provided material for important revisions in
constitutional, administrative and economic history; and they have
done so, on the whole, with commendable precision and lack of preconceived ideas. In the circumstances, one can forgive the slightly
excessive enthusiasm with which they appear to claim for themselves
the very discovery that proclamations were issued and constituted a
major instrument of government; the 'conclusion that proclamations
are a source material for a more complete and accurate history of the
period' (p. xxxvii) strikes one as a trifle naïve. But the manifest pride
of achievement is engaging.[2]

* [Review of *Tudor Royal Proclamations*, vol. I, ed. Paul L. Hughes and James F. Larkin
  (New Haven, 1964), in *HJ* 8 (1965), 266–71.]
[1] *Tudor and Stuart Proclamations 1485–1714*, ed. R. R. Steele (2 vols., Oxford, 1910).
[2] The extraordinary claims to originality, and the animadversions on English scholars,
  put into Mr Hughes's mouth in the *Chicago Sunday Tribune* of 12 June 1964, should no
  doubt be blamed on the interviewing journalist rather than the interviewed professor.

The editors' introduction, however, is less satisfactory. There are some hints of a strange conviction that the proclamations (perfectly lawful documents justified by the common-law prerogative of the Crown) prove Tudor government to have been less 'constitutional' and more arbitrary than has been supposed. A reference to charters issued 'prior to the establishment of the House of Commons as a legislative body' (p. xxiii) suggests a false view of the history of that institution. It is not right to call the enforcing council of the 1539 Proclamations Act a 'committee of the King's Council' (p. xxvii): that 'committee' was a good deal larger than the Council itself. Altogether, the editors have nothing very useful to say on the question of enforcement; but while in part this is the result of wrong criteria and lack of strictness in the analysis, it is also true that the problem requires a study of an order too large for any introduction. The class of record office materials curiously described as Exchequer of Treasury Receipts should be called Exchequer, Treasury of the Receipt (the error suggests an insufficient acquaintance with Tudor administration); and the improbable assertion (p. xxiv) that warrants for the issue of proclamations carried both the sign manual and the privy seal[1] is not, as claimed, borne out by the warrant reproduced opposite p. 84 which surprisingly mentions no seal of warranty. The description of proclamations and the manner of their production is acceptable; but the larger analysis of purpose and effect, of policy and scope, commands less assent. What evidence is there, for instance, that 'licences and monopolies [an odd pair] account for some of the most effective early Tudor proclamations' (p. xxxi)? At present we know almost nothing about the effectiveness of these orders, and Hughes and Larkin certainly do not add to our knowledge. Or again, it is strange to be told that the very few proclamations dealing with the consequences of Henry VIII's establishment of the royal supremacy are 'more sharply pointed' than the statutes of the period (p. xxxv): these statutes created new treasons and felonies, while the proclamations tidied up a few enforcement problems. Altogether, the analysis of these documents offered in the introduction barely starts on the many issues involved.

The documents themselves have on the whole been well edited, especially if one accepts the principle that they will be more readily accessible in modern spelling. This may well be true, though an edition ought to reproduce the originals, and the dangers of altering the spelling are not negligible. On p. 82 the original has been repunc-

---

[1] Sign manual warrants issued under the signet.

tuated till the sense is lost.[1] Two king's councillors are called out of their names on p. 383, John Dudley (Viscount Lisle) appearing quaintly as 'John Lord, Viscount Lisle', and Sir Richard Lister, the judge, as Listen. It is by no means always clear on what evidence the confident dating rests. The head notes give useful information concerning both the bibliography and, occasionally, the circumstances of the proclamations, but they are not as free of error as one could wish.[2] Some of the titles supplied by the editors mislead. Thus in no. 42 the reader is surprised to be told that clipped coin is declared legal tender; the proclamation itself ordered the acceptance of all coins, 'so that they may be silver and whole'. The threat in no. 168 is one of war, not, as stated in the heading, of martial law. 'Redistricting Western Shires' is a very odd title for a proclamation which organizes the shiring of the Welsh Marches (no. 172). No. 324, 'Announcing Payment of King's Debts', hides the interesting fact that the document deals with purveyance.[3]

How complete is the list? Some more proclamations apparently came to light too late for inclusion. One proclamation missing is that of 16 February 1541, which prohibited the export of victuals; the editors regret that they could not trace it, which is a pity since it was one of the informers' favourite weapons in the courts. However, no doubt it closely resembled others made for a like purpose. On the other hand, I cannot agree with the presence of quite a few of the proclamations included in the canon. Technically, a proclamation was no more than any announcement of a royal order: the bulk of them covered such technicalities as outlawries proclaimed in the shire court or forfeited goods proclaimed by order of the Exchequer. These are naturally and rightly excluded here. But their dismissal should carry with it the local proclamation of fugitives. Some of the proclamations included were proclaimed by commissioners or in the court of Chancery and do not seem to me to belong here because they were not of

---

[1] For 'misusing of apparel statute; labourers for all unlawful games', read 'misusing of apparel; statute [of] labourers; for all unlawful games'. If the text of this document is taken from the source stated, the beginning of it is mistranscribed.

[2] E.g. no. 75, there is no evidence that the passage cited from the Ellesmere MSS had anything to do with this proclamation; no. 60, the date is derived from a mention in Holinshed but this refers to no. 59 (in which treason and murder are excepted from the general pardon, while in 60 they are included); no. 376, the reference to *APC*, either by page or by date (the two do not coincide), yields nothing to the purpose.

[3] The index entry 'purveyors' mixes up the technical problem of royal purveyance and the general meaning of the word (= purchaser). Altogether, the subject index contains some idiosyncrasies.

general import; if they did, so would every proclamation of a commission of oyer and terminer. The editors include some licences to beg alms, circulars to Justices of the Peace or bishops, and straightforward letters patent, none of which are proclamations in the sense defined by them and generally agreed. Some documents appear twice because their issue was authorized on different dates for different shires. No doubt there are some tricky borderline decisions to be made in this, but I have removed 27 items from the list, for the following reasons:[1]

(1) Purely local orders (8, 14, 15, 41, 78, 98, 99).
(2) Alms placards (32, 82, 84).
(3) Proclaimed in Chancery only (109, 113, 114, 119).
(4) Circulars to select groups, not proclaimed (158, some Justices of the Peace; 285, customs officers; 353, bishops).
(5) Ordinary letters patent (192, 210, 251).
(6) Schedule of instructions to certain commissioners (338).
(7) A draft – no evidence of issue (191).
(8) Duplicates (79 = 76, 103 = 102, 132 = 131, 180 = 178, 232 = 231).

This still leaves 361 proclamations issued in these sixty-eight years, and it remains to have a look at what emerges from a preliminary study of them.

The first point of importance is the clear evidence that the number of proclamations issued increased quite rapidly in the course of the period. The twenty-four years of Henry VII yield 54, the thirty-six of Henry VIII 197, and the six of Edward VI 110. Up to a point, no doubt, losses of records help to distort the picture, but there is no reason to think this indication of a trend anything but accurate. Table 1 gives totals for five-year periods, slightly modified by adherence to reigns. Proclamations, very rarely used by Henry VII, did not really come into their own until the beginning of the new order in the 1530s, and they ran riot after 1540. Interestingly enough, the repeal of the 1539 Proclamations Act did nothing to stop the acceleration; indeed, only five of the proclamations issued in the seven years that the Act was in force cited its authority (205, 211. 217, 231, 242). The figure for Edward VI hides the fact that of the early Tudor governments that of the Protector Somerset relied most lavishly on proclamations: the two and a half years of his ascendancy account for 75, a fifth of the total.

---

[1] From now on, figures in brackets refer to the numbers of documents.

Table 1

(1)	1485–90	22	(8)	1521–5	19
(2)	1491–5	7	(9)	1526–30	20
(3)	1496–1500	16	(10)	1531–5	28
(4)	1501–5	8	(11)	1536–40	34
(5)	1506–9	1	(12)	1541–6	74
(6)	1509–15	19	(13)	1547–53	110
(7)	1516–20	3			

The problems of the new dynasty drove up numbers in Henry VII's early years; war, with its concomitants of musters, martial law, logistics and peace treaties, boosted the figures in periods 6, 8 and 12.

However, these quinquennial figures do not tell the whole story. Any classification of proclamations must to some extent remain a matter of personal opinion, but it is nevertheless necessary to undertake one. In Table 2, I have broken down the totals from two points of view. The first criterion is the authority on which proclamations rested: declaratory (announcing a fact and requiring no special authority), prerogative (adding to the body of regulations by authority of the king alone, with or without the advice of the Council), and statutory (either enforcing acts of Parliament or resting on their authority). The second criterion looks to their purpose. The distinctions are not always easy to make, but I have tried to separate proclamations which concerned economic problems (victuals, enclosure, coinage, manufacture) from those dealing with general administration.

This reveals some very interesting points. Wolsey's administration did not use proclamations very much, but the bulk of those issued rested on the prerogative. The same was true in the very active period after 1540. The 1530s, on the other hand, are the only period when a very large proportion of proclamations rested on statute. Of the seven suspensions of acts of Parliament by prerogative action, five postpone the act of 1536 (27 Henry VIII, c. 12) which regulated the manufacture of cloth (166, 175, 198, 202, 207); they did so under pressure from the weaving interests. The other two likewise freed sections of the community from burdens imposed by Parliament (195, 226). There appear to be only four proclamations which specifically decree something *non obstante* any statute to the contrary. One of them, in the Cromwell period, freed the exchanges (181); the other three, from Edward's reign, permit the export of grain (280, 301) and allow merchants to

Table 2

	H. VII to 1509	Wolsey to Oct. 1529	Cromwell to March 1540	to 1546	Somerset to Oct. 1549	Northumberland to 1553
Declaratory	15*	11*	10*	9	12*	4
Prerogative	34	36†	27‡	57§	54	21
Statutory	5	11	24‖	12‖	9	10
Total	54	58	61	78	75	35
Administration	27	35	18	52¶	43	15
Economic	13	13	26	17**	19	18
Religious	—	1	7	6	7	1
Announcement	14	9	10	3	6	1

* 2 pardons. † 8 arising out of 1512 war. ‡ 2 suspend acts of Parliament. § 5 cite 1539 Proclamations Act; 25 arise out of 1542 war; 5 suspend acts of Parliament. ‖ 8 issued by authority of Parliament but not enforcing an act. ¶ 27 arise out of the war. ** 9 rest on acts of Parliament.

take £4 in cash out of the realm (387). Evidently, the prerogative of the early Tudors made no attempt to attack the supremacy of statute; in the Cromwell era it was manifestly employed to back up and enforce acts of Parliament; and though the bulk of proclamations rested on the king's authority alone, this perfectly well-known fact does not entitle us to suppose, with the editors, that this flow of orders from the Crown in some way contradicts the view that the Tudor monarchy governed under the law. The 1539 Act seems to have no visible effect: during the remainder of Henry VIII's reign, at least, the rise in number resulted in large part from the war. Nor did its repeal make any difference to Somerset's determination to govern by edict, the contrast between him and Northumberland being pointed further by the fact that of the latter's thirty-three proclamations no fewer than ten arose from the debasement and revaluation of the coinage. Somerset's real purpose in multiplying proclamations must await a thorough analysis of his seventy-seven pronouncements; for what it is worth, I may record my impression that the government reflected in them is paternalistic rather than paternal, vicious rather than generous, and that A. F. Pollard's picture of the duke seems to bear little resemblance to his doings.

It may also just be noted that the present analysis would seem to bear out the traditional view that proclamations were used in the ordinary government of the realm, to regulate and administer, entirely within the lawful and customary powers of the Crown. The very small number of proclamations dealing with matters religious must surprise: the supreme head does not seem to have had much use for the potentially despotic powers taken over from the papacy.

Professors Hughes and Larkin rightly comment on the punishments laid down in proclamations. A good many carried no penalties or threatened only the king's displeasure in general terms; of those that do, the great bulk impose fines or forfeitures or imprisonment. This subject requires proper analytical and statistical study, but the question of penalties remains in any case meaningless until we know more about enforcement. All this is too much for a review article. But one part of the subject can be managed and must find a place here. The editors state that 'contrary to a formal proviso in the Statute of Proclamations . . . an unexpected number of proclamations carry the death penalty' (p. xxix). I do not know how many they expected, nor is it clear why proclamations issued before 1539 should be read as contradicting an act passed in that year. In any case, what of these death-dealing proclamations? If the editors' analysis were correct, it would indeed force us to think again about the textbook generalization that proclamations 'could not (and did not) touch life or members'.[1] As to 'member', one proclamation of 1551 (378) authorizes the cropping of the ears of a rumour-monger unable to pay a fine; there is no other example, and one may doubt if ears are, technically, members.

That leaves the death penalty. I may have missed the odd instance, and the index (which, for instance, lists a pardon as though it inflicted the punishment of death) is no help; at any rate, I have noted seventeen proclamations in which death is decreed in some way or other.[2] This total is made up of seven which in effect proclaim martial law or deal with rebellions (1, 13, 73, 190, 244, 341, 342), and one which threatens rebels against the king's ally, the emperor Maximilian (52): these prove only that proclamations were a proper instrument to use in case of war or its equivalent. Six more proclaim offences which carry the death penalty at common law (71, 179, 182, 323, 326, 334); these do not demonstrate any innovatory force in the proclamation, though one (323) comes close to it by including aiders of pirates among the pirates liable to death by statute, while another (179) removes the chance of escaping a common-law punishment by means of a pardon or benefit of clergy. Two proclamations impose the death penalty for anabaptist opinions, the first (155) on aliens refusing to leave the country, and the

---

[1] Cf. *Tudor Constitution*, 22. [2] As against the editors' eleven on p. xxix.

other (186) on all who, not being learned, dispute of the eucharist: this last, the only truly drastic step, was revoked a few months later (188). One proclamation which might be read as introducing a new capital offence is one of 1549 (336: Somerset again) which makes it treason to take the law into one's own hands against profiteers and price-riggers; but even this in fact only extends the concept of rebellion to cover major rioting. The traditional conclusion must stand: proclamations could not and did not create new offences punishable by loss of life.

Many very interesting points, both great and small, are brought out in these pages. To list a few: Wolsey employing secret spying to get information about enclosure (119: not a proclamation), or Northumberland offering a cash reward to informers (358); the use of 'surname' to mean kin (p. 6); the description of heresy procedure used in 1529 (pp. 184–5);[1] a reference showing that the act of proclamations was taken to have 'dilated and confirmed' the king's powers (p. 310); a list of the king's courts in 1546 which omits Requests (p. 371); a reference to the first prayer book as the king's act and 'the act of the whole state of our realm assembled together in parliament' (p. 485). In the 1530s several proclamations seem to have later been replaced by statutes (145, 152, 153). Lenten fasts were ordered in the reign of Edward VI for practical, not religious, reasons – to save foodstuffs (368). Perhaps the most dramatic proclamation of the lot is that in which Somerset tried to gather forces for his own protection when it was already too late (351): the editors rightly print a facsimile of that. The questions that remain to be investigated are many, and – to say it once again – that of enforcement should be tackled soon. It might be worth while analysing the instances in which the Council's consent is quoted. And there is the subject-matter of proclamations, of interest to every historian of the period. Despite all the critical remarks made in this review, the last word must once more be of gratitude to the scholars who ventured so bravely and energetically into these thickets.

---

[1] [Actually 1530; cf. *Policy and Police*, 218, n. 5.]

18

WHY THE HISTORY
OF THE EARLY-TUDOR COUNCIL
REMAINS UNWRITTEN*

I

In England, as in most parts of sixteenth-century Europe, the King's Council was the centre of administration, the instrument of policy making, the arena of political conflict, and the ultimate means for dispensing the king's justice. One would suppose that so essential, so inescapable, an institution would be well known; surely, it should have a book to itself. But this is not so. In 1922, A. F. Pollard noted that the history of the Tudor Council had been ignored by historians;[1] and although this neglect has not continued unaltered, it is still true that the most important institution of Tudor England as yet lacks the sort of treatment which has been given to such bodies as the king's Chamber or the shortlived court of Augmentations.[2] Of course, it has been written about. There are even books which claim to treat specifically of it, but for one reason or another they will hardly do. A. V. Dicey's *The Privy Council* (London, 1887) is a short and out-of-date sketch by a brilliant lawyer; that is to say, it has insight and understanding, but it does not even realize how many historical problems beset the question. Dorothy M. Gladish's *The Tudor Privy Council* (Retford, 1915) collects a good deal of material and says some useful things about the work of the Elizabethan Council, but it begs the whole question of institutional development by treating the Council of 1500 as though it were identical with that of 1600. Over E. R. Turner's *The Privy Council of England in the 17th and 18th centuries, 1603–1784* (Baltimore, 1930–2), with its preliminary outline of Tudor developments, it will be only charitable to draw a veil.

Nevertheless, there have been several important contributions to the study of the nature, composition, growth and function of the

* [*Annali della Fondazione Italiana per la storia amministrativa*, 1 (1964), 268–96.]
1 A. F. Pollard, 'Council, Star Chamber and Privy Council under the Tudors', *EHR* 37 (1922), 337.
2 W. C. Richardson, *Tudor Chamber Administration*, and *History of the Court of Augmentatons 1536–1554* (Baton Rouge, 1961).

early-Tudor Council, all of which have advanced understanding to some degree without ever achieving really firm or final answers, and all of which have of necessity committed themselves to premature conclusions. This review of them should not be seen as an assertion of superiority at the expense of earlier writers; it is undertaken because it can usefully do two things. It can make reasonably plain where we stand and where we need to advance further. And secondly it can act as a warning against certain assumptions which have bedevilled the study of the Council, so that present views on it are a disconcerting mixture of unjustifiably firm assertions and needless vagueness. Our predecessors can teach us not only much sound understanding but also caution us against the pitfalls which are scattered across the road which the historian of the early-Tudor Council must travel.

The serious study of the Council began with J. F. Baldwin who allowed his monumental history of the medieval Council to run out in an epilogue on the Tudor institution.[1] He came to the conclusion that the absence of proper records between 1460 and 1540 testified to a very real decline in the Council's activity. These records, he believed, had never existed rather than been lost, a supposition which he did not succeed in justifying and which was unfortunate not only because a good many such records have since been found but because even then some bits were known from the use made of them in Cora Scofield's pioneer work on the court of Star Chamber.[2] Baldwin did not deny that the Yorkists and early Tudors had their Councils and councillors, but he played the Council's importance down almost to extinction, even though he himself listed some of its activities and attempted to classify some of its institutional manifestations. There would be no point in drawing attention to ancient errors long since exposed,[3] if Baldwin's mistakes had not in great part arisen from the two fundamental troubles lying in wait for the historian of the Council: fixed preconceived ideas, and failure to analyse the records thoroughly and imaginatively. Baldwin was so convinced that only a Council of the particular magnate type, acting as a control on royal power, which he had found under the Lancastrians, could be a true Council, and so sure that the keeping of surviving registers was essential to the identification of such a Council, that he effectively ignored the very plentiful

[1] J. F. Baldwin, *The King's Council in England during the Middle Ages* (Oxford, 1913), 419 ff.

[2] C. L. Scofield, *A Study of the Court of Star Chamber* (Chicago, 1900).

[3] For a criticism of Baldwin on the Yorkist Council cf. J. R. Lander, 'The Yorkist Council and Administration', *EHR* 73 (1958), 27 ff.

evidence of the Council's constant activity and general importance under the early Tudors which was before him. In looking at the registers he made some very odd statements. Thus he claimed that the new minute book of 1540 demonstrated, in name and form, 'that the traditions of Henry VI had not been forgotten'.[1] Yet the 1540 register, which at its inception had no official title, differed in almost every respect from anything seen under Henry VI. The entries in the new book record the place and date of meeting, the councillors present, and then, in a series of paragraphs, the work done.[2] The Lancastrian book (when it existed)[3] did not, as a rule, record the presence and ran the dating clause into the substance of the entry.[4] No two sets of registers could be more different in appearance. Baldwin was presumably misled by the editor of these records, Sir Harris Nicolas, who supposed that the book covering the years 1540–3 represented a resumption, after eighty years' interruption, of the fifteenth-century records which he had found among the Cotton Manuscripts at the British Museum. Curiously enough, the error seems to have left some relic in much more recent work. Even C. G. Bayne, whose important study of Henry VII's Council shall be mentioned in a moment, supposed that this first minute book of a reformed Privy Council was a register of the unreformed older Council; he thought its existence proved that not all the older Council's records had disappeared, as was alleged in the early seventeenth century.[5]

The first attempt to sort out the confusion in which Baldwin's treatment of the Council and earlier studies of Star Chamber[6] had left the subject was made by A. F. Pollard in three articles in 1922 and 1923.[7] Pollard's virtues as an historian never shone more brightly than

---

[1] Baldwin, *Council*, 449.

[2] Printed in *Proceedings and Ordinances of the Privy Council of England*, vol. vii., ed. N. H. Nicolas (1837), and *APC*.

[3] It ceased in 1435, not 1460, as Baldwin might lead one to suppose (Nicolas, *Proceedings*, vi. 1).

[4] E.g. the minutes of 12 Nov. 1434 start straightaway with 'Under protestation that it is not the entente of any of the lordes of the Kinges counsail here present . . .'; those of 7 Feb. 1435 begin 'vij die Februar' anno xiij apud Westm' ordinatum et concessum fuit . . .' and 'The viij day of Fev'er the xiij of the King oure sov'ein lord it is accorded and assented by the lordes of his conseil . . .' (Nicolas, *Proceedings*, iv. 287, 293–4).

[5] *Select Cases in the Council of Henry VII*, ed. C. G. Bayne and W. H. Dunham (1958), p. xii.

[6] In addition to Miss Scofield's book (above, p. 309, n. 2) see the introduction to I. S. Leadam's edition of *Select Cases in the Star Chamber 1477–1509* and *1509–44* (Selden Soc., 1903, 1910). Leadam's introductions contribute remarkably little to the analysis of the Council's history, though they remain useful on the subject of the Council's work as a court. [7] Pollard, *EHR* 37 (1922), 337 ff., 531 ff.; 38 (1923), 42 ff.

in this analysis of a complex problem, even though it would be unfair to use them in order to judge him as a writer. He certainly succeeded in clarifying some issues. In particular he demonstrated that 'the medieval king's council . . . continued its existence under the Elizabethan disguise of the court of star chamber'; this remains essentially true, though one would not put it in quite that way today. He freed the history of Star Chamber from the troublesome burden of the so-called Star Chamber Act of 1487 (3 Henry VII c. 7) which even in the reign of Henry VIII had misleadingly been linked with the Court;[1] and he realized that the initiation of a new register in 1540 marked a significant moment of institutional innovation. But he did not by any means settle everything clearly or determinedly, in part because he would not reduce the confusion of his evidence to a point of precision which to him seemed unwarranted, and in part because he had relied on much too small a range of sources.

The stage now reached in the history of the Council's history was exemplified in two attempts at general synthesis. Sir William Holdsworth, describing the Tudor constitution by way of introducing his account of Tudor law, rashly generalized on very insufficient grounds and brought in some additional confusions. Thus he made inadmissibly clear distinctions between greater and lesser councillors, while at the same time remaining very vague about the institutional growth of the central Council itself. He also caused trouble to himself and others by using French parallels of no relevance and by reviving the mistaken supposition that Henry VII borrowed his ideas concerning the Council from the writings of Chief Justice Fortescue – even though Fortescue's overrated advice and Henry VII's practice differed in almost every detail.[2] A much better account was given by Sir Kenneth Pickthorn whose grasp of practical politics made him see several points in the true light, though he accepted Pollard's mistake of supposing that Henry VII's Council, because it was large, could not have been a true Council. To say, as Pickthorn did, that Henry VII's councillors 'were the king's superior servants, diversified with a few harmless noblemen',[3] sounded well but was certainly not accurate.

By this time it had in fact become quite plain that no more progress could be made with the history of the Council by merely mulling over

---

[1] For the full story of this problem, irrelevant in the present context, cf. *Select Cases* . . . *Henry VII*, pp. xlix ff., and *Tudor Constitution*, 159 ff.
[2] Holdsworth, *Hist. of Eng. Law*, iv. 56 ff.
[3] Pickthorn, *Early Tudor Government*, i. 30 ff.

the oft-used and not very extensive evidence; a search for additional material was manifestly necessary. Part of that need was supplied by two scholars who may be treated together. In 1943–4, Professor W. H. Dunham Jr published three articles based on the discovery, among the Ellesmere Manuscripts at the Huntington Library in California, of Elizabethan transcripts from the early-Tudor Council registers which added greatly to those already known from certain British Museum collections.[1] These transcripts were also used in C. G. Bayne's edition of cases heard in Henry VII's Council; or rather, Bayne (whose work appeared posthumously in 1958 but was really completed by 1947) printed as full a reconstruction as possible of what survives of Henry VII's Council registers, but did not succeed in amalgamating their information with his study of the Council as a court of justice which he had completed before he saw the transcripts.[2] Between them, Dunham and Bayne enormously advanced our understanding of the early-Tudor Council. Bayne mainly assisted by clarifying its work as a court: he ended the legend of a royal tribunal against troublemakers and introduced us to a court for private persons' suits which responded not to royal policy but to pressure from below. This, however, is a little marginal in the present context. He also went some way towards sorting out the membership of Henry VII's Council and confirmed Dunham's chief, and vital, assertion (against Pollard) that 'there was a king's council, not just king's councillors, that the king's council functioned as an institution and was not just a loose body of royal advisers'. This is certainly borne out by the evidence of the Ellesmere extracts and puts the whole history of the Council on a new level of accuracy and precision.

Unfortunately, Dunham also introduced some new confusions, the result of both excessive precision and cautious vagueness. Like his predecessors, he remained vague about the growth of an organized Privy Council out of the early-Tudor mists. His precision is a little more dangerous to an understanding of the problem. His whole analysis turned on one fundamental point: the alleged existence of a body known institutionally as 'the King's Whole Council', from which other manifestations of conciliar activity may be distinguished. He claimed that 'in 1509 the clerk of the Council could describe the

---

[1] W. H. Dunham, Jr, 'The Ellesmere Extracts from the "Acta Consilii" of King Henry VIII,' *EHR* 58 (1943), 301 ff.; 'Henry VIII's Whole Council and its Parts,' *Huntington Library Quarterly* 7 (1943), 7 ff.; 'Wolsey's Rule of the King's Whole Council,' *Amer. Hist. Rev.* 49 (1944), 644 ff. The transcripts are discussed below, p. 334.

[2] Cf. above, no. 16.

institution whose records he kept as all the Whole Council. His expression reflects the importance medieval men attached to magnitude and completeness, but it also implies that at times the King's Council might be something less than whole.'[1] Thereafter the 'Whole Council' runs right through his treatment of the question, and the term is getting to be accepted in general usage as a truly institutional, and contemporary, description.[2] It must therefore be said very firmly that it never existed. Dunham's single example occurs on 11 November 1509 when the clerk recorded that concerning a certain matter something was thought 'by all the hole Counsayll'; and that this means no more than unanimity among the councillors present, not a reference to a body to be called 'the Whole Council', is confirmed by the note later on the same day that 'it is thoughte to all his sayde Counsayle and Judges', as well as by the entry of 2 May 1515 when Wolsey made a speech 'in the name of the hole Counsellors'.[3] Even Dunham has not supposed that one can make a distinction between councillors called whole and councillors who were less than whole; it is quite obvious that the word means no more than 'all'. The Whole Council (never otherwise found in the record) must be abandoned. This does not invalidate Dunham's treatment of Council activities, though (a point discussed further below) he tried too hard to reduce these to schematic order, but it does mean that we need not add yet another institution to the discussion or seek excessive organized precision in the committees and commissions – less than whole – which did much of the Council's work. We are dealing with one body known, as it were, to the law: the King's Council.

Since then, the only further contribution to the history of the Council has come from me. I have endeavoured to show that the Privy Council proper – the small, organized and institutional body of leading ministers and advisers so different from the larger, mixed body which earlier formed the only conciliar institution – was deliberately created by administrative reform some time between 1534 and 1536;[4] and I have given a short account of the Council's history which in the main stresses the view that there was never at any time more than one king's

[1] *Hunt. Lib. Qu.* 7 (1943), 8.
[2] Before I saw the Ellesmere transcripts I so accepted it: *Tudor Revolution*, 319.
[3] Huntington Library, MS El. 2655. I possess microfilms of these manuscripts which unfortunately do not indicate the pagination used by Dunham who saw the originals. However, the contents are arranged in chronological order, so that reference to the whole document makes it easy to find the particular passage.
[4] *Tudor Revolution*, 317 ff.

Council at the centre of government. The organized Privy Council did not split off from the parent body but replaced it, being created not by fission but by contraction.[1] After all this belabouring of other historians, it is a pleasant duty to offer some criticism of my own earlier views. In general, I admit to still thinking these two major conclusions correct, but I am coming to realize that in seeking clarity and precision I have underestimated both the complexity of the problems and have overlooked the willingness, especially of Henry VII, to use instruments as he pleased, without much regard for the feelings of constitutional historians compelled to understand them when they no longer exist. I am less certain than I used to be that we shall ever be able to bring the whole question into the light of day and comprehension; but I am not yet totally discouraged, and this paper is by way of being a progress report, a sorting out of a few specific points, and an indication of what the available materials may or may not allow us to grasp.

It may now be clear why, at heart, the history of the early-Tudor Council remains unwritten, even though so much has been written about it. There are two major obstacles in the way. In the first place, the Council, its members, and its parts acted in so varied and often haphazard a manner that it is extremely dangerous to be too precise about many aspects of it. It is in this respect that I plead guilty to some oversimplifications. The interrelation of the Privy Council, the Council courts of Star Chamber and Requests, and of special com-mittees (such as Henry VII's Council learned in the law discussed by Sir Robert Somerville[2]) may turn out to defy description, even if it should prove possible to keep the central institution always quite clear from the other royal councils such as those at Calais or Dublin, in the Welsh Marches or in the North. The activities of individual councillors, alone or in small groups of two or three, as arbiters and investigators in disputes, further complicate the issue since it is not always clear whether they acted by delegation from the Council or as private persons called in by the disputants. The difficulties posed by all this have been aggravated by the growth of certain fixed ideas – convictions derived from partial evidence and necessary, but necessarily premature, inferences, as well as from certain *a priori* assumptions. Some of these ideas have been eliminated; more persist. It will help to review some of

---

[1] *Tudor Constitution*, 87 ff. The present article is in a manner an elaboration of and com-mentary on my footnote on p. 87.

[2] *EHR* 54 (1939), 427 ff.; and cf. *Tudor Constitution*, 89, 91, and no. 3 above.

them, not for the sake of proving how much cleverer we are than our predecessors but in order to remove a few obstacles to understanding. This treatment will also illustrate some of the difficulties which beset the writing of administrative history. Furthermore, however, it is plain that the real difficulties lie in the sources from which a full history of the early-Tudor Council must be written, and a discussion of them shall conclude this paper.

II

First, then, some of the assumptions which have been made but can be shown to be wrong, however reasonable in themselves.

A large Council cannot be a working Council. Ever since it was realized that Henry VII put a large number of men on his Council, this point has been reiterated. If anything up to forty, or even more, councillors attended specific meetings, obviously those meetings can have been only formal. Pollard maintained that under the first Tudor the word 'counsellors' described 'his civil service rather than his cabinet' and that 'his counsellors did not constitute a council, great or small'.[1] 'It is certain,' he added in another place, 'that only some of the scores of counsellors of Henry VII and Henry VIII sat in the star chamber, and that Wolsey and Henry VIII on occasion made the selection.'[2] That 'it is certain' admittedly hid the fact that he offered no evidence for his statement, but on the face of it it seemed reasonable enough. Pickthorn echoed this view when he called Henry VII's councillors 'too numerous to have been an effective consultative body',[3] and Holdsworth remarked that its size prevented it from doing business in the manner of a modern Cabinet,[4] though in point of fact nobody quite knows how a modern Cabinet does its business. Even Dunham, with the new evidence before him, held that when the Council met in anything like its full size it dealt with formal business only.[5] Much depends on the meaning given to 'only formal'. Let us cite a few examples. On 7–9 June 1486, forty councillors are recorded as being present to attend to a variety of matters ranging from the decision to send for the lord mayor of London to explain security precautions in the capital and from the obtaining of news from Calais, to the issue of summons in private suits.[6] It may be that the actual presence on the separate days was smaller. But twenty-eight councillors debated ordinary business

[1] *EHR* 37 (1922), 356.
[2] Ibid. 531.
[3] Pickthorn, *Early Tudor Gov.* i. 30.
[4] Holdsworth, *Hist. of Eng. Law*, iv. 67.
[5] *Hunt. Lib. Qu.* 7 (1943), 12.
[6] *Select Cases . . . Henry VII*, 13.

on 30 January 1488, twenty-three considered Anglo-Flemish trade on 7 May 1488, twenty-nine heard a private suit on 5 February 1489, forty-two settled a dispute between the Merchant Adventurers and the Staplers in 1503, thirty-five discussed relations with Spain on 16 November 1504, and the same number reassembled three days later to consider further of the same subject.[1] Though of course there is no telling how many of these men spoke up, or how far the king, present (as Henry VII usually was) at all these meetings, merely used the occasion to announce his policy, such doubts are highly improbable. On several of the occasions mentioned there was no point in the king meeting his Council at all unless he wanted them to work, nor was there any need for so large a presence unless all the councillors had a purpose to serve.

Things did not change much under Henry VIII. At the beginning of his reign the Council shrank a little, though not necessarily to the mere eleven men whom, according to Lord Herbert, the Lady Margaret Beaufort selected for her grandson's first Council.[2] The important business of handling the anti-monarchical reaction in the first months of the reign was discussed in meetings of sixteen and about twenty;[3] the even more exciting claim of the duke of Buckingham to be hereditary high constable of England assembled an increasing number of councillors as the business went forward – eight, fifteen, eighteen.[4] Even in Wolsey's heyday meetings a good deal larger than this were not confined to formal business. True, thirty-four came to hear him deliver 'a notable and Elegant Oration in Englishe' on 2 May 1515, and fifty-three to hear another of his speeches on 27 October 1519;[5] but there were twenty-six present when the enforcement of certain statutes was considered,[6] thirty-four to think about illegal retaining,[7] twenty-eight to attend the swearing in of sheriffs and justices of the peace, a matter certainly not 'purely formal' in Tudor estimation, whatever modern historians may think.[8] Many meetings were smaller, but it is plain that a presence beyond what one would expect to be manageable could perfectly well consider and decide ordinary and significant Council business. The mere number of councillors must no longer be used to argue against the probability that they composed a

---

[1] Ibid. 16, 18, 22, 34, 38, 40.
[2] Lord Herbert of Cherbury, *Henry VIII*, 2.
[3] MS El. 2655: 11 and 14 Oct. 1509.
[4] Ibid.: 19 and 21 June, 2 July 1510.
[5] Ibid.   [6] Ibid.: 26 Jan. 1518.
[7] Ibid.: 14 Oct. 1519.   [8] Ibid.: 21 Nov. 1519.

fully institutional and active Council; nor is there much point in the sort of classification, co-ordinating size of presence with type of business, which Dunham has attempted.[1]

In so large a Council it is further usually taken for granted that *a mixed membership necessarily meant a distinction between the more and the less important councillors* – between what some would already call privy councillors and the 'ordinary councillors' of lesser standing. Again, this is reasonable on the face of it. A Council which includes both the archbishop of Canterbury and obscure doctors of law, both the premier duke and a king's serjeant-at-law, looks so mixed that profound differences in importance must be concluded to have existed between groups of councillors. Baldwin supposed that 'ordinary councillors' (appointed by that name and not members of the true Council) existed from early in Henry VIII's reign, and in this Holdsworth followed him;[2] neither realized that the very term only occurs after the formal organization of the Privy Council which, by restricting the Council to a part of its earlier membership, left over some sworn councillors from the earlier body.[3] In stating that Henry VII's Council was really his civil service, Pollard assumed this distinction and asked what we are to make of certain men who are but names to us and who cannot have been important enough to be true councillors. Minute research, he thought, might some day tell us more about them, but he could not conceive that men so obscure could really have been members of a quasi-Cabinet.[4] Minute research has done what it could, which is not very much, but at least it shows that Pollard was unfortunate in his examples. The three men he singled out – Geoffrey Simeon, Edmund Chatterton, John Wallys or Wells – were all clerics very much involved in that part of the Council's work which came later to be the court of Requests: the hearing of private pleas, especially of poor men.[5] That is to say, they were among the more active councillors in concerns which at the time at least seemed important; Simeon was dean of the Chapel Royal from 1491 to 1502, an office always held by one of the leading equity judges in the early-Tudor Council. After all, it depends what one means by importance. If one takes it for granted, with Bayne, that personal status is the thing to look at, then one concludes that the ecclesiastical and common lawyers formed a second rank in

[1] *Hunt. Lib. Qu.* 7 (1943), 12–13.
[2] Baldwin, *Council*, 450–1; Holdsworth, *Hist. of Eng. Law*, iv. 64.
[3] *Tudor Revolution*, 336.   [4] *EHR* 37 (1922), 343.
[5] *Select Cases in the Court of Requests*, ed. I. S. Leadam (Selden Society, 1898), p. cxi, n. 15; *Select Cases . . . Henry VII*, pp. xx, xxxviii, lxxxvi, 54.

the Council, only wanted for legal business.[1] If one follows Pickthorn, bemused by the false textbook generalization that Henry VII preferred 'middleclass' men to noblemen, one reverses the inference and supposes that his Council was, to cite the phrase once more, 'the king's superior servants diversified with a few harmless noblemen'.[2] Either way one makes inadmissible distinctions within the undifferentiated body. As Dunham has stressed,[3] the evidence of Council meetings and attendances permits no conclusion except that men of all types and standing formed equal members of a single Council.

There is a distinction by importance in the Council: the difference between all councillors on the one hand and those specially trusted or favoured on the other. This inner ring, as is now recognized, formed no identifiable 'Council Attendant', though Dunham was reluctant to admit the fact.[4] A quick look at the groups shows how little personal status had to do with this inner ring: neither noble blood, nor lowly origin and specialized training, either eased or barred a man's way into the king's particular favour. This is plain in the temporarily important inner ring of Henry VIII's early years, until Wolsey's engrossing of the Council's functions deprived the councillors attending on the King first of work and then of existence. The Council contained the usual mixture: lords, bishops, doctors of law and other lesser clerks, household knights and other lay administrators, and common lawyers from the chief justices downward. The inner ring contained representatives of all these types, as they were selected or, more probably, were free to attend away from Westminster. For instance, during the Michaelmas term 1510, the earl of Surrey, the bishops of Winchester and Durham, the lord chamberlain, the vice-chamberlain, the treasurer of the Household, the comptroller of the Household, and Sir Thomas Englefield (a lawyer elected Speaker of the Commons in 1510 but not apparently yet a serjeant-at-law) were the councillors regularly in attendance at court.[5] But this lists omits men necessarily at Westminster during term, such as the lord chancellor, the councillors engaged in dealing with petitions for redress received in Star Chamber, and the judges of the common-law courts. That some of them were quite as

---

[1] Ibid. p. xxxii. His other reason – economy – is even less convincing. Ecclesiastical lawyers – the 'doctors' – were essential in a policy-making body dealing with foreign policy.   [2] Pickthorn, *Early Tudor Gov.* i. 30.

[3] *Hunt. Lib. Qu.* 7 (1943), 11 ff.

[4] Ibid. 40 ff. But cf. *Tudor Revolution*, 320–1. I was, however, wrong to regard the true Privy Council as simply the inner ring organized. The inner ring was larger, and also too little defined in membership to make this widely held view adequate.

[5] *LP* i. 596, 602, 604 (18, 25, 26, 44).

much at the centre of things as the men attending the king is shown by the deliberations early in the reign concerning the general enquiry set on foot to offer remedies to any who thought they had grievances against Henry VIII's father. This was discussed on 11 October 1510 in the Star Chamber by sixteen men, including the lord chancellor (Archbishop Warham), three other bishops, the earls of Surrey and Shrewsbury, the prior of St John of Jerusalem, the under-treasurer of the Exchequer, and eight judges. The entry is full and long, and shows how very real this Council meeting was.[1] The Council resumed the discussion on the 14th; this time there were present three bishops, four lay lords, the prior of St John, two Household officers, five judges, the king's serjeants, the attorney and solicitor general.[2] The discussion, though less prolonged, was as searching and important. Yet when the decision to abolish the special commissions was carried into effect, only ten men signed the order of whom four were judges and two those relatively minor officials, the attorney and solicitor general. Only three really 'leading Councillors' – the earls of Surrey and Shrewsbury, and the bishop of Winchester – put their names to the letter.[3] In short, the inner ring must not be identified with the councillors who happened to be with the king. Really important business could engage the whole body of some accidental selection of Councillors, or it could be dealt with by those chosen to accompany the king on progress; attendance at court was not the privilege of a special section, nor did the attendant Councillors constitute an even informally *more important* group – only one more active at that particular time. The differences between individual councillors cannot be inferred from either their personal status or from their being chosen to accompany the king; insofar as differences existed, they must be discovered from a detailed analysis of the individuals involved.

Even more disturbing than these sufficiently confusing assumptions about a Council that happened to be rather large are the clouds which for long hung about (and to some extent continue to hang about) the problem of distinguishing between the Council as a board of administrators and the Council as a court – between what by the reign of Elizabeth were unquestionably the Privy Council and the court of Star Chamber. Some have refused to admit that the two ever became separate, a view one would have thought dead if it had not been revived quite recently.[4] Holdsworth accepted the distinction from

---

[1] MS El. 2655.   [2] Ibid.   [3] *LP* i. 257 (85).
[4] C. Ogilvie, *The King's Government and the Common Law 1471–1641* (Oxford, 1958), 100 ff.

about 1600, and Tanner would agree to its existence by about 1570.[1] The problem was confused by the difficulty of keeping apart two institutions of nearly identical membership. How tough the notion was that *two bodies of this kind can be thought separate only if they were staffed by different people* was rather disquietingly demonstrated by both Holdsworth and Dunham. Holdsworth could say in one place that the Privy Council and the Star Chamber 'were practically the same body', while in another he followed Baldwin's totally erroneous analysis which spoke of 'co-ordinate boards' at Westminster (future Star Chamber) and with the King (future Privy Council).[2] Dunham, who throughout seems aware that the same body of men administered both policy and justice in the early-Tudor Council, suddenly, as he comes to the emergence of the true Privy Council, provides a strong suggestion that for him the Star Chamber would appear to have consisted of non-privy councillors.[3] I have elsewhere explained what I believe to be the truth of the matter.[4] The sole King's Council, whether large and 'medieval' or reorganized into the Privy Council, did the work of both a board of government and a court of law, though in the latter function the Privy Council, which had no judges on it, had to afforce itself by calling in the chief justices. From 1540 the two aspects of the work done by these men were embodied in separate institutions; whether they were so embodied before that date remains still to be settled by further research. At the moment it looks improbable.

Related to this confusion about the emergence of separate institutions from one earlier King's Council is the conviction that *the Privy Council developed gradually from the body of more intimate advisers.* This view comes naturally enough when there is no evidence of specific creation, but it seems to me to reflect a total failure to visualize the realities. 'As the privy council became a more definite body', says Holdsworth;[5] 'in time,' says Pollard, 'these consultations [with men whom the king was in the habit of selecting for private discussions] grew into an institution called the king's private or privy council';[6] 'gradually,' as

---

[1] Holdsworth, *Hist. of Eng. Law*, i. 497 ff.; *Tudor Constitutional Documents 1485–1603*, ed. J. R. Tanner (Cambridge, 1922), 261.

[2] Holdsworth, iv. 60; i. 495–6. Though volume i was originally published in 1903, i.e. twenty-three years before volume iv, these errors were retained in the 1927 revision and not amended in the edition of 1956, or in S. B. Chrimes's revisionary essay prefaced to that edition.

[3] *Hunt. Lib. Qu.* 7 (1943), 43–4. His language is not very clear, but I can read no other meaning into it. [4] *Tudor Constitution*, 91, 158 ff.

[5] Holdsworth, *Hist. of Eng. Law*, iv. 64. [6] A. F. Pollard, *Wolsey* (1929), 106.

Dunham puts it, 'the group of councillors about his person hardened into an instrument of political and administrative power'.[1] I am afraid that to me such expressions demonstrate nothing less than a failure of the historical imagination. If it is agreed that the king's close advisers at one time formed a fluid and uninstitutional group, and at another a formal body from which other earlier Councillors, now called 'ordinary' or 'at large', were excluded, how could the first possibly develop gradually into the second, how could it grow (those dangerous biological metaphors) or harden (physics, not history) into a new state? We are dealing with a group of men engaged in a task to be discharged through an agency of government. Are we to suppose that after a lapse of time the men meeting round the Council Board suddenly looked upon each other with a wild surmise, saying: 'Good heavens, we have gradually grown, or hardened, into a Privy Council!' If the distinction between an unorganized, non-exclusive inner ring and an organized, specific Privy Council is valid – and on this Pollard, Dunham and myself, for instance, are agreed – the change must have resulted from deliberate action: action so deliberate that men hitherto equally members of the Council could be told that in future they would play no part in its work. It may well be true that in the absence of the actual order making the change we shall never be able to date it precisely, but that does not entitle us to smudge the necessary facts of reasonable practice.

The other side of the question demonstrates a similar failure of insight. That is to say, the frequently expressed doubt whether the Star Chamber can, before some date in Elizabeth's reign, be described as a true court institutionally distinct from the Council, ought not to survive a little thought and a little study of the documents. Of course, it is true that to the end of its days the court continued to bear the official title of 'the Lords of the king's Council in the Star Chamber at Westminster' or some variant on this, and the phrase exemplifies both the composition and the origin of the court. But what distinguished it as a court from the Privy Council was curial organization – regularity of meetings, fixity of procedure, publicity, formality in its decisions and their enforcement – together with the general and public recognition that it was a court. What people held it to be matters much more than historians, lost in the contradictions of the evidence, have been willing to admit: those who used the court to get their difficulties resolved must have known whether or not it deserved the name. Thus

[1] *Hunt. Lib. Qu.* 7 (1943), 41–2.

when as early as 1494 a man notes that the Council have been so busy on the king's affairs 'that my Lord Chawnsler kept not the Star Chawmber thys viij days',[1] the casual phrase suggests some measure of court-like existence even at this date; Bayne's caution in seeing here only an association of the room with trials of cases seems excessive.[2] Such caution would, I suppose, justify doubts whether as late as Wolsey's rule the Star Chamber may be distinguished even from Chancery: for a curious entry of June 1517 records that the lords of the Council had appointed four days of the week to sit in Star Chamber and the other two (Wednesday and Friday) in Chancery.[3] This might suggest that the two courts were then in some way identical. Fortunately there is plenty of evidence to the contrary, such as that provided by the complainant who recalls litigation before Wolsey 'in the kynges most honorable courte of Chancery' which he wishes to outflank by getting his opponent to appear 'afore your grace [Wolsey] in the Sterr Chamber'.[4] As for recognition that the Star Chamber is a true court, references come thick and fast from the 1530s onwards. The earliest I have so far found speak of a bill 'in the Curte of the Sterre Chambre' (1517–18) and of an appearance before Wolsey and 'the other lordes of [the] kynges most honerabyll Councell in the kynges Court of sterred Chamber' (c. 1521).[5] Thereafter some such phrase occurs sufficiently often to justify the party who some time later in the reign spoke of 'your graces [Henry's] high Court comonly called the Sterre Chamber'.[6] Though for the present it must remain an open question whether there was any institutional divorcement between Council and Star Chamber before 1540, it must not be doubted that the existence of a Court of Star Chamber was long before this generally recognized by those to whom this mattered most – the parties to suits before it.

Lastly, we may take a look at some generalizations of recent date which have been put forward in place of earlier orthodoxy, seem to me only dubiously true, and are relevant here because they rest on an inadequate criticism and mistaken use of the sources. They all concern the judicial (or 'Star Chamber') work of the early-Tudor Council and occur in the valuable contributions of Bayne and Dunham. Bayne has sufficiently proved that the Council under Henry VII was not

[1] *Paston Letters 1422–1509*, ed. J. Gairdner (1872), iii. 385.
[2] *Select Cases . . . Henry VII*, p. lxxvii.   [3] BM, Lansdowne MS 1, fo. 108.
[4] PRO, St Ch 2/7/19.   [5] Ibid. 3/79, 2/9.
[6] Ibid. 15/282. For other references see ibid. 3/6, 56, 97, 261; 5/97; 6/218; 20/220; 21/243; 23/309 (award of costs, in 1532–3, by 'the Courte of the Sterre Chamber'), etc.

primarily a royal tribunal enforcing the king's policy against over-mighty subjects, keepers of unlawful retainers, breakers of the peace and so forth, as used traditionally to be supposed. But when he maintained that the Council dealt with such matters hardly at all, he rested this conclusion on the surviving Star Chamber cases of the reign, a mere 194 in all, and though he recognized that so small a number may be thought insufficient for an argument *ex silentio*, he claimed that natural losses cannot have distorted the balance of the evidence.[1] This is a very rash assumption, the more so because the evidence of the registers, which he himself printed, contradicts it. Here we find the Council dealing with an arrested outlaw, deciding to punish retaining and rioting, summoning breakers of the peace, investigating a corrupt jury, debating the law concerning riot.[2] This was early in the reign, but a later sample shows no change. There are more cases of rioting, binding over to keep the peace, robberies, the troubles of great men, contempt, and so on.[3] Moreover, what survives of the registers are extracts made the best part of a century later. Some indication of what was left out appears in the transcriber's important introductory note prefaced to several copies of this so-called *Liber Intracionum* (as it has been called).[4] Written with the full register before it, this says that in Henry VII's time the court dealt with riots, routs, unlawful assemblies, forcible entries, misdemeanours, deceits, forgeries, falsehoods, perjury, maintenance, contempt 'and other comoun crymes comitted to the offence of the kinges lawes'.[5] Later on it even mentions heresy, murder and treason, though there is nothing of such things in the extracts and capital offences were not triable in the fully established court of Star Chamber. Bayne was right to point out that the surviving cases are overwhelmingly civil suits between party and party, and it is very probable that the growth of this business did most to turn the judicial sessions of the Council into the court of Star Chamber. But when he goes on from there to maintain that the Council heard almost no cases in which the king was party and policy was in question, he relies on partial evidence and misinterprets the situation.

Bayne's mistake arose because he put too much trust in the surviving proceedings. Dunham, looking only at the surviving extracts from the register for Henry VIII's reign, in effect came to the opposite conclusion. Asking, quite fairly, how the 5,000 or so suits of the reign

---

[1] *Select Cases ... Henry VII*, p. cxlviii. [2] Ibid. 8, 11, 14, 17, 19.
[3] Ibid. 33, 37, 39, 41–5. [4] Cf. below, p. 332.
[5] *Select Cases ... Henry VII*, 6–7.

for which evidence survives in the proceedings could ever have been dealt with by the court in its restricted term time sittings (possibly sixty days a year), he decided that they must have been settled by commissioners, either parts of the Council deputed for the purpose or people in the shires specifically commissioned to see to the matter.[1] Assuredly there is evidence, during Wolsey's ascendancy, of attempts made to devolve some of the Council's work upon commissions and committees, and Dunham usefully assembles it.[2] But there is no evidence that this decentralization removed all civil cases from the parent body, and Dunham's general argument includes several misconceptions which tend to invalidate it. He notes that the Ellesmere extracts contain no references to any private suits before the Council in Henry VIII's day and that he has not been able to find a single case in the published list of proceedings of which note is taken in the register, insofar as it survives.[3] Therefore, he says, it is probable 'that cases between private parties were not recorded in the *Acta*'. But the probabilities are unfortunately the other way. The Elizabethan extracts were taken from the registers, and the selection was severe. Dunham's material covers eighteen years (1509–27) or approximately (if, as he says, the court sat for sixty days a year) a thousand sessions; yet in the extracts we have evidence of only forty-eight of these. It is thus quite impossible to argue anything from the absence of matters among them. Moreover, one of the Ellesmere manuscripts gives a long list of things done in the Council, with folio references to the original registers which prove whence this evidence was derived. This includes such things as taking away a ward, supporting thieves, spreading tales and false rumours, private requests for process, jury offences, maintenance and the like, or in other words the staple diet of the court as reflected in its extant proceedings.[4] One entry actually reads 'hurtes to priuate persons'. This very mixed list, mingling matters of high policy and ordinary disputes, contains a great deal that is not traceable in the fuller extracts of the other Ellesmere manuscripts and proves how selective the transcriber had been.

Dunham has further confused various quite distinct forms of delegation. That the Council of the North held a commission of oyer and terminer is off the point: such a commission empowered a court

---

[1] *Hunt. Lib. Qu.* 7 (1943), 22 ff.
[2] Ibid. 7 ff.   [3] Ibid. 21 and n. 4.
[4] MS El. 2768. Star Chamber bills in private suits commonly alleged offences against the public peace, so that the business could be regarded as a 'Star Chamber matter'.

to hear the felonies and treasons which the Council was not competent to try. Delegation to bodies of councillors, either subcommittees at Westminster or in the local Councils in Wales and the North, certainly must have eased the burden of the central Council's work, but it is also known that a good deal of business was remitted by the local Councils to the centre. Even delegation at Westminster did not necessarily help; the repetition of such efforts suggests their futility, and the list just mentioned includes a note of 'Iudgementes given in the White Hall [Requests] examined', as though the Council had to go over the work of one of its committees. Above all, the very frequent commissions of *dedimus potestatem* are quite different from the use of Council committees. Here local worthies were instructed to deal with any given stage of a dispute (from the taking of respondent's answer or witnesses' depositions to the final settlement in the case), but this common attempt to delegate very often failed of its purpose. Plenty such commissions survive among the proceedings, endorsed to the effect that the commissioners found their task beyond them and returned the matter to the court. A commission might even come to a definite conclusion in a dispute and yet report: 'And the further order & determynacion of the sayd matter & the fynall iugement therof we referre vnto the discrete wysdomes of your honorable lordshyppys.'[1]

A good example of the use of the *dedimus potestatem* is provided by a case of 1544. The bill complained of an offence committed on 12 February that year. On 4 June, a commission issued to take respondent's sworn answer, and the answer is endorsed with the fact of its delivery into Star Chamber by the commissioners' messenger. On 4 December a further *dedimus potestatem* delegated the interrogation of witnesses and gave power to end the matter by an order, but the interrogatory forwarded with the writ has a note saying 'commissioners to here and determyn if the[y] can; if nott, to examyn witness & to certifye'. The depositions, taken on 22 January 1545, are accordingly endorsed as having been brought in on 11 February. Despite all this commissioning, the Council still had to decide the case and issue its decree.[2] It is true that in the nature of things we only know of the issue of a commission if the commissioners could not end the matter themselves; there may well have been successful delegations of this sort. But the large number of commissions returned to the court and

[1] PRO, St Ch 2/15/208 (c. 1530). The commissioners were powerful enough: two leading London merchants (Sir Richard Gresham and Sir John Aleyn) and the lieutenant of the Tower. [2] Ibid. 2/18/272.

the frequent reference in bills to the refusal of one party to abide by commissioners' rulings do not encourage belief that the Council could rid itself of the bulk of private suits by sending them elsewhere. The duties remaining to the Council after a commission had done its work, Dunham is inclined to regard as purely formal,[1] a point which cannot be proved but in any case still contradicts his view that the absence of private suits from the Ellesmere extracts shows that none appeared in the original register. However freely the Council spread the mass of work before it to committees and commissioners, it clearly dealt very often, as a Council, with the suits of private persons. The Star Chamber of Wolsey and Henry VIII was quite as much a court for both the king's and the subject's business as the Star Chamber of Henry VII; that pressure of work produced experiments in the quicker disposal of cases does not in the least alter that fact.

The foregoing arguments will have shown how doubtful and contested many points in the history of the early-Tudor Council have been and still are. Even where a measure of agreement is possible on the general outlines of a problem, the exact details, and often the real issues, are liable to remain in the dark. The reason is plain enough: it lies in the nature of the evidence, though an understandable inclination to premature generalizations or fixed convictions has sometimes created additional difficulties. The history of this institution remains unwritten because the sources from which it can be written make the task difficult rather than possible. I propose to conclude this paper with a survey of these sources and a discussion of some of the problems they set.

III

The materials from which the history of the early-Tudor Council must be written fall into three categories. In order of importance they are: the records produced by the Council itself in its various manifestations, comments or references made incidentally by contemporaries, and accounts given of the institution by near-contemporaries who had before them material no longer available to us. These are best reviewed in the reverse order, eliminating the less fundamental before discussing the essential. Turning first, then, to accounts given of the Council and the court of Star Chamber in the Tudor and early-Stuart periods, we may ignore Sir Thomas Smith's *De Republica Anglorum* (1565) which says nothing on the Council and nothing important on Star Chamber,

---

[1] *Hunt. Lib. Qu.* 7 (1943), 26 ff.

though it does usefully draw attention to Wolsey's part in establishing that court. Sir Edward Coke, too, did no more than summarize the history and powers of that court in a manner which helps little in the real investigation; his brief notes have too often served in place of a genuine study.[1] More important are two treatises by officers of the court, William Mill's unprinted account produced for the use of Lord Burghley, and William Hudson's fuller description of which a slightly compressed version has been printed.[2] Both these writers, concerned to prove the antiquity and pre-eminence of the Council's judicial activity, used the lost Council Registers of the early Tudors; thus they occasionally say something that we can get only from them, but nothing they say should be taken as gospel unless it can either be confirmed or makes sense in the light of more primary sources. References to the Council's existence, membership and activities are found quite frequently in contemporary letters, especially from foreign ambassadors, and the various collections of state papers provide a good deal of information for our purpose; at times this is all we have, but of necessity it suffers from various faults. It is casual, unsystematic, often conjectural, frequently inaccurate, and very difficult to check. Still, it helps to fill in some gaps in the story: thus the activities of Henry VIII's Council are at times known only from the reports of people who had dealings with it.[3]

However, it is obvious that the most important material is to be found in the actual products of the Council's own activities. These, again, are of three kinds. In the first place, there is such evidence as survives of action taken by the Council. Occasionally letters or other documents demonstrate the work of the Council. Early in the reign of Henry VIII a good many papers bear the signatures of the councillors authorizing them;[4] for a few months in 1536–7 we possess, unfortunately only in later copies, letters signed by the Council;[5] from 1540 onwards, the state papers increasingly preserve original letters of this sort.[6] This is obviously first-rate evidence for anything

[1] Smith's and Coke's remarks are printed in *Tudor Constitution*, 164 ff., 172 f. They mislead, especially as to the composition of the court.

[2] Mill's treatise is in BM, Hargreaves MS 216; Hudson's, in BM, Harleian MS 1226, is printed (not too accurately) in *Collectanea Juridica*, ed. F. Hargrave (1792), vol. ii.

[3] Cf. e.g. *Tudor Revolution*, 325 ff.

[4] E.g. *LP* i. 11 (12), 54 (33), 94 (43, 44), 118, 168, 190 (19, 25, 34, 35), 257 (12, 88), 313, 555, 596, 602, 604 (18, 25, 26, 44), 651 (7, 13), 716, 731 (20, 52), 749 (3, 16, 24), 784 (15), 820, 845, 1003 (15, 17), 2441.

[5] *Tudor Revolution*, 338–9.

[6] E.g. the index to *LP* xvi. (Sept. 1540–Dec. 1541) lists 42 letters from the Privy Council.

to do with the Council, and the problems raised by it are few, mostly connected with membership. Thus on 15 October 1510, the Council, sitting at Windsor, authorized two pieces of business; but one of them was signed by five and the other by six councillors,[1] making one wonder why this should have been so and whether the signatures on a letter can safely be taken to represent the full presence on the occasion of signing. Unfortunately, such evidence of positive action taken by the Council is extremely patchy; for long stretches of years, none seems to survive at all. A further search is assuredly required. In the nature of things, these letters are most likely to have survived in the place of receipt, and since the age rarely kept copies of outletters (though first drafts are not uncommon) one cannot hope for much among the state papers themselves. Most of the recipients would have been men in the shires, private persons or such officials as sheriffs or local receivers or customs men, and local archives and collections should be investigated; but enough has been done to indicate that the harvest is unlikely to be notable. There may be copies of instructions received at the Exchequer in the Memoranda Rolls there, but so far I have found no Council letters among their entries of letters and *brevia*. In short, though the attempt must be made, we are not likely ever to find much more of this kind of evidence than is calendared in the *Letters and Papers of Henry VIII*; and at present I know of none for the father's reign. One other possibility exists. Mr Lander has shown how much Council activity may be deduced from a study of the original authority behind certain grants and orders, annotated as 'per concilium' by the receiving clerks,[2] but it must be said that it looks very much as though from 1485 little care was taken to distinguish warrants authorized by the Council from those authorized by the king, a lapse of practice which presumably reflects a change in the Council's relationship with the monarch. Important and instructive as this first-hand evidence of Council activity must be, it will never be systematic or remotely exhaustive.

The second group of documents directly derived from the Council's activities are the *Proceedings of the Courts of Star Chamber and Requests*.[3] These are the papers produced by litigation in these courts, or rather in those judicial sessions of councillors which at some time become identifiable as separate courts. Theoretically, every suit should consist of complainant's bill, respondent's answer, the further exchanges of

---

[1] *LP* i. 604 (25, 26).   [2] See above, p. 309, n. 3.
[3] PRO, record classes Star Chamber 1 and 2, Requests 2.

the parties (replication, rejoinder), interrogatories and depositions, and the court's decree.[1] In addition one can expect to find some other matters. Writs of summons (subpoena followed, if necessary, by attachment and proclamation) would not survive, since these went forth from the court; but when issues were committed away from the court and then returned there, writs of *dedimus potestatem* and commissioners' certificates should exist. In practice, however, the records are nothing so tidy as this description suggests. Once the case was over, the proceedings ceased to have any evidential value, and no care was taken to preserve them properly; over the centuries much has been lost and the rest has been roughly bundled up. Papers belonging to a single suit may be scattered through the bundles; many are mutilated and more are illegible. Nevertheless, just under 200 cases before the Council in Star Chamber survive for the reign of Henry VII and round about 5,000 for Henry VIII; something like 3,000 cases in the 'court of Requests' have left extant evidence for the period 1485–1547. This mass is daunting in itself, and the condition of the material raises every sort of difficulty; nevertheless, all of it must be gone through if the history of the early-Tudor Council is ever to rest on knowledge as full as it can be made. There is much incidental information of great value to be found there. Endorsements on documents tell something about procedure, and stray papers – drafts of orders or letters from individuals – are occasionally found there. Perhaps half the surviving cases provide casual evidence by which they may be dated. Slow and unrewarding though the work may be, it will have to be done; even partial study of these Proceedings has already revealed a good deal that was before either unsuspected or even denied.[2]

However, quite apart from their condition and the obscurity attaching to fragmentary evidence, there is a fundamental problem involved in the use of these Proceedings. They are now described as belonging to the two Council courts of Star Chamber and Requests, but one can by no means be certain that their present location accurately describes their origin. There are certainly some Requests cases among the Star

[1] I have described these documents in a short paper, 'The Records of the Conciliar Courts in the 16th Century,' *Amateur Historian* 4 (1959), 89 ff.
[2] So far I have found time to go through 25 of the 33 volumes and bundles of Star Chamber cases for Henry VIII's reign, and evidence from that source has been used in the course of this paper. Bayne analysed the 194 cases of Henry VII. As for Requests, I have so far seen only the cases datable to the years 1529–40. [Since this paper was written, additional material found at the PRO has been collected there as St Ch 10 and Req 3.]

Chamber bundles, and some of the documents appear to have been produced in disputes heard and arbitrated informally by councillors to whom the parties had agreed to submit themselves. Worse, there may be genuine Chancery cases mixed up in the mass; at any rate, many bills are addressed to the chancellor (instead of the king, as was proper in cases before the Council), and this occurs even after Wolsey's fall when the sovereign informality of that prince of lord chancellors had given way to a more precise observance of the rules. It is therefore far from easy to use these Proceedings in order to prove what sort of matters could properly be tried in the prerogative courts. What makes the problem particularly exasperating is that we cannot now tell whether the confusion is simply the result of later neglect and inadequate record-keeping, or whether it reflects a genuine absence of institutional differentiation at that early date between bodies which a little later were clearly distinct. Quite possibly a bit of each has contributed to create the present state of affairs. Thus even when all these materials have been worked over, it is not likely that we shall have fully dispelled the darkness which at present hangs over such fundamental questions as whether in the early-Tudor Council administrative and judicial – cabinet and court – functions were institutionally distinct.

Thus despite these Proceedings, important enough in themselves and in addition full of unexpected finds, the vital records are the third group of those produced by the Council: the registers and minutes kept of meetings. These unfortunately pose quite as many questions as they solve. In particular, some have vanished, and conjecture about what once existed and has left only odd shadows behind is always likely to result in differences of opinion. However, what have we got, and what may safely be presumed once to have been there?

We still possess two series of Council registers, and the fact that there are gaps in both, though unfortunate, is less important than the certain existence of such identifiable sets of records. From 10 August 1540 the Privy Council kept a book of minutes which is thereafter continuous;[1] whether anything resembling it existed before is doubtful,[2] and certainly as a fullblown register the book begun on that day represented an innovation. It is sufficient proof that from that time at the latest a separate institution, staffed only by the nineteen councillors listed in the first entry and served by the clerk then appointed, existed as the

[1] Cf. above, p. 310, n. 2. The order instituting this register is printed in *Tudor Constitution*, 95. [2] *Tudor Revolution*, 360.

only true governing Council of the realm. The other series of registers are the so-called 'Books of Orders and Decrees of the Court of Requests'.[1] Several serious gaps in the sequence make these books less useful than they might have been for an analysis of the work of that part of the Council; but it is more important to be sure that they do in fact record the activities of an identifiable subdivision of the whole body. Is it correct to call them the books of the court of Requests? The first volume opens with a very interesting order of 12 February 1494 according to which the king appointed seventeen councillors to accompany him on his forthcoming progress; some are given special months of attendance, while against others stands the word 'continue'. Insofar as the book notes the councillors present at meetings (a point in which it is inconsistent), it appears that the register records the doings – all judicial – of these 'attendant councillors'. Meeting places range around the country. In other words, this is a book kept by the Council with the king wherever he might be, and usually out of term, as distinct from the Council sitting at Westminster in term time, though the first book, at least, includes some meetings at Westminster too. This is not the place to investigate the origin of the court of Requests: whether it was simply the institutionalized form of this kind of undifferentiated Council, attendant on the King, or whether it owed more to specific orders setting up committees. What is clear is that the series later quite rightly described as the Books of the Court of Requests begins with at least one volume which cannot be properly given that name. Just when a regular court emerged has still to be definitely settled,[2] the more so as I would question the readiness with which the court of Requests has been identified with any body of councillors dealing with the suits of private parties. As far as I can see at present, in the reign of Henry VII at least it is wrong to speak of either Star Chamber or Requests. One should instead speak of judicial

---

[1] Described in *Select Cases . . . Requests*, pp. lii–liii.

[2] Ibid. p. xiii: Leadam suggests that the years 1497 (beginning of term time meetings) and 1516 (Wolsey's setting up of committees) were the crucial ones. Though he may be right, his dates depend on his conviction that the court of Requests grew straight out of the attendant Council's judicial sessions. I am inclined to think that the later court was the survivor of the various and conflicting experiments to provide justice for clamant suitors and to free the Council of much of this work. If that is so, the formal organization of the Privy Council in 1534–6 is the important date, as it is in the history of Star Chamber but even more so: from that time the real (privy) councillors are distinguishable from the nominal councillors who sat as judges in Requests. [In his dissertation on the court of Requests under Edward VI (Cambridge, 1973), D. A. Knox has established that the crucial dates were 1529, when the committee experiments ceased, and 1538–9 when the court was settled.]

sessions of the Council, either in the Star Chamber at Westminster or wherever the king might be; and the books under discussion would appear to have begun life as the register kept on the latter occasions. Though as time went on certain councillors seem to have specialized in the work recorded here, down to the disappearance of the un-differentiated large Council in the 1530s there is no evidence of fixity of membership. It is almost certainly true that up to that time we should think not of various institutions but of one only, doing its work as the King's Council, either in Star Chamber or with the King or by means of temporary and evanescent committees. But this, very likely, is to run ahead of the present state of knowledge. Nevertheless it has to be said because on the face of it the existence of this series of 'Requests books' suggests the existence of an identifiable institution producing the books. The documents do not support such a notion, at any rate under Henry VII; the problem is completed by the fact that during the crucial years of Wolsey's and Cromwell's administrations the gaps are large.

It will have become clear by now that the one thing we lack is any series of registers recording the doings of the true central Council before 1540. The Requests books, whatever their meaning, are a side issue; what of the Council as a whole? Fortunately we can at least say, as against Baldwin, that it certainly kept regular registers or *Acta*, though all that survives are extracts made from them in the reign of Elizabeth. The fullest set of these are the Ellesmere extracts already referred to, but there are additional copies of this so-called *Book of Entries* or *Liber Intracionum* among the British Museum manuscripts.[1] These transcripts enable us to say a good deal about these registers. Probably several volumes, individually of small size, covered the reign of Henry VII.[2] A new one started in 1509 and ran down to 1527.[3] The series did not end there, though the extracts nearly do: the one started in 1527, or its successor, certainly extended beyond the inception of the Privy Council register, so that after 1540 two separate series recorded the business of what was still one Council, now operating through two distinct institutions: Privy Council and Star Chamber. This is proved by two points. In the first place, the book started in 1527

---

[1] *Select Cases . . . Henry VII*, pp. xiii ff., for the fullest discussion. The term *Liber Intracionum* would appear to have been first used in 1590 by William Mill (ibid. pp. xi–xii) and, despite Bayne, is suitable. In sixteenth-century usage, a book of entries was a lawyer's precedent book, and the extracts, though manifestly taken from a daily record of proccedings or 'Acta', were themselves selected as examples and precedents.

[2] Ibid. pp. xvii–xviii.   [3] Dunham, *EHR* 58 (1943), 308.

opened with a list of the 'Counsellers sworn to the king anno regni regis Henrici VIII decimo octauo'.[1] The list gives forty-two separate names, plus an unknown number of king's serjeants-at-law. We therefore have here the old undifferentiated Council of nobles, bishops, doctors, lawyers and Household officials, only some of whom survived the reform which produced the Privy Council proper. The transcriber also noted that this body 'sate in the starchamber'. Secondly, a few extracts from Council cases made after August 1540 prove the continued existence of another book by the side of the Privy Council minute book.[2] That is to say, this record – the continuation of the *Acta Consilii* found in the main Ellesmere transcripts – is a Star Chamber book of orders and decrees, comparable to the surviving Books of the court of Requests. What had been two series of Council registers kept respectively at Westminster and at Court had now become the master records of fully organized courts, while the political and administrative business had been transferred to the new series begun in August 1540.

There cannot, then, any longer be any doubt that before the Council reform the early-Tudor Council kept a register in which was recorded the business it did in formal session at Westminster in term time, including both political and judicial matters;[3] nor can anyone seriously doubt that after the reform this older series continued as the register of the court of Star Chamber. This point, which Pollard in effect divined from the British Museum manuscripts alone when he said that 'the medieval king's council . . . continued its existence under the Elizabethan disguise of the court of star chamber',[4] was put beyond dispute by the discovery of the Ellesmere transcripts.[5] It is a pity that we have neither originals nor transcripts from the Elizabethan Star Chamber books, to tell us whether the form of the register changed. It may be that this lack, in part at least the result of the court's demolition by the Long Parliament when its records were lost, also reflects a decline in efficient record-keeping. At any rate, Hudson, writing in the reign of James I, claimed that the registers were much more complete and careful in the days of Henry VII and Henry VIII than in the second half of the century.[6] However that may have been, it is certain that a real Council book existed which, probably from the mid-1530s, became the record only of the Council sitting as a court.

[1] Quoted Scofield, *Star Chamber*, 31–2. [2] MS El. 436.
[3] [Mr D. A. Knox has now found a draft page for the Council register for Hillary 1525 (in Req 3) which shows that justice and administration were indeed mingled there in the manner here conjectured.] [4] *EHR* 37 (1922), 531.
[5] *Select Cases . . . Henry VII*, p. xii. [6] BM, Harleian MS 1226, fos. 3–4.

Of course, when a record survives only in later copies one wants to know how far one can trust it. Both Bayne and Dunham have argued, quite convincingly, that the transcripts are accurate; but while Bayne recognizes that they usually appear to summarize the originals, Dunham seems to think that they give them in full.[1] Here Bayne would seem to have the right of it, since (as he says) certain duplicated entries prove his point. At the same time, in justice to Dunham, it is possible that the much less plentiful extracts from Henry VIII's reign give a fuller text. I cannot agree with Bayne that the language of the extracts is Elizabethan rather than early Tudor, nor do I share his feeling that the fact that they were either made or used by a lord chancellor automatically ensures their accuracy. However, the internal and external evidence in itself gives one confidence in these copies. Yet they are not quite as trustworthy as Bayne and Dunham suppose. It may not matter much that a certain Richard Mitchell, proclaimed an outlaw, is variously described in two copies as of the town and of the county of Northampton, though this sort of thing opens the way to doubt.[2] But it is tiresome to find that the lists of councillors present are not necessarily accurate, even in Lord Chancellor Ellesmere's own copies. Thus for the meeting of 23 November 1504, El. 2655 lists thirty-eight councillors of whom El. 2654 omits four; while for those of 28 November and 2 December 1504 the latter adds six to the thirty-nine given by the former. Indeed, El. 2655 does not give these dates, nor any indication that both the presence and the matter listed would appear to pertain to two meetings, not one.[3] It is therefore clear that some caution is necessary in the use of these documents. Ordinarily they date entries and give the presence; but the fact that on occasion they omit to do so does not prove the absence of such details from the lost originals. One can trust the transcripts to provide sufficiently accurate information on that small part of the Council's transactions that was copied from forty-two years of registers; but one cannot easily argue to the precise appearance of the record or especially to the significance of anything omitted. As we have seen, Dunham fell into the trap implied in this.

The real appearance of the original register becomes a matter of importance because there is additional evidence of *Acta Consilii*, this time in originals. The probabilities are that most entries in the lost

---

[1] *Select Cases . . . Henry VII*, pp. xiv ff.; Dunham, *EHR* 58 (1943), 303 ff.
[2] *Select Cases . . . Henry VII*, 2, 11.
[3] These points are obscured ibid. 42 ff.

books followed a common pattern. A date line across the top gave sometimes the place and always the day of meeting. If the King was present, the word *Rex* appeared underneath it. Down the left-hand margin the clerk listed the ecclesiastical councillors present, from bishops to doctors, and down the right-hand margin he put the lay councillors from dukes to common lawyers. The business done that day was set down in the box thus framed. This arrangement is usually adopted in the Ellesmere extracts, and it is also found in a copy from the original register certified by William Mill, clerk of the Star Chamber in the last decades of Elizabeth's reign.[1] We may take it that this was the usual style adopted, though some entries in the copies of the register do not follow it, leaving out the presence or conflating several days' meetings into one. On the whole it is more probable that the copyist was responsible for these variations than that the originals occasionally abandoned common form.

What, then, are we to make of the quite numerous entries of Council decisions which are scattered, on loose slips, through the bundles of Proceedings? Of those so far found only three give the presence and would appear to be complete drafts for a proper Council book.[2] All the rest have a date line, which does not always mention the year, and an entry beginning with some such phrase as 'It is orderid' or 'Memorandum that', with some variants, sometimes in Latin and sometimes in English. Some of them are manifestly copies, even if they do not expressly indicate the fact. Others are equally manifestly drafts, being plentifully corrected. Thus on 26 November 1529 a draft was made of two orders in different suits issued that day; the first of them further survives in a paper marked *Vera copia*.[3] A list of five entries for 20–23 November (*c.* 1533–40) looks like a draft.[4] At other times we can be sure that we are dealing with a copy because the paper lists orders made on widely differing days but all belonging to the same dispute.[5] That leaves a large number which can be judged to be drafts or copies only from internal evidence; most of them are final decrees rather than intermediary orders for subpoenas and the like.[6] The copies present no serious problem: they were made to be sent, with the papers in the

---

[1] BM. Lansd. MS 1, fos. 108.
[2] PRO, St Ch 2/17/399 (18 Feb. 1530); 17/405 (1 Feb. 1530); 17/406 (c. 1526–8).
[3] Ibid. 12/51, 65.   [4] Ibid. 19/178.
[5] Ibid. 12/258 (four entries from July 1539 to May 1543); 4/100 (from a 'Requests-type' of committee, June and October 1523).
[6] Ibid. 7/17, 172; 9/186; 13/46, 135, 137(b), 204; 14/45–6; 16/96A, 387; 17/395, 396, 398, 403, 407; 18/330; 19/304, 372; 20/164, 220; 23/261, 368; 24/82, 97.

case, to commissioners appointed by the court; in fact, one of them is signed by the commissioners before whom it was entered.[1] In such cases it may be conjectured that only the essentials were copied out – the date and the substance – while the list of councillors present, of no interest to the recipients, could be omitted. The copies could therefore very well have been made from the known *Acta Consilii* as exemplified in the Ellesmere extracts.

This conclusion would be more satisfactory if more links could be established between the copies or drafts and the Ellesmere transcripts. So far I have found only two rough papers reflected in the *Acta*. One of them is straightforward. Two copies were made of the entry of 11 October 1518 which recorded a decree awarded against two priests whose fines were to contribute to an extension of the Star Chamber building.[2] In this case the clerk transcribed the decree in full and accurately but omitted the presence, thus proving that the practice we have conjectured could in fact be followed. The other instance raises difficulties. According to the Ellesmere extracts, Henry Standish, bishop of St Asaph, appeared in the Star Chamber on 27 October 1518 to make his submission – standing at the bar – to a charge of having fallen into a *praemunire* by being consecrated before sending his papal bulls of appointment to the king and doing homage for his temporalties.[3] According to a slip found in the Proceedings, Standish made his confession – kneeling at the bar – on 6 November 1518,[4] on which day the Ellesmere extracts record that the Council was 'also' ordering the punishment of a slanderer (no other entry), thus leaving it open whether an earlier minute of that date and referring to the Standish affair had been left out. The rough memorandum says that the submission was made in the presence of Wolsey, Norfolk, the bishop of Durham (Ruthal) and others of the Council; but the Ellesmere extracts do not record Ruthal's presence on either 27 October or 6 November, though they show him to have sat in the Council on 29 October. The texts of extract and memorandum differ in important details; especially, the latter includes a plea for mercy on Standish's part of which there is nothing in the former. It is not very probable that the extracts got the date wrong, especially as they have an entry for 6 November and interpolate another for 29 October. Their failure to note Ruthal's presence is surprising only because he was a most

---

[1] Ibid. 12/51.   [2] MS El. 2655; St Ch 2/1/94–6.
[3] MS El. 2655. All this was really Wolsey's revenge for Standish's part in the humbling of the clergy in 1515–16.   [4] St Ch 2/2/75.

regular member of the Council; we have seen that the transcriber could be casual about the presence lists. It would thus seem that Standish appeared twice before the Council. On the first occasion he stood at the bar and acknowledged his offence; on the second Wolsey rubbed his nose in it by making him kneel and ask the Council to intercede with a justly incensed king. The fact that the extracts omit the dramatic second occasion further shows how patchy they are: not only minor or routine matters could be left uncopied. In view of its contents the memorandum in the Proceedings was clearly derived from the Act Books of the Council.[1] Surviving copies, at any rate, may be read as representing samples of the lost registers.

On the other hand, we are less sure of the precise significance of the drafts. There is nothing surprising in rough drafts and notes made for transcription into a clean register, and one such paper, endorsed as 'notes of orders & decrees in Mich' terme anno xxvto [1533]' suggests just that.[2] But if these pieces were the clerk's rough minutes one might expect them to carry a list of the presence which he would also have to enter into the register; and, as we have seen, only three of them have such a list. It is, of course, perfectly possible that he noted the presence in some other way; perhaps he employed the most convenient method of keeping a roll-call of the Council and ticking off those attending on a given occasion, a possibility reinforced by the fact that something very like this seems to have been the practice in the House of Lords at the time.[3] The supposition that the drafts were meant for the main Council register is only hampered by one piece of evidence. When Francis Bacon in 1608 became clerk of the Star Chamber, he found among its archives 'one Booke of the *Kalendar of Orders beginning anno primo et secundo Henr. Septimi'*,[4] and Bayne conjectured that this re-presented a second register, reserved for those entries in private suits which Hudson said were kept so carefully in the first half of the century. A single entry, preserved in a British Museum manuscript, seemed to Bayne to come from this secondary Council book.[5] If he were right, the drafts in the Proceedings, concerned as they are with private suits, could have been meant for this calendar of orders rather

[1] It was more probably a copy than a draft because the memorandum, instead of giving the councillors in a list, refers only to the leading ones 'and other of the kinges most hon'able councell' in the middle of its account of the event.

[2] St Ch 2/7/172.

[3] A. F. Pollard, 'The Authenticity of the Lords' Journals in the Sixteenth Century,' *TRHS* (1914), 17 ff.; at p. 29.

[4] *Select Cases . . . Henry VII*, p. xii.   [5] Ibid. 7.

than for the main register or *Acta*, a point which might explain the omission of the presence. However, interesting though the suggestion is it cannot really carry conviction, and I have every doubt whether Bayne's second register ever existed. Bacon's use of the word calendar does not suggest a regular and full-scale register but rather something in the nature of an abstract, possibly either a book of precedents or more probably an index to the register proper. He speaks of a single book beginning in 1485–6; though he does not tell us how far its entries extended, it is impossible to suppose that the drafts of the 1530s and 1540s, found among the Proceedings, could still have been accommodated in a volume of court orders begun forty or fifty years earlier. There is no good reason for believing that the Council sitting in Star Chamber kept two registers, and we must prefer the explanation that the rough drafts were for the single book which down to 1540 was the only true record of *Acta Consilii*, and which thereafter (after the inception of the Privy Council register) we have decided to call the Star Chamber Books of Orders and Decrees. The drafts, being orders and decrees, fit such a book well, and they can therefore be treated as additional evidence of the proceedings of the unreformed Council, sitting in the Star Chamber in term time; incidentally they thus help to underline that the Council's business included those private suits whose absence from the Ellesmere extracts led Dunham into error.

From these various materials the history of the early-Tudor Council – its structure, membership, functions, procedure, manifold manifestation and changing nature – will have to be reconstructed. It will be seen that no single body of records provides systematic evidence of Council activities; everything is either haphazard, or utterly confused, or very patchy, or all three. In the circumstances, it is no wonder that the story of this central institution of government remains obscure and beset by error. Some conclusion, some opinion concerning the Council, has always been demanded from any historian trying to understand the reigns of the two Henries. If in consequence he has made mistakes, that is little enough blame to him; though it is still necessary to correct error that the truth may be brought closer. The state of the evidence is such that a truly well-based understanding will be hard to come by. Indeed, anyone who surveys this range of booby-trapped materials might well be tempted to retire and keep bees.

19

HENRY VIII'S
ACT OF PROCLAMATIONS*

It may well be thought that enough has been written about the famous
act of 1539 which dealt with royal proclamations and was at one time
regarded as the highwater mark of Tudor despotism.[1] Over forty years
ago Mr E. R. Adair published an article which disposed of the more
extravagant misstatements concerning it and suggested a truer interpretation.[2] Since then we have had authoritative comment from
Pollard,[3] Pickthorn,[4] and Holdsworth,[5] all of whom at least agree
that the angry denunciations listed by Adair were wrong and that the
act did nothing towards creating a royal despotism in England. The
present writer has before this had occasion to refer briefly to some
aspects of the statute, expressing views with which he is no longer
altogether satisfied.[6] However, two things may excuse yet another
attack on what must always be an important historical problem.
Adair's article did not find general acceptance; above all, Tanner,
whose words on this are probably read more widely than anyone
else's, was rather tart about his attempt to play down the act's importance and sat on the fence to such good purpose that an untenable older
view has been allowed to survive behind a cloak of mistaken caution.[7]
Holdsworth had his doubts about Adair's suggestion that the act was
not at all concerned with the validity of proclamations,[8] and Mr Stone
has rightly charged Adair with failing to explain the opposition to the
bill.[9] Quite recently, a new red herring has been introduced: it has
been maintained that section vi of the statute authorized the king's

---

* [EHR 75 (1960), 208–22.]

[1] 31 Henry VIII, c. 8 (*Statutes of the Realm*, iii. 726 ff.). Maitland (*English Law and the
Renaissance*, 19), perhaps inspired by Froude's evocation of the Roman dictator (*Hist. of
England*, iii. 200), attached the tag 'the English *lex regia*' to this act which still somehow
clings to it here and there.

[2] 'The Statute of Proclamations', *EHR* 32 (1917), 34 ff.

[3] A. F. Pollard, *Evolution of Parliament* (2nd ed., 1934), 266 ff.

[4] Pickthorn, *Early Tudor Gov.* ii. 414 ff.

[5] Holdsworth, *Hist. of Eng. Law*, iv. 102 f.

[6] *Tudor Revolution*, 340 ff.

[7] *Tudor Constitutional Documents*, ed. J. R. Tanner (Cambridge, 1922), 530, and esp. n. 6.

[8] Holdsworth, iv. 103, n. 7.

[9] L. Stone, 'Thomas Cromwell's Political Programme', *BIHR* 24 (1951); 2, n. 11.

Council to inflict the punishment for treason on those who by fleeing abroad tried to escape the consequences of offending under the act.[1] Before the legend of a tyrannical measure is thus revived, it must be said that the charge rests on an error. In making it treason to avoid trial by voluntary exile, the act did not entrust the enforcement of this clause to the Council but, by its silence, left it to the ordinary courts competent to deal with treason, which the Council was not. If these continuing doubts and conflicting views justify another investigation, the case becomes clearer still if it can be shown that not all the available evidence has hitherto been used and that some of that which has could do with a more precise and rigorous interpretation.

Strictly speaking, we are concerned with two bills – that which was enacted (having been produced in the Commons to replace one sent down by the Lords) and the original bill promoted by the government which had experienced changes during its passage in the Lords.[2] But only the former now exists, and it is here that one must start. The evidence does not permit certainty: one has a choice of either throwing up the sponge or trying to make a little sense of the bits of knowledge available. It is proposed first to establish what the act tried to do; then to see how it came to be in its present form; and lastly to attempt, as far as may be, to reconstruct the original proposals.

Adair maintained that the statute 'was concerned not at all with the legality of proclamations, but merely with the manner of trying offenders against them'.[3] He could have found better supporting evidence still than a casual, if contemporary, list of acts passed in 1539 which, as he says, calls the Proclamations Act simply 'breakers of king's proclamations'.[4] The *Lord's Journals* always treat the bill as 'concernens Punitionem eorundem qui Proclamationes Regio nomine fiendas in posterum violabunt aut infringent',[5] and the official title of this alleged piece of despotism was no more than 'an Acte that Proclamacions made by the King shall be obeyed'. Lest memories of the so-called Star Chamber Act of 1487 intrude, it should be said that the session of 1539 witnessed a remarkable if temporary change in the Parliament Roll. The new deputy clerk, Thomas Soulemont (a product of Cromwell's office) began with a descriptive list of the acts of the session, divided into public and private and given contemporary titles, which confirms the other evidence as to the official name of the

---

[1] Ogilvie, *King's Government*, 62 n.
[2] For the vicissitudes of the act cf. Adair, 35, and below, p. 346.
[3] Adair, 42 f.   [4] Ibid. 44, n. 38.   [5] *LJ* i. 108a, etc.

statute.[1] Unquestionably, therefore, the problem of enforcement struck those who made the act or witnessed its making as its chief purpose. Yet Holdsworth was quite right: it will not do to regard this as its sole purpose. The preamble ranges wider, and so, in part, does the enactment.

The preamble makes it plain enough that no one thought of creating a royal right to issue proclamations, for it begins by explaining the established practice. It specifies three causes for which proclamations have been issued: the settlement of religious doctrine, the preservation of 'unytie and concorde' in the realm, and 'the advauncement of his comon wealth and good quiett of his people'. The reasons which now compel action are also three. In the first place, 'froward, wilfull and obstinatt persons . . . not consideringe what a Kinge by his royall power may doe' have, in the absence of 'a directe statute and lawe to cohart offenders to obey the saide proclamacions', ignored and broken such ordinances. The phrase about the royal power has been read as a high assertion of mystic kingship,[2] but it was no more than a plain statement of fact; within their proper sphere, which excluded life and property, the king's proclamations had always had legal validity. Secondly, the occurrence of emergencies which cannot await the calling of a Parliament makes it necessary for the Crown to possess limited powers of legislation. Lastly, it is undesirable that the king – who by his regal power derived from God 'may doe many thinges in such cases' – should be 'driven to extend the libertye and supremacye of his regall power and dignytye by wilfulnes of frowarde subjectes'. It is therefore thought right that the king, by the advice of his Council, shall make proclamations 'as the cases of necessitie require' and that 'an ordynarie lawe' (enforcing statute) should be enacted to provide for their effectiveness. Both the reasons and the deductions are interesting enough. The trouble about proclamations was in part that they were being evaded, but in part too that their basic validity seems to have been called in doubt; and the striking assertion that continued evasion might lead to an unwelcome extension of prerogative action may be read either as a concealed threat from the Crown or a frank revelation of suspicion on Parliament's part.

The preamble thus made a clear distinction between validity and enforceability, mentioning both, but assigning only the second to the proposed act. So far Adair would have the right to it. However,

---

[1] PRO, C 65/147. The innovation was abandoned a year later.
[2] Tanner, 530.

section i of the enactment goes further. It provides 'that alwayes the Kinge . . . may set forth at all tymes by auctoritie of this Acte his proclamacions', and that these shall be obeyed 'as thoughe they were made by Acte of Parliament' unless dispensed with by letters patent. This last phrase was responsible for the act's bad reputation in the past; it used to be read as saying that proclamations could take the place of statute. However, anything but the most cursory reading must make it plain that what is in question here is enforcement only. It is the first part of the section which deals with validity, and that, being silent on the powers of proclamations, left them in fact as they were at common law. Adair suggested that for proclamations to be obeyed like acts of Parliament could only mean that, like statutes, they should be enforced in the courts of common law, and – admittedly conjectural though this inference must be since no such provision survived into the extant form of the act – it is very plausible. However, in view of the preamble's lamentations, it is also possible that the act only meant to allude to the respect generally given to statute and to demand that the same respect be accorded to proclamations. In any case, much the most significant part of section i is the first which takes an unquestioned royal prerogative (based, according to the preamble, on powers given to the king by God) and rests it on the authority of a parliamentary statute. So far from asserting an independent royal right to make law to the detriment of parliamentary privilege, this act ignored the divinely derived power of the Crown and subjected the prerogative to the sovereignty of the king in Parliament. Section i, therefore, does embody a very definite statement about the nature of proclamations: it contains – one would have thought without much concealment, were it not for the centuries of misinterpretation – a striking declaration of constitutional principle.

Section ii consists of an important proviso which exempts freehold of all kinds ('enheritaunces, laufull possessions, offices, libertyes, privileges, franchesies, goodes or catalles') and life from the operation of proclamations which were also specifically barred from affecting existing statutes, common law, and even the customs of the realm. An exception was made for those who offended against proclamations dealing with heresy. The drafting of this clause leaves something to be desired. As it stands, it does not protect subsequent legislation from infringement by proclamations, which could have been a very serious matter if the act had lasted. Nor is it at all plain what the exception about heresy meant. Did it empower proclamations to inflict the death penalty (in any case applicable under the old act *de haeretico comburendo*) and also forfeiture of property; or did it mean, which is as likely and perhaps more so, that the clause was not to debar the Crown from later defining doctrine differently from the scheme of things in existence when the act was passed? The second interpretation seems the more convincing because at this very time the problem of religion was alive enough and plans for settlement by the supreme head were being contemplated; if it is correct, it altogether disposes of any notion that the act gave proclamations any powers they had not had before.

Section iii, which defines the duty of sheriffs and others to publish any proclamations they receive with every degree of publicity, is of little import. On the other hand, great attention must be paid to sections iv and v which concern themselves with the machinery of enforcement. They create a statutory body of twenty-six judges, consisting in effect of councillors and office-holders and including not only the chief justices and chief baron but also such higher civil servants as the general surveyors of crown lands and the treasurer of the chamber. Thirteen were to be a quorum, provided two of the greater officers named were present. As has been pointed out elsewhere, this large body should be studied in connection with the reconstruction of the Council which was going on in the 1530s.[1] By 1539 the organized Privy Council was in existence,[2] and it seems very likely that the statutory body was made so big in order to ensure that the tribunal for trying offences against proclamations could always be readily constituted. If only two privy councillors were required and the other eleven could be judges or administrators, it might be hoped that the machinery would work.[3] As Adair has shown, it did not in fact do so.[4] An act of 1543 (34 & 35 Henry VIII, c. 23) reduced the quorum to nine. It has been assumed that the tribunal never actually met to exercise its powers under the act, and this may have been so. However, it is the case that these sections of the act did not escape notice; several bills concerning breaches of proclamations were formally addressed to the tribunal.[5] They are found among the files of Star Chamber papers,

---

[1] *Tudor Revolution*, 343 f.   [2] Ibid. 342 f.

[3] In ibid. 344, I regarded as convincing Adair's suggestion that the tribunal was the Commons' substitution for the government's desire to use the common-law courts. I no longer think that this is so: the setting up of such a statutory body is too clearly in line with other early-Tudor practice to come from anyone but the government. Since Adair could offer no evidence, however slender, and since I now feel that probability is against the notion, I prefer to abandon it.   [4] Adair, 43.

[5] E.g. PRO, St Ch 2/28/14, 24; 29/26. There may well be others.

and we cannot now tell whether the Council in Star Chamber made any distinction between bills brought before it in its ordinary capacity (which were addressed to the king) and bills addressed to the tribunal for proclamations. It has recently been shown that, contrary to received opinion, some plaintiffs addressed the special committee set up by the so-called Star Chamber Act, and there is good reason to suppose that that earlier tribunal did have some sort of life for a while.[1] So far, the study of the Council under Henry VIII has not progressed sufficiently to reveal what happened to the 1539 tribunal. However, there may be a pointer in the complaint of the 1543 act that it had in practice been found difficult to assemble the court as constituted by the act; it looks as though attempts were made.

Section v, which authorizes the issue of process under the great or privy seal by either the chancellor or the lord privy seal with the consent of six other members of the tribunal, also recalls the 1487 act, as well as the Statute of Liveries (1504). Time and again, early-Tudor legislation for the Council embodied in a statute what was already common practice in the court. Despite the complaints of the preamble, someone must have been trying to enforce proclamations before 1539, and as far as we know this someone was the Council sitting as a court in Star Chamber. Even while the act operated, plaintiffs did not all change their habits, and informations are known which were laid not before the statutory tribunal but addressed (like Star Chamber bills) to the king, though they refer to the Proclamations Act as the basis of the action.[2] These two sections, iv and v, should be seen in the light of such facts and parallels. They created machinery for enforcement, but they also in effect endorsed the traditional and insufficient machinery; in consequence suitors did not always quite know to whom to apply. What they did know was that the act gave a statutory basis to proclamations and encouraged actions by announcing the government's eagerness to punish offenders.

These are the parts of the statute which matter here. The remainder is less to the point. Section vi, which applies the penalties of treason to flight abroad in avoidance of the act, has already been mentioned. In all probability it was designed to deal with those who revolted against the Henrician Church; for proclamations not concerned with religion could never impose penalties to which abjuration of the realm was

---

[1] *Select Cases . . . Henry VII*, pp. liv. ff.
[2] This was the practice of that busy informer, George Whelplay (Elton, *Star Chamber Stories*, 94 ff.).

preferable.[1] Anyone avoiding trial by concealing himself inside the realm for long enough to exploit the eighteen months' limitation clause inserted in section iv was to stand convicted of the offence alleged against him, his contumacy acting as proof (section vii). Section viii deals with proclamations issued during the reign of Henry VIII's successor if he should be a minor. These were to be issued in his name, but his councillors (the real 'devisors or settors forth') were to sign each one of them. Moreover, while the ordinary Privy Council was meant in the section (i) which authorized a king who was of age to make proclamations with the advice of his Council, in this special case a majority of the large council named in the act was required. Surely it is in this clause viii, and not in any libertarian reaction against a *lex regia* or in the failure of the statutory committee,[2] that one finds Somerset's reasons for repealing the act in 1547. Not only would it be very difficult to make any proclamations if at least fourteen of the varied councillors named in the act had to be gathered together every time; it is even more to the point to remember that Somerset had no intention of allowing the other councillors to rival or diminish his outstanding position as protector. The Act of Proclamations had to go because it in effect (and, what is more, unquestionably by design) operated against the ascendancy of one man during the reign of a boy.

The last two sections (ix and x) describe the manner in which justices of the peace were to see to the enforcement of proclamations and empower the tribunal to reduce the penalties specified in proclamations at their discretion, provided they first obtain the king's consent.

That this interesting statute cannot be described as a weapon of despotism, or even of the prerogative, should now be plain. It was in

[1] Pollard (*Evolution of Parliament*, 267 f.) argued that the real purpose of the act was to provide for the enforcement of the supreme head's jurisdiction in matters of heresy. This is not impossible, and it is indeed clear from the act that the point was in the minds of its promoters. But if Pollard were right in making it the only or chief point, one would expect to find some use made of proclamations on religious matters while the act was in force. Of the 118 proclamations listed by R. R. Steele, *Tudor and Stuart Proclamations* for the years 1539–47 only four deal with religion. Of these one orders the placing of a bible in every church (no. 192); another permits the eating of white meat in Lent because fish is short (no. 226); a third published the act of 1543 concerning the reading of Scripture by the common people (no. 229); only the last – an injunction for the use of the primer (no. 271) – comes near to the purpose which Pollard divined behind the act. It seems very unlikely that the government should have gone to all the trouble of this statute if they had no use for it on the terms conjectured. In any case, Pollard entirely failed to consider the questions of validity and enforceability.

[2] The two reasons advanced respectively by A. F. Pollard, *Pol. Hist. of England*, vi. 16, and Adair, 46.

the main an attempt to reorganize the machinery for the enforcement of proclamations, but it also provided a general statutory justification for proclamations and in the process limited the independent power of the Crown by resting them on parliamentary authority. However, it is well known that the act had a difficult, or at least a peculiar, passage in both Houses of Parliament, and we must now once again, and in greater detail than has heretofore been done, rehearse its history there.[1] On 12 May 1539, Lord Chancellor Audley introduced the Bill in the Lords.[2] Though it at once received a first reading, nothing further happened till 7 June when it was read a second time.[3] Even allowing for an adjournment from 23 to 30 May, so timed and so long that ill-informed observers reckoned Parliament would not assemble again until the autumn,[4] this leaves three weeks between the two readings. The Lords were at the same time busy with the religious problem; on 10 May Norfolk raised the six points of doctrine in order to break the deadlock reached by a committee appointed five days earlier to study the issue, and the Whitsun adjournment was mainly designed to allow a solution to be found behind the scenes.[5] But even so a three weeks' delay argues that difficulties were encountered. On the 10th, the bill, engrossed in parchment, was read a third time.[6] But this, though it should have been, was not the end. For no discoverable reason the House reverted to the bill on the 12th when it was ordered to be committed for revision to the two chief justices, the master of the rolls, and the king's attorney and solicitor, 'quibus articuli in eadem continendi in plena Curia declarabantur'. That is to say, only the redrafting was left to the legal experts; the substance of the changes was settled by the House. The business did not take long: on the day after (the 13th) the reformed bill was read anew and handed to the clerk for a fresh engrossing, and on the 14th it was expedited after receiving altogether five readings.[7]

The bill's passage in the Lords alone is thus mysterious enough. We know from a later remark of Stephen Gardiner's that it ran into trouble there: in its passing, he says, it provoked 'many liberall wordes',[8] and since he was present in the Lords on all the days in question he must be referring to protesting voices in the Upper House. One might readily suppose that these debates helped to hold the bill

---

[1] Both Adair (p. 35) and Pickthorn (*Early Tudor Gov.* ii. 414) give only the bare outline.   [2] *LJ* i. 108a.   [3] Ibid. 116b.
[4] Marillac to Francis I, 9 June 1539 (*LP* xiv. I. 1091).
[5] Cf. above, pp. 207–8.   [6] *LJ* i. 116b.   [7] Ibid. 118a–b.
[8] *The Letters of Stephen Gardiner*, ed. J. A. Muller (Cambridge, 1933), 391.

up for some three weeks of actual sittings after it was first introduced; but what then is the meaning of that curious by-play after the third reading? The number of readings was by no means invariable at this time; yet three were usual, and it is very surprising to find a bill engrossed before there was certainty of agreement. The fact that the government draftsmen called in to recast the bill were given strict instructions by the House also suggests strongly that the changes were pushed through at a late stage against the wish of the government who could surely have supervised the work of redrafting without solemnly expounding 'in plena Curia' what matter was to be included. The only thing certain in the whole affair is the difficulty experienced in getting the bill through the Lords: the Lords, be it noted, and not the Commons, as some accounts might make one think. For what it is worth, one might conjecture some such sequence as this: prolonged debate failed to prevent a second reading, and the Crown managers (that is, Cromwell and Audley) then decided to take the House by storm and produced an engrossed bill for the third reading. Although they got it through, the opposition rallied next day and forced their amendments into the bill. In the end they carried the day; but we cannot tell how large or fundamental their objections were.

On 14 June the bill was carried to the Commons where (in the absence of Journals) it disappears from sight for ten days. On the 25th, John Hussee reported to his master, Lord Lisle, that Parliament had been sitting on a proclamations act for fifteen days but would soon be done now.[1] His figures were a little inaccurate, and he was a trifle behindhand with his information, for on the 24th the Commons presented the Lords with the upshot of their deliberations; but writing when he did he must have had the Commons in mind rather than the earlier business in the Lords. Certainly, except for the bill for proclamations, nothing of great importance engaged the Commons in those ten days, for they had returned the Act of Six Articles to the Upper House on the very day that they received the Proclamations Act.[2] They, too, had debated to some purpose: on the 24th they returned to the Lords their bill which they had rejected, together with a new one they had framed in its place.[3] There followed what was in some ways the strangest part of the whole story. The Lords, who had laboured so long in amending the government's original proposals, took precisely two days (the 24th and 25th of June) to give three readings to the Commons' bill, sending it down on the second day

---

[1] *LP* xiv. I. 1158.   [2] 14 June: *LJ* i. 118b.   [3] Ibid. 122b.

with a few amendments they wanted the Commons to insert. This
the Commons did, and on the 26th the long business was at last over.

Counsels are now properly darkened. It seems possible, at first sight,
to offer three conjectural explanations of what had taken place. Either
the Lords had at first been deprived of their full criticisms and joyfully
accepted the Commons' victory over the government's plans; or they
had been drilled back into order by the 24th and would, under government direction, accept what the Crown had had to concede to the
Commons; or the government had used the Commons as a last-ditch
defence against the Lords' opposition, had in effect revived its original
bill there, and had then presented the Lords with an accomplished fact
which they had neither the time nor the stomach to fight again. This
last possibility – which would in effect reverse the later practice of
Elizabeth with her reliance on a docile House of Lords – may sound
the least likely but happens to be the only one for which a few scraps
of evidence can be adduced. After all, this was the notorious Parliament
for which Cromwell had organized electoral influence on an unprecedented scale, so as to produce what he himself called a tractable
Commons.[1] One ought not to be surprised to see a House so influenced
and presumably manageable used in the government interest. That the
Lords raised major difficulties in the first place is certain: the bill they
sent to the Commons was the product of their opposition. Further we
know that they did not take the Commons' new bill without some
amendment, and the changes they demanded survive as interlineations
on the original act in the Parliament Office.[2] And very interesting they
are too. Apart from a few insignificant alterations they all trend one
way: they limit the independent vigour of royal proclamations. In the
well known passage in section i – 'that alwayes the Kinge for the
tyme being . . . may set forth at all tymes by auctoritie of this Acte
his proclamacions' – the words 'by auctoritie of this Acte' were put
in by the Lords; and in three passages in section ii the Commons'
drafting, which had left open later arbitrary action by the Crown,
was so amended as to restrict the king by the act itself.[3] These were not

[1] For the fullest discussion of this point see above, pp. 200–5.
[2] Some, but not all, the interlineations are noted in *Statutes of the Realm*.
[3] The act prohibits the death penalty except where it 'shall be hereafter in this Acte
declared'; 'in this Acte' is inserted. The Lords added the words 'to be made by vertue
of this Acte' to 'any proclamacion', and later the words 'hereafter shalbe set forth by
auctoritie of the same [act]' to 'everie proclamacion whiche'. One change in section i
was administrative rather than fundamental. The Commons' bill had authorized the
making of proclamations with the advice of the Council, but only the Lords' amendments added the necessary 'or with thadvise of the more parte of them'.

world-shaking changes, nor would one expect any when merely small alterations in a bill itself acceptable were in question. But they all stress one aspect of the act which has already been described: the recognition that the statute embodied a definition of, and therefore a limitation upon, a function of the prerogative.

However, while these pointers suggest that the only serious opposition was encountered in the Lords, there is a hint elsewhere which brings us back to the Commons. It is indeed so dark a hint that Adair could make nothing of it,[1] and his example should warn us not to drive it too hard. On 5 July 1539, the French ambassador in England, Marillac, reported to his king the conclusion of the session, and described one statute which, he said, had received its assent 'avec grandes difficultez qui ont esté débatues longtemps en leurs assemblées et avec peu de contentment'.[2] His account would certainly justify every degree of opposition, for, as he had it, the act compelled the king's subjects 'sans aucune excuse ni délay' to pay whatever money-tax should be imposed upon them, 'quant le bon plaisir de leur roy seroit en faire imposition sur eux pour son affaire et besoing'. Refusal meant treason with its attendant penalties 'sans aultre procès'. Of course, there is no such act among those passed, and Marillac's report rests manifestly upon some extremely garbled rumours. But perhaps it may be possible to guess at some of the facts which rumour perverted. His mention of long delays in Parliament makes plain that he had either the Act of Six Articles or the Proclamations Act in mind; no other in this session caused difficulties. Of the two, the former will not fill the bill at all; besides, Marillac had earlier shown himself aware of the settlement of religion.[3] And the Act of Proclamations does include, in section vi, a reference to the penalties of treason. It is not, therefore, unreasonable to deduce from this letter that part of the trouble over the act was connected with matters of property – fears that proclamations might be used to invade property rights and even to tax at pleasure. If such fears had been freely expressed in the debates, Marillac, writing (as he says) before the act was printed and therefore before he had seen it, might readily confuse what he had heard from his usual unreliable sources about the business in Parliament and produce his version of the statute. In this connection, section ii is worth another look. It protects the nation against precisely such uses of proclamations

---

[1] Adair, 43, n. 37.

[2] *Correspondence Politique de MM. de Castillon et de Marillac*, ed. J. Kaulek (Paris, 1885), 107 (and cf. *LP* xiv. I. 1207).   [3] Ibid. 1091 (9 June 1539).

as may be conjectured to lie behind Marillac's report. And it is a
proviso: it begins with the words 'provided always that' and, in a
revealing phrase in the section itself, is kept separate from the act – 'as
yf this acte or proviso had never bene had or made'. In addition (as
has already been said) it is curiously imprecise in its drafting, in which
it contrasts with the rest of the act and especially with section i. There
are therefore at the least some strong hints that it was not part of the
original draft but was inserted at some later stage. Though it would
be too much to claim that in this period provisos were always appended
at the end of acts this was certainly their usual place, and the appearance
of one immediately after the main enacting clause would seem to
throw something like light on the subject of the debates which delayed
the act for so long. If these important reservations were added in
Parliament, one would on the whole suppose them to be the work of
the Commons who throughout the 1530s were never more likely to
oppose the Crown than on matters of property and taxation. A whole
proviso would be difficult to add to an existing parchment bill except
at the end, and if the Commons wished to put one in the middle they
would almost have to do what in fact they did – write the thing out
afresh. And if the only material alteration made by them consists of
section ii, one can see why the Lords had no difficulty in accepting the
new bill.

Thus the safest conclusion, conjectural as it must necessarily be,
would be that there was opposition in both houses but that the more
serious opposition to the principle of the bill occurred in the Lords.
They concentrated on preventing any extreme claims for the authority
and sweep of proclamations, while the Commons were more concerned to protect property rights. That brings us back to the question
of the government's original proposals. On the face of it, neither point
of debate should have worried them overmuch; despite the delays
(for which other business was in any case partly responsible) it does not
look as though in the end there was very much between the parties.
By the very fact of introducing a statute on which to rest proclamations,
the Crown accepted the principle that the king in Parliament was
superior as a legislator to the king in Council; and there is no sign
whatever that the sort of fears suggested in section ii had any basis in
fact. In Henry VIII's reign no proclamation before or after the act
evaded the common-law limitations upon their range, and it is quite
possible that debate over section ii would be prolonged not because
the government resisted a limitation which would deprive it of taxing

powers but because the Commons tried to get away without the saving clause which enfranchised the Crown in matters of heresy.

What, indeed, did the government wish to obtain from the act? Clearly – if only because the bill's title confirms this from the very beginning – they were concerned with enforceability. The clauses which deal with this are more than likely to have been in the act from the first, though no one can say whether amendment took place in Parliament. But secondly there is reason to suppose that the government also wished to clear up the constitutional point concerning the authority of proclamations. We have in effect three statements, of a sort, about the origin of the statute. Burnet, giving no evidence in support, says that injunctions issued by the supreme head had caused resentment because they altered law and taxed the spiritualty without parliamentary consent; the act was therefore introduced to provide general authority.[1] Gardiner, recalling matters a few years after the event, alleged that proclamations forbidding the export of corn had proved unenforceable because the judges declared them illegal while wheat remained below the price fixed by statute, and that therefore the statute was made.[2] He may well have been right in remembering that this sort of problem came up in the Council, but the act did nothing to solve it because it contained the subjection of proclamations to statute. Thirdly we know that as early as 1535 Cromwell had been concerned about the authority behind proclamations.[3] The Council, wishing to prohibit the export of coin, had taken legal advice and discovered a statute of Richard II on which it would ground a proclamation. However, Cromwell had gone on to ask the experts what the position would be if no such act had been found. The answer he got (and was delighted to get) was that

the Kynges highness by the aduyse of his Cownsayll myght make proclamacyons and vse all other polecyes at his pleasure as well in this Case as in Anye other lyke For the avoyding of any suche daungers and that the sayd proclamacyons . . . sholde be of as good effect as Any lawe made by parlyament or otherwyse.

This was assuredly good law, especially as coin was in question, always a prerogative matter; and it is worth noting that the ominous phrase equating proclamations and statutes was used here by the judges

[1] G. Burnet, *History of the Reformation* (ed. N. Pocock, 1865), i. 422.
[2] *Letters of Stephen Gardiner*, 391.
[3] His letter to Norfolk, 15 July 1535 (Merriman, i. 409 f.). [This letter is now known to belong to 1531: *Reform and Renewal*, 117, n. 70.]

themselves. However, the later production of an act to provide general authority suggests that Cromwell continued to prefer a statutory basis to a common-law one. This, after all, was a common feature of the legislation passed in the 1530s and under his aegis.[1]

We may well believe, therefore, that both validity and enforcement – the points of the preamble – were in the government's mind when it introduced the act. Indeed, the preamble, with its assertions of what the king could do, looks rather like government drafting. The most curious phrase in it distinguishes between 'disobedyence of the preceptes and lawes of Almightie God' and 'synn to[o] much to the great dishonor of the Kinges most royall Majestie'; here one almost hears the supreme head himself at his most pompous. But what is not clear is whether the original proposal made much larger claims than the enacted statute. Adair, concentrating on enforcement, did not seem to think it likely, but he ignored the stray pieces of evidence which suggest a tradition of great dangers averted by a vigilant Parliament. In 1559, John Aylmer, discussing the nature of constitutional monarchy in England, stressed how important it was that Parliament should look to its privileges:

Wherefore, in my judgement, those that in King Henry the viii dais, would not grant him that his proclamacions shuld haue the force of statute, were good fathers of the countri, and worthy commendacion in defending their liberty.[2]

Much later, James I, addressing a Commons' deputation, took occasion to praise a system where 'usage consonant to reason hath given the subject free consent of denyal and rejection':

and therefore I comend Bacon who when Hen. 8th sought by parliament to make his proclamation a law, and this with such violence thrust on your house as none durst stir a finger; then did Bacon as reason would stand up and speak with boldness against it, for the king's seeking in that point was tyrannical.[3]

Neither of these statements carries full conviction. Aylmer says that Parliament refused to do what 300 years of historiography alleged it did; but here Aylmer was right. In the sense that proclamations were not made interchangeable for all purposes with statute, the 1539 act refused to admit that proclamations had 'the force of statute'. But Aylmer's words must even leave it open whether he thought that no

---

[1] An outstanding example is the treasons act of 1534 which turned the common law of treason by words into parliamentary enactment: I. D. Thornley, 'Treason by Words...', *EHR* 32 (1917), 556 ff.
[2] *An Harborowe for faithfull and trewe Subiectes* (Strasbourg, 1559), sig. H.3.
[3] 'Narrative of Sir Henry Yelverton,' *Archaeologia*, 15 (1806), 43.

act was passed at all; as they stand they do not very well describe an act which did order obedience to proclamations as though they had been made by Act of Parliament. Nor do we know where he got his information or how good it was. It is to the point that the act was repealed twelve years before he wrote. King James's account is difficult to assess, for we cannot even confirm that any Bacon sat in the 1539 parliament for which at present no list of members exists.[1] The history of the act, as far as we have been able to reconstruct it, does not suggest that the bill was 'thrust' violently on the Commons: a ten days' debate sounds like rather more than one brave man standing up amongst his abashed fellows, and in any case the bill had suffered already in the Lords. Nevertheless, together with Marillac's letter, these allusions make it difficult to think that the original bill was quite as innocuous as Adair has, by and large, supposed. The chances are that it did not expressly bar proclamations from invading life and property, and it may have said more simply than the final act that proclamations were to have the same force as statute. If the first bill used some such form of words as that which Cromwell reported was used by the judges (and after all Cromwell and the judges were foremost among government draftsmen), then the careful drafting of section i – authorizing the king to issue proclamations but reserving the comparison with statute to the matter of enforcement only – could be the work of the Lords; and the earlier form of words, if it ran as we conjecture, could easily give rise to the sort of report which reached Aylmer and James I.

But these are not points as vital as might be supposed. How little difference the statute made in practice is well brought out by Adair,[2] and much additional evidence could be adduced to support his point that Elizabeth without the act – relying on her common-law prerogative which was available also to her father – exploited proclamations much more dangerously. The whole history of Henry VIII's reign after 1529 makes it difficult to suppose that anyone wished to govern by ordinance or tax without consent. This is not to say that Parliament

---

[1] Mr Stone (*BIHR* 24, 2, n. 11) identifies this Bacon as Nicholas, the later lord keeper, but there appear to be no grounds for doing so. If Nicholas Bacon really sat in this Parliament and spoke against the Crown, it would throw some light on problems of management; he was already in the king's service and very much a government man.

[2] Adair, 41. In the 1550s, a legal textbook stated outright that the repeal of the act had not affected the validity of proclamations provided they were 'in supplement or declaracion of a lawe', i.e. provided they obeyed the definitions of the act: *A Discourse upon the Exposicion & Understandinge of Statutes*, ed. S. E. Thorne (San Marino, 1942), 103 ff.

were not right to watch with care and express fears which may well have been exaggerated: Aylmer's commendation was, no doubt, deserved. However, what real fears and real opposition could achieve in the 1530s is demonstrated by the long years of negotiations over the Statute of Uses, not by the Proclamations Act. The story of this act is incomprehensible unless, on the one hand, there were serious differences between the Crown's views and those of both Lords and Commons, and unless, on the other, these differences were not so fundamental as to make a compromise between them impossible. After all, the bill was redrafted, not thrown out; after all, it received the king's assent.

One thing, however, is clear. Adair was wrong when he said that 'the act of proclamations was the work of the commons'.[1] Its history was much more complicated than that and in part must always remain outside the realm of discoverable certainty. Furthermore, while enforcement of proclamations was the most obvious purpose of the act, their validity and scope entered fully into its drafting, and there is every reason to suppose that it was this constitutional and legal question, rather than the machinery for trying offenders, which caused the trouble in Parliament.

[1] Adair, 43.

20

THE ELIZABETHAN EXCHEQUER:
WAR IN THE RECEIPT*

In the government of Elizabeth, the Exchequer, reformed in 1554, once again handled the bulk of the Crown's revenues; it was the dominant ministry of finance, though two lesser offices, the court of Wards and the Duchy of Lancaster, remained outside its control.[1] The Exchequer was divided into two departments, a treasury and pay-office (Exchequer of Receipt) and a court of audit (Exchequer of Account), which had almost developed into separate institutions. The administration of the Queen's money was indeed shared by them, but each operated as a unit, contacts between them were interdepartmental rather than casual, and only one man (the chancellor of the Exchequer who was also always undertreasurer of the Receipt) had a standing in both sections. The various early-Tudor experiments in financial administration, which had in the end produced the reformed Exchequer, had left that office with an increased jealousy of irregular or novel procedure and a more specific interest in its own venerable methods; respect for their indisputable safety would admit no recognition of their devilish clumsiness and soon grew into an unthinking affection for any established practice. The feeling appeared in the number of notes and accounts of the Exchequer's vast organization and esoteric ways scattered through the papers of the time; one of these, written by Thomas Fanshawe who was queen's remembrancer under Elizabeth, appeared in print in 1658.[2] Departmental devotion was further encouraged by the needs of the Exchequer's staff. Next to the royal Household, the Exchequer was easily the largest department in existence; served by men who usually entered young and worked their way up by seniority, it constituted the most complete example of a civil service structure in the Queen's government. Like nearly all Tudor officers, those of the Exchequer drew their income from three sources: they had official salaries, took fees from revenue officers and

---

* [*Elizabethan Government and Society: essays presented to Sir John Neale*, ed. S. T. Bindoff, J. Hurstfield, C. H. Williams (1961), 213–48.]   [1] *Tudor Revolution*, 223 ff.

[2] *The Practice of the Exchequer Court and its Several Officers.* The book enjoys a not altogether deserved reputation for correctness and completeness. [The author was probably not Thomas Fanshawe, but Peter Osborn, lord treasurer's remembrancer.]

others for such requirements of the accounting process as the making out of documents or of certified copies from the record, and could hope for perquisites and bribes intended to dispose them favourably to those who got involved in the Exchequer's machinery. On the whole it seems clear that this last source of income did not amount to much among the rank and file of officials, and salaries were certainly never adequate. In consequence the fees, levied on a fixed scale, provided the chief means of livelihood and attraction of office; conservatism in procedure was assisted by the fact that reforms, if efficient, would probably reduce the chances of earning them. Nothing so well illustrates the facts of life in the Exchequer as the war over precedence, duties and fees waged throughout Elizabeth's reign between two officers in the Receipt, the writer of the tallies and the clerk of the pells, a war which left behind a mass of complex materials.[1]

The medieval Receipt was in the charge of the treasurer and the two chamberlains of the Exchequer, and its organization was therefore determined by the existence of three head-officers designed to act as checks upon one another. The only public records in the Receipt consisted of rolls of receipts and issues, called pells, one of each being kept on behalf of each officer. There were thus six rolls, two treasurer's pells and four chamberlains' counterpells. These were, in theory, made up on the spot, each item of money received and paid being entered as it came in or went out; they were really journal books from which it was both difficult to establish accurate totals and impossible to analyse either the items of revenue or the nature of government expenditure. Such money as there was in the Exchequer was supposed to be in the custody of the treasurer and chamberlains whose representatives kept the keys to the money-chests. In practice two things had happened to modify this theoretical picture. One was the emergence of the treasurer's clerk (or deputy) as the effective head of the Receipt with the title of undertreasurer, an event which Elizabethans liked to link with Henry VII's reforms[2] but which had taken place by the middle of the fifteenth century.[3] The other – which alone made the system workable

---

1 The bulk of the papers is found in one bundle of Miscellanea of the Receipt, PRO, E 407/71; most documents in this are numbered individually but in no sort of order. The next five bundles (72–76) of unnumbered papers consist of the office correspondence of one writer of the tallies and contain some helpful details. In addition material is found in BM, Lansdowne MSS and in Hist. MSS Com. *Salisbury MSS.* In the compass of this paper it will be necessary to omit many of the often fascinating details.

2 E.g. BM, Lansd. 151, fos. 103 ff.

3 J. L. Kirby, 'The Rise of the Under-Treasurer of the Exchequer,' *EHR* 72 (1957), 666 ff.

– was the near-disappearance of cash from the Exchequer, whose transactions came to consist predominantly in the issuing and auditing of tallies of assignment (anticipations of revenue), so that a detailed record of revenue and expenditure proved the less necessary.[1]

However, the reorganization of government begun in the late fifteenth century touched also the Exchequer, and certain reforms had been carried out before the accession of Henry VIII. Sir Vincent Skinner, writer of the tallies, describing them in the course of his war with Chidiock Wardour, clerk of the pells, put them down to Henry VII, 'being, as he is right worthily styled in story, a prince of prudent and politic government'.[2] The king, we are told, found the pells a useless record which did not enable him to plan an increase in revenue and decrease in expenditure, or to 'understand thereby what remained due and answerable to him'; he regarded the cost of these various rolls as excessive; and he therefore instituted the 'formal and orderly course of account' since in use. He retained one pell of receipt 'as a ledger and coucher in court to serve as a double voucher for his more security', but abolished the issue roll altogether; this was done also because he did not wish too many people to know how his money was spent. Secondly he transferred the actual custody of money to the four tellers who were to pay it out only on a warrant from the lord treasurer and undertreasurer, an order which in turn must rest on a warrant under the great or privy seal. Allegedly the establishment of the undertreasurership was another part of the reforms. Lastly, he instituted the making and presenting of annual 'Declarations of the State of the Treasury' in which all receipts and payments, in cash or by tally, were reduced into digested form, giving a clear view of the nature of both revenue and expenditure as well as making plain at a glance what the reserves were.

These reforms certainly took place: were they Henry VII's? The habit now is to see in him nothing but the heir of Yorkist practice, and it is certainly true that the office of undertreasurer was older. Moreover, the last medieval pell of issue now extant is that of 19 Edward IV (1479), and it is claimed that no later one was known even by the end of Elizabeth's reign.[3] Yet this cannot quite be: Wardour discovered

---

[1] For the fifteenth-century Receipt cf. A. Steel, *The Receipt of the Exchequer 1377–1485* (Cambridge, 1954), pp. xxix ff.; J. L. Kirby, 'The Issues of the Lancastrian Exchequer,' *BIHR* 24 (1951), 121 ff.

[2] There are several drafts of Skinner's discourse, written between 1601 and 1604: E 407/71/13; E 405/75 (unnumbered); BM, Lansd. 151, fos. 103 ff.

[3] *Third Report of the Deputy Keeper of the Public Records*, App. II. 173.

a writ of 20 Edward IV ordering the entry of certain payments on the issue roll and transcribed it for his purposes.[1] He also thought that the custody of money was not transferred to the tellers until early in Henry VIII's reign,[2] but in this he postdated events. It certainly seems that the institution of the vital 'Declarations' only began about 1504: Skinner claimed to have the first of them in his office and that it belonged to 20 Henry VII.[3] In all probability the duplicated pells ceased to be kept in course of time and without any specific orders of reform; the surviving series are patchy enough throughout, and even in 1550 (and later), when no counterpells had been known for decades, officers were still paid a nominal fee for writing them.[4] The more precise reforms which put the tellers, controlled by the undertreasurer, in charge of the cash, and which relied on the annual statements to the king and lord treasurer – these may safely be left to Henry VII's credit.[5]

Though these reforms do not look big, they did in fact amount to an upheaval in the Receipt. The chamberlains' deputies ceased to have any controlling influence; everything fell on the treasurer's deputy, the undertreasurer. But he in turn had to depend on active officers in the Receipt, especially from 1543 onwards when his office came to be held jointly with the chancellorship of the Exchequer, a post in the upper or audit court.[6] And since the roots of the quarrel with which this paper is concerned lie precisely here, it will be necessary to say a few words about the working of the Receipt – its so-called 'course'.[7] When an officer accountant, or a debtor, paid money into the Receipt, he set in motion a complicated machinery designed to produce a tally which he could present in the Exchequer of Account to have his payment or debt discharged. He paid the money to a teller who (having entered the receipt in his own book) put a bill 'down a trunk' into the Receipt (later known as the tally court) on which he had

---

[1] E 407/71/11.   [2] BM, Lansd. 106 fo. 4.

[3] E 406/71/13. The earliest extant now is E 405/183, for 23–24 Henry VII (1507–8).

[4] Each chamberlain had a deputy in the Receipt, with a fee of £10, for the striking of tallies, and a clerk to write the counterpell who got £6: E 405/212 (1550).

[5] Sir Julius Caesar thought that 'a new establishment' in the Receipt dated from 20 Henry VII and that the pell of issue was discontinued in 21 Henry VII: BM, Lansd. 168 fo. 284. But it is possible that he relied on, and misinterpreted, Skinner's discourse which was certainly available to him since the fair copy is among his papers: BM, Lansd. 151, fos. 103 ff.   [6] Cf. *Tudor Revolution*, 254.

[7] This description, reduced to essentials, is in great part derived from two documents: E 407/17/82 ('an old report found in the Receipt of the service there used by the officers attendant') and ibid. no. 3 (based on this but with some variations in detail and annotated by Skinner). Other descriptions occur among the papers.

entered the date, year and term, the payer's name and county, and the sum received. This was now in effect entered three times. It was transcribed for record into the pell of receipt; it was transferred onto a tally (the sum being cut in notches and the other matter written on the sides of the wooden stick); and it was also registered in a book kept by the officer called writer of the tallies. The tally was then struck (split), and the accountant could depart for his audit.[1] The teller's bill remained in the Receipt and came to be kept by the writer of the tallies. Payments out of the Receipt rested ultimately upon Crown warrants, either dormant (for recurring payments) under the great or privy seal, or special warrants under the privy seal only. The tellers, however, could not pay any money except on receiving letters grounded upon the royal warrants. In the case of recurring payments, the patent, registered in a book kept in the Receipt, was retained by the payee who obtained and deposited a dormant writ of *liberate*; each individual payment then required a debenture to the teller. Privy seals for special payments, addressed to the treasurer and chamberlains, resulted in letters from the lord treasurer and undertreasurer (usually made up into weekly statements) to the Receipt where an order assigning the payment to a specified teller was then made out. The privy seals were filed in the department, which also kept an entry book of the lord treasurer's weekly orders.

The essential problem in the Receipt consisted in controlling the tellers who alone handled the money for which they rendered half-yearly account. There had to be one officer in the Receipt who kept the material for auditing their books. The old treasurer's clerk, out of whose office the exalted undertreasurer had grown, had kept the rolls and written the tallies himself;[2] by the late fifteenth century these duties had come into the charge of the clerk of the Receipt of whom there is no trace under the Tudors;[3] but from the middle of the fifteenth century anyway one can trace two sets of officers who were respectively responsible for keeping the pells of receipt and issue, and

---

[1] In fact, revenue officers usually came to their account much later, and there were careful rules about the transfer of the countertallies or foils to the custody of the deputy chamberlains in the Upper Exchequer, there to await the production of the tally and the joining which constituted the chief proof of payment accepted by the Exchequer.

[2] R. L. Poole, *The Exchequer in the Twelfth Century* (Oxford, 1912), 73 ff.; J. Willard, 'The Treasurer's Issue Roll and the Clerk of the Treasurer,' *BIHR* 8 (1935), 129 ff., esp. 133.

[3] Kirby, 'Under-Treasurer,' *EHR* 72 (1957), 676. Does the absorption (re-absorption?) of this office into the undertreasurership explain the conviction that Henry VII has instituted this last office?

for writing the tallies.[1] On the face of it, the first was a much more weighty office, and Dr Steel considered the clerk of the pells to be the treasurer's true representative in the fifteenth century Receipt.[2] Yet it is curious to find that certain clerks of the pells appeared later as writers of the tallies, a point not missed by the embattled tally writers of Elizabeth's reign.[3] These men had evidently been promoted to a higher and more profitable office. The explanation lies almost certainly in a fact which appears at first to contradict it. The Tudor 'Declarations of the State of the Treasury' used somewhat surprising terms in describing these various officers.[4] The undertreasurer appeared as *clericus thesaurarii Anglie*, the writer of the tallies as *unus clericorum ex parte thesaurarii Anglie*, and the clerk of the pells as *alter clericus thesaurarii Anglie* (in that order). In other words, this official record, using, in the Exchequer manner, an old-fashioned terminology, equated as treasurer's clerks two officers whose salaries were £173 6s. 8d. and £17 10s. respectively; while the tally writer, earning at that time £28 6s. 8d., seemed in title inferior to the lowest paid. All this suggests that the clerk of the pells had a longer independent history and that the tally writer had risen to prominence as a special agent of the undertreasurer, the titular head of the Receipt. Certainly he had come to be relied on for the keeping of the papers and records to audit the tellers' accounts and for the preparation of the material needed for treasury statements.

Two events in the first half of the sixteenth century assisted these developments, which reduced the clerk of the pells to inferiority in the Receipt. One was a purely personal matter. In July 1517 Thomas Danyell became writer of the tallies, while five months later, in November, John Uvedale obtained the clerkship of the pells. Danyell was succeeded by Thomas Felton in May 1550; Uvedale held his office till he died in 1549. During this long common tenure Danyell was nothing except an Exchequer official, while Uvedale, a Yorkshireman, held a variety of other offices, culminating in the active secretaryship of the Council of the North from 1536 onwards.[5] He can never have attended in person to the pells at all, and it is known that he exercised his office through his son-in-law.[6] At this very time the need for

---

[1] I have easily compiled lists of them from the admissions registered in the Black Book of the Exchequer (E 36/266). [2] Steel, *Receipt*, 3.

[3] E.g. John Leyton, clerk 1460 and writer 1464; Thomas Bulkley, clerk at an unknown date and writer 1471; John Lewes, clerk 1486 and writer 1489.

[4] E.g. E 405/183, Declaration of 23-24 Henry VII.

[5] *DNB*. Uvedale served in the north with short interruptions from 1528 to his death.

[6] E 407/71/96.

someone connected with the accounts to take charge grew urgent as the undertreasurership passed from such professional hands as those of Sir John Cutt (1506–21) to the hands of lawyers and courtiers like Sir Thomas More (1521–6), Sir Richard Weston (1526–42), and Sir John Baker (1543–58). The writer of the tallies, active in person and relied on by his superiors, necessarily took over. Secondly, there was the growing practice of introducing new sources of revenue into the Exchequer, culminating in the reforms of 1554 which, while they restored Exchequer supremacy in the finances, also meant that the bulk of Exchequer revenue was new and no longer handled by the 'old course' of the Exchequer.[1] That is to say, it stood outside the tally system proper, and since the old pells were designed for a register of tallies the clerk of the pells had ever greater difficulties in asserting supervisory powers. All this came to a head with Thomas Felton, tally writer from 1550 to 1556, who (according to Sir Julius Caesar)[2] was first called by the novel but descriptive title of auditor of the Receipt.

From this time, however, the counterattack began. Behind it there lay complex and obscure relationships between these Exchequer officials and the great officers of state. Both the writership of the tallies and the clerkship of the pells were in the gift of the lord treasurer, and it appears that while most treasurers relied more on the writer, one of them, the marquess of Winchester (1550–72), leaned towards the clerk. At any rate, trouble seems to have begun with Edmund Cockerell's appointment as clerk of the pells late in 1555,[3] and his successors Robert Hare (1560–70) and Chidiock Wardour (1570–1611) appear to have been clients of the 'old treasurer', as he was later called.[4] On the other hand, the important writers of the tallies were both Burghley's men. Robert Peter (1569–93), appointed nominally still by Winchester but in fact apparently a servant of that good Cecilian, Sir Walter Mildmay, chancellor of the Exchequer since 1566,[5] had the closest ties with Burghley, who consistently relied on him for the running of the

---

[1] *Tudor Revolution*, 254 ff.

[2] BM, Lansd. 168, fo. 353*b*. Skinner thought that the title first appeared in 1566 when Humphrey Skelton took over from Felton: E 407/71/96.

[3] Below, p. 371.

[4] Letters from Winchester to Hare describe the clerk specifically as his servant and are signed 'your master': SP 12/8/62; 12/83/138. They required Hare to do the sort of thing for which Burghley relied on the auditor of the Receipt.

[5] Mildmay was later described as Peter's 'especial good master' who had assisted him in various usurpations 'without the consent of the old lord treasurer who then [1572] lay at Basing and never returned hither again': E 407/71/51.

Receipt.[1] Peter's successor, Vincent Skinner, was a much more striking case. He had no previous professional experience of the Exchequer but was a trusted servant of Burghley's, employed by him from at least 1578 onwards in many affairs: making peace at Cambridge, dealing with prisoners in the Fleet, devilling for him on the subject of prohibitions at common law (for which purpose he read the subject up in Fitzherbert and Brooke), investigating the history of negotiations over contraband.[2] From 1584 Skinner sat in the Cecil interest in Parliament,[3] and his appointment as writer of the tallies was very much a personal reward to a favourite servant. A copy of the treasurer's patent appointing him survives among Burghley's papers;[4] and Skinner was admitted to the office, not (as was proper) at the Receipt but at Court, on 11 November 1593, taking the oath of supremacy (the first holder of the office to do so) with Burghley signing the entry.[5] In office he continued a Cecil client, a fact to which Burghley's death and the lord treasurership of Lord Buckhurst made no difference.[6] In 1599 he acknowledged to Robert Cecil Burghley's 'honourable favour and goodness' by which 'I received the place, though with small desire and less affection unto it, being unknown to me then how painful and otherwise troublesome it was and hath proved since, saving that it was a continuation of my service under him'.[7] He no doubt regarded himself in great part recompensed when he was among the first knights dubbed, on 7 May 1603 at Belvoir castle, by James I.[8]

Thus out of these gradual but marked changes in administrative practice grew the war between the two most important officers in the Receipt, a war for control of affairs on the one hand and over the fees paid by the public on the other. The first shot, however, was fired, early in Elizabeth's reign, not by a clerk of the pells but by an anonymous deputy to the earl of Shrewsbury as chamberlain of the Exchequer.[9] He demanded a full restoration of the ancient course so that

---

[1] SP 12/105/90; 12/192/art. 9; cf. Hist. MSS Com. *Salisbury*, ii. 106, 107, 187, 217, 264, 339; iii. 105.

[2] Hist. MSS Com. *Salisbury*, xiii. 156 ff., 158, 446; SP 12/233/art. 29; 12/238/142-3.

[3] J. E. Neale, *The Elizabethan House of Commons* (London, 1949), 207, 243.

[4] Hist. MSS Com. *Salisbury*, iv. 377.

[5] Black Book, E 36/266/89b.

[6] This is shown by his correspondence with Robert Cecil: Hist. MSS Com. *Salisbury*, ix. 131, 298; x. 83, 281, 292 ff.; xii. 435.

[7] SP 12/271/177. It should be noted that despite all these personal attachments both officers, holding for life, were civil servants who stayed on regardless of changes at the top.   [8] W. A. Shaw, *Knights of England*, ii. 104.

[9] BM, Lansd. 106, fos. 8-15.

the chamberlains' clerks should once again exercise some control over the lord treasurer's clerks. Things seem to have been bad in the Receipt under Mary. An usher who allegedly sold half a cart-load of treaties and other records in St Paul's Churchyard was never punished till executed for a treason in which he had also got involved; the tellers had embezzled much money and died in debt to the Queen. The author of this memorandum relied heavily on Cockerell, who (according to Robert Peter) had begun the recovery of his office by improperly obtaining custody of the old pells records;[1] he also attacked Felton. Most interesting is the story with which he concludes. In the previous Michaelmas term, lord treasurer Winchester had declared in full court that the departures from the ancient course had resulted in nothing but abuse and had sworn that he would have it reintroduced 'or else he would give up his staff and leave his office'. However, he was blocked by his own chancellor of the Exchequer, Sir John Baker, with whom he appears to have been on bad terms – Baker who (our writer says) calls himself by the new-fangled name of undertreasurer. Winchester, when 'at great contentation' with him, had been heard to assure his underofficer that before Henry VII there was no better title than treasurer's clerk. Anyway, Baker managed to persuade the Queen that Winchester was merely working off his resentment over certain land sales which he had opposed, and she would not permit the restoration of the discarded rolls.

This story throws some light on the history of the Receipt in the first ten years of Elizabeth, when there is otherwise little evidence. All we know is that in the three years 9–11 Elizabeth (1567–9) the issue roll suddenly reappeared.[2] It therefore looks as though, with Baker and Queen Mary gone (they both died in 1558), Winchester got his way in the end. That he was acting on behalf of his special servant, Robert Hare, is also clear enough. Peter later told how Hare 'revived' the issue roll: he borrowed from the writer of the tallies the fully audited tellers' accounts and copied them into a parchment roll which he then pretended was the true record of payments made.[3] 'This he did to make a show of some service in respect of the great allowances that he a little before had procured.' Hare, in fact, got his fee increased from the traditional £17 10s. to £67 13s. 4d.,[4] and the tally writers thereafter maintained that that increase was granted to pay for the labour

---

[1] E 407/71 (unnumbered), Peter's memo. of January 1584.
[2] E 403/858–60.   [3] E 407/71 (unnumbered).
[4] BM, Lansd. 28, fo. 2.

and costs of an issue roll the making of which was again abandoned in 1572 without any surrender of fee. What they did not stress was that in the same year they too obtained an increase of £50, to raise their salary to £91 13s. 4d.[1] Having got his extra fee, Hare allegedly sold the office 'at the best' to Chidiock Wardour. The charge was therefore that Hare had artificially inflated its value in order to get a good price; it is very probably true and explains something about Wardour's immediate and never-ending endeavours to get the most for and out of his purchase.

The real war began with Wardour's appointment to the pells in April 1570, coming as it did on top of Peter's succession as auditor to the colourless Humphrey Skelton (July 1569): and its first stage lasted from 1570 to 1584, when Wardour secured a favourable verdict from a committee of Exchequer officials. Many of the vast number of memoranda are hard to date, a difficulty aggravated by Skinner's habit of scribbling marginalia against his predecessor's papers when he was constructing minutes of his own out of them. But the arguments were nearly always the same, with minor variations, and it will be as well to summarize the main ones here. Until 1597 things turned in the main on Wardour's demand that the pell of issue be restored, though he kept a few lesser hares (custody of records, matters of fees, the making out of certificates of payments, etc.) running with his leading entry. A fair summary of his position is found in a document which belongs to shortly after 1584 but clearly adds nothing new to what he must have put forward in the previous dozen years.[2] This begins by stating that 'there ought to be two principal records kept daily in the Receipt of her majesty's Exchequer', a 'pell of introitus' or receipt and one of 'exitus' or issue. The former records all money paid in, from whom and for what cause and on what day it was received, and the name of the teller who took it. The latter should record all payments of fees, annuities, pensions, rewards or other money, with details of day, cause and warrant, as well as all money paid on imprest. The officer responsible for keeping these records is the lord treasurer's clerk, otherwise now called clerk of the pells of receipt and issue, an office dating back to Henry II. Wardour thus claimed to be the true heir of the clerk mentioned in the *Dialogus de Scaccario*. Skinner's marginal note against this sums up the repeated arguments of Peter and himself: the old treasurer's clerk was 'superintendent over all the officers and under-ministers of the Receipt' and was in the sixteenth

---

[1] Ibid.   [2] E 407/71/51. It has later marginal notes by Skinner.

century really represented by the undertreasurer. That this is correct has already been shown. But we have also seen that conservative practice preserved a nomenclature in the early-Tudor records which gave some colour to Wardour's claim by seeming to equate his office with that of the undertreasurer.[1] Nevertheless, it can be said at once that Wardour's desire to inherit the office of lord treasurer's clerk *par excellence* was at best a piece of mistaken antiquarianism. Peter was fond of pointing out also that Wardour's office was properly clerk of the pell, only Wardour himself having invented the plural (a point I have been unable to establish); from this Peter argued that the writing of the issue roll had never been part of his duties. In the declaration of receipts and issues which Robert Hare rendered in 1568, the clerk called himself the treasurer's clerk, but another hand on the cover described him as *clericus pellis*.[2] It is in truth hard to discover who wrote the fifteenth-century issue rolls; there were then three under-clerks on the treasurer's side in the Receipt who no doubt divided the actual work between themselves.[3]

Wardour went on to state that he kept the receipt roll, though Peter's jealousy prevented him from making it perfect: the tellers received money and tallies were cut that were never brought to his notice. Against this Skinner noted another standard reply of the tally writer's: the receipt roll, which had used to be written day by day in court and kept locked up when the court was not in session, was now being copied from rough notes and entirely open to falsification. As for the issue roll, Wardour complained that it had been totally discontinued 'without cause, warrant, or order', which left the payments in the sole control of one man – 'so as her majesty for the state of her treasure is subject to the particular honesty of the said Mr Peter'. He then went on to claim the rights of his office which he rested on the title conferred by his patent which described him as *clericus thesaurarii ad scribendas pelles recepti et exitus*. Here he touched on a tricky point. That his patent ran this way was admitted, but Peter asserted that Hare's patent, the precedent for Wardour's, had been altered from standard form. He ascribed this to Hare's influence over Winchester in his declining years.[4] Cockerell's, certainly, said nothing of the issue roll.[5] In this connection the admissions registered in the Black Book of the Receipt are of some assistance. There is no mention of the issue roll

[1] Above, p. 360.
[2] E 405/379.
[3] Kirby, *EHR* 72, 668.
[4] E 407/71/75.
[5] Ibid. no. 18.

after its cessation until Richard Browne came to be admitted on 11 February 1550 when a later hand inserted ' & de exitu' above the line in a record which originally spoke only of the receipt roll.[1] Cockerell was admitted 'ad officium scriptoris pellis',[2] but in Hare's case the traditional formula was again amended by the later addition of '& de exitu', and for Wardour the full duties of keeping both rolls were carefully noted.[3] Of course, when he took office the issue roll had temporarily been revived. But there seems no doubt that Hare and Wardour deliberately saw to the inclusion of the issue roll in the latter's patent (and probably tampered with the Black Book as well), so that Wardour's reliance on his patent was at best the exploitation of a prepared line of attack. Peter once analysed his rival's patent for the lord treasurer's benefit: it entitled him to call himself treasurer's clerk, to write tallies and enter them in the receipt and issue roll, to put the seals to the bags of money, to oversee the Receipt and know all things there, to be responsible for supplying its financial needs. (That is to say, it granted the office of the thirteenth-century treasurer's clerk.) In this way, Peter went on, 'he seeketh to intrude' on the undertreasurer's title, on the writer of the tallies, on the ushers, on the undertreasurer's duties twice over, and even on the lord treasurer who would not do without a warrant what Wardour here arrogated to himself in his patent. He concluded that the patent was therefore void.[4] But there could be no question that, however they had got it out of Winchester, Hare and Wardour had staked a strong claim. Their office was in Winchester's gift, and Skinner had cause to note at the end of one of Wardour's plaints the dubious ' Quere whether an office being in the gift of a superior the grantor may alter the form from the ancient grants'.[5]

The question – to which the answer surely is, yes, he may – was the more serious because the writer of the tallies could not usefully rely on his patent which granted him nothing but the writing of tallies.[6] He was therefore inclined to fall back on his oath of office and on lists of duties performed in the past. But the latter – though they might be used to justify his taking more fees than Wardour[7] – could not con-

---

[1] E 36/266/73.   [2] Ibid. fo. 74b.   [3] Ibid. fos. 75b, 78.
[4] E 407/71/16.   [5] Ibid. no. 51: dorse of last sheet.
[6] Ibid.: several examples cited by Wardour without comment from Skinner.
[7] This was the purpose of the list in E 407/71/79. Others (ibid. nos. 14 and 45) recorded Peter's office work. He made (1) a book of entry in which he personally entered all tellers' bills; (2) an entry book of payments in which he entered transcripts of the treasurer's warrants; (3) the equivalent of a year's entries in that he wrote all orders for

stitute a title, and so everything turned on the oath.[1] By this he swore
to write tallies; to help discharge accounts 'according to the ancient
custom of this court'; to make declarations of all receipts and payments
to the lord treasurer and undertreasurer; and to have a special care and
charge of the treasury of the Receipt, the main record depository of the
Crown where treaties and other important state documents were kept.
On the second and third of these promises the writer rested his claim
to audit the tellers' accounts and act as the general link between the
head-officers and the Receipt. Wardour had much formal right on his
side when he maintained that 'all men are officers by their patents and
admittances and not by their oaths'.[2] Peter could only protest, un-
convincingly, that his office 'by the grant of the lord treasurer is *ad
scribenda tallia et contratallia, ac ad facienda et exercenda omnia alia que ad
officium predictum pertinent*, the which by mine oath is explained': the
oath justified the vast expansion of activities which the phrase *omnia
alia* was perhaps intended to cover.[3] Since Wardour had cited patents
of the tally writers (and a copy of Skinner's survives),[4] it seems mere
subterfuge on Peter's part to pretend that his case was one of those
where an office was granted by a superior officer for life and without
patent; in such cases, he claimed, Exchequer practice was to regard
oath and admittance as perfect definitions.[5] In any case, Wardour had
a larger argument against the oath: he charged Felton with having
deliberately torn it out of the Black Book and replaced the missing
sheet with a new one on which he had written an oath of his own
devising.[6] This charge Peter evaded rather than refuted by showing
evidence that earlier predecessors of his had done all the things which
in his own oath he had sworn to do.[7] An inspection of the Black Book
suggests that Wardour was right,[8] but the point is not material. At

payment himself; (4) a half-yearly audit of the tellers' accounts; (5) half-year books of
views (views of tellers' accounts); (6) translations into Latin of all dormant privy seals,
entered in a ledger in the office; (7) a book of annuities and fees on which debentures
were based; (8) payments by assignment engrossed on parchment and added to the
tellers' accounts yearly; (9) paper drafts, transcribed into a ledger by his clerks, of prests
which were engrossed and delivered to the queen's remembrancer; (10) two entry books
of patents and privy seals for payments; (11) a weekly certificate to the lord treasurer
of receipts, payments, and remain, a matter so secret it could not be delegated to a clerk.
[1] Transcribed in E 407/71/79.
[2] This, he said, Peter was told by the chief baron: ibid. no. 51.
[3] Ibid., unnumbered.   [4] Above, p. 361.
[5] E 407/71 (unnumbered).   [6] Ibid. no. 51; BM, Lansd. 106, fo. 4.
[7] E 407/71 (unnumbered).
[8] E 36/266/98, which contains the oaths of both the writer of the tallies and the clerk
of the pells, looks to have been glued into the book. The two oaths, each at the head of

most Felton found it necessary, perhaps under instruction, to revise the oath in accordance with changing practice, and practice had changed because of far-reaching reforms in the Receipt which unfortunately had been carried through without regard to bureaucratic record and precision.

In the document which has guided us so far, Wardour followed his exposition of the old course and his list of helpful precedents by what he himself called his demands. He wanted the custody of all warrants for payment, claiming that he could produce in his office his predecessors' warrants down to the first year of Henry VIII. This, of course, once again ignored more recent developments: in 1576, one of the tellers told Sir Walter Mildmay that privy seals and accounts 'ever remained with the auditor of the Receipt' who by an order of Sir Richard Sackville's (chancellor of the Exchequer 1558–66) always got all warrants because he alone knew which teller had enough money to pay them.[1] Wardour wished to make the weekly reports of payments, revenue and reserves which, according to him, had been the clerk's duty till Peter filched it from him in 1572. He wanted to enrol patents and warrants, with allowance for so doing, to sign debentures to the tellers (with allowance), and to make constats for prest money and for 'tallies missing or not joined'.[2] In other words, he demanded that after the restoration of the issue roll he should be equipped with independent powers not only to share in controlling the transactions of the Receipt but also to supersede the writer of the tallies. He reminded the lord treasurer that his office was 'a clerk's office that maketh a special record for her majesty's service . . . and that Mr Peter's office is but a single office that maketh no record . . . And by this ground of truth your lordship may easily judge what right he hath to the fees he now taketh so far exceeding mine. . . .' Wardour constantly claimed to be fighting for the proper functions of his office, for the Queen's service, and for safeguards against peculation; as constantly, his mind was really fixed on increasing the income of his office by either duplicating, or preferably by taking from the auditor, such duties as carried fees payable by the public.

This document was drawn up after 1584, but the same demands

---

the page (fos. 98 and 98*b*) are written in a fifteenth-century Exchequer hand, which could of course be a deliberate copy. Underneath each there are entries in a mid-sixteenth-century hand. Fo. 97 is later in purport than 98; fos. 99 ff. contain pre-Tudor entries.   [1] E 407/71/26.

[2] Constats were certificates from the Lower to the Upper Exchequer, testifying to the receipt of a payment.

and arguments were clearly being pressed on Burghley between 1572 and 1584. In January of this latter year Peter produced a counter-statement in which he made no very good historical case for himself (since he was a necessary innovation, there could hardly be one) but convincingly disproved Wardour's claim to be the true treasurer's clerk.[1] In another paper he stated some of the fees he took, to show that Wardour was thirsting after a poorish brew.[2] At some time or other he put together the auditor's four standard arguments against reviving the pell of issue.[3] The pell had been replaced by better and more significant records in the form of the annual 'Declarations' and the half-yearly engrossed tellers' accounts, all produced or audited by the writer of the tallies; the revival of the pell, involving necessarily the revival of the chamberlains' counterpells, would acquaint too wide a range of officials with the state of her majesty's finances; the clerk of the pells having got an increment for keeping the issue roll, the chamberlains' deputies would also seek one, to the detriment of the Queen's service;[4] since the pell would be written (as Hare's antics had proved) from the audited tellers' accounts, it would serve no purpose whatsoever.

Although the writer was of course pleading a case, it should be admitted that it was a good one administratively. This, however, availed him little in the face of official conservatism. Sometime in the 1570s Burghley was told by an officer connected with the chamberlains' side in the Exchequer that Peter was monopolizing the work of the Receipt and earning good money from it, while Wardour did little and got little; the informant, though satisfied that the system recorded receipts accurately enough, thought payments too much in Peter's sole control and therefore asked for a return to the old course.[5] About 1580–1, Burghley asked Mildmay, as chancellor of the Exchequer, and Sir Roger Manwood, chief baron, to investigate Wardour's complaints; their report does not survive but, according to Peter, found for the tally writer.[6] Wardour was not deterred; his long memoranda continued, and on 21 January 1584 he secured a hearing by a committee

---

[1] E 407/71 (unnumbered).

[2] Ibid. no. 79. He claimed that his fees amounted to just over £40 a year, no doubt an underestimate. The subject of fees, too big for a footnote, deserves the separate treatment it shall have elsewhere.

[3] E.g. ibid. no. 17 which seems to belong to the early part of the reign.

[4] At other times the increased charges to the public were also used against the whole notion.   [5] BM, Lansd. 106, fos. 18–20.

[6] Hist. MSS Com. *Salisbury*, iv. 455 ff.

of Exchequer officials which reported greatly to his liking.[1] He went well prepared, with a list of precedents and arguments,[2] and the officials were entirely overwhelmed by his historical learning. They informed the treasurer that Wardour was clerk of both pells and Peter only writer of the tallies. They wished the issue roll to be restored, no tally to pass until entered in the pell and counterpells of receipt, the money to be in the chamberlains' charge. In fact, they wished to go right back behind Henry VII's reforms, and their loving preference for the full security of the ancient course promised to clog the machinery of a modern state by devices of extreme complexity and slowness. On fees, they judiciously recommended an equal division between the contending clerks. With regard to two of Wardour's more outrageous complaints, however, they were less single-minded: the keys of the treasury belonged to neither officer by right and could be assigned by the lord treasurer as he pleased, and if the queen's remembrancer chose, at the end of each term, to confer with Peter rather than anyone else about outstanding debts, that was his business. The remaining seven points dealt with a variety of practices in the office – the checking of the tellers' accounts, the keeping of warrants, the making of certificates of payment, and the like – on all of which the committee on the whole took Wardour's view, though they leant towards giving both officers a half-share in the work so that one might control the other. All told, therefore, they recommended the revival of the pell of issue, a return to stricter and much more cumbersome procedure, and the strengthening of the pells office as against the auditor's.

Peter at once riposted with a statement addressed to the lord treasurer which once again recited the work of his office and produced the evidence which, he said, had been put before the committee but ignored by them.[3] This consisted of the testimony of certain old and experienced officers of the Receipt.[4] William Walter, a man of nearly eighty who had entered the department in 1533 and served as a deputy chamberlain under three undertreasurers,[5] deposed that all that time

---

[1] A copy of the report exists: BM, Lansd. 171, fos. 356–7b. The committee were: Manwood (chief baron), Robert Shute (baron), John Sotherton (foreign apposer; later baron), Thomas Fanshawe (queen's remembrancer), Peter Osborn (lord treasurer's remembrancer), Thomas Morison (auditor). They sat for several days and 'heard at length all that Mr Wardour and Mr Peter did speak or show'.

[2] BM, Lansd. 106, fos. 4–6.   [3] Hist. MSS Com. *Salisbury*, iv. 455 ff.

[4] Peter briefly summarizes it; it was later used again by Skinner and survives in greater detail from that occasion: E 407/71/96.

[5] Alleged to be Wyatt, Weston and Baker, but Wyatt was never undertreasurer. If Walter's service began in 1533 he came in under Weston.

Mr Danyell was chief officer next to the undertreasurer, taking the tellers' accounts, making certificates and declarations, keeping tellers' bills and accounts, keeping the warrants and the keys to the treasury. Uvedale's 'substitute', his son-in-law Gilbert Claydon, did nothing but write. the pell of receipt. Thomas Burrow, in the Receipt these forty years since he was fifteen, a deputy chamberlain from 1545 to the present day, said much the same. In Danyell's time the pell was at the day's end committed to Danyell and the chamberlains' deputies for safe keeping, 'which pell I very well also remember was by Mr Cockerell through the favour of the old lord treasurer in Queen Mary's time got to be kept by himself', since which time it was neither written in public nor kept in indifferent hands, as it used to be. As for fees, he only remembered that Danyell and Felton used to take the lot 'and pay the clerk of the pell a part', giving him much less than they kept for themselves. William Stanton, who had been first a teller's and later Cockerell's clerk, confirmed this and added that Cockerell had failed in an attempt to gain 'some addition to his place' out of Felton. Others who spoke to the same effect included Richard Stonley, a teller since 1553 and by 1580 senior of the four.

All this only goes to show that the reign of Henry VIII, in part because of Uvedale's absence, had witnessed a great expansion of the tally writer's activities and power; on the whole it is plain that this expansion did not so much rob the clerk of the pells as result from the changes initiated by Henry VII – the new position of the tellers and the new need to have an officer to supervise them. Wardour was trying to capture at least some of the new ground, and the Exchequer committee took his side in part because they believed his precedents which identified the clerk of the pells with the old treasurer's clerk, and in part because the trained Exchequer mind distrusted any official who seemed to have sole control of any important section of the work.

Burghley, however, was less impressed. Whether he agreed with Peter that to revive the issue roll now would be to brand the auditor as a bad and inefficient servant, we cannot tell,[1] but at any rate he did nothing further in the matter. That did not stop Wardour, but it made him turn to another court of appeal. He began to petition the Queen. Outflanking Burghley in Exchequer matters can never have been an easy task, but the persistent clerk of the pells achieved it. The next stage of the business began on 5 August 1589, with a signet

[1] Hist. MSS Com. *Salisbury*, iv. 456.

warrant signed by the Queen at Nonsuch.[1] Peter later asserted that Wardour had got it by false charges of mismanagement in the Receipt to which he, unaware of these machinations, was never allowed to reply; he hoped Burghley would enlighten the Queen about the true state of affairs.[2] After telling her treasurer that 'we are given to understand by our servant Chidiock Wardour, gentleman, that there is yet no final orders set down by you to authorize him to keep our record called the pell of exitus' as anciently kept by his predecessors, Elizabeth ordered immediate steps to restore the pell to its 'pristine state'. Wardour accompanied this deceptively peremptory command with another long bill, received by Burghley on 22 November 1589, to which Peter made an answer.[3] Matters dragged on. On 5 June 1590 Peter produced yet another set of replies.[4] He suggested that if the Queen wanted an issue roll, she should at least be spared the cost of parchment (which would come to £40 a year), a useful point to put before her and one which Wardour could never stomach; even the receipt roll was 'no use but an expense of parchment'. By Burghley's recent instructions (of which we are otherwise ignorant) Wardour was empowered to obtain a copy of the order and acquittance after payment, which was enough to secure a cross-check; his demand for enrolment of the order in the pells office before payment was made offended custom and had nothing in mind but gain and spite. All his ideas only tended 'to division and delays'. *Clericus pellium* was found in no record; he was appointed to write the one pell of receipt and should stop thinking of himself as the successor to the *clericus thesaurarii*. Wardour had apparently suggested that patentees and annuity holders should obtain a quarterly writ of *mandamus* for their instalments; Peter justly remarked on the burden this would be to them and defended the existing system with its dormant *liberate* kept by himself and its regular debentures made by himself for each payment.[5] As for debentures being a dangerous innovation, the only innovation would be to accede to Wardour's request that none should issue without his inspection and signature.

Peter's comments on a draft set of articles prepared by Wardour for Burghley's signature and sent to his rival for his views were equally

---

[1] E 407/71/53, a copy in Wardour's hand. There is no doubt that he submitted a warrant drawn by himself for the signet and sign manual.   [2] Ibid. no. 65.

[3] Hist. MSS Com. *Salisbury*, xiii. 417.

[4] E 407/71/77.

[5] Peter's papers are full of requests for debentures and orders from the holders of pensions and annuities: E 407/72-6.

clear-cut.¹ The articles would have restored the issue roll; subjected payments out of the Receipt to the control of the clerk of the pells; arranged for the sharing of fees paid for debenture (Peter: 'that which is given in this respect is voluntary and is so small as is not fit to be apportioned'); authorized Wardour to audit the tellers' accounts; and ordered that all constats or certificates of money received at the Receipt (needed in audit) should rest on the pell and not on the documents retained by the writer of the tallies. A particularly devastating last paragraph reserved Wardour's right to renounce his compromise with Peter when a new writer of the tallies should succeed, a claim which Peter rightly described as prejudicial to the powers of the lord treasurer. But the tide would for the moment not be resisted. On 7 December 1590 the head-officers issued a tentative set of articles largely based on Wardour's, on which Peter again commented.² For clarity's sake, and so as for once to get the full flavour of this business, it will be best to follow the orders through by the numbers they bear in the document.

1. Wardour is to keep a pell of issue. – Peter: This will cost the Queen a lot, especially as the chamberlains will raise similar demands next.

2. No payment except of regular fees and annuities is to be made without special warrant signed by the lord treasurer and undertreasurer, which order (written by Peter but addressed to him and Wardour jointly) shall specify which teller shall pay; no teller shall make payment until the order is entered on the pell. – Peter: This will cause 'manifest delay . . . abridging wholly the power of the tellers', and all this just to satisfy Wardour's desire for superiority.

3. All patents, privy seals and warrants, though remaining with Peter, are to be registered with Wardour. – Peter: The delay will be much disliked by patentees.

4. Debentures are to be signed by both Peter and Wardour, provided that neither delay nor new fees are thereby incurred. – Peter: What value is there in Wardour's signature since he has no materials against which to check the debentures?

¹ E 407/71/8. These purport to be articles made on a date left blank by Burghley and John Fortescue (who succeeded Mildmay in 1589) in response to the signet letter of August 1589. They were drawn up by Wardour and have marginal notes by Peter.
² E 407/71/52, a set of articles with marginal notes by Peter; ibid. no. 65, Peter's counter-suit of 14 Dec. 1590 in which he attacked the articles.

5. The tellers are to cast orders and acquittances[1] into the Receipt for entry with the clerk of the pells who shall afterwards redeliver these documents to them. – Peter: The effect of this is contained in Art. 2.

6. No teller is to make payments without Wardour's knowledge; if he does he shall be liable to the Queen for the money; provided no delay is caused by the pells office. – Peter: This must cause delay, as well as great danger to any tellers who act 'for the more speedy furtherance of her highness' said service'.

7. Wardour is to examine the tellers' books every half year against the pells, and also weekly for his weekly report. – Peter: He cannot do any good because he has neither the tellers' bills[2] by which 'they are and will be charged' nor the warrants by which they are discharged.[3]

8. Constats and certificates are to be made by either Peter or Wardour, as the officer requiring such documents shall choose. – Peter: This belongs to my office; I cannot submit to an article which 'toucheth my office both in credit and profit so near'. The 'simplicity of Mr Wardour is such' that he cannot understand how well protected payments are by the system of warranty in operation.

9. These orders are at once to cease if it be proved that they cause any delay or new charge, or an imposition on the Queen's subjects. To this point was added a further proviso, protesting that no fee was to be taken from any officer who had so far enjoyed it; this was drafted separately and annotated by Burghley himself – 'It is not meet to make any change of these things so claimed by him'.[4]

Even without Peter's vigorous protests, Article 9 really disposed of these orders. It did not need Peter to prove to Burghley that another parchment roll could hardly be produced without some cost to the Queen, and even if one could believe that all this red tape would lead to no delays in the transaction of business, it is hard to see how Wardour could have his greater share of the fees if Peter lost nothing and the public paid no more. In fact, the orders of December 1590 were never signed, and Wardour's great assault of 1589–90 was beaten off. But

---

[1] I.e. the orders to pay received from Peter, and the acquittances signed by the parties paid.

[2] The parchment certificate recording receipt of money which the teller cast down through a trunk into the Receipt and with which the whole accounting process began.

[3] In the department's technical language, 'charging' meant only demanding an account of money received of which proof of payment-in existed, and 'discharging' only allowing payments-out for which proof was supplied. Peter's point was that the tellers would not admit the authority of any records which Wardour controlled.

[4] E 407/71/39.

since he had got so far with Elizabeth by persuading her that all was
not well in the Receipt while its auditor had sole control, we ought,
before turning to Peter's counterattack and the troubles of Vincent
Skinner, to see what can be discovered of conditions in the office. The
overriding question is whether the tellers, in charge of all the Queen's
money, were really sufficiently supervised or liable to run off the rails.
As one would expect, there are some indications that things were not
always as they should have been. In 1555, for instance, Sir Robert
Rochester, controller of the Household, was engaged with one of the
tellers in trying to alleviate the chronic financial difficulties of the
Household.[1] He hoped the teller would not be blamed for letting
certain money go out of his hand and promised that 'for as much
money as you deliver unto Mr Cofferer I shall save you harmless'. But
though it is impossible to reconstruct the whole affair from one short
letter, it looks as though the difficulties in question were caused by the
needs of the royal service, not in defiance of them. More suspicious is
a letter from Robert Tailor, teller, to Sir Walter Mildmay, of 9 April
1576.[2] Mildmay was angry with Tailor for not keeping his entry books
properly and failing to record the terms of the warrants on which he
had paid in the past; to this Tailor replied that he had not had any
privy seals but only orders from the lord keeper and 'my lord treasurer
that now is then being secretary[3] (the old lord treasurer and Sir Richard
Sackville signing these orders)'. This was certainly irregular, but Tailor
was sure that no harm had been done; he had 'made the less haste' to
put the books straight (they had been locked up with Peter for five or
six years) because he knew that no cheating had taken place. Now he
would go at once and complete the entries 'according to our orders in
the Receipt'. If no harm was done, it was still very unsatisfactory that
the apparently foolproof rules could cover up some very irregular
practice, though it should be noted that the trouble dated back before
Peter's time to the ascendancy of Robert Hare and the dotage of lord
treasurer Winchester. Still, it is not surprising to find that as soon as
they got their hands on the controls, in the Easter term 1572, Burghley
and Mildmay drew up some stringent orders for the tellers.[4]

Tailor was once more in trouble in 1588 when one of his clerks, one
Raven, robbed a money chest.[5] He did this by only pretending to
turn the key in Peter's presence, so that the chest remained open

---

[1] Rochester to Brigham, 9 Oct. 1555: E 407/72.
[2] E 407/71/23.   [3] Burghley.
[4] E 36/266/80–80b.   [5] Tailor to Burghley, 23 Sept. 1588: SP 12/216/art. 35.

even when the auditor had the key. But it appears that Tailor himself had been in the habit of using the Queen's money for his own purposes, though he had always put it back in time; he begged Burghley to distinguish between Raven's 'horrible practice' and his own 'over-boldness', promised to make the loss good, and only hoped the Queen would not have to be told until at least part had been repaid. In the same year, the senior teller, Richard Stonley, got obscurely into Burghley's bad books; there appears to have been a deficiency in his office, and he was forbidden, through Peter, to make any payments till the matter was cleared up.[1] These are surely disquieting pointers, but if things had been seriously wrong in so long a period of time one would expect more and worse instances. Moreover it is quite clear that the lord treasurer was throughout content to rely on Peter to manage the Receipt for him, and that he had no cause to regret his trust. There survive quite a few of Burghley's and his undertreasurers' orders to the auditor which simply entrust him with finding the money for often important business of state;[2] one paper shows how an order signed by the head-officers would bear a signed note from Peter allocating the payment to a teller chosen by himself.[3] Though things were not altogether perfect in the Receipt, they were – especially by sixteenth-century standards – remarkably good, and the writer of the tallies carried out his heavy duties well.

Minor irregularities of course occurred. The lord privy seal's clerk once wrote in some agitation to demand back a privy seal for new assignments to Ireland, issued in error for a signet warrant which would permit the balance of a previous allocation to be spent.[4] Sir Henry Radcliffe, anxious to sail from Portsmouth and unable to get an order signed because Burghley and Mildmay were not together, asked Stonley for some money and gave him a letter authorizing him to set it against the next lot due.[5] A complicated situation arose when a teller refused to accept £25 from a collector of the 1589 privy seal loan on the grounds that the sum was too small; when the collector offered this excuse, Burghley growled that the teller 'would have taken it if it had been much less'.[6] But when pressed, the treasurer could himself

---

[1] Hist. MSS Com. *Salisbury*, iii. 377; iv. 401. The business thus lasted at least from 1588 to 1593.

[2] E.g. SP 12/199/art. 27; 12/239/128; 12/244/art. 114; Fortescue to Peter, 27 July 1591: E 407/76.   [3] BM, Egerton 895, fo. 4.

[4] Fr. Mylles to Peter, 19 Feb. 1578: E 407/74.

[5] Radcliffe to Peter, 27 Dec. 1575: E 407/73.

[6] John Brokettes to Peter, 11 Dec. 1589: E 407/72.

break the rules: in the middle of the Armada preparations he asked Peter to pay out £1,435 on his letters only and he would get a Council order later; a postscript reveals how much he depended on the civil servant for a knowledge of the detailed procedure: 'I pray you, certify me whether I am to have my warrant for payment hereof from the lords of the Council or from the officers of the Admiralty, that the same may be accordingly procured'.[1] Yet such anomalies really only confirm the general impression of an efficiently and honestly run department, of an administration firmly in control and enjoying the services of reliable officers.

This is supported by a lesser point which yet has some significance. Among the aspects of Elizabethan administration more obviously capable of being turned into a ramp, the widespread system of rewarding service or friendship by pensions and annuities out of the Exchequer was clearly one. The recipients, who usually got their money quarterly, normally lived far away from Peter's office at St Stephen's, Westminster, and in the conditions of the time one might expect to find money collected for dead men, and similar tricks. That this happened was hinted by Wardour and denied by Skinner.[2] No pension could be paid except on a debenture from the auditor who held the dormant writ authorizing it, and he soon refused to issue one without proof that the beneficiary was alive. The masses of certificates – ranging from solemn documents to a few roughly scrawled words – which survive among Peter's files testify to the rigour with which this order was carried out. It was in force by October 1574, and by October 1575 at the latest Peter would accept no certificate unless it was signed by two justices of the peace, though he could make an exception for a man whose handwriting he knew well. Some of the pensioners, sending in a note so signed every quarter, clearly got pretty tired of the necessity, but they complied. Peter was a good bureaucrat, and in his position it was better so for the state.[3]

---

[1] Burghley to Peter, 2 June 1588: E 407/76. In another ticklish situation, when money was to be paid for antipapist measures of which nothing must be known, a later treasurer (Buckhurst) was more careful: 'I will keep the privy seal myself and . . . no man shall know it but myself and Mr Chancellor, Mr Skinner and Mr Wardour, as all these of necessity must; but to pay her majesty's money without warrant of privy seal never was nor can be done, without an act of Parliament': SP 12/283/art. 69.

[2] E 407/71/92, 94.

[3] Evidence for the statements here made is scattered through the unnumbered documents in E 407/72-6. Some proofs were necessarily a little dubious: thus Walsingham testified on 16 March 1578 that one of his agents, Richard Cavendish, was alive on the previous 8 January when he had written from Heidelberg.

Thus Peter defended a sound position against Wardour, and if he was moved by some self-interest – less for the fees which were usually safeguarded even when reforms were contemplated than for his ascendancy in the Receipt – it is also true that he stood for an efficient and sensible system against a more blatant and vastly more pointless self-interest. In 1591 he had once more to spare time from his duties to draft long memoranda. First Wardour, waiting for the issue roll to be restored, initiated a comprehensive attack on Peter's fees, which angered Peter greatly: his restraint at last broke down in such phrases as 'this man careth not what he informeth', or that Wardour 'might have been satisfied in this his ignorance'. Peter asked 'that neither the tellers nor myself may be further troubled with him', which would benefit the Queen's service.[1] An idle hope: Wardour replied with all the old arguments about his descent from the medieval treasurer's clerk and the rest, and continued to appeal to the Queen's and Burghley's 'honourable justice' for a fairer division of the fees. Peter's comments referred the lord treasurer to his previous paper.[2] Wardour was especially hard on Peter's 'man', Edmund English ('who plays Friar Rush's part between us for fear of his downfall'). He maintained that quarterly debentures for pensions were an extortionate practice for English's benefit and that the tellers used to pay 'upon sight of the party'; yet, as we have seen, many pensioners could not come in person, and in such cases control by debentures was highly desirable. One wonders whether Burghley ever read these mountains of paper of which only an inkling can be given here. The business about fees was the last straw for Peter: in April 1591 he went over to the offensive with various charges against his tormentor.[3] Wardour had allegedly promised, in his suit to the Queen, that his proposals would cost nothing; but now he had increased his claims for stationery. He is enlarging his demands on fees. He says he is entitled to a penny of all fees taken by the tellers in excess of 4*d*., yet claims that anything over 4*d*. is extortionate. On 29 June 1591, Peter sent Burghley a formal petition in which he asked that Wardour's patent be revoked and reissued in a form more consonant with precedent; thus his encroachments on the lord treasurer, the undertreasurer, and the writer of the tallies would be stopped.[4] Nothing, of course, came of this, but at least as far as the evidence goes Peter was not troubled further for the

---

[1] Peter's reply to Wardour's charges, c. March 1591: E 407/71/103.
[2] Ibid. no. 71 (26 March 1591).   [3] Ibid. no. 37.
[4] Two copies: ibid. nos. 78 and 101.

two remaining years of his life. Though he had had to spend much more time than can have been convenient in beating off these attacks, he had not given an inch.

The succession of Vincent Skinner altered the situation for Wardour. On the one hand he now faced a foe – for the thought of giving up never entered his head – who knew little about the Receipt; the fact that Skinner diligently studied, annotated and used Peter's papers as the war progressed is proof of that.[1] On the other, Skinner was Burghley's particular servant and a man of higher social standing than Peter had been. Perhaps for this reason, Wardour did not immediately revive his demand for the restoration of the issue roll but first tested the ground upon the lesser issue of constats, a point which he had often raised before but on which he now concentrated his formidable fighting qualities. Constats (certificates of payments made into the Receipt) were something of an innovation and had grown out of the financial reforms between 1534 and 1554.[2] The old course of the Exchequer relied at the audit on the proof supplied by the joining of the tally brought by the accountant with the foil kept in the Exchequer. But the newer revenue incorporated in the Exchequer in 1554 – the accounts taken by the auditors of the land revenue and the auditors of the prests – did not proceed to this joining of tallies.[3] The accountant still brought the tally which he had obtained when paying the Queen's money into the Receipt, but the auditor did not seek out a foil from the chamberlains' custody; instead he required an independent note, a constat, from the writer of the tallies, certifying that the payment claimed had been made. Wardour now raised a double demand: constats should be made for all payments, even when tallies were joined, and the clerk of the pells should share in the business.[4] In order to defend what was a most obvious search for more money, Wardour seems to have argued that tallies – used without question for hundreds of years and always praised for their certainty – could be tampered with by enlarging of the notches; he told the story of one Lawson, a clerk

---

[1] In June 1595 Skinner sent Burghley a constat made by himself in response to Wardour's challenge 'to pose me with, as some elementary scholar and not so deeply seen in parchment as he': E 407/71/90.

[2] Cf. Skinner's statement in one of the papers composing a bundle concerning this stage of the dispute: E 407/71/77.

[3] E.g. in July 1579, E. Fetiplace, auditor, about to declare the accounts of the treasurer of Berwick before the lord treasurer and chancellor of the Exchequer, found that he had 'mislaid' Peter's constats which he required to prove his audit; he asked for new ones for which he would pay: E 407/73.

[4] For what follows cf. E 407/71/77, a collection of several papers by Skinner.

in the pipe office, who had thus conspired with one Langworth, collector of a subsidy. What he omitted in this story was that the fraud was discovered by the secondary of the pipe who in joining the tallies found that the notches did not match. In fact, as Skinner rightly pointed out, since no man could hope to falsify both tally and foil the system was entirely safe and required no cross checks.

Skinner continued to produce reasoned statements confuting Wardour's ever more extravagant claims and explaining convincingly that in the Receipt original documents rather than rolls – not necessarily made up at the time and often amended later – must be the fundamental record. Since Wardour was trying to acquire a duty which had, by good proof, always been carried out by the writer of the tallies, he could only hope to succeed by showing that his rolls, on which he proposed to rest his constats, were a better record than the tellers' bills used for the purpose by the writer; and this, Skinner said, he could not do. Burghley once again committed matters for investigation: on 12 February 1594 the chancellor of the Exchequer, the chief baron and others sat to hear the dispute. It was agreed that constats were not required when tallies were joined, this being only a cause of cost and delay; that constats were not 'of any long continuance' or 'antiquity'; and that the evidence pointed to Skinner as the proper officer to make them. But Skinner had still to learn about Wardour. This defeat in no way abashed him, and by October 1596 he had somehow obtained a letter from the Queen committing the making of constats to himself alone,[1] the result of which, according to Skinner, was delay and chaos in the passing of accounts. To illustrate the mess, and also the unreality of Wardour's position, he related what had happened on 18 October 1596 when the son and executor of the famous Mr Customer Smyth came to the exchequer to settle a debt of his father's alleged to be £3,000. He produced constats from Wardour to show that £2,400 of this had been paid as long ago as 1571. Thus he went to the Upper Exchequer, but since he no longer had those twenty-five-year old tallies he got an order for 'innovates' (new tallies struck to replace lost ones).[2] This necessitated the production of the old foils for destruction. Wardour's clerk entered the transaction in the

[1] E 407/71/33.
[2] When an accountant had lost any tallies he could make an affidavit before a baron of the Exchequer ('the ordinary use in such cases') and could obtain a writ from the Exchequer of Pleas authorizing the Receipt to issue 'innovate' tallies based on the foils in the Upper Exchequer. These foils were then destroyed and replaced by the innovate foils.

innovate roll, but when the new tallies were examined with this roll and with the old foils it was found that the entry in the roll differed from all the rest: where the correct form read 'pretextu obligationis', the roll had 'pretextu recognitionis'.[1] The clerk explained that he had remembered making the constats from the receipt roll and that there it stood 'recognitionis'; he had merely intended to keep the rolls in agreement. Upon this the chamberlains' deputies refused to deliver the tallies until the roll was amended: to them the old foil, not the receipt roll, was the true record. The clerk then cheerfully altered both rolls and also the constats. This, as Skinner said, threw a pretty murky light on Wardour's assertion that only his rolls were a good record in the Receipt. Yet the old campaigner, however bad his case and however much he bedevilled the running of the Receipt, knew his way about too well; he had won over constats and was about to win over the pell of issue.

On 24 March 1597, a privy seal, addressed to Burghley and Fortescue (chancellor of the Exchequer since 1589), expressed the Queen's desire that 'our ancient record, called the pell of exitus, be immediately restored'. It was to be written and kept by Wardour who was to have the necessary 'fees and commodities for the same', and the Queen's command was to be published to all the Exchequer.[2] This time there was to be no evasion and little delay, though on 28 May Skinner tried a last protest.[3] On 9 June Burghley presented the privy seal in the Exchequer court and ordered Wardour to revive the pell. On the 13th the writ was read again in open court, and on the 17th Fortescue commanded Thomas Agarde, deputy chamberlain, to have it published in the Receipt and entered in the Black Book there. This was done next day.[4] Triumphantly Wardour made up his first issue roll at Michaelmas 1597, putting – an unprecedented step – his own name in the superscription.[5] In his book of annual declarations, where hitherto he had been able to return receipts only, he wrote with glee: 'This was the first declaration that I made both of the Introitus and the Exitus.'[6] The long struggle seemed over: Wardour had achieved the real core of his war aims. However, wars are said never to settle

---

[1] Obligations – bonds given in respect of a future duty; recognizances – bonds recognizing an existing duty or debt.

[2] E 407/71/34, a copy in Skinner's hand.   [3] Ibid. no. 86.

[4] Ibid. no. 36, copy by Fanshawe from the memoranda roll, with Fortescue's holograph note to Agarde; E 36/266, fos. 94–94*b*, entry in the Black Book.

[5] E 403/865; neither the medieval rolls nor those of 1569–71 mentioned the name of the clerk of the pells at the top: ibid. 850, 858.   [6] E 405/243/138.

anything, and the restoration of the issue roll (kept thereafter until its final abolition exactly 200 years later),[1] proved to be only a stage in the conflict. On 23 June Skinner received Burghley's more detailed orders designed to take account of the new situation.[2] The clerk of the pells was to be given means of making his shared control felt: he was to enrol all warrants for payment, to have a direct hand in the issue of money by the tellers, to sign debentures together with the writer of the tallies, and to inspect the tellers' accounts. Skinner protested at once,[3] and things in a way returned to the embattled state.

As Wardour discovered soon enough, it was one thing to get the pell revived and another to wrest from the auditor a power of control established over eighty years of administration. Thus he resumed operations with yet another memorandum, once again sent to Skinner for comment, in which he demanded that no payment be made to the tellers without entry on the receipt roll, that payments follow the course established by Burghley's orders, that he be given a chance of enrolling all warrants, that prest money be certified by constats out of the pell and not otherwise, and that he be permitted to see the tellers' accounts.[4] Skinner swept these plaints aside by referring to the by now established practice and charging that Wardour's demands were only meant 'to give colour to the reviving of such a pell'. Wardour, in some despair now that his ends were ostensibly won without a reality in the victory, asked the lord treasurer to assist him in getting co-operation from Skinner and the tellers.[5] Then Skinner found an opportunity to draw attention to the consequences of Wardour's victories. The needs of war were again forcing the Crown to sell lands, and Wardour wanted the money so obtained to be recorded on the receipt roll and accounted for by tallies. Skinner argued that a muddle had been made in the recent changes when insufficient thought had been given to 'the difference grown by change of times'; in other words he was, quite rightly, pleading for a sensible understanding of the realities in preference to Wardour's kind of antiquarian researches.[6] In his opinion, the sales money was in the same category as the surplus paid into the Exchequer by the court of Wards and the Duchy of Lancaster which, it had been decided, should not pass by tally because

---

[1] The roll was never again a serious record, being made up at leisure from rough books kept in court. These books continued to the abolition of the Exchequer in 1834: M. S. Giuseppi, *Guide to the Public Records*, i. 184 ff. [2] E 407/71/12.

[3] A badly mutilated letter from Skinner to Burghley's clerk Maynard, 26 June 1597: E 407/71/59. [4] E 407/71/63.

[5] Ibid. no. 88. [6] Ibid. no. 20.

those departments had nothing to do with the course of the Exchequer and tallies were not recognized by their auditors.[1] Money from sales and loans appeared in the tellers' accounts and the tellers were charged by confession and acquittance, 'the two usual, ordinary and only means of charging any accountants in any courts her majesty hath besides the Exchequer'. Since the tellers would not accept a charge based on the rolls and would recognize only their own bills, acquittances and accounts, there was no point in entering in the rolls any transactions not designed to lead to the joining of tallies.

Not content with restricting Wardour to the least important part of the Exchequer's work, Skinner, deprived after 1598 of his old master Burghley, tried to get the new treasurer, Buckhurst, to see how disastrous the 1597 reforms had been.[2] He renewed the old plea that the existence of the pell gave too many people a chance to know the state of the Queen's finances. Perhaps discouraged by the change of treasurer he offered to resign: 'wherein that I make thus bold to enlarge myself I humbly crave pardon and beseech you to consider that as I only served in one house so I never sought dependence elsewhere'. But the threat was not real; the next year, when Wardour suddenly renewed the war, found Skinner alert at his post.

Wardour had by this time clearly decided that his victory of 1597 was hollower than he had supposed; alternatively one may see him determined, after consolidating his bridgehead, to break out into Skinner-held territory beyond. At any rate he launched a fresh attack on 10 July 1600 which included matters both new and familiar. As usual, they were replied to, point for point, by Skinner.[3] Wardour first asked the head-officers fully to define the spheres of the two disputing officers. As to this, Skinner produced much history. Though Wardour seems to have agreed that events since Henry VII's reign favoured his rival, he rested his case on the earlier precedents. Skinner pointed out that even in the fifteenth century some men had been promoted from Wardour's office to his, which showed clearly whose was the more important; he drove the point home by citing respective

[1] Cf. Edmund English to Edward Latymer, 13 June 1598: SP 46/25/241–2. English could not remember that any tally ever passed for Wards' or Duchy money paid into the Exchequer by the Queen's warrant, the only (and sufficient) record being the teller's bill which remained with Mr Peter. He advised Latymer that a tally was only necessary if expressly demanded in the warrant, but that he would now have to get the bill registered in the pell as well as with Skinner.

[2] E 407/71/60, 7 July 1599.

[3] E 407/71/57, an abstract of the articles submitted by Wardour to Burghley and Fortescue; ibid. nos. 55, 75, 98, three papers embodying Skinner's answers.

salaries, the granting of rewards for special work, and payments by the Crown for assistant clerks in the writer's office while none were allowed to the clerks of the pells. An interesting addition to these recurring arguments gives some indication of the effect which the Exchequer reforms of 1554 had had on the Receipt.[1] Wardour, of course, could not accept an exposition which rested the auditor's superiority on the developments of the last century. Yet while he may have had some ancient and dubious precedents on his side, he was in a real sense the innovator because he was trying to get control of business that at the time of his precedents had not existed.

Others among Wardour's points are also only too familiar. Once again we hear that he has a claim to the custody of privy seals, certificates and other working papers of the Receipt; that constats for prests should be made out of the pell; that patents for pensions must be registered with him; that the tellers must certify him at once of their receipts and payments so that he can render the weekly certificate which now he wants to make side by side with the auditor's; that he wants to keep the entry book in which the weekly orders for payment from the head-officers were registered. Skinner's replies, to the effect that all this work is and ought to be his, are equally familiar. Two of Wardour's demands broke new ground. He wanted an authoritative ruling on the custody of all bonds and obligations taken in the Receipt, to which Skinner returned that such bonds for payments as were kept there had to be in the keeping of the tellers because from the accounting point of view the bonds were treated as cash and charged to the tellers at their account. Lastly, and very outrageously, Wardour suddenly claimed that debentures were more properly issued by his office than by Skinner's. Since debentures were in effect introduced by the writer of the tallies, Skinner was rightly contemptuous of the claim. It seems, however, than in the bad years in the middle of the century there had been some lapses when tellers had paid annuities without debentures, with the result that Mr Lichfield, under Burghley's instructions, recovered some lost money for the Queen;[2] then Peter revived debentures and all was well.

[1] Ibid. no. 98: 'when the court of Augmentations was dissolved and united to the exchequer, as the matters fell out most properly pertinent some were distributed into Mr Fanshawe's office [queen's remembrancer], some to the pipe office, some to other places. And the books of enrolments of letters patent for grants of fees and annuities were delivered over to mine office, and nothing to his.'

[2] Cf. BM, Lansd. 28, fos. 2–3, for a fragment of evidence relating to Lichfield's investigations in 1579.

It does not appear that Buckhurst listened to Wardour on this occasion, for about a year later, on 27 June 1601, the indefatigable clerk was at it again.[1] His last bill repeated the points about the spheres of office, obligations, custody of privy seals, enrolling of patents, the weekly certificate, and debentures; on all this Skinner's replies, too, added nothing fresh. There is perhaps a little less disguising in Wardour's memorandum of his real desire – fees – and a little more exasperation in Skinner's. Wardour had also thought up one new complaint. Since, he says, he now has to attend at the Receipt as much as the other officers (itself a consequence of his campaign), he wants a part of the house occupied by Skinner and the tellers. He argued that the building – St Stephen's[2] – must be big enough to hold them all because in Peter's time even Mildmay had had offices in it. Skinner was highly indignant: the house was 'little enough for his own use for the service of her majesty and the matters that concern his office, and but competent and necessary for receipt of his family [staff]'. It was true that Mildmay had used it, but he had had the 'help of some other rooms' and had never brought in the sort of numbers contemplated by Wardour. By this time Skinner must have been even fuller of the sort of despair he had described to Robert Cecil two years earlier: 'The distraction I have had about quarrels to my place have hindered me much and now so utterly discouraged me that the service I intended to have done I could not. . . .'[3] Still, so far he had prevented Wardour from ruining the efficiency of the Receipt by making a reality of the revived pell of issue.

But the head-officers were still thinking things over. On 28 October 1601, the lord treasurer, chancellor, chief baron, and the other barons heard what Wardour, Skinner, and their learned counsel had to say, and on 1 February 1602 Buckhurst and Fortescue alone once more went over the ground with the two disputants. Then, on 26 February, they at last produced a large parchment of orders. The war had drifted into an exhaustion where arbitration could take over, and these orders endured.[4]

1. All bonds in the Receipt to be taken by Skinner and enrolled by Wardour, each of them taking 2*s*. per bond.

[1] E 407/71/56 and 92, Wardour's articles; ibid. 94 and 95, two drafts of Skinner's answers.
[2] Described in a letter of W. Fitzwilliam to Peter, 2 Dec. 1577, as 'beside the Star Chamber stair': E 407/74.
[3] Skinner to Cecil, 7 July 1599: SP 12/271/177.
[4] E 407/75. The heading to this paper describes the history of meetings and hearings.

2. Privy seals to be enrolled in the pells office but to be kept by 'him who shall have the custody of the tellers' accounts' (that is, the auditor). No fees for copies, except 'where it tendeth to the private and particular benefit of the subject', when both may take 3*s*. 4*d*. for the copy and the enrolment respectively.

3. The tellers not to make payment on any order before it is entered in the issue roll, but orders as hitherto to be made by Skinner.

4. Both officers to render independent certificates of all imprest money every Trinity term.

5. Constats for imprest money to be made by either, as the officer accountable shall choose; patents of fees and annuities to be endorsed in future by the lord treasurer himself with the name of the teller who is to pay.

6. All warrants dormant for recurring payments to be first enrolled by Skinner and then by Wardour, the first taking 6*s*. 8*d*. and the other 3*s*. 4*d*. The writs to remain with Skinner.

7. Debentures to be made by Skinner, with the usual fees, but the tellers to have no allowance for payments made on any debenture not first entered with Wardour.

The document ended with a promise to settle outstanding differences soon. On the face of it Wardour had won some further small victories; though he did not gain control of either the tellers' accounts or the papers used in auditing them, his office was now indispensable to those using the Receipt to pay in or take out money. In particular, the pells office now had a part in the profitable dealings with private persons – annuitants and holders of fees. Buckhurst seems to have intended to establish the clerk of the pells simply as a control on the auditor, but in effect he allowed him to settle parasitically upon the course of the Receipt: all the essential work and the real supervision remained with the auditor, while the clerk of the pells acquired the sort of income which made his office significant in the age of sinecures about to begin. Skinner, admittedly, was not satisfied and tried to reopen the whole business when the accession of James I, his knighthood, and the promotion of his patron, Cecil, to the treasurership seemed to make this worth while;[1] but there is no sign that any further changes were made by order, though no doubt the years brought adjustments in practice.

[1] Skinner's petition to Salisbury, Caesar (chancellor of the Exchequer), Sir Laurence Tanfield (chief baron), and others, giving a brief and one-sided résumé of the whole war: E 407/71/33.

The two officers now existed side by side, in theory overlapping and controlling each other in the best Exchequer manner, delaying especially payments out of the Exchequer now that no teller could pay until the order bore the *recordatur* of the pells office, and charging the public double for their often needless services.[1] That in practice the auditor remained the much more important official cannot be in doubt; though after the Restoration both of them were sinecurists, the auditor's office continued to do a great deal of vital work.[2]

The thirty years' war in the Receipt naturally tells us a great deal about the Elizabethan administration and bureaucracy, but also something about Elizabethan society. The great reforming era of Henry VII and Cromwell came to an end with the restoration of Exchequer supremacy in 1554, and Burghley could do no more than fight a rearguard action on behalf of what to him were sensible innovations, an action which just before his death he had to acknowledge had failed. The notorious persistence of 'medievalism' in English government would seem to have been largely due to the power of certain interests and individuals and the respect paid to them in the reign of Elizabeth, though Winchester must bear his share of the blame; if Burghley had had a free hand he would probably have developed rather than arrested the tendencies of Henry VIII's reign. There was nothing in the running of the Receipt that demanded the restoration of the pell of issue, nor did that pell serve any useful function when it was restored. Corruption was to be feared not from the auditor's alleged independence, but, as the reign of James I proved, from the failings of kings and ministers. The means by which Wardour won his victory are also highly significant. His arguments depended on distant and selected precedents, amalgamated into bad history; yet against them the voice of sense and good history, which Skinner kept trying to use, availed nothing. What is more, Wardour managed to impose his errors on later generations. In the nineteenth century it was authoritatively held that 'the Auditor of the Receipt appears to have succeeded in keeping up the jealous policy of Henry VII, by procuring the suppression of the Pell of Issues until 1597',[3] though if 'reforming' be substituted for 'jealous' this statement makes sense. The view of the Public Record Office seems still to be that the auditor was at fault in resisting the

[1] The developed dual procedure was set out in the act 8 & 9 Will. III, c. 28; its so-called 'old' course is that established after 1597.
[2] S. Baxter, *The Development of the Treasury 1660–1702* (1957), 124 ff.
[3] *Deputy Keeper's Third Report*, App. II, 173.

clerk's demands.[1] More surprisingly, even R. L. Poole was deceived
into believing that the clerk of the pells was the true continuator of
the treasurer's clerk mentioned in the *Dialogus*.[2] Nor is it too fanciful
to see a likeness between the precedent-hunting of Chidiock Wardour,
intent only on increasing the profits of an office which he had bought
somewhat dearly from his predecessor,[3] and the sort of historical
arguments which were soon to beset the controversies over the nature
of the constitution. Peter, of course, was no better: he, too, believed
in this typical search for 'good title' in documents produced by quite
different conditions. Vincent Skinner stands out as the one man
capable of seeing and saying that arguments from the past can be only
part of the story, that changes made in the course of history must
affect the meaning of precedents, and that the efficiency of the service
should in any case be studied first.

[1] Giuseppi, *Guide*, i. 180.   [2] Poole, *Exchequer*, 73 ff.

[3] His concern with fees bore noble fruit, for he built not for himself alone, the clerkship
of the pells becoming virtually hereditary in his family for a century: Baxter, *Treasury*,
124.

GENERAL INDEX

INDEX OF AUTHORS CITED

Includes only passages in which writers' views are discussed or assessed; writers of antiquity, and those contemporary with the events with which they deal, are listed in the General Index.